EDUCATION AS
ENFORCEMENT

THE MILITARIZATION
AND CORPORATIZATION OF SCHOOLS

KENNETH J. SALTMAN & DAVID A. GABBARD
EDITORS

RoutledgeFalmer

NEW YORK AND LONDON

Published in 2003 by
RoutledgeFalmer
29 West 35th Street
New York, NY 10001
www.routledge-ny.com

Published in Great Britain by
RoutledgeFalmer
11 New Fetter Lane
London EC4P 4EE
www.routledgefalmer.com

Design and typesetting: Jack Donner

Printed in the United States of America on acid-free paper.

10 9 8 7 6 5 4 3 2 1

Library of Congress Cataloging-in-Publication Data

Education as enforcement : the militarization and corporatization of schools / Kenneth J. Saltman & David A. Gabbard, editors.
      p. cm.
   Includes index.
   ISBN 0-415-94488-0 — ISBN 0-415-94489-9 (pbk. : alk. paper)
   1. Educational sociology—United States. 2. Education and state—United States. 3. Commercialism in schools—United States. 4. Militarism—United States. I. Saltman, Kenneth J., 1969- II. Gabbard, David A.

LC191.4 .E36 2003
306.43—dc21

                                                                    2002036798

CONTENTS

ACKNOWLEDGMENTS

Sometimes it can be difficult to generate discussion on a new or underexplored theme in an academic field. The relationship between militarization and corporatization in education is such a theme that has not seen a great deal of books or conference panels. We are optimistic that this book will encourage future study. The editors owe an enormous debt of gratitude to Joe Miranda at RoutledgeFalmer for his tremendous faith in the project as well as his help in realizing this volume. The editors would also like especially to thank Michael Apple, Enora Brown, Noam Chomsky, Henry Giroux, Robin Truth Goodman, Pepi Leistyna, Pauline Lipman, and Peter McLaren, not only for their contributions to this book but also for their generous interest, exchange, and encouragement on its creation. Thanks also to David Gregg for his help in preparing the manuscript.

FOREWORD

Democracy, Schooling, and the Culture of Fear after September 11[*]

HENRY A. GIROUX

As a wartime president, George W. Bush enjoys incredibly high popularity ratings, but beneath the inflated ratings and the president's call for unity, there is a disturbing appeal to modes of community and patriotism buttressed by moral absolutes in which the discourse of evil, terrorism, and security works to stifle dissent, empty democracy of any substance, and exile politics "to the space occupied by those discontented with the West, and dispossessed by it."[1] Shamelessly pandering to the fever of emergency time and the economy of fear, President Bush and his administrative cohorts are rewriting the rhetoric of community so as to remove it from the realm of politics and democracy. In doing so, Bush and his followers are not only concentrating their political power, they are also pushing through harsh policies and regressive measures that cut basic services and public assistance for the poor, offering school children more standardized testing without providing them decent health care and adequate food, and sacrificing American democracy and individual autonomy for the promise of domestic security at the same time that they allocate resources and tax breaks to the rich through airline bailouts and retroactive tax cuts. Under the auspices of a belligerent nationalism and militarism, community is constructed "through shared fears rather than shared responsibilities," and the strongest appeals

Henry A. Giroux holds the Waterbury chair professorship at Pennsylvania State University. He is currently the director of the Waterbury Forum in education and cultural studies at Penn State University. His most recent books include: *Channel Surfing: Racism, the Media and the Destruction of Today's Youth* (St. Martin's Press, 1997), *Pedagogy and the Politics of Hope* (Westview/HarperCollins, 1997), *The Mouse that Roared: Disney and the End of Innocence* (Rowman & Littlefield, 1999), *Stealing Innocence: Youth, Corporate Power, and the Politics of Culture* (St. Martin's Press, 2000), *Impure Acts: the Practical Politics of Cultural Studies* (Routledge, 2000), *Public Spaces/Private Lives: Beyond the Culture of Cynicism* (Rowman & Littlefield, 2001), *Breaking Into the Movies: Film and the Culture of Politics* (Basil Blackwell, 2002), and *The Abandoned Generation* (Palgrave, 2003).

[*]Many of the ideas for this foreword draw from *The Abandoned Generation: Democracy Beyond the Culture of Fear* (Palgrave, 2003).

to civic discourse are focused primarily on military defense, civil order, and domestic security.[2] Given the increasing militarization of public space, the disconnection of security from liberty, and the erosion of crucial civil freedoms, *Education as Enforcement: The Militarization and Corporatization of Schools* appears at a critical juncture for educators and others concerned about the fate of democracy in the aftermath of September 11.

Within the rhetoric and culture of shared fears, patriotism becomes synonymous with an uncritical acceptance of governmental authority and a discourse "that encourages ignorance as it overrides real politics, real history, and moral issues."[3] The longing for community seems so desperate in the United States, steeped as it is in the ethic of neoliberalism with its utter disregard for public life, democratic public spheres, and moral responsibility, that in such ruthless times any invocation of community seems nourishing, even when the term is invoked to demand an "unconditional loyalty and treats everything short of such loyalty as an act of unforgivable treason."[4] How can any notion of democratic community or critical citizenship be embraced through the rhetoric of a debased patriotism that is outraged by dissent in the streets? What notion of community allows Peter Beinart, editor of *The New Republic*, to wrap himself in the flag of patriotism and moral absolutism while excoriating those who are critical of Bush policies? He says: "This nation is now at war. And in such an environment, domestic political dissent is immoral without a prior statement of national solidarity, a choosing of sides."[5] Charges of unpatriotic dissent are not restricted to either protesters in the streets or to those academics who incurred the wrath of Lynne Cheney's American Council of Trustees and Alumni for not responding with due Americanist fervor to the terrorist attacks of September 11. It was also applied to Senate majority leader Tom Daschle when he offered a mild critique of President Bush's plan to launch what appears to be a never-ending war against terrorism. Trent Lott, the Republican leader, responded with a crude rebuke, suggesting that Daschle had no right to criticize President Bush "while we are fighting our war on terrorism."[6] It appears that the leadership of the Republican party, along with its strong supporters, has no qualms about dismissing critics by impugning their patriotism. Tom Davis of Virginia, the head of the GOP's House campaign committee branded those who criticize Bush's policies as "giving aid and comfort to our enemies."[7] The Family Research Council went even further by running ads in South Dakota "likening Tom Daschle to Saddam Hussein because the Senate majority leader opposed oil drilling in the Arctic National Wildlife Refuge."[8] Community in this instance demands not courage, dialogue, and responsibility but silence and complicity.

Eric Hobsbawm has observed that "never was the word 'community' used more indiscriminately and emptily than in the decades when communities in the sociological sense became hard to find in real life."[9] Maybe the absence of viable communities organized around democratic values and basic freedoms accounts for the way in which the language of community has currently "degraded into the currency of propaganda."[10] How else can one explain the outrage exhibited by the dominant media against anyone who seems to question, among other things, the United States' support of friendly dictatorships, including Afghanistan and Saudi Arabia, the "USA Patriot Act" with its suppression of civil liberties, or even suggest the need for a serious discussion about how U.S. foreign policy contributes to the widespread poverty, despair, and hopelessness throughout the world, offering in return terrorist nihilism the opportunity "to thrive in the rich soil of exclusion and victimhood."[11] Actual democratic communities are completely at odds with a smug self-righteousness that refuses to make a distinction between explaining events and justifying them. As Judith Butler points out:

> [T]o ask how certain political and social actions come into being, such as the recent terrorist attack on the U.S., and even to identify a set of causes, is not the same as locating the source of the responsibility for those actions, or indeed, paralyzing our capacity to make ethical judgments on what is right or wrong . . . but it does ask the U.S. to assume a different kind of responsibility for producing more egalitarian global conditions for equality, sovereignty, and the egalitarian redistribution of resources."[12]

Such questions do not suggest that the United States is responsible for the acts of terrorism that took place on September 11. On the contrary, they perform the obligatory work of politics by attempting to situate individual acts of responsibility within the broader set of conditions that give rise to individual acts of terrorism while simultaneously asking how the United States can intervene more productively in global politics to produce conditions that undercut rather than reinforce the breeding grounds for such terrorism. At the same time, such questions suggest that the exercise of massive power cannot be removed from the practice of politics and ethics, and such a recognition demands a measure of accountability to be responsible for the consequences of our actions as one of the most powerful countries in the world. As Lewis Lapham observes, "[i]t is precisely at the moments of our greatest peril that we stand in need of as many questions as anybody can think to ask."[13]

The rhetoric of terrorism is important not only because it operates on many registers to both inflict human misery and call into question the delicate balance of freedom and security crucial to any democratic society, but also because it carries with it an enormous sense of urgency that often redefines community against its most democratic possibilities and realized forms. Rising from the ashes of impoverishment and religious fundamentalism, terrorism, at its worst, evokes a culture of fear, unquestioning loyalty, and a narrow definition of security from those who treat it as pathology rather than politics. In part, this is evident in Bush's war against terrorism, which, fueled by calls for public sacrifice, appears to exhaust itself in a discourse of moral absolutes and public acts of denunciation. This all-embracing policy of antiterrorism depoliticizes politics by always locating it outside the realm of power and strips community of democratic values by defining it almost exclusively through attempts to stamp out what Michael Leeden, a former counterterror expert in the Reagan administration calls "corrupt habits of mind that are still lingering around, somewhere."[14]

The militarizing of community and the perpetuation of a harsh culture of fear and insecurity results in the narrowing of community and the ongoing appeal to jingoistic forms of patriotism in order to divert the public from addressing a number of pressing domestic and foreign issues; it also contributes to the increasing suppression of dissent and what Anthony Lewis has rightly called the growing escalation of concentrated, unaccountable political power that threatens the very foundation of democracy in the United States.[15] This is evident in Attorney General John Ashcroft's recent decision to relax restrictions on the FBI's ability to conduct domestic spying as part of its stepped up counterterrorism campaign. Dispensing with probable cause restrictions in order to begin counterterrorism investigations, the new FBI regulations allow federal agents to search commercial databases, monitor the World Wide Web, examine phone and library records, and compile dossiers on people and groups, without the need to show that a crime has been committed. According to officials at the American Civil Liberties Union, the new guidelines "say to the American people that you no longer have to be doing something wrong in order to get that FBI knock at your door."[16]

At the core of Bush's notion of community and hyperpatriotism is a notion of temporality that detaches itself from a sense of public deliberation, critical citizenship, and civic engagement. Jerome Binde refers to this view of temporality as "emergency time" and describes it as a "world governed by short-term efficacy," which under the imperatives of utter necessity and pragmatism, eschews long-term appraisals, and gives precedence to the "logic of 'just in time' at the expense of any forward-looking deliberation."[17] According to Binde, emergency time opens the way for what he calls "the tyranny of emergency." He explains:

> Emergency is a direct means of response that leaves no time for either analysis, forecasting, or prevention. It is an immediate protective reflex rather than a sober quest for long-term solutions. It neglects the fact that situations have to be put in perspective and that future events need to be anticipated. Devising any durable response to human problem . . . requires looking at a situation from a distance and thinking in terms of the future.[18]

Lacking any reference to democratic collective aims, the appeal to emergency time both shrinks the horizon of meanings and removes the application of governmental power from the fields of ethical and political responsibility. Emergency time defines community against its democratic possibilities, detaching it from those conditions that prepare citizens to deliberate collectively about the future and the role they must play in creating and shaping the conditions for them to have some say it how it might unfold. Under such conditions, cynical reason replaces reasoned debate with the one-way gaze of power and popular resistance to the "war" is dismissed as "a demagoguery of the streets, while dictators are offered up to us as responsible representatives of their countries."[19] But emergency time in the context of Bush's war against terrorism also rejects the radical secularism at the heart of a substantive democracy in favor of a religious vocabulary. The metaphysics of religious discourse dispenses with the task of critically engaging and translating the elaborate web of historical, social, and political factors that underscore and give meaning to the broader explanations for terrorism. Instead, the complexity of politics dissolves into the language of "crusades," "infidels," "goodness," and "evil." Under such conditions, as Steven Lukes and Nadia Urbinati point out: "A rhetoric of emergency has arisen in which a Manichean impulse is given free range, in which 'our' (American? Western?) values are seen as threatened by an enemy that is seen as the incarnation of evil and variously identified as 'fundamentalist' and 'Islamist' as embodied in Al-Quaida and personified by Osama bin Laden."[20]

It is the displacement of politics and the weakening of democratic public spaces that allow for religious ideology and excess to define the basis of community, civic engagement, and the domain of the social. Against this notion of emergency time, educators, cultural workers, and others need to posit a notion of public time. According to democratic theorist Cornelius Castoriadis, public time represents "the emergence of a dimension where the collectivity can inspect its own past as the result of *its own actions,* and where an indeterminate future opens up as domain for its activities."[21] For Castoriadis, public time puts into question established institutions and dominant authority. Rather than maintaining a passive attitude toward power, public time demands and encourages forms of political agency based on a passion for self-governing, actions informed by critical judgment, and a commitment to linking social responsibility and social transformation. Public time legitimates those pedagogical practices that provide the basis for a culture of questioning, one that provides the knowledge, skills, and social practices that encourage an opportunity for resistance, a space of translation, and a proliferation of discourses. Public time unsettles common sense and disturbs authority while encouraging critical and responsible leadership. As Roger Simon observes, public time "presents the question of the social— not as a space for the articulation of pre-formed visions through which to mobilize action, but as the movement in which the very question of the possibility of democracy becomes the frame within which a necessary radical learning (and questioning) is enabled."[22] Put differently, public time affirms a politics without guarantees and a notion of the social that is open and contingent. Public time provides a conception of democracy that is never complete and determinate and constantly open to different understandings of the contingency of its decisions, mechanisms of exclusions, and operations of power.[23] At its best, public time renders governmental power explicit, and in doing so it rejects the language of religious rituals and the abrogation of the conditions necessary for the assumption of basic freedoms and rights. Moreover, public time considers civic education the basis, if not essential dimension, of justice because it provides individuals with the skills, knowledge, and passions to talk back to power while simultaneously emphasizing both the necessity to question that accompanies viable forms of political agency and the assumption of public responsibility through active participation in the very process of governing.

Against Bush's disregard for public discussion of his policies, his fetish for secrecy, his clamoring for a notion of patriotism that is synonymous with a mindless conformity, and his flaunting of presidential power, public time gives credence to a notion of democracy that calls for the establishment of unbounded interrogation in all domains of public life. Democratic politics and viable notions of community are created and affirmed when public spaces are created that enable individuals and social movements to exercise power over the institutions and forces that govern their lives. Under such conditions, politics is not relegated to the domain of the other as a form of pathology, but is central to what it means to build vibrant public spheres and democratic communities.[24]

What has become clear both in Bush's 2001 State of the Union Address and in the policies enacted by his administration is that there is no discourse for recognizing that a democratic society has an obligation to pay its debts to past generations and fulfill its obligations to future generations, especially the young who are being increasingly abandoned at all levels of government. His tax cuts privilege the commercial interests of the rich over public responsibilities to the poor, the elderly, the environment, and to children. His call for military tribunals for trying noncitizens, his detaining in secrecy over 1,200 Arabs and Muslims for extended periods, and willingness to undermine the basic constitutional freedoms and rights by enhancing the power of the police and other enforcement groups pose a grave threat to those civil liberties that are fundamental to democracy.[25] Edward Said argues more specifically that

> Bush and his compliant Congress have suppressed or abrogated or abridged whole sections of the First, Fourth, Fifth and Eighth Amendments, instituted legal procedures that give individuals no recourse either to a proper defense or a fair trail, that allow secret searches eavesdropping, detention without limit, and, given the treatment of the prisoners at Guantanamo Bay, that allow the US executive branch to abduct prisoners, detain them indefinitely, decide unilaterally whether or not they are prisoners of war and whether or not the Geneva Conventions apply to them—which is not a decision to be taken by individual countries.[26]

Most important, Bush's war against terrorism camouflages the undermining of democracy effected through its relentless attempts to depoliticize politics itself. What began as the demonization of political Islam has now been extended into the demonization of politics itself as Bush and his cohorts put forth policies that attempt to erase the possibility of imagining a democratic future, the democratic space of the social, the meaning of democratic community, or the practices that anchor democratic life. As Barnor Hesse and S. Sayyid insightfully observe:

> Through such processes, politics seems exiled. While the centre is reoccupied by a naturalised world order, politics is proscribed from the domain of order itself. Paradoxically, cynical reason becomes a dominant ideology within an apparently post-ideological West. In a Western world apparently deprived of political alternatives to corporate capitalism, neoliberalism and global social inequalities, what once passed for politics has been exclusively transposed to the space occupied by those discontented with the West, and dispossessed by it.[27]

By depoliticizing politics, the war on terrorism becomes both an empty abstraction and a strategic diversion. Empty because terrorism cannot be either understood or addressed through the discourse of moral absolutes and religious fervor. Militarism does not get to the root of terrorism, it simply expands the breeding grounds for the conditions that give rise to it. Military intervention may overthrow governments controlled by radical fanatics such as the Taliban, but it does not address those global conditions in which poverty thrives, thousands of children die every day from starvation or preventable diseases, where 250 million are compelled to work under harsh conditions, or some 840 million adults are without adequate shelter and access to health care.[28] As long as such inequalities exist, resistance will emerge and terrorism will be the order of the day. Dropping thousands of bombs on poor countries (with or without accompanying packets of food) will not only fail to solve the problem, it will only exacerbate the conditions that gave rise to it. Instead of looking to militarism as a solution, we ought to be rethinking how U.S. policies actually contribute to these conditions through its support of military dictatorships, its unilateral disregard for international coalitions, and its ongoing support for the ruthless policies of global neoliberalism. Such honest reassessment could help us recognize how the rhetoric of antiterrorism cleanses Bush and his cohorts of the obligations of political and ethical responsibility on a global level by ignoring the complex bonds that tie the rich and the powerful to the poor and the powerless. Such ties cannot be explained through the language of a rabid nationalism, hyped-up patriotism, or religious zeal. As Judith Butler points out, fatuous moralism is no substitute for assuming responsibility for one's actions in the world. She writes:

> [M]oralistic denunciation provides immediate gratification, and even has the effect of temporarily cleansing the speaker of all proximity to guilt through the act of self-righteous denunciation itself. But is this the same as responsibility, understood as taking stock of our world, and participating in its social transformation in such a way that non-violent, cooperative, egalitarian international relations remain the guiding ideal?[29]

Moralism may offer Bush and his cohorts the grounds of innocence, but it does nothing to further the dynamics of democracy or civic engagement and may, as John Edgar Wideman suggests, even serve to "terrorize" those Americans it claims to benefit.

> By launching a phony war [Bush] is managing to avoid the scrutiny a first-term, skin-of its teeth presidency deserves. Instead, he's terrorizing Americans into believing that we require a wartime leader wielding unquestioned emergency powers. Beneath the drumbeat belligerence of his demands for national unity, if you listen you'll hear the bullying, the self-serving, the hollowness, of his appeals to patriotism. Listen carefully and you'll also hear what he's not saying: that we need, in a democracy full of contradictions and unresolved divisions, opposition voices.[30]

If Wideman is correct, and I think he is, then Bush's innocent posturing wrapped in the righteous rhetoric of antiterrorism also provides a massive diversion from addressing those political issues at the heart of what it means to measure the reality against the promise of a substantive democracy. Bush commits us to the dark world of emergency time, a world divided between good and evil, one in which "issues of democracy, civil comity and social justice—let alone nuance, complexity and interdependence simply vanish."[31] In this world of emergency time, politics assumes a purity that posits only one right answer, one side to choose. Not only does emergency time provide Bush with a political identity that closely resembles a kind of martyrdom, it certifies him as the proper authority for speaking the only admissible language and holding down the only acceptable position.[32] Emergency time not only refuses to question its own assumptions, it also refuses to acknowledge its glaring absences—those issues or points of view it either ignores or marginalizes. Hence, in the name of "fighting freedom's fight," Bush constructs a worldview in which the growing gap between the rich and the poor is ignored, massive unemployment is disregarded, the war against youth marginalized by class and color does not exist, poverty and racial injustice become invisible, the folly of attacking the public sector is passed over, the shameful growth of the prison-industrial complex is overlooked, Enron is easily forgotten, and government-sanctioned threats to the environment evaporate.

Bush's notion of community depoliticizes politics and makes a sham of civic complexity and responsibility. If we are to challenge his policies, particularly his willingness to wage a war against Iraq, educators and others need to reclaim a notion of politics and pedagogy that embraces a notion of public time, one that fosters civic engagement and public intelligence. This means at the very least creating the conditions for rendering governmental authority accountable for its actions while also mobilizing the conditions for citizens to reclaim the power necessary to shape the regimes of power and politics that influence their lives on a daily basis. The greatest struggle Americans face is not terrorism, but a struggle on behalf of justice, freedom, and democracy for all of the citizens of the globe, especially youth. This is not going to take place, as Bush's policies will tragically affirm, by shutting down democracy, eliminating its most cherished rights and freedoms, and deriding communities of dissent. On the contrary, the struggle for democracy has to be understood through politics, not moralism, and if politics is to be reclaimed as the center of individual and social agency, it will have to be motivated not by the culture of fear, but by a passion for civic engagement and ethical responsibility and the promise of a realizable democracy.

The invocation of emergency time profoundly limits the vocabulary and imagery available to us in developing a language of critique, compassion, and possibility for addressing the relationship between the crisis of democracy and the crisis of youth. Limiting civil liberties, cutting back social programs, and defining democracy as expendable as part of the discourse of emergency time and the appeal to the culture of fear shut down the opportunity for adults to both focus on young people as a symbol of the future and to create the symbolic and material conditions for increasing the scope of those values and freedoms necessary for them to become active and critical citizens willing to fight for a vibrant democracy.

The Challenge to Educators

Though *Education as Enforcement* was conceptualized long before the events of September 11, 2001, those events and the events transpiring since have elevated the poignancy of the book's primary themes—the militarization and corporatization of schools. The events of September 11 provide educators with a crucial opportunity to reclaim schools as democratic public spheres in which students can engage in dialogue and critique around the meaning of democratic values, the relationship between learning and civic engagement, and the connection between schooling, what it means to be a critical citizen, and the responsibilities one has to the larger world.[33]

Defined largely through an appeal to fear and a call to strengthen domestic security, the space of the social has been both militarized and increasingly commodified. As such, there is little public conversation about connecting the social sphere to democratic values, justice, or what the public good might mean in light of this horrible attack as a moral and political referent to denounce mass acts of violence and to attempt to secure freedom and justice for all people. But such a task would demand, in part, addressing what vocabularies and practices regarding the space of the social and political were actually in place prior to the events of September 11, and what particular notions of freedom, security, and citizenship were available to Americans—the legacy and influence of which might prevent them from assuming the role of critical and engaged citizens capable of addressing this national crisis. The contributing authors of this volume meet this challenge. Instead of seeing the current crisis as a break from the past, it is crucial for the American public to begin to understand how the past might be useful in addressing what it means to live in a democracy in the aftermath of the bombings in New York and Washington, D.C. Public schools should play a decisive role in helping students configure the boundaries between history and the present, incorporating a critical understanding of those events that are often left out of the rendering of contemporary considerations that define the roles students might play as critical citizens. Of course, this will be difficult since many public schools are overburdened with high-stakes testing and harsh accountability systems designed to get teachers to narrow their curriculum and to focus only on raising test scores. Consequently, any struggle to make schools more democratic and socially relevant will have to link the battle for critical citizenship to an ongoing fight against turning schools into testing centers and teachers into technicians.

Education and the Challenge of Revitalizing Democratic Public Life

As the state is increasingly relieved of its welfare-providing functions, it defaults on its capacity to provide people with the most basic social provisions, extending from health care to public transportation, and simultaneously withdraws from its obligation to create those noncommodified public spheres in which people learn the language of ethics, civic courage, demo-cratically charged politics, and collective empowerment. Within such a turn of events, schools are increasingly defined less as a public good than as sites for financial investment and entrepreneurial training, that is, as a private good.

As those public spaces that offer forums for debating norms, critically engaging ideas, making private issues public, and evaluating judgments disappear under the juggernaut of neoliberal policies, it becomes crucial for educators to raise fundamental questions about what it means to revitalize public life, politics, and ethics in ways that take seriously such values as patri-otism, "citizen participation, . . . political obligation, social governance, and community,"[34] especially at a time of national crisis when such terms become less an object of analysis than uncritical veneration. The call for a revitalized politics, grounded in an effective democracy substantively challenges the dystopian practices of neoliberalism—with its all-consuming emphasis on market relations, commercialization, privatization, and the creation of a worldwide economy of part-time workers—against its utopian promises. Such an intervention confronts educators with the problem as well as the challenge of analyzing, engaging, and developing those public spheres the media, public education, and other cultural institutions—that provide the conditions for creating citizens who are equipped to exercise their freedoms, competent to question the basic assumptions that govern political life, and skilled enough to participate in shaping the basic social, political, and economic orders that govern their lives. It is precisely within these public spheres that the events of September 11 and military action against Afghani-stan and Iraq, the responsibility of the media, the civic obligation of educa-tors, and America's role in the world as a superpower should be debated rather than squelched in the name of a jingoistic patriotism.

Two factors work against such a debate on any level. First, there are very few public spheres left that provide the space for such conversations to take place. Second, it is increasingly difficult for young people and adults to appropriate a critical language, outside of the market, that would allow them to translate private problems into public concerns or to relate public issues to private considerations. For many young people and adults today, the private sphere has become the only space in which to imagine any sense of hope, pleasure, or possibility. Reduced to the act of consuming, citizenship is "mostly about forgetting, not learning."[35] The decline of social capital can be seen in research studies done by the Justice Project in 2001, in which a substantial number of teenagers and young people were asked what they thought democracy meant? The answers testified to a growing depoliticiza-tion of the social in American life and were largely along the following lines: "Nothing," "I don't know," or "My rights, just like, pride, I guess, to some extent, and paying taxes" or "I just think, like, what does it really mean? I know it's like our, like, our government, but I don't know what it techni-cally is."[36] Market forces focus on the related issues of consumption and safety, but not on the economic, cultural, and political meaning of a vibrant democracy.

When notions of freedom and security are decoupled and freedom is reduced to the imperatives of market exchange, and security is divested from a defense of a version the welfare state distinguished by its social provisions and "helping functions," not only does freedom collapse into brutal form of individualism, but also the state is stripped of its helping functions while its policing functions are often inordinately strengthened. Even as the foundations of the security state are being solidified through zero tolerance policies, antiterrorist laws, soaring incarceration rates, the criminalization of pregnancy, racial profiling, and antiimmigration policies, it is crucial that educators and scholars take up the events of September 11 not through a one-sided view of patriotism that stifles dissent and aids the forces of domestic militarization, but as part of a broader effort to expand the United States' democratic rather than repressive possibilities.

Unlike some theorists who suggest that politics as a site of contestation, critical exchange and engagement has either come to an end or is in a state of terminal arrest, the authors who have contributed to *Education as Enforcement* join me in the belief that the current, depressing state of politics points to the urgent challenge of reformulating the crisis of democracy as part of the fundamental crisis of vision, meaning, education, and political agency. If it is possible to "gain" anything from the events of September 11, it must be understood as an opportunity for a national coming together and soul searching—a time for expanding democratic possibilities rather than limiting them. Politics devoid of vision degenerates into either cynicism, a repressive notion of patriotism, or it appropriates a view of power that appears to be equated almost exclusively with the militarization of both domestic space and foreign policy initiatives. Lost from such accounts is the recognition that democracy has to be struggled over—even in the face of a most appalling crisis of political agency. Educators, scholars, and policymakers must redress the little attention paid to the fact that the struggle over politics and democracy is inextricably linked to creating public spheres where individuals can be educated as political agents equipped with the skills, capacities, and knowledge they need not only to actually perform as autonomous political agents, but also to believe that such struggles are worth taking up. Central to my argument is the assumption that politics is not simply about power, but also, as Cornelius Castoriadis points out, "has to do with political judgements and value choices,"[37] indicating that questions of civic education-learning how to become a skilled citizen—are central to both the struggle over political agency and democracy itself. Finally, there is the widespread refusal among many educators and others to recognize that the issue of civic education—with its emphasis on critical thinking, bridging the gap between learning and everyday life, understanding the connection between power and knowledge, and using the resources of history to extend democratic rights and identities—is not only the foundation for expanding and enabling political agency, but also takes place across a wide variety of public spheres through the growing power of a mass-mediated culture.[38] For many educational reformers, education and schooling are synonymous. In actuality, schooling is only one site where education takes place. As a performative practice, pedagogy is at work in a variety of educational sites—including popular culture, television and cable networks, magazines, the Internet, churches, and the press—where culture works to secure identities; it does the bridging work for negotiating the relationship between knowledge, pleasure, and values and renders authority both crucial and problematic in legitimating particular social practices, communities, and forms of power. As a moral and political practice, the concept of public pedagogy points to the enormous ways in which popular and media culture construct the meanings, desires, and investments that play such an influential role in how students view themselves, others, and the larger world. Unfortunately, the political, ethical, and social significance of the role that popular culture plays as the primary pedagogical medium for young people remains largely unexamined by many educators and seems almost exclusively removed from any policy debates about educational reform. Educators also must challenge the assumption that education is limited to schooling, and that popular cultural texts cannot be as profoundly important as traditional sources of learning in teaching about important issues framed through, for example, the social lens of poverty, racial conflict, and gender discrimination. This suggests not only expanding curricula so as to allow students to become critically literate in those visual, electronic, and digital cultures that have such an important influence on their lives, but it also suggests teaching students the skills to be cultural producers. For instance, learning how to read films differently is no less important than learning how to produce films. At the same time, critical literacy is not about making kids simply savvy about the media so they can become better consumers, it means offering them the knowledge, skills, and tools to recognize when the new technologies and media serve as either a force for enlarging democratic relations or when it shuts down such relations. Becoming media literate is largely meaningless unless students take up this form of literacy within the larger issue of what it means to be a critical citizen and engaged political agent willing to expand and deepen democratic public spheres. Within this expanded approach to pedagogy, both the notion of what constitutes meaningful knowledge as well as which conditions of critical agency might point to a more expansive and democratic notion of civic education and political agency.

Educators at all levels of schooling need to challenge the assumption that either politics is dead or that any viable notion of politics will be determined exclusively by government leaders and experts in the heat of moral frenzy to impose vengeance on those who attacked the Pentagon and the World Trade Center. Educators need to take a more critical position, arguing that critical knowledge, debate, and dialogue grounded in pressing social problems offers individuals and groups some hope in shaping the conditions that bear down on their lives. Public engagement born of citizen engagement is urgent if the concepts of the social and public can be used to revitalize the language of civic education and democratization as part of a broader discourse of political agency and critical citizenship in a global world. Linking a notion of the social to democratic public values represents an attempt, however incomplete, to link democracy to public action, and to ground such support in defense of militant utopian thinking (as opposed to unadorned militancy) as part of a comprehensive attempt to revitalize the conditions for individual and social agency, civic activism, and citizen access to decision making, while simultaneously addressing the most basic problems facing the prospects for social justice and global democracy.

Educators within both public schools and higher education need to continue finding ways of entering the world of politics by both making social problems visible and contesting their manifestation in the polity. We need to build on those important critical, educational theories of the past in order to resurrect the emancipatory elements of democratic thought while also recognizing and engaging their damaged and burdened historical traditions.[39] We need to reject both neoliberal and orthodox leftist positions, which dismiss the state as merely a tool of repression in order to find ways to use the state to challenge, block, and regulate the devastating effects of capitalism. On the contrary, educators need to be at the forefront of defending the most progressive historical advances and gains of the state. French sociologist Pierre Bourdieu is right when he calls for collective work by educators to prevent the right and other reactionaries from destroying the most precious democratic conquests in the areas of labor legislation, health, social protection, and education.[40] At the very least, this would suggest that educators defend schools as democratic public spheres, struggle against the deskilling of teachers and students, and argue for a notion of pedagogy that is grounded in democratic values rather than those corporate-driven ideologies and testing schemes that severely limit the creative and liberatory potential of teachers and students. At the same time, such educators must resist the reduction of the state to its policing functions, while linking such a struggle to the fight against neoliberalism and the struggle for expanding and deepening the freedoms, rights, and relations of a vibrant democracy. Postcolonial theorist Samir Amin echoes this call by arguing that educators should consider addressing the project of a more realized democracy as part of an ongoing process of democratization. According to Amin, democratization "stresses the dynamic aspect of a still-unfinished process" while rejecting notions of democracy that are given a definitive formula.[41] Educators have an important role to play in the struggle to link social justice and economic democracy with the equality of human rights, the right to education, health, research, art, and work. On the cultural front, teachers as public intellectuals can work to make the pedagogical more political by engaging in a permanent critique of their own scholasticism and promoting a critical awareness to end oppression and forms of social life that disfigure contemporary life and pose a threat to any viable notion of democracy. Educators need to provide spaces of resistance within the public schools and the university that take seriously what it means to educate students to question and interrupt authority, recall what is forgotten or ignored, make connections that are otherwise hidden, while simultaneously providing the knowledge and skills that enlarge their sense of the social and their possibilities as viable political agents capable of expanding and deepening democratic public life. At the very least, such educators can challenge the correlation between the impoverishment of society and the impoverishment of intellectuals by offering possibilities other than what we are told is possible. Or as Alain Badiou observes "showing how the space of the possible is larger than the one assigned—that something else is possible, but not that everything is possible."[42] In times of increased domination of public K–12 education and higher education it becomes important, as George Lipsitz reminds us, that educators—as well as artists and other cultural workers—not become isolated "in their own abstract desires for social change and actual social movements. Taking a position is not the same as waging a war of position; changing your mind is not the same as changing society."[43]

Resistance must become part of a public pedagogy that works to position rigorous theoretical work and public bodies against corporate power and the militarization of visual and public space, connect classrooms to the challenges faced by social movements in the streets, and provide spaces within classrooms and other sites for personal injury and private terrors to be transformed into public considerations and struggles. This suggests that educators should work to form alliances with parents, community organizers, labor organizations, and civil rights groups at the local, national and international levels to better understand how to translate private troubles into public actions, arouse public interests over pressing social problems, and use collective means to more fully democratize the commanding institutional economic, cultural, and social structures of the United States and the larger global order.

In the aftermath of the events of September 11, *Education as Enforcement* serves to remind us that collective problems deserve collective solutions, and that what is at risk is not only a generation of minority youth and adults now considered to be a threat to national security, but also the very promise of democracy itself. As militarism works to intensify patriarchal attitudes and antidemocratic assaults on dissent, it is crucial for educators to join with those groups now making a common cause against those forces that would sacrifice basic constitutional freedoms to the imperatives of war abroad and militarism at home.

Notes

1. Barnor Hesse and S. Sayyid, "A War against Politics," *Open Democracy*, (November 28, 2001): 3, available at openDemocracy@opendemocracy.net.
2. Anatole Anton, "Public Goods as Commonstock: Notes on the Receding Commons," in *Not for Sale: In Defense of Public Goods*, edited by Anatole Anton, Milton Fisk, and Nancy Holmstrom (Boulder, Colo: Westview Press, 2000), 29.
3. Edward Said, "Thoughts about America," *Counterpunch* (March 5, 2002): 5, available at www.counterpunch.org/saidamerica.html.
4. Zygmunt Bauman, *Community: Seeking Safety in an Insecure World* (Cambridge, UK: Polity, 2001), 4.
5. Cited in Lewis H. Lapham, "American Jihad," *Harper's Magazine* (January 2002): 7.
6. Cited in Frank Rich, "The Wimps of War," *New York Times* Op-Ed (March 30, 2002): A27.

7. Ibid.
8. Ibid.
9. Eric Hobsbawm, *The Age of Extremes* (London: Michael Joseph, 1994), 428.
10. Lapham, "American Jihad," 8.
11. Susan George, "Another World is Possible," *The Nation* (February 18, 2002): 12.
12. Judith Butler, "Explanation and Exoneration, or What We Can Hear," *Theory & Event* 5, no. 4 (2002): 8, 16.
13. Lewis H. Lapham, "Innocents Abroad," *Harper's Magazine* (June 2002): 7.
14. Ledeen cited in Douglas Valentine, "Homeland Insecurity," *Counterpunch* (November 8, 2001); available online at www.counterpunch.org/homeland1.html.
15. Anthony Lewis, "Taking Our Liberties," *New York Times* (March 9, 2002), A27.
16. Dan Van Natta, Jr., "Government Will Ease Limits on Domestic Spying by F.B.I." *New York Times* (May 20, 2002): A1.
17. Jerome Binde, "Toward an Ethic of the Future," *Public Culture* 12, no. 1 (2000): 52.
18. Ibid.
19. Hesse and. Sayyid, "A War against Politics."
20. Steven Lukes and Nadia Urbinati, "Words Matter," *Open Democracy* (November 27, 2001): 1 available at openDemocracy@opendemocracy.net
21. Cornelius Castoriadis, "The Greek Polis and the Creation of Democracy," in *Philosophy, Politics, Autonomy: Essays in Political Philosophy* (New York: Oxford University Press, 1991), 113–14.
22. Roger I. Simon, "On Public Time," Ontario Institute for Studies in Education. Unpublished paper (April 1, 2002), 4.
23. Simon Critchley, "Ethics, Politics, and Radical Democracy—The History of a Disagreement," *Culture Machine*, available at www.culturemachine.tees.ac.uk/frm_f1.htm
24. Cornelius Castoriadis, "The Crisis of the Identification Process," *Thesis Eleven* 49 (May 1997): 85–98.
25. Critical reactions to the Bush administration's holding of secret hearings for immigrants detained in the weeks after September 11 are not limited to "unpatriotic" dissenters. A federal judge in New Jersey recently rejected the government's blanket suppression of the rights of immigrant detainees. See Susan Sachs, "Judge Rejects U.S. Policy of Secret Hearings," *New York Times* (May 30, 2002): A21.
26. Said, "Thoughts about America," 2.
27. Hesse and Sayyid, "A War against Politics," 3.
28. These figures are taken from Thomas W. Pogge, "The Moral Demands of Global Justice," *Dissent* (Fall 2000): 37–43.
29. Judith Butler, "Explanation and Exoneration," 19.
30. John Edgar Wideman, "Whose War," *Harper's Magazine* (March 2002), 33–38.
31. Benjamin R. Barber, "Beyond Jihad vs. Mcworld: On Terrorism and the New Democratic Realism," *The Nation* (January 21, 2002): 17.
32. I want to thank Jane Gordon for helping me think through the relationship between politics and purity, which cuts across ideological boundaries.
33. For some excellent examples of such teaching practices, see the special issue of *Rethinking Schools*, 16, no. 2 (Winter 2001/2002), titled "War, Terrorism, and America's Classrooms."
34. Carl Boggs, *The End of Politics* (New York: Guilford Press, 2000), ix.
35. Zygmunt Bauman, *Globalization: The Human Consequences* (New York: Columbia University Press, 1998), 82.
36. Cited in Anna Greenberg, "What Young Voters Want," *The Nation* (February 11, 2001): 15.
37. Cornelius Castoriadis, "Institution and Autonomy," in *A Critical Sense: Interviews with Intellectuals*, edited by Peter Osborne (New York: Routledge, 1996), 8.
38. See Henry A. Giroux, *Public Spaces, Private Lives: Beyond the Culture of Cynicism* (Lahnam, Md.: Rowman & Littlefield, 2001).
39. I am referring to works that extend from John Dewey to some of the more promi-

nent contemporary critical educational theorists such as Paulo Freire and Amy Stuart Wells.

40. Pierre Bourdieu, *Acts of Resistance* (New York: Free Press, 1998).
41. Samir Amin, "Imperialization and Globalization," *Monthly Review* (June 2001): 12.
42. Alain Badiou, *Ethics: An Essay on the Understanding of Evil* (London: Verso, 1998), 115–16.
43. George Lipsitz, "Academic Politics and Social Change," in *Cultural Studies and Political Theory*, edited by Jodi Dean (Ithaca, NY: Cornell University Press, 2000), 81.

Introduction

KENNETH J. SALTMAN

Military generals running schools, students in uniforms, metal detectors, police presence, high-tech ID card dog tags, real time Internet-based surveillance cameras, mobile hidden surveillance cameras, security consultants, chainlink fences, surprise searches—as U.S. public schools invest in record levels of school security apparatus they increasingly resemble the military and prisons. Yet it would be a mistake to understand the school security craze as merely a mass media spectacle in the wake of Columbine and other recent high-profile shootings. And it would be myopic to fail to grasp the extent of public school militarization, its recent history, and its uses prior to the sudden interest it has garnered following September 11.

This book argues that militarized education in the United States needs to be understood in relation to the enforcement of global corporate imperatives as they expand markets through the material and symbolic violence of war and education. As an entry into the themes of the book this introduction demonstrates how militarism pervades foreign and domestic policy, popular culture, educational discourse, and language, educating citizens in the virtues of violence. This chapter demonstrates how, prior to September 11, a high level of comfort with rising militarism in all areas of U.S. life, particularly schooling, set the stage for the radically militarized reactions to September 11 that include the institutionalization of permanent war, the suspension of civil liberties, and an active hostility of the state and mass media toward attempts at addressing the underlying conditions that gave rise to an unprecedented attack on U.S. soil.

Militarized schooling in America can be understood in at least two broad ways: "military education" and what I am calling "education as enforcement." Military education refers to explicit efforts to expand and legitimate military training in public schooling. These sorts of programs are exemplified by JROTC (Junior Reserve Officer Training Corps) programs, the

Kenneth J. Saltman is an assistant professor in Social and Cultural Foundations in Education at DePaul University. He is the author of *Collateral Damage: Corporatizing Public Schools—A Threat to Democracy* (Rowman & Littlefield, 2001) and co-author with Robin Truth Goodman of *Strangelove, Or How We Learn to Stop Worrying and Love the Market* (Rowman & Littlefield, 2002).

Troops to Teachers program that places retired soldiers in schools, the trend of military generals hired as school superintendents or CEOs, the uniform movement, the Lockheed Martin corporation's public school in Georgia, and the army's development of the biggest online education program in the world as a recruiting inducement. The large number of private military schools such as the notorious Valley Forge Military Academy that service the public military academies and the military itself could be thought of as a kind of ideal toward which public school militarization strives. Military education seeks to promote military recruitment as in the case of the 200,000 students in 1,420 JROTC army programs nationwide. These programs parallel the Boy Scouts and Girl Scouts by turning hierarchical organization, competition, group cohesion, and weaponry into fun and games. Focusing on adventure activities these programs are extremely successful as half (47 percent) of JROTC graduates enter military service.

In addition to promoting recruitment, military education plays a central role in fostering a social focus on discipline. In short, to speak of militarized schooling in the United States context it is inadequate to identify the ways that schools increasingly resemble the military and prisons. This phenomenon needs to be understood as part of the militarization of civil society exemplified by the rise of militarized policing, increased police powers for search and seizure, antipublic gathering laws, "zero tolerance" policies, and the transformation of welfare into punishing workfare programs. The militarization of civil society has been intensified since September 11, as conservatives and most liberals have seized upon the "terrorist threat" to justify the passage of the USA Patriot Act. As Nancy Chang of the Center for Constitutional Rights explains, the Patriot Act sacrifices political freedoms and dangerously consolidates power in the executive branch.

> It achieves these undemocratic ends in at least three ways. First, the act places our First Amendment rights to freedom of speech and political association in jeopardy by creating a broad new crime of "domestic terrorism" and denying entry to noncitizens on the basis of ideology. Second, the act reduces our already low expectations of privacy by granting the government enhanced surveillance powers. Third, the act erodes the due process rights of noncitizens by allowing the government to place them in mandatory detention and deport them from the United States based on political activities that have been recast under the act as terrorist activities.[1]

As Chang persuasively argues, the Patriot Act does little to combat terrorism yet it radically threatens basic constitutional safeguards, most notably the freedom of political dissent, which is, in many ways, the lifeblood of democracy as it forms the basis for public deliberation about the future of the nation. The repressive elements of the state in the form of such phenomena as militarized policing, the radical growth of the prison system, and intensified surveillance accompany the increasing corporate control of daily life. The corporatization of the everyday is characterized by the corporate domination of information production and distribution in the form of control over mass media and educational publishing, the corporate use of information technologies in the form of consumer identity profiling by marketing and credit card companies, and the increasing corporate involvement in public schooling and higher education at multiple levels. The phrase Education as Enforcement attempts to explain these merging phenomena of militarization and corporatization as they are shaping not only the terrain of school but the broader society. The term refers both to the ways that education as a field is being transformed by these trends but also it refers to the extent to which education is central to the workings of the new forms that power is taking.

What I am calling "Education as Enforcement" understands militarized public schooling as part of the militarization of civil society that in turn needs to be understood as part of the broader social, cultural, and economic movements for state-backed corporate globalization that seek to erode public democratic power and expand and enforce corporate power locally, nationally, and globally. In what follows here I lay out these connections. Then, by reading news coverage of NATO's attack against Kosovo in relation to the shooting at Columbine High School, the latter half of this introduction shows how both events were driven by the same corporate-driven cultural logic of militaristic violence. I continue by discussing how the movement against militarism in education must challenge the many ways that militarism as a cultural logic enforces the expansion of corporate power and decimates public democratic power.

Educating to Enforce Globalization

Corporate globalization, which should be viewed as a doctrine rather than as an inevitable phenomenon, is driven by the philosophy of neoliberalism. The economic and political doctrine of neoliberalism insists upon the virtues of privatization and liberalization of trade and concomitantly places faith in the hard discipline of the market for the resolution of all social and individual problems. Within the United States neoliberal policies have been characterized by their supporters as "free market policies that encourage private enterprise and consumer choice, reward personal responsibility and entrepreneurial initiative, and undermine the dead hand of the incompetent, bureaucratic and parasitic government, that can never do good even if well intended, which it rarely is."[2] Within the neoliberal view, the public sphere should either be privatized as in the call to privatize U.S. public schools, public parks, social security, health care, and so on, or the public sphere should be in the service of the private sphere as in the case of U.S. federal subsidies for corporate agriculture, entertainment, and defense.

As many critics have observed, globalization efforts have hardly resulted in more just social relations either in terms of access to political power or democratic control over the economy. While corporate news media heralded economic boom at the millennium's turn, disparities in wealth have reached greater proportions than during the Great Depression,[3] with the world's richest three hundred individuals possessing more wealth than the world's poorest forty-eight countries combined, and the richest fifteen have a greater fortune than the total product of sub-Saharan Africa.[4]

According to the most recent report of the United Nations Development Programme, while the global consumption of goods and services was twice as big in 1997 as in 1975 and had multiplied by a factor of six since 1950, 1 billion people cannot satisfy even their elementary needs. Among 4.5 billion of the residents of the "developing" countries, three in every five are deprived of access to basic infrastructures: a third have no access to drinkable water, a quarter have no accommodation worthy of its name, one-fifth have no use of sanitary and medical services. One in five children spend less than five years in any form of schooling; a similar proportion is permanently undernourished.[5]

Austerity measures imposed by world trade organizations such as the World Bank and the International Monetary Fund ensure that poor nations stay poor by imposing "fiscal discipline" while no such discipline applies to entire industries that are heavily subsidized by the public sector in the United States. While the official U.S. unemployment rate hovers around 5 percent, the real wage has steadily decreased since the 1970s to the point that not a single county in the nation contains one bedroom apartments affordable for a single minimum wage earner.[6] Free trade agreements such as NAFTA (and the FTAA that aims to extent it) and GATT, have enriched corporate elites in Mexico and the United States while intensifying poverty along the border.[7] Free trade has meant capital flight, job loss, and the dismantling of labor unions in the United States, and the growth of slave labor conditions in nations receiving industrial production such as Indonesia and China. But perhaps the ultimate failure of liberal capitalism is indicated by its success in distributing Coca-Cola to every last niche of the globe while it has failed to supply inexpensive medicines for preventable diseases, or nutritious food or living wages to these same sprawling shanty towns in Ethiopia, Brazil, and the United States. Forty-seven million children in the richest twenty-nine nations in the world are living below the poverty line. Child poverty in the *wealthiest* nations has worsened with real wages as national incomes have risen over the past half century.[8] The effects of globalization on world populations are a far cry from freedom.

Neoliberalism as the doctrine behind global capitalism should be understood in relation to the practice of what Ellen Meiskins Wood calls the "new imperialism," that is "not just a matter of controlling particular territories. It is a matter of controlling a whole world economy and global markets, everywhere and all the time."[9] The project of globalization according to *New York Times* foreign correspondent Thomas L. Friedman "is our overarching national interest" and it "requires a stable power structure, and no country is more essential for this than the United States," for "[i]t has a large standing army, equipped with more aircraft carriers, advanced fighter jets, transport aircraft and nuclear weapons than ever, so that it can project more power farther than any country in the world ... America excels in all the new measures of power in the era of globalization." As Friedman explains, rallying for the "humanitarian" bombing of Kosovo, "[t]he hidden hand of the market will never work without the hidden fist—McDonald's cannot flourish without McDonnell Douglas, the designer of the F-15. And the hidden fist that keeps the world safe for Silicon Valley's technologies is called the

United States Army, Air Force, Navy, and Marine Corps."[10] The Bush administration's new military policies of permanent war confirm Wood's thesis. The return to cold war levels of military spending approaching $400 billion with only 10–15 percent tied to increased antiterrorism measures can be interpreted as part of a more overt strategy of U.S. imperial expansion facilitated by skillful media spin amid post-September 11 anxiety. The framing of those events enabled not only a more open admission of violent power politics and defiant U.S. unilateralism but also an intensified framing of democracy as consumer capitalism. Who can forget the September 12 state and corporate proclamations to be patriotic and go shopping. Post-September 11 spin was a spectacularly successful educational project. Suddenly, in teacher education courses, students who would have proudly announced that they could see no relationship between U.S. foreign policy and U.S. schooling now proudly announced that teachers must educate students toward the national effort to dominate, control, and wage war on other nations who could threaten our economic and military dominance because we have the best "way of life," because "they are jealous of our freedoms," because "they are irrational for failing to grasp that our way of life benefits everybody." Yet, the new Bush military expenditures are part of a longer legacy of World War II military spending that has resulted in a U.S. economy that is, in the words of economist Samir Amin, "monstrously deformed," with about a third of all economic activity depending directly or indirectly on the military complex— a level, Amin notes, only previously reached by the Soviet Union during the Brezhnev era.[11]

The impoverishing power of globalization is matched by the military destructive power of the new imperialism that enforces neoliberal policy to make the world safe for U.S. markets. However, weapons are not the predominant means for keeping Americans consenting to economic policies and political arrangements that impoverish the world materially and reduce the imaginable future to a repetition of a bleak present. Rather, education in the form of formal schooling and predominantly the cultural pedagogies of corporate mass media have succeeded spectacularly in making savage inequalities into common sense, framing issues in the corporate interest, producing identifications with raw power, presenting history in ways that eviscerate popular struggle, and generally shifting the discussion of public goods to the metaphors of the market.[12]

Though initially received as a radical and off-beat position by liberals and conservatives at the time of its promotion by Milton Friedman during the Kennedy administration, neoliberalism began to take hold with the Reagan/Thatcher era. Significantly, the Reagan era is also the origin of the landmark *A Nation at Risk* report published in 1983. This formulated a crisis of U.S. public education through the language of global business and military competition. It began, "If an unfriendly foreign power had attempted to impose on America the mediocre educational performance that exists today, we might well have viewed it as an act of war." The report suggested that there was a crisis of education requiring radical reform. Because the crisis was framed in economic and militaristic terms, the solution would be sought in those domains. This marked a turning point in the public conversation of American education. While such earlier initiatives as the GI Bill and Sputnik indicated a strong link between the military and education, what can be seen as new is the way that militarism was tied to the redefining of education for the corporate good rather than the public good. In other words, this marked a new conflation of corporate profit with the social good, the beginnings of the eradication of the very notion of the public. Corporate CEOs became increasingly legitimate spokepersons on educational reform. Such high-profile corporate players as Louis Gerstner of IBM began declaring that education needs to serve corporate needs. Increasingly, as David Labaree has noted, this trend marked a shift toward defining the role of schools as preparing students for upward social mobility through economic assimilation. So, while on a social level, schools were suddenly thought to exist for the good of the national economy, that is the corporate controlled economy, on an individual level, schools came to be justified for inclusion within this corporate-controlled economy.

The case of Michael Milken nicely exemplifies the relationship between the neoliberal redefinition of the goals of public schooling and the privatization movement. Upon release from prison for ninety-eight counts of fraud and insider trading that resulted in the milking of the public sector of billions of dollars, junk bond king Michael Milken immediately began an education conglomerate called Knowledge Universe with his old pals from investment bank Drexel. As he bought up companies engaged in privatizing public schooling, he declared on his website that schools should serve corporate needs. He was wildly lauded throughout the press by such respectable papers as the *New York Times,* and was declared a greater figure than Mother Teresa by *Business Week* for redeeming himself from a tainted past by such good works in education. In addition to Knowledge Universe, Milken established the Milken Institute that propagandizes neoliberal social policy, and he set up the Milken Family Foundation that funds research and lobbies for privatization of Israel's economy and education system through the Jerusalem Center for Public Affairs. He also funded Justus Reid Weiner's slanderous attack in *Commentary Magazine* on Palestinian human rights spokesperson and progressive intellectual Edward Said. Milken was instrumental in the growth to monopolistic proportions of Time Warner, which included Time's swallowing of Warner Brothers and Turner Broadcasting, and the growth of MCI. As Robert W. McChesney, Edward Herman, and others have shown, the radical consolidation of corporate media with its stranglehold on knowledge production has contributed significantly to the success of neoliberal ideology.[13]

Neoliberal ideals were not taken seriously until the 1990s, in part because of the fall of the Soviet Union in 1991. This began a tide of claims that we live in the best and only social order. This is a social order marked by what Zygmunt Bauman calls the TINA thesis: There Is No Alternative to the present system.[14] The TINA thesis was started by Francis Fukuyama's "End of History" argument and runs through Thomas Friedman's *The Lexus and the Olive Tree* with its circular logic: everyone in the world wants to be American because this is the best of all possible systems, and if anyone does not want to be American, this proves their irrationality and we must bomb them into realizing that this is the best of all possible systems. The dissolution of the Soviet system as a symbol of a possible alternative allows a growing insistence on the part of neoliberals that since the present order is the only order, then the task should be one of enforcing the ideals of the order, aligning institutions and social practices with these ideals. So for example, you get Washington Post columnist William Rasberry (who favors full-scale public school privatization) writing that scripted lessons may seem harsh but after all "it works."[15] Such an instrumentalist approach to schooling, which overly relies on supposedly value-free and quantifiable measures of "success," fails to account for how efficacy needs to be understood in relation to broader social contexts, histories, and competing notions of what counts as valuable knowledge. So, for example, how did the canon championed by E. D. Hirsch, Jr., with his Core Knowledge Schools come to be socially valued knowledge? Whose class, racial, and gender perspectives does such knowledge represent? There are high social costs of measures such as scripting, standardization, and the testing fetish. Citizenship becomes defined by an anticritical following of authority; knowledge becomes mistakenly presented as value-free units to be mechanically deposited; schooling models the new social logic that emphasizes economic social mobility rather than social transformation—that is, it perceives society as a flawed yet unchangeable situation into which individuals should seek assimilation in the New World Order.

This criticism of instrumental schooling would seem not to be a terribly new insight. In education, the tradition of critical pedagogy that includes Freire, Apple, Giroux, and others made this critical insight a basic precept. However, what is distinct about instrumentalism under the neoliberal imperative is that prior taken-for-granted ideals of an education system intended to ameliorate, enlighten, and complete the individual and society no longer hold. For neoliberalism is not simply about radical individualism, the celebration of business, and competition as a virtue; it is about a prohibition on thinking the social in public terms. In the words of Margaret Thatcher "there is no such thing as English society," there are only English families.[16] The insidiousness of the TINA thesis cannot be overstated. When there is no alternative to the present order then the only question is the method of achieving the goal—the goal being the eradication of anything and anyone that calls the present order into question. This is why it has been so easy following September 11 to discuss methods that are radically at odds with the tradition of liberal democracy in the war on terrorism. (It is no coincidence that the new war is declared on a *method of fighting* rather than an ideological opponent or another nation. Precisely because there is no alternative to the present order, the values, ideologies, and beliefs of the opponent are not discussable. Ethics can only be a matter of strategy.) Torture of prisoners, disappearances of suspects, spying on the population without limit, and an unprecedented level of secrecy about the workings of the government are a few of the proto-fascist developments that have been achieved within the first year since September 11. But the destruction of the trade towers did not itself make this rush to fascism possible so much as did the success of neoliberal ideology's prohibition on thinking, discussing, and creating another more just system of economic distribution, political participation, and cultural recognition.

Ronald Reagan entered office with plans to dismantle the U.S. Department of Education and implement market-based voucher schemes. Both initiatives failed largely due to teachers' unions and the fact that public opinion had yet to be worked on by a generation of corporate-financed public relations campaigns to make neoliberal ideals appear commonsensical.[17] Despite this failure, in his second term Reagan successfully appropriated the racial, equity-based, magnet school voucher model developed by liberals to declare that the market model (rather than authoritative federal action against racism) was responsible for the high quality of these schools.[18] What should not be missed here is that the real triumph of such rhetoric was to shift the discussion of U.S. public schooling away from political concerns with the role that education should play in preparing citizens for democratic participation. The market metaphors redefine public schooling as a good or service that students and parents consume like toilet paper or soap. Despite a history of racial and class oppression, that owes in no small part to the fact that U.S. public schooling has been tied to local property wealth and hence unequally distributed as a resource, public schooling has been a site of democratic deliberation where communities convene to struggle over values. Despite the material and ideological constraints that teachers and administrators often face, the public character of these schools allows them to remain open to the possibility of being places where curricula and teacher practices can speak to a broader vision for the future than the one imagined by multinational corporations. Thus, to speak of militarized public schooling in the United States, it is not enough to identify the extent to which certain schools (particularly urban nonwhite schools) increasingly resemble the military or prisons, nor is it adequate to point out the ways public schools are used to recruit soldiers. Militarized public schooling needs to be understood in relation to the enforcement of globalization through the implementation of all the policies and reforms that are guided toward the neoliberal ideal. Globalization gets enforced through privatization schemes such as vouchers, charters, performance contracting, and commercialization; standards and accountability schemes that seek to enforce a uniform curriculum and emphasize testing and quantifiable performance; assessment, accreditation (in higher education), and curricula that celebrate market values and the culture of those in power rather than human and democratic values. Such curricula and reforms are designed to avoid critical questions about the relationships between the production of knowledge and power, authority, politics, history, and ethics. While some multinational corporations, such as Disney in their Celebration School, and BPAmoco (see chapter 2), with their middle-level science curriculum, have appropriated progressive pedagogical *methods*, these curricula, like ads, strive to promote a vision of a world best served under benevolent corporate management.

Selling War

JROTC and standard recruitment, prior to September 11, proved insufficient to keep the voluntary U.S. military stocked with enough soldiers to wield, in the words of Thomas Friedman, "the hidden fist that keeps the world safe for Silicon Valley's technologies and McDonald's."[19] In fact, military recruiting in the United States has seen a crisis in the past few years. As of 1999 the army suffered its worst recruiting drought since 1979 with a shortage of 7,000 enlistees to maintain a force size of 74,500. The air force fell short by 1,500–1,800, while the navy had to cut its target numbers and lower its requirements to make numbers,[20] As recruitment target numbers have not been met, the military has invested heavily in a number of new advertising campaigns that radically redefine the image of the military and use "synergy" to promote the branches of the service in Hollywood films and on television. For example, navy ads use clips from the film *Men of Honor*, with military advertising preceding the film. Because the U.S. military must rely fully upon consent rather than coercion to fill its ranks, the military is portrayed in ads as fun and exciting, and the heroism of service is tied to the most sentimental depictions that play on childhood innocence and family safety to sell youth on the business of killing.

The new campaign for the air force titled "Lullaby" promotes its new slogan "No One Comes Close." Quadrupling its advertising budget to $76 million (all the services are spending $11,000 per recruit on advertising),[21] buying national television slots for the first time, and using a "brand identity" based approach, the new marketing seeks to induce recruitment by filling the airwaves with "value-based" advertising that emphasizes the "intangibles" of military service.[22] For example:

> An ad called "Lullaby," for example, shows home videos of happy children and their mother with a soft voice singing in the background. At the words "guardian angels will attend thee all through the night," the visual image shifts to an F-117 "stealth" fighter roaring across a dark sky. The only explicit appeal to recruits comes in the final second, when the Air Force's new slogan, "No One Comes Close," appears on a black screen followed for an instant by the words "Join Us."[23]

A central strategy of this campaign as well as the army's new "Army of One" campaign is to suggest a heroic exclusivity of service in this particular branch. All of the branches are following the marine corps' successful campaign that "portrayed enlistment as a chance to become a dragon-slaying knight in shining armor. The macho ads were designed to convince young people that joining the Marines was not merely a career choice but a powerful statement about what kind of adults they intended to become."[24]

The Air Force advertisement draws on Judeo-Christian imagery of an angry and protective techno-god. By joining the air force one can be the protector of the innocent and approach the infinite power of the almighty—interchangeably God and the unmatchable techno-power of Lockheed Martin, Boeing, McDonnell-Douglas, and Raytheon. To be in the air force, the ad suggests, is to be in an elite and exclusive, powerful, and moral position. Another set of public service announcement ads aimed at adults seeks to "ensure that parents, teachers and other 'adult influencers' know about the educational programs so that they, in turn, can advise young people."[25] These ads stress tangible rewards such as educational opportunities, high-tech skills training, and managerial expertise, which can later translate into cash in the corporate sector.

While the United States offers no public universal higher education program in civil society, it does so through the military. Ryan's statement about the higher calling of serving our nation is hardly a sentiment reserved for a conservative military establishment. Liberals and conservatives join in proclaiming the virtues of a military form of public service at a time when public spending goes increasingly for militarized solutions to civic social problems. These militarized solutions have translated into the United States having by far the largest prison system in the world with over two million inmates. Rapidly rising investment in the prison industrial complex, which includes for-profit prisons and high-tech policing, is matched by rapid privatization of the public sector.[26] As U.S. citizens enjoy few of the social safety nets of public health care, education, or welfare, enjoyed by citizens of most industrialized nations, U.S. public institutions such as hospitals, schools, and social security are subject to the fevered call to privatize. At the same time that public investment in militarizing civil society has come into vogue, the world of the corporate class has discovered military chic. The first issue of *Harper's Bazaar* for the new millennium shows a serious looking fashion model goose stepping down the runway in uniform. The accompanying text sounds off: "Military Coup. Never thought you would crave camouflage? Think again . . . fashion's military scheme will have even the most resistant shopper succumbing to the latest protocol."[27] The model's designer jacket is listed for $1,500, and the cotton skirt runs $370. Military chic for corporate elites extends to the nationwide trend for private boot-camp style exercise classes.

The same marketing strategies designed to lure recruits are used by weapons manufacturers Lockheed Martin and Boeing (along with a lot of money) to lobby the U.S. Congress to continue funding such miserably failed and unbelievably expensive and unnecessary weapons programs as the F-22 joint strike fighter and "Star Wars."[28] As Mark Crispin Miller observes, the defense industry's advertisements not too subtly suggest that the public better fund the weapons projects or American family members will die in foreign wars and from terrorist attacks at home.[29] The weapons manufacturers also use the ads to propose that peace is a result of heavy military investment, thereby obviating the need for social movements for peace such as those that influenced the end of the Vietnam War.

The new campaign for the army, "An Army of One," replaces the "Be All That You Can Be" slogan that was the number two jingle of the twentieth century behind McDonald's "You Deserve a Break Today."[30] The "Army of One" campaign, like its predecessor, stresses individual self-actualization, yet goes a step further to insist upon the ideal of radical individualism. A lone recruit runs across a desert in full gear as troops pass in the opposite direction. Such images would seem to chafe against the necessity of self-sacrifice and teamwork, which more accurately characterizes the military. The new ads insist that every soldier is a hero, is an army. The promise is not merely one of becoming the "best" that one can be, a promise that implies there might still be someone better; the "Army of One" slogan promises that one incorporates the army into oneself, one renounces oneself and actually becomes the army with all of its power and technology. The Army slogan is consistent with the virtual tour offered by the marine corps. This tour begins by explicitly linking the militaristic renunciation of self to economic metaphors:

> One must first be stripped clean. Freed of all the notions of self. It is the marine corps that will strip away the façade so easily confused with the self. It is the corps that will offer the pain needed to *buy* the truth. And at last each will *own* the privilege of looking inside himself to discover what truly resides there.[31]

One renounces oneself. One's body undergoes torments of the flesh. Yet this pain inflicted through training is currency that allows one to buy knowledge of one's new self. At the end of the tour one learns that self-renunciation, pain, the breaking and remaking, and ultimate purchase of self-knowledge results in the privatized social unit: "We came as orphans, we depart as family," concludes the marine tour.

Just as family restoration becomes the aim of war in the marine ad, so too does it appear in such blockbuster films as *Saving Private Ryan, Men of Honor, Three Kings,* and *The Thin Red Line.* The brilliant innovation of *Saving Private Ryan* was to make the goal of the good war not the protection of the public so much as the preservation of the private family unit. *Saving Private Ryan* simultaneously shifted democratic ideals onto the market metaphor. Freedom, we are told in the end of *Saving Private Ryan,* needs to be *earned* by individuals. When they have earned their freedom they can go home.

Coming Home to Kosovo

> Fifty years ago, movies were homogenous, meant to appeal to the whole family. Now pop culture has been Balkanized. . . . Recent teen films, whether romance or horror, are really about class warfare. In each movie, the cafeteria is like a tiny former Yugolsavia, with each clique its own faction: the Serbian jocks, Bosnian bikers, Kosovar rebels, etc. And the horror movies are a microcosm of ethnic cleansing.
>
> —*Time* magazine reporting on the shootings at Columbine

> We must teach our children . . . to resolve their conflicts with words, not weapons.
>
> —President Bill Clinton responding to the Columbine High School shooting as the U.S. dropped more bombs on former-Yugoslavia than were dropped in World War II.

This section[32] illustrates how the corporate-produced violent culture of mass media and competitive sports informs both U.S. public schooling and U.S. foreign policy. As mass-mediated news accounts of the war in Kosovo were expressed through stories of families abroad, the school shooting in Littleton, Colorado, refocused the nation's attention on violence at home. As the story unfolded "The Littleton Massacre" and "The Kosovo Massacre" began to merge, elements of one bleeding into the other. On April 20, 1999, Hitler's 110th birthday, two white boys, calling themselves the Trenchcoat Mafia, shot and killed twelve of their fellow students and one teacher before turning their guns on themselves. This event was a tragedy that caused terrible, even devastating sadness for many people. The enormous, spectacular coverage of the event, of the magnitude of the 1992 L.A. uprising, however, participates in broader public dialogues, particularly in the way it works to assign blame variously to errant parents, crazy kids, lack of adequate policing, and violent video games while exonerating the institutions of power, particularly in the ways they configure economic, political, and social agency. How many black kids died in the United States that day because of violence and guns, and why is that information so comparatively hard to access, particularly during a media spectacle that is highlighting the dangers that kids confront in public schools? In reality, violence in schools has diminished in the past ten years even while people perceive there to be more violence in schools.[33] Even more relevant, how many Serbian and ethnic Albanian kids were killed in NATO bombings that day? Adults pose a far greater threat to youth than youth do.[34] How and in whose interests are these perceptions manufactured?

The December 20, 1999, issue of *Time* magazine featured exclusive coverage of "The Columbine Tapes: The Killers Tell Why They Did It, The Five Home Videos They Made Before Their Death, What the Families Are Doing to Prevent Another Tragedy." The cover shows Eric Harris and Dylan Klebold assessing their damage from a frame of the school cafeteria surveillance video. Open *Time* magazine and immediately following the contents page is a two-page advertisement for Internet search engine AltaVista. The advertisement displays the Lockheed Martin F-16 fighter plane in an exploded blueprint diagram with every part labeled and with the external body of the plane invisible so that the interior is revealed, as in Wonder Woman's aviational aesthetic. The Altavista search box overlaying the schematic reveals a search for "Who will guide my sleigh tonight?" Another box headed "AltaVista shopping" contains a first category "find product" and is filled in "F-16"; the second category "compare with" is filled in with "Reindeer." Turn the page and the advertisement continues with Santa's sled being pulled by an F-16, a weapon that U.S.-led NATO used to bomb Serbia "back to the stone ages."

> Thanks to the F-16s top speed of 1,320 mph, Santa will be delivering your presents faster this holiday season. Furthermore, the F-16's armament of one 20mm M61A1 three-barrel cannon with 515 rounds and 20,450 pounds of ordnance guarantees the safe arrival of those presents.

At the top of the page an elf sips a soda and accompanying text reads,

> Who needs elves when you have AltaVista Shopping.com? At AltaVista Shopping.com you can research products you know nothing about: stereos, computers, TV's, digital cameras and Pokemon toys, for example. There are 126

different Pokemon characters and over 2,000 licensed Pokemon toys on the market. Only one of them is going to win you most-favored parent status for the coming year. We can help you find out which.

At the bottom of the page, eight cute out-of-work, clearly nonunionized reindeer are accompanied by a search box that reads, "Where can I sell eight tiny reindeer?" Between the three pages of AltaVista ads, *Time* Managing Editor Walter Isaacson editorializes on "Why We Went Back to Columbine." The title, which references a slew of recent stories on returning to Vietnam after a quarter of a century, is headed by a photograph of triumphant white high school football players with the caption: "Healing the Wounds: Columbine Celebrates Its Recent State Championship."

On one level there is nothing particularly new here in *Time*'s spread. The white male violence of football, toy weapons, violent video games, and global imperialist ventures such as Vietnam and Kosovo arise as the tools for recovering the health of youth and family threatened by the insane and random joyride of the gun-toting Columbine murderers. The AltaVista ad restores the innocence of technology and violent aggression—Internet technology that Klebold and Harris used in their little war. The ad returns the web technology to innocence by associating it with the destructive NATO attack done in the name of love or at least humanitarian intervention, but also by associating it with consumerism.

A large part of the public incredulity over Columbine stems from the very fine line between the "innocent" yet pervasive culture of violence that sells consumer goods and the "pathological" culture of violence that does not sell consumer goods or expand markets. The "innocent" culture of violence transforms imperialist slaughter into Christmas morning family love and fuzzy cuteness. It portrays as healing and recovery violent team sports that emulate war—Columbine High School football team's "state conquest." It mutates military hardware into a fashion show for viewers to identify with destructive power (AltaVista's motto adorning the F–16 blueprint is "Smart Is Beautiful"). Central to this recovery of the "innocent" culture of violence is the transformation of justice into the act of consumption. The final text of the ad reads:

> *Can I really purchase military aircraft online?* Let's put it this way: if military aircraft were available for purchase by the general public, we'd not only find it for you, we'd find you a deal that would make the Defense Department jealous. That said, AltaVistaShopping.com lets you scour the entire Web for just about anything you can buy, even if we don't sell it.

What is so shocking and even terrifying in this spread is an open admission that U.S. military aggression in such places as the Balkans and Iraq is fundamentally about the expansion of markets.

Yet the big lie at work here is the suggestion that the dropping of bombs is the same as the dropping of consumer goods (the expansion of markets), done all in the name of the preservation of childhood innocence as the stronghold of a civilization severely menaced when these values go awry. The ad suggests that destruction is really about the enrichment of the place being bombed because it is about the expansion of American wealth, markets, and consumer goods. While multinational corporations did line up to take advantage of infrastructural rebuilding, some estimates placed former Yugoslavia's recovery time from the bombing at fifty years. Perhaps more pertinently, those places that have agreed to Americanization without bombs have also suffered terribly from "structural adjustment." If Isaacson's interceding headline "Why We Went Back to Columbine" resonates with a spate of articles about why we went back to Vietnam, that is because the bombing of Kosovo as a part of the new imperialism really is a return to Vietnam, and Isaacson's headline is simultaneously about how *Time* magazine's return to Columbine is also a return to Vietnam.

In fact, the imperialist venture of bombing Kosovo is replicated in the call for increased discipline, mostly in inner cities, which followed the Columbine massacre. As Harris and Klebold let a slew of bullets loose on the suburban kids who were calmly eating their lunches or studying chemistry before the attack, the tragedy of a cruel Milosevic performing ethnocide came home. The need for the intervention to defend the defenseless Albanians blurred into the need to defend our kids at home through increasing police enforcement of inner cities. Reflected in the coverage of the Columbine massacre, Kosovo thus appeared as the exporting of the inner city. Columbine coverage entered a discourse on youth innocence that is essentially an imperialist discourse assigning criminality to the colonized. It thus treats youth differently depending on race and class. As Harris and Klebold created public website paeans to Hitler, declared hatred for blacks, Asians, and Latinos, still no one believed white kids from the suburbs were capable of such violence. As Henry Giroux points out,

> If these kids had been black or brown, they would have been denounced not as psychologically troubled but as bearers of a social pathology. Moreover, if brown or black kids had exhibited Eric Harris and Dylan Klebold's previous history of delinquent behavior, including breaking into a van and sending death threats to fellow students over the Internet, they would not have merely been given short-term counseling. On the contrary, they would have been roundly condemned and quickly sent to prison.[35]

In the words of Patricia Williams, Klebold and Harris,

> seem to have been so shrouded in presumptions of innocence—after professing their love for Hitler, declaring their hatred for blacks, Asians and Latinos on a public Web site no less, downloading instructions for making bombs, accumulating the ingredients, assembling them under the protectively indifferent gaze (or perhaps with the assistance) of parents and neighbors, stockpiling guns and ammunition, procuring hand grenades and flak jackets, threatening the lives of classmates, killing thirteen and themselves, wounding numerous others and destroying their school building—still the community can't seem to believe it really happened "here." Still their teachers and classmates continue to protest that they were good kids, good students, solid citizens.[36]

What *Time* and AltaVista add to this scenario is that the presumption of innocence saturating the Columbine coverage promotes the innocence of the imperialist mission in Kosovo.

Returning to Vietnam in Kosovo

Similar to the public conversation at the beginning of the Gulf War, endless articles debating the Kosovo air war focused on the danger of a ground war that would get the United States embroiled in "another Vietnam." As Noam Chomsky points out, there has been a long project in mass media of getting the public to overcome the "Vietnam Syndrome." That is, the conservative restoration of the past three decades has involved making global aggression and the murder of combatants and non-combatants in foreign nations once again palatable to the public. Yet, Kosovo is different from Vietnam and the hot wars of the cold war in that the ventures of militarized globalization since the end of the cold war are still not viewed by the public as worth U.S. lives. Writes Ellen Meiskins Wood,

> In his Manifesto [for the Fast World], [Thomas L.] Friedman explains that Americans, who "were ready to pay any price and bear any burden in the Cold War," are unwilling to die for that "abstract globalization system." That's why "house-to-house fighting is out; cruise missiles are in." He could just as easily have said "that's why ground troops are out and high-tech bombing is in. We don't want to die ourselves for globalization, but we don't mind killing others."[37]

For Wood, part of what successfully undercut popular and particularly left opposition to Kosovo, unlike Vietnam, was the pretense of humanitarian intervention that mystified the imperialism.

> We now have what some have called "human rights imperialism," based on a conception of human rights in which the particular interests of the U.S. and its arbitrary actions have effectively displaced the common interests of humanity and the international instruments designed to represent them. The notion of "human rights imperialism" nicely captures the mystification that seems to have swayed a lot of people on the left in the case of Kosovo.[38]

Open claims in news outlets as to the humanitarianism of the bombing were matched by a spate of popular war films such as *Saving Private Ryan* and culminating in *The Patriot*, which brought the "good war" theme back after a long stretch of "bad war" Vietnam films.

If pre-Kosovo *Saving Private Ryan* reinvented the public and political motives for World War II as the redemption of the private and apolitical maintenance of the family, then post-Kosovo *The Patriot* took this theme even further, suggesting that the American Revolution, the good war par excellence, was about nothing but family. "What difference does it make if I'm ruled by a tyrant three thousand miles away or by three thousand tyrants one mile away," orates Mel Gibson's character at the South Carolina meeting about whether to enter the war on the side of the colonies, just before joining up to defend his southern plantation family. In other words, fighting for the politics of democracy poses dangers to the preservation of the family and, in fact, Gibson's two eldest sons get killed in the fray.

The film further marks the disruption of the family through the British enslavement of the black plantation farmhands who claim to be working as free labor, the system many characters in the film insist the revolutionaries are defending. In the film, the black plantation laborers explicitly claim to be working as free labor rather than as slaves (until the tyrannical British arrest them and turn them into slaves), even though the images of black labor are surely borrowed from a cultural repertory of traditional, familiar images from slavery. The film suggests that the war was about freeing the slaves in defense of ideas about self-determination and free will (represented in the defense of the family against state authoritarianism), the goal of the "good war." It is only when the British threaten this self-determination—by entering the home and killing one of the kids, and by enslaving black labor—that a defense campaign can be taken up. Just as the AltaVista ad replaces fanciful toy reindeer with real fighter planes, in *The Patriot* Mel Gibson's character melts down his dead son's toy lead soldiers into bullets. The campaign against Kosovo involved getting over the "Vietnam Syndrome" to return to the "good war" by reinventing imperialist aggression as a loving gift, associating it with the childhood innocence of Rudolph the Red-nosed Reindeer and Santa Claus himself. Merry Christmas, Kosovo. Merry Christmas, Serbia.

War Games: Returning to Vietnam in Littleton

The Columbine shooting coverage was also a return to the battlefield. As mentioned, Isaacson's title "Why We Went Back to Columbine" references the return to Vietnam after twenty-five years in order to open markets. It is contextualized with a photo of Columbine's football team conquest. Isaacson begins:

> I want to explain why we returned to Columbine this week, running a chilling cover photo and stories about killers we would rather forget . . . we sent a team back to Littleton, Colo., to investigate what actually motivated the killers and find out what they were really like. What could we learn about how to spot— and deal with—the demons that can lurk inside the souls of seemingly average kids? . . . Assistant managing editor Dan *Goodgame*, who led our team, is the father of three schoolkids and the husband of a teacher, and he was sympathetic to the concerns of the survivors and others in the community.[39]

It is, perhaps, a coincidence that the leader of *Time*'s team that went in search of "answers" about Columbine is named "Goodgame." It is not, however, a coincidence that Isaacson uses the metaphor of the "good game" to discuss the Columbine recovery, health, and healing. The AltaVista ads link global trade and military competition between nations to parental competition for children's love: "Only one [Pokemon toy] is going to win you most-favored parent status for the coming year."

It is not only the editorial and the AltaVista spread that refer to gaming. Page after page of *Time* is filled with "news" and advertisements that tout the salubrious power of gaming as well as its dangers: Headline page eight— "Is Your Dog an Athlete?" "Border collies ... get psychotic if they don't have work."[40] Page nine: "Enter to win the APC Home Power Protection Package." Two-page spread on twelve and thirteen advertising ClearStation.com: "I'm simply going to move to the sidelines until the trend becomes more clear." Turn the page and Mohegan Sun Casino asks, "Who needs caffeine? Experience the rush of 190 gaming tables, over 3,000 slot machines. . . . All in a setting that'll blow you away." Turn the page and see James Bond, the regal and suave gamer extraordinaire who blows away his opponents, pitching an Omega watch. Turn the page and find a colorful two-page spread with a man on the Olympic rings transforming into mercury and information for a web application called Akamai, "Why embrace mediocrity and risk indifference when intensity and impact are at your fingertips." Turn two pages and a girl shoots hoops in an idyllic black and white photo of the heartland as State Farm Insurance tells us that "She learned about life in a world of broken glass and blacktop where nothing is given. Especially to those trying to play a man's game. . . . State Farm is a proud supporter of women's sports and women's dreams. Little girls have big dreams too." Turn the page and the daily game of the stock market advertises Compaq computers. Turn again and the new ExxonMobil oil conglomerate tells us that their anticompetitive merger is in fact "A future where the best combination of ideas, technology and talent will win." A page turn later and an arthritis drug has a two-page spread of a father and son on a soccer field, "Vioxx can help make it easier for you to do the things you want to do. Like sitting down on the grass to watch your kid's game." But you may not be sitting too long as, "Commonly reported side effects included upper respiratory infection, diarrhea, nausea, and high blood pressure." Other news content of *Time* is, of course, also framed in terms of competition from the education article on the dangers of cheating to the "Winners and Sinners of 1999" column to the Columbine tapes feature itself.

The difficulty that parents, teachers, and the police had in identifying the violent outbursts of Harris and Klebold owes, in part, to the normalcy of such competitive violence that saturates not only *Time* magazine's reporting and advertisements but pervades mass media more generally, particularly as it sells the public on globalization. Such a fine line between "healthy" and "pathological" competitive violence became particularly blurry as Bill Clinton himself said after the tragedy, while continuing the bombing campaign on Kosovo, refusing diplomatic solutions, "We must teach our children . . . to resolve their conflicts with words, not weapons."

The Columbine story involves regularly repeated acts of playing: "Eric Harris adjusts his video camera a few feet away, then settles into his chair with a bottle of Jack Daniels and a sawed-off shotgun in his lap. He calls it Arlene, after a favorite character in the gory Doom video games and books that he likes so much. He takes a small swig. The whiskey stings, but he tries to hide it, like a small child playing grownup." "It's going to be like f—ing Doom. Tick, tick, tick, tick-Haa! That f—ing shotgun is straight out of

Doom." "It's easy to see the signs: how a video-game joystick turned Harris into a better marksman like a golfer who watches Tiger Woods videos."[41] Whereas Clinton equates "playing grown-up" with playing with words, Harris and Klebold equate "playing grown-up" with the violence of adults like Clinton and the valorization of violent competition more generally.

News coverage downplayed the fact that Harris and Klebold were resolving a conflict in a way consistent with the competitive violence surrounding them. Instead *Time* opts to emphasize the shooters' thirst for fame. A photo in the *Time* coverage of angry and imposing-looking football players is titled, "The classmates Harris and Klebold felt immense rage toward all, not just jocks." Yet later commentary reveals the extent to which the shooters did seek revenge against the violent culture that targeted them.

> Evan Todd, the 255-lb. Defensive lineman who was wounded in the library, describes the climate this way: "Columbine is a clean, good place except for those rejects," Todd says of Klebold and Harris and their friends. "Most kids didn't want them there. They were into witchcraft. They were into voodoo dolls. Sure, we teased them. But what do you expect with kids who come to school with weird hairdos and horns on their hats? It's not just jocks; the whole school's disgusted with them. They're a bunch of homos, grabbing each other's private parts. If you want to get rid of someone, usually you tease 'em. So the whole school would call them homos, and when they did something sick, we'd tell them, "You're sick and that's wrong."[42]

Time's commentary, in the tradition of nineteenth-century sciences of race, positions Harris and Klebold as uppity, mutinous colonized subjects practicing magical curses against the righteous, governing elite. Because they practice voodoo and because they are "homos," the jocks, like nineteenth-century colonials, serve as defenders of the morality on which civilization is founded and which was threatened by the evil superstitious practices and the unlawful, ungodly sexual proclivities. The superstitious violence of Harris and Klebold is used to justify the disgust and then the violence of the morally upholding jocks.

Remarkably, *Time* uses the above quote as evidence that the shooters were not responding to systematic cruelty by other students. Instead, the article emphasizes a desire for celebrity. However, in the following article, "The Victims: Never Again," the father of victim Daniel Rohrbough says, "jocks could get away with anything. If they wanted to punch a kid in the mouth and walk away, they could. Had I known this, my son wouldn't have been there. They did nothing to protect the students from each other."[43] Rohrbough's statement clearly attests to how the thin facade of innocence barely covered a vicious culture of violence. The tapes themselves reveal the killers' motive to settle a score at being unable to compete: " 'Harris recalls how he moved around so much with his military family and always had to start over, "at the bottom of the ladder." People continually made fun of him—'my face, my hair, my shirts.' As for Klebold, 'If you could see all the anger I've stored over the past four f—ing years' "[44]

The *Time* coverage charges that the police, parents, and the community failed to see how Harris's and Klebold's violent fantasies were motivated not so much by the desire for revenge as ultimately the desire for celebrity. "Because this may have been about celebrity as much as cruelty. 'They wanted to be famous,' concludes FBI agent Mark Holstlaw. 'And they are. They're infamous.' It used to be said that living well is the best revenge; for these two, it was to kill and die in spectacular fashion."[45] The emphasis on the killers' desire for fame in the coverage downplays the extent to which the shootings were politically motivated, as Giroux and Williams show; but the emphasis on fame as an alibi also effaces the extent to which the shootings took the competitive culture of violence to its logical extension, even turning themselves into commodities, notorious for an instant. Harris and Klebold were even willing to sacrifice their own lives to win at the game they had been losing for years.

There is an overwhelming sense in the coverage that police and parents lost the competition with the kids by failing to see the signs, failing in the shootout at the school, and, due to the suicides, even losing the satisfaction of a legal trial to see authority restored symbolically. Just as endless Vietnam films of the 1970s and 80s brought to national consciousness a notion of the Viet Cong as an enemy that cannot be seen, everywhere and nowhere, simultaneously culpable aggressors and innocent victims, media coverage surrounding Columbine and Kosovo framed youth simultaneously as innocent victims in need of saving and as violent aggressors hell-bent on destruction. These Vietnam films produced a nostalgia for a good war in which the enemy was visible, thereby replacing a meaningful public discussion of the motives for U.S. imperial aggression with a suggestion that the real problem behind a war that caused roughly sixty thousand U.S. and over two million Vietnamese lives, was that the U.S. was denied an opportunity to fight the good fight. That representation both denies the politics undergirding U.S. global aggression and it transforms the aggressor into the victim. Similarly, Columbine coverage produced nostalgia for the "good school" with its innocent culture of violence exemplified by white warriors on the football field. The coverage denies the relationship between the pervasive culture of violence that structures the lived realities of school for many students and the broader social structures that such violence serves. It is precisely this connection that *Time*'s editor denies in the "Why We Returned to Columbine" editorial. Says *Time* editor-in-chief Norman Pearlstine, defending *Time*'s sensationalist coverage, "It's not our tendency to sensationalize crime or do covers on the crime of the week. Sometimes, however, a shocking picture—of a wartime execution, a brutality, a kid with a gun—along with an analysis of the tale behind it serves to focus our eyes on things we would prefer to ignore but instead should try to understand."[46] Yet, not unlike the Vietnam War practice of measuring success through body counts, understanding and even justice ultimately become the compilation of the most possible minute details of the event by *Time*'s team, thereby replacing with spectacle a meaningful discussion of the role that the innocent culture of violence plays in maintaining a social order in the service of the corporation.

Within the climate of the innocent culture of violence the endlessly repeated images of collapsing twin towers were nearly seamlessly contextualized as a complete surprise, a fall from American innocence. Rather than confronting the problem with U.S. intervention in the Middle East, central and South America, and elsewhere as the originary violence that has been some of the most brutal of the past century, the event was interpreted as unthinkable and irrational rather than as a political response, thereby justifying an escalation of violence in the Middle East, central and south Asia, and South America. In the declaration of permanent war not on a specific enemy but on a method of warfare, mindless vengeance trumps understanding the history of U.S. imperial violence overseas that brought about such brutal reaction. Moreover, the enemy's ideological commitments, basic values, and historical relation to the U.S. cannot be discussed as the ground of discussion in the war on terrorism is shifted to the methods of struggle. The enemy is anyone in the world who does not pledge allegiance.

Education is becoming increasingly justified on the grounds of national security. This can be seen in the Hart-Rudman commission that in 2000 called for education to be classified as an issue of national security, in the increase of federal funding to school security simultaneous with cuts to community policing, in the continuation of the Troops to Teachers program, as well as the original *A Nation at Risk* report. Why is this? It is tied to the attack on social spending more generally, the antifederalist aspect of neoliberalism, a politics of containment rather than investment, the political efficacy of keeping large segments of the population uneducated and miseducated, the economic efficacy of keeping funds flowing to the defense and high-tech sectors and away from the segments of the population that are viewed as of little use to capital. As well, the working class, employed in low-skill, low-paying service sector jobs, would be likely to complain or even organize if they were encouraged to question and think too much. Education and literacy are tied to political participation. Participation might mean that noncorporate elites would want social investment in public projects or at least projects that might benefit most people. That won't do. There is a reason that the federal government wants soldiers rather than say the glut of unemployed Ph.D.s in classrooms. Additionally, corporate globalization initiatives such as the FTAA seek to allow corporate competition into the public sector at an unprecedented level. In theory, public schools would have to compete with corporate for-profit schooling initiatives from any corporation in the world. By redefining public schooling as a national security issue, education could be exempted from the purview of this radical globalization that such agreements impose on other nations. Consistent with the trend, education for national security defines the public interest through the discourse of discipline that influences reforms that deskill teachers, inhibiting teaching as a critical and intellectual endeavor that aims to make a participatory citizenry capable of building the public sphere.

What to do? As Seymour Melman argues in *After Capitalism*, a central task for the future is to transform a war economy to a civilian one not only for former Soviet states but for the United States as well. Considering the ways that the global financial system maintains poverty and the military system produces war, a key task for educators is to imagine the role of education as a means of mobilizing citizens to understand and transform these systems toward a goal of global democracy and global justice. Militarized schooling can be resisted at the local level. Many activists and critical educators already do so. For example, Kevin Ramirez started and runs the Military Out of our Schools campaign that seeks to eject JROTC programs from public schools. Ramirez points out to parents, teachers, administrators, and newspaper reporters that school violence is an extension of social violence, which is taught. Like Ramirez, other civic and religious organizations work to eliminate military recruiting in schools. I have argued that militarized education in the United States needs to be understood in relation to the enforcement of corporate economic imperatives and in relation to a rising culture of "law and order" that pervades popular culture, educational discourse, foreign policy, and language. The movement against militarism in education must go beyond challenging militarized schooling so as to challenge the many ways that militarism as a cultural logic enforces the expansion of corporate power and decimates public democratic power. Such a movement against education as enforcement must include the practice of critical pedagogy and also ideally links to multiple movements against oppression such as the antiglobalization, feminist, labor, environmental, and antiracism movements. These movements and critical educational practice and theory need to form the basis for imagining and implementing a just future.

Notes

1. Nancy Chang, *Silencing Political Dissent: How Post-September 11 Anti-Terrorism Measures Threaten Our Civil Liberties* (New York: Seven Stories, 2002).
2. Robert W. McChesney "Introduction," in *Profit Over People* Noam Chomsky (New York: Seven Stories Press, 1999), 7.
3. "Since the mid-1970's, the most fortunate one percent of households have doubled their share of the national wealth. They now hold more wealth than the bottom 95 percent of the population." "Shifting Fortunes," Chris Hartman, ed., "Facts and Figures" (September 18, 2000), available at http://www.inequality.org/factsfr.html. In a report to the World Bank's Board of Governors, James D. Wolfensohn attests, "Across the world 1.3 billion people live on less than $1 a day; 3 billion live on under $2 a day; 1.3 billion have no access to clean water; 3 billion have no access to sanitation; 2 billion have no access to power." "The Other Crisis," October 6, 1998 available at www.worldbank.org/html/extdr/am98/jdw-sp/am98-en.htm. In the United States alone, "by far the richest country in the world and the homeland of the world's wealthiest people, 16.5 per cent of the population live in poverty; one fifth of adult men and women can neither read nor write, while 13 per cent have a life expectancy shorter than sixty years." Zygmunt Bauman, The Individualized Society (Cambridge, UK: Polity, 2001), 115.
4. Bauman, *The Individualized Society,* 115.
5. Bauman, *The Individualized Society*, 114.
6. "Index," *Harper's Magazine* (July 2000).
7. "According to data from the 2000 consensus, fully 75 percent of the population of Mexico lives in poverty today (with fully one-third in extreme poverty), as compared with 49 percent in 1981, before the imposition of the neoliberal regimen and, later, NAFTA. Meanwhile, the longstanding gap between the northern and southern regions, as manifested in poverty, infant mortality and malnutrition rates, has grown wider as the latter has borne the brunt of neoliberal adjustment policies.

Chiapas, for example, produces more than half of Mexico's hydroelectric power, an increasing portion of which flows north to the maquiladora zone on the Mexico–US border. Yet, even including its major cities of Tuxtla Gutiérrez and San Cristóbal de las Casas, only half of Chiapanecan households have electricity or running water. Additional water sources have been diverted to irrigate large land-holdings devoted to export-oriented agriculture and commercial forestry, while peasant farmers have suffered reductions in water and other necessities as well as an end to land reform, even as they have endured a flood of US agribusiness exports that followed the NAFTA opening. According to the Mexican government's own official estimates, 1.5 million peasants will be forced to leave agriculture in the next one to two decades, many driven northward to face low-wage maquiladoras on one side of the border and high-tech militarization on the other." Jerry W. Sanders, "Two Mexicos and Fox's Quandary." *The Nation* (February 26, 2001): 18–19.

8. John Williams, "Look, Child Poverty in the Wealthy Countries Isn't Necessary," *International Herald Tribune* (July 24, 2000). See also Chris Hartman, ed., "Facts and Figures": nine states have reduced child poverty rates by more than 30 percent since 1993. These states include Tennessee, Michigan, Arkansas, South Carolina, Mississippi, Kentucky, Illinois and New Jersey. Michigan is a prime example of a national trend, in that even the recent dramatic improvement did not counter the losses of the previous 15 years, in which its poverty rate increased 121%. In California, the number of children living in poverty has grown from 900,000 in 1979, to 2.15 million in 1998.

9. Ellen Meiksins Wood, "Kosovo and the New Imperialism," in *Masters of the Universe?*, edited by Tariq Ali (New York: Verso, 2000), 199.

10. Thomas L. Friedman, *The Lexus and the Olive Tree* (New York: Farrar Straus Giroux, 1999), 304, 373.

11. Samir Amin, *Capitalism in the Age of Globalization* (New York: Zed Books, 2000), 48.

12. Public schooling has come increasingly to be described in the language of monopoly, accountability, choice, and efficiency, and decreasingly described in the language of the public, the civic, community, and solidarity. For a longer discussion of the political use of market language in educational policy see Kenneth J. Saltman, *Collateral Damage: Corporatizing Public School—a Threat to Democracy* (Boulder, Colo.: Rowman & Littlefield, 2000).

13. Robert W. McChesney, *Rich Media Poor Democracy* and McChesney and Edward Herman *The Global Media: The New Missionaries of Corporate Capitalism* (Washington, D.C.: Cassell, 1997).

14. Zygmunt Bauman, *In Search of Politics* (Malden, Mass.: Polity, 1999).

15. William Raspberry, "Sounds Bad, but It Works," *Washington Post* March 30 1998, 25A.

16. Zygmunt Bauman, *Liquid Modernity* (Malden, Mass.: Polity) 2000, 30.

17. McChesney "Introduction," 7.

18. See Jeffrey Henig's *Rethinking School Choice* (Princeton, NJ: Princeton University Press, 1994) for an excellent history of the appropriation of equity-based programs by privatization advocates.

19. Friedman, 373.

20. Steven Lee Myers, "Drop in Recruits Pushes Pentagon to New Strategy," *New York Times*, (September 27, 1999): A1.

21. Robert Suro, "Army Ads Open New Campaign: Finish Education," (*Washington Post*, September 21, 2000): A3.

22. Robert Suro, "Army Ads Open New Campaign: Finish Education," (*Washington Post*, September 21, 2000): A3.

23. Ibid.

24. Ibid.

25. Ibid.

26. Noam Chomsky, *Profits Over People* (New York: Seven Stories Press, 1999).

27. *Harper's Bazaar* (January 2001): 35.

28. See Ken Silverstein's *Washington on $10 Million a Day* for a detailed expose on the way the lobbying industry ensures that weapons manufacturers keep politicians voting in favor of their projects.
29. *Marketing Tomorrow's Weapons* video produced by America's Defense Monitor.
30. News Services, "Army to Try New Advertising Manuever to Boost Recruiting," *Star Tribune* (Minneapolis) (January 8, 2000): 12A.
31. Available at http//:www.marines.com.
32. This section is reprinted from Goodman and my *Strange Love, or How We Learn to Stop Worrying and Love the Market*, (Lanham, MD: Rowman & Littlefield, 2002) which offers a book length analysis of the ways that the public is educated to embrace neoliberal ideology through depictions of family sentimentality and private life.
33. See "Facts about Violence among Youth and Violence in Schools," a study published by the National Centers for Injury Prevention and Control and the 1999 annual School Safety Report published by the U.S. Department of Education, both showing decreases in school violence in the 1990s. Both reports suggest that schools are some of the safest places that kids can be. See also, Mike Males, *Scapegoat Generation* (Monroe, Maine: Common Courage Press, 1996).
34. Mike Males, *Framing Youth: Ten Myths About the Next Generation* (Monroe, Maine: Common Courage Press, 1999), 10.
35. Henry A. Giroux, *Stealing Innocence* (New York: St. Martin's Press, 2000), 8.
36. Patricia J. Williams, "The Auguries of Innocence," *The Nation* (May 24, 1999): 9.
37. Ellen Meiskins Wood, "Kosovo and the New Imperialism," 196–7.
38. Ibid., 195 (italics added).
39. Walter Isaacson, "Why We Went Back to Columbine," *Time* (December 20, 1999), 6.
40. Kenneth Miller, "Is Your Dog an Athlete?" *Time* (December 20, 1999), 8.
41. Nancy Gibbs and Timothy Roche, "The Columbine Tapes," *Time* (December 20, 1999): 40–41, 42, 44.
42. Ibid., 50–51.
43. Andrew Goldstein, "The Victims: Never Again," *Time* (December 20, 1999): 53.
44. Gibbs and Roche, "The Columbine Tapes," 44.
45. Ibid., 42.
46. As cited in Isaacson, "Why We Went Back to Columbine," 6.

INTRODUCTION TO CHAPTER 1

In *Deterring Democracy*, Chomsky writes that from the perspective of those in power,

> The rascal multitude are the proper targets of the mass media and a public education system geared to obedience and training in needed skills, including the skills of repeating patriotic slogans on timely occasions.[1]

Noam Chomsky's prominent long-standing presence in the field of education, resulting from his revolutionary work in linguistic theory, has been recently expanding due to the publication of a number of works that bring together his commentary on the social and political function of schooling. *Chomsky on Mis-Education*[2] and *Chomsky on Democracy and Education*[3] are representative, though his insights on the politics of education can be found in more of his books than can be listed. His edited volume *The Cold War and the University* focused on the relationship between corporatization and militarization in higher education. In this chapter, reprinted from *Understanding Power: The Indispensable Chomsky*,[4] Chomsky emphasizes the current roles that schooling takes as an instrument of state and corporate control by producing, framing, and filtering knowledge, and encouraging social relations that are fundamentally authoritarian and antidemocratic. In this selection Chomsky succinctly explains the role schools take to teach subservience, docility, and political nonparticipation as well as the relation of higher education to the Pentagon system. The discussion emphasizes the relation between the structure of the economy and the function of schools. The analysis of the politics of schooling highlights insights emphasized by both early reproduction theorists of schooling (such as Bowles and Gintis, Bourdieu, Althusser, and others) and theorists of the hidden curriculum that elaborate the relations between economic structure and the cultural and social functions of schooling. Chomsky's clear analysis emphasizes the political function of schools as instruments of class warfare and the management of knowledge and dispositions rendering people useful and compliant to the material and ideological interests of those in power.

Notes
1. Noam Chomsky, *Deterring Democracy* (New York: Hill and Wang, 1991), 370.
2. Noam Chomsky, *Chomsky on Mis-Education* (Landham, Md.: Rowman & Littlefield, 1999).
3. Carlos Otero, ed., *Chomsky on Democracy and Education* (New York: Routledge, 2002).
4. Noam Chomsky, *Understanding Power: The Indispensable Chomsky* (New York: New Press, 2002).

CHAPTER 1

The Function of Schools

Subtler and Cruder Methods of Control

NOAM CHOMSKY

Woman: How is it that the schools end up being an indoctrination system? Can you describe the process in more detail?

Well, the main point I think is that the entire school curriculum, from kindergarten through graduate school, will be tolerated only so long as it continues to perform its institutional role. So take the universities, which in many respects are not very different from the media in the way they function—thought they're a much more complex system, so they're harder to study systematically. Universities do not generate nearly enough funds to support themselves from tuition money alone: they're parasitic institutions that need to be supported from the outside, and that means they're dependent on wealthy alumni, on corporations, and on the government, which are groups with the same basic interests. Well, as long as the universities *serve* those interests, they'll be funded. If they ever *stop* serving those interests, they'll start to get in trouble.

So for example, in the late 1960s it began to appear that the universities were *not* adequately performing that service—students were asking questions, they were thinking independently, they were rejecting a lot of the Establishment value-system, challenging all sorts of things—and the corporations began to react to that, they began to react in a number of ways. For one thing, they began to develop alternative programs, like I.B.M. began to set up a kind of vocational training program to produce engineers on their own: if M.I.T. wasn't going to do it for them the way they wanted, they'd do it themselves—and that would have meant they'd stop funding M.I.T. Well, of course, things never really got out of hand in the Sixties, so the moves in that direction were very limited. But those are the kinds of pressures there are.

And in fact, you can even see similar things right now. Take all of this business about Allan Bloom and that book everybody's been talking about, *The Closing of the American Mind*. It's this huge best-seller, I don't know if

Noam Chomsky is institute professor and professor of linguistics at the Massachusetts Institute of Technology in Cambridge, Massachusetts. A major figure in the field of linguistics, Chomsky has also written extensively on matters of U.S. foreign and domestic policy. Some of his best-known works include: *Power and Prospects: Reflections on Human Nature and the Social Order, Year 501: The Conquest Continues*, and *Necessary Illusions: Thought Control in Democratic Societies*.

you've bothered looking at it—it's mind bogglingly stupid. I read it once in the supermarket while my . . . I hate to say it, while my wife was shopping I stood there and read the damn thing; it takes about fifteen minutes to read.

Man: You read two thousand words a minute?

I mean, "read"—you know, sort of turn the pages to see if there's anything there that isn't totally stupid. But what that book is basically saying is that education ought to be set up like a variant of the Marine Corps, in which you just march the students through a canon of "great thoughts" that are picked out for everybody. So some group of people will say, "Here are the great thoughts, the great thoughts of Western civilization are in this corpus; you guys sit there and learn them, read them and learn them, and be able to repeat them." That's the kind of model Bloom is calling for.

Well, anybody who's ever thought about education or been involved in it, or even gone to school, knows that the effect of that is that students will end up knowing and understanding virtually nothing. It doesn't matter how great the thoughts are, if they are simply imposed on you from the outside and you're forced through them step by step, after you're done you'll have forgotten what they are. I mean, I'm sure that every one of you has taken any number of courses in school in which you worked, and you did your homework, and you passed the exam, maybe even you got an "A"—and a week later you couldn't even remember what the course was about. You only learn things and learn how to think if there's some purpose for learning, some motivation that's coming out of *you* somehow. In fact, all of the methodology in education isn't really much more than that—getting students to want to learn. Once they want to learn, they'll do it.

But the point is that this model Bloom and all these other people are calling for is just a part of the whole method of imposing discipline through the schools, and of preventing people from learning how to think for themselves. So what you do is make students go through and sort of memorize a canon of what are called "Great Books," which you force on them, and then somehow great things are supposed to happen. It's a completely stupid form of education, but I think that's why it's selected and supported, and why there's so much hysteria that it's been questioned in past years—just because it's very functional to train people and discipline them in ways like this. The popularity of the Bloom thing, I would imagine, is mostly a reaction to the sort of liberating effect that the student movement of the Sixties and other challenges to the schools and universities began to have.

Woman: All of Allan Bloom's "great thoughts" are by elite white males.

Yeah, okay—but it wouldn't even matter if he had some different array of material, it really wouldn't matter. The idea that there's some array of "the deep thoughts," and we smart people will pick them out and you dumb guys will learn them—or memorize them at least, because you don't really learn them if they're just imposed on you—that's nonsense. If you're serious about, say, reading Plato, it's fine to read Plato—but you try to figure out what's right, what's wrong, what's a better way of looking at it, why was he saying this when he should have been saying something else, what grotesque error of reasoning did he make over here, and so on and so forth. That's the way you would read serious work, just like you would in the sciences. But you're not supposed to read it that way here, you're supposed to read it because it's the truth, or it's the great thoughts or something. And that's kind of like the worst form of theology.

The point is, it doesn't matter *what* you read, what matters is *how* you read it. Now, I don't mean comic books, but there's a lot of cultural wealth out there from all over the place, and to learn what it means to be culturally rich, you can explore almost anywhere: there's no fixed subset that is the basis of truth and understanding. I mean, you can read the "Good Books," and memorize what they said, and forget them a week later—if it doesn't mean anything to you personally, you'd might as well not have read them. And it's very hard to know what's going to mean something to different people. But there's plenty of exciting literature around in the world, and there's absolutely no reason to believe that unless you've read the Greeks and Dante and so on, you've missed things—I mean, yeah, you've missed things, but you've also missed things if you haven't learned something about other cultural traditions too.

Just take a look at philosophy, for example, which is a field that I know something about: some of the best, most exciting, most active philosophers in the contemporary world, people who've made a real impact on the field, couldn't tell Plato from Aristotle, except for what they remember from some freshman course they once took. Now, that's not to say that you shouldn't read Plato and Aristotle– sure, there are millions of things you should read; nobody's ever going to read more than a tiny fraction of the thing you wished you knew. But just reading them does you no good: you only learn if the material is integrated into your own creative processes somehow, otherwise it just passes through your mind and disappears. And there's nothing valuable about that—it has basically the effect of learning the catechism, or memorizing the Constitution or something like that.

Real education is about getting people involved in thinking for themselves—and that's a tricky business to know how to do well, but clearly it requires that whatever it is you're looking at has to somehow catch people's interest and make them *want* to think, and make them *want* to pursue and explore. And just regurgitating "Good Books" is absolutely the worst way to do it—that's just a way of turning people into automata. You may call that an education if you want, but it's really the opposite of an education, which why people like William Bennett [Reagan's Secretary of Education] and Allan Bloom and these others are so much in favor of it.

Woman: Are you saying that the real purpose of the universities and the schools is just to indoctrinate people—and really not much else?

Well, I'm not quite saying that. Like, I wouldn't say that *no* meaningful work takes place in schools, or that they only exist to provide manpower for the corporate system or something like that—these are very complex systems, after all. But the basic institutional role and function of the schools, and why they're supported, is to provide an ideological service: there's a real selection for obedience and conformity. And I think that process starts in kindergarten, actually.

Let me just tell you a personal story. My oldest, closest friend is a guy who came to the United States from Latvia when he was fifteen, fleeing from Hitler. He escaped to New York with his parents and went to George Washington High School, which in those days at least was the school for bright Jewish kids in New York City. And he once told me that the first thing that struck him about American schools was the fact that if he got a "C" in a course, nobody cared, but if he came to school three minutes late he was sent to the principal's office—and that generalized. He realized that what it meant is, what's valued here is the ability to work on an assembly line, even if it's an intellectual assembly line. The important thing is to be able to obey orders, and to do what you're told, and to be where you're supposed to be. The values are, you're going to be a factory worker somewhere—maybe they'll call it a university—but you're going to be following somebody else's orders, and just doing your work in some prescribed way. And what matters is discipline, not figuring things out for yourself, or understanding things that interest you—those are kind of marginal: just make sure you meet the requirements of a factory.

Well, that's pretty much what the schools are like, I think: they reward discipline and obedience, and they punish independence of mind. If you happen to be a little innovative, or maybe you forgot to come to school one day because you were reading a book or something, that's a tragedy, that's a crime—because you're not supposed to think, you're supposed to obey, and just proceed through the material in whatever way they require.

And in fact, most of the people who make it through the education system and get into the elite universities are able to do it because they've been willing to obey a lot of stupid orders for years and years—that's the way I did it, for example. Like, you're told by some stupid teacher, "Do this," which you know makes no sense whatsoever, but you do it, and if you do it you get to the next rung, and then you obey the next order, and finally you work your way through and they give you letters: an awful lot of education is like that, from the very beginning. Some people go along with it because they figure, "Okay, I'll do any stupid thing that asshole says because I want to get ahead" others do it because they've internalized the values—but after a while, those two things tend to get sort of blurred. But you do it, or else you're out: you ask too many questions and you're going to get in trouble.

Now, there are also people who *don't* go along—and they're called "behavior problems," or "unmotivated," or things like that. Well, you don't want to be too glib about it—there *are* children with behavior problems—but a lot of them are just independent-minded, or don't like to conform, or just want to go their own way. And they get into trouble right from the very beginning, and are typically weeded out. I mean, I've taught young kids too, and the fact is there are always some who just don't take your word for it. And the very unfortunate tendency is to try to beat them down, because they're a pain in the neck. But what they ought to be is encouraged. Yeah:

why take my word for it? Who the heck am I? Figure it out for yourself. That's what real education ought to be *about*, in fact.

Actually, I happen to have been very lucky myself and gone to an experimental-progressive Deweyite school, from about the time that I was age one-and-a-half to twelve [John Dewey was an American philosopher and educational reformer]. And there it was done routinely: children were encouraged to challenge everything, and you sort of worked on your own, you were supposed to think things through for yourself—it was a real experience. And it was quite a striking change when it ended and I had to go to the city high school, which was the pride of the city school system. It was the school for academically-oriented kids in Philadelphia—and it was the dumbest, most ridiculous place I've ever been, it was like falling into a black hole or something. For one thing, it was extremely competitive—because that's one of the best ways of controlling people. So everybody was ranked, and you always knew exactly where you were: are you third in the class, or maybe did you move down to fourth? All of this stuff is put into people's heads in various ways in the schools—that you've got to beat down the person next to you, and just look after yourself. And there are all sorts of other things like that too.

But the point is, there's nothing *necessary* about them in education. I know, because I went to an alternative to it—so it can certainly be done. But given the external power structure of the society in which they function now, the institutional role of the schools for the most part is just to train people for obedience and conformity, and to make them controllable and indoctrinated—and as long as the schools fulfill that role, they'll be fine.

Now, of course, it doesn't work a hundred percent—so you do get some people all the way through who don't go along. And as I was saying, in the sciences at least, people have to be trained for creativity and disobedience—because there is no other way you can *do* science. But in the humanities and social sciences, and in fields like journalism and economics and so on, that's much less true—there people have to be trained to be managers, and controllers, and to accept things, and not to question to much. So you really do get a very different kind of education. And people who break out of line are weeded out or beaten back in all kinds of ways.

I mean, it's not very abstract: if you're, say, a young person in college, or in journalism, or for that matter a fourth grader, and you have too much of an independent mind, there are a whole variety of devices that will be used to deflect you from that error—and if you can't be controlled, to marginalize or just eliminate you. In fourth grade, you're a "behavior problem." In college, you may be "irresponsible," or "erratic," or "not the right kind of student." If you make it to the faculty, you'll fail in what's sometimes called "collegiality," getting along with your colleagues. If you're a young journalist and you're pursuing stories that people at the managerial level above you understand, either intuitively or explicitly, are not to be pursued, you can be sent off to work at the Police desk, and advised that you don't have "proper standards of objectivity." There's a whole range of these techniques.

Now, we live in a free society, so you don't get sent to the gas chambers and they don't send the death squads after you—as is commonly done, and not far from here, say in Mexico. But there are nevertheless quite successful devices, both subtle and extreme, to insure that doctrinal correctness is not seriously infringed upon.

Subtler Methods of Control

Let me just start with some of the more subtle ways; I'll give you an example. After I finished college, I went to this program at Harvard called the "Society of Fellows"—which is kind of the elite finishing school, where they teach you to be a Harvard or Yale professor, and to drink the right wine, and say the right things, and so on and so forth. I mean, you had all of the resources of Harvard available to you and your only responsibility was to show up at a dinner once a week, so it was great for just doing your work if you wanted to. But the real point of the whole thing was socialization: teaching the right values.

For instance, I remember there was a lot of anglophilia at Harvard at the time—you were supposed to wear British clothes, and pretend you spoke with a British accent, that sort of stuff. In fact, there were actually guys there who I thought were British, who had never been outside of the United States. If any of you have studied literature or history or something, you might recognize some of this, those are the places you usually find it. Well, somehow I managed to survive that, I don't know how exactly—but most didn't. And what I discovered is that a large part of education at the really elite institutions is simply refinement, teaching the social graces: what kind of clothes you should wear, how to drink port the right way, how to have polite conversation without talking about serious topics, but of course indicating that you *could* talk about serious topics if you were so vulgar as to actually do it, all kinds of things which an intellectual is supposed to know how to do. And that was really the main point of the program, I think.

Actually, there were much more important cases, too—and they're even more revealing about the role of the elite schools. For example, the 1930s were a period of major labor strife and labor struggle in the U.S., and it was scaring the daylights out of the whole business community here—because labor was finally winning the right to organize, and there were other legislative victories as well. And there were a lot of efforts to overcome this, but one of them was that Harvard introduced a "Trade Union Program." What it did was to bring in rising young people in the labor movement—you know, the guy who looks like he's going to be the Local president next year—and have them stay in dorms in the Business School, and put them through a whole socialization process, help them come to share some of the values and understandings of the elite, teach them that "Our job is to work together," "We're all in this together," and so on and so forth. I mean, there are always two lines: for the public it's, "We're all in this together, management and labor are cooperating, joint enterprise, harmony" and so on—meanwhile business is fighting a vicious class war on the side. And that effort to socialize and integrate trade union activists—well, I've never measured its success, but I'm sure it was very successful. And the process was similar to what I experienced and saw a Harvard education to be myself.

Or let me tell you another story I heard about twenty years ago from a black civil rights activist who came up to study at Harvard Law School—it kind of illustrates some of the other pressures that are around. This guy gave a talk in which he described how the kids starting off at Harvard Law School come in with long hair and backpacks and social ideals, they're all going into public service law to change the world and so on—that's the first year. Around springtime, the recruiters come for the cushy summer jobs in the Wall Street law firms, and these students figure, "What the heck, I can put on a tie and a jacket and shave for one day, just because I need that money and why shouldn't I have it?" So they put on the tie and the jacket for that one day, and they get the job, and then they go off for the summer—and when they come back in the fall, it's ties and jackets, and obedience, a shift of ideology. Sometimes it takes two years.

Well, obviously he was over-drawing the point—but those sorts of factors are also very influential. I mean, I've felt it all my life: it's extremely easy to be sucked into the dominant culture, it can be very appealing. There are a lot of rewards. And what's more, the people you meet don't look like bad people—you don't want to sit there and insult them. Maybe they're perfectly nice people. So you try to be friends, maybe you even are friends. Well, you begin to conform, you begin to adapt, you begin to smooth off the harsher edges—and pretty soon it's just happened, in kind of seeps in. And education at a place like Harvard is largely geared to that, to a remarkable extent in fact.

And there are many other subtle mechanisms which contribute to ideo-logical control as well, of course—including just the fact that the universities support and encourage people to occupy themselves with irrelevant and innocuous work.

Or just take the fact that certain topics are unstudiable in the schools—because they don't fall anywhere: the disciplines are divided in such a way that they simply will not be studied. So for example, take a question that people were very worried about in the United States for years and years—the economic competitiveness of Japan. Now, I always thought the talk about "American declinism" and "Japan as Number 1" was vastly overblown, just as the later idea of "Japanese decline" is wildly exaggerated. In fact, Japan retains a very considerable edge in crucial areas of manufacturing, especially in high tech. They did get into trouble because of a huge stock market and real estate boom that collapsed, but serious economists don't believe that Japan has really lost competitiveness in these areas.

Well, why has Japan been so economically competitive? I mean, there are a lot of reasons why, but the major reason is very clear. Both Japan and the United States (and every other industrial country in the world, actually) have essentially state-coordinated economies—but our traditional system of state coordination is less efficient than theirs.

Remember, talk about "free trade" is fine in editorials, but nobody actu-ally practices it in reality: in every modern economy, the taxpayers are made to subsidize the private corporations, who then keep the profits for them-selves. But the point is, different countries have different ways of arranging those subsidies. So take a look at the competitive parts of the U.S. economy, the parts that are successful in international trade. Capital-intensive agriculture is a well-known case: American capital-intensive agriculture is able to compete internationally because the state purchases the excess products and stores them, and subsidizes the energy inputs, and so on.

Or look at high-technology industry: research and development for high technology is very costly, and corporations don't make a profit off it directly—so therefore the taxpayer is made to pay for it. And in the United States, that's traditionally been done largely through the Pentagon system: the Pentagon pays for high-tech research and development, then if something comes out of it which happens to be marketable, it's handed over to private corporations so they can make the profits. And the research mostly isn't weapons, incidentally—it's things like computers, which are at the center of any contemporary industrial economy, and were developed through the Pentagon system in the United States. And the same is true of virtually all high tech, in fact. And furthermore, there's another important subsidy there: the Pentagon also purchases the output of high-technology industry, it serves as a state guaranteed market for waste-production—that's what contracts for developing weapons systems are; I mean, you don't actually *use* the weapons you're paying for, you just destroy them in a couple years and replaced them with the next array of even more advanced stuff you don't need. Well, all of that is just perfect for pouring continuous taxpayer subsidies into high-tech industry, and it's because of these enormous subsidies that American high-tech is competitive internationally.

Well, Japan has run its economy pretty much the same way we do, except with one crucial difference. Instead of using the military system, the way they've worked their public subsidies in Japan is they have a government ministry, M.I.T.I. [the Ministry of International Trade and Industry], which sits down with the big corporations and conglomerates and banking firms, and plans their economic system for the next couple of years—they plan how much consumption there's going to be, and how much investment there's going to be, and where the investment should go, and so on. Well, that's more efficient. And since Japan is a very disciplined and obedient society culturally, the population there just does what they tell them, and nobody ever asks questions about it.

Alright, to see how this difference played out over the years, just look at the "Star Wars" program in the United States. Star Wars [the Strategic Defense Initiative] is the pretext for a huge sum amount of research and development spending through the Pentagon system here—it's our way of funding the new generation of computer technology, lasers, software, and so on. Well, if you look at the distribution of expenses for Star Wars, it turns out that it was virtually the same allocation of funding as was made through the Japanese state-directed economic system in the same time period: in those same years, M.I.T.I. made about the same judgments about how to distribute their resources as we did, they spent about the same proportion in lasers, and the same proportion in software, and so on. And the reason is that all of these planners make approximately the same judgments about the likely new technologies.

Well, why was Japan so competitive with the U.S. economically, despite highly inauspicious conditions? There are a lot of reasons. But the main reason is that they directed their public subsidy straight to the commercial market. So to work on lasers, they tried to figure out ways of producing lasers for the commercial market, and they do it pretty well. But when we want to develop lasers for the commercial market, what we do is pour the money into the Pentagon, which then tries to work out a way to use a laser to shoot down a missile ten thousand miles away—and if they can work that out, then they hope there'll be some commercial spin-offs that come out of it all. Okay, that's less efficient. And since the Japanese are no dumber than we are, and they have an efficient system of state-coordination while we have an inefficient one, over the years they succeeded in the economic competition.

Well, these are major phenomena of modern life—but where do you go to study them in the universities or the academic profession? That's a very interesting question. You don't go to the economic department, because that's not what they look at: the real hot-shot economics departments are interested in abstract models of how a pure free-enterprise economy works—you know, generalizations to ten-dimensional space of some non-existent free-market system. You don't go to the political science department, because they're concerned with electoral statistics, and voting patterns, and micro-bureaucracy—like the way one government bureaucrat talks to another in some detailed air. You don't go to the anthropology department, because they're studying hill tribesmen in New Guinea. You don't go to the sociology department, because they're studying crime in the ghettos. In fat, you don't go anywhere—there isn't any field that deals with these topics. There's no journal that deals with them. In fact, there is no profession that is concerned with the central problems of modern society. Now, you can go to the *business school*, and there they'll talk about them—because those people are in the real world. But not in the academic departments: nobody there is going to tell you what's really going on in the world.

And it's extremely important that there *not* be a field that studies these questions—because if there ever was such a field, people might some to understand too much, and in a relatively free society like ours, they might start to do something with that understanding. Well, no institution is going to encourage *that*. I mean, there's nothing in what I just said that you couldn't explain to junior high school students, it's all pretty straightforward. But it's not what you study in a high school civics course—what you study there is propaganda about the way systems are supposed to work but don't.

Incidentally, part of the genius of this aspect of the higher education system is that it can get people to sell out even while they think they're doing exactly the right thing. So some young person going into academia will say to themselves, "Look, I'm going to be a real radical here"—and you *can* be, as long as you adapt yourself to these categories which guarantee that you'll never ask the right questions, and that you'll never even *look* at the right questions. But you don't *feel* like you're selling out, you're not saying "I'm working for the ruling class" or anything like that—you're not, you're being a Marxist economist or something. But the effect is, they've totally neutralized you.

Alright, all of these are subtle methods of control, with the effect of preventing serious insight into the way that power actually works in the society. And it makes very good sense for a system to be set up like that: powerful institutions don't want to be investigated, obviously. Why would they? They don't want the public to know how they work—maybe the people inside them understand how they work, but they don't want anybody else to know, because that would threaten and undermine their power. So one should *expect* the institutions to function in a way as to protect themselves— and some of the ways in which they protect themselves are by various subtle techniques of ideological control like these.

Cruder Methods of Control

Then aside from all that, there are also crude methods of control. So if some young political scientist or economist decides they *are* going to try to ask these kinds of questions, the chances are they're going to be marginalized in some fashion, or else be weeded out of the institution altogether. At the extreme end, there have been repeated university purges in the United States. During the 1950s, for example, the universities were just cleaned out of dissident thought—people were fired on all kinds of grounds, or not allowed to teach things. And the effects of that were very strong. Then during the late 1960s, when the political ferment really got going, the purges began again— and often they were just straight firings, not even obscured. For example, a lot of the best Asia scholars from the United States are now teaching in Australia and Japan—because they couldn't keep jobs in the U.S., they had the wrong ideas. Australia has some of the best Southeast Asia scholars in the world, and they're mostly Americans who couldn't make it into the American academic system, because they thought the wrong things. So if you want to study Cambodia with a top American scholar, you basically have to go to Australia. One of the best Japan historians in the world (Herbert Bix) is teaching in a Japanese university—he's American, but he can't get a job in the United States.

Or let me just tell you a story about M.I.T., which is pretty revealing. A young political science professor—who's by now one of the top people in the field, incidentally [Thomas Ferguson]—was appointed as an assistant professor right after he got his Ph.D. from Princeton; he's very radical, but he's also extremely smart, so the department just needed him. Well, one day I was sitting in my office and he came over fuming. He told me that the chairman of his department had just come into his office and told him straight out "If you ever want to get tenure in this department, keep away from anything after the New Deal; you can write all of your radical stuff up to the New Deal, but if you try and do it for the post–New Deal period, you're never going to get tenure in this department." He just told him straight out. Usually, you're not told it straight out, but you get to understand it—you get to understand it from the reactions you receive.

This kind of stuff also happens with graduate students. I'm what's called an "Institute Professor" at M.I.T., which means I can teach courses in any department of the university. And over the years I've taught all over the place—but if I even get *near* Political Science, you can feel the bad vibes starting. So in other departments, I'm often asked to be on students' Ph.D.

committees, but in Political Science it's virtually never happened—and the few times it has happened, it's always been Third World women. And there's a reason for that: Third World women have a little bit of extra space to maneuver in, because the department doesn't want to appear *too* overtly racist or *too* overtly sexist, so there are some things they can do that other people can't.

Well, a few years ago, one very smart woman graduate student in the Political Science Department wanted to do her dissertation on the media and Southern Africa, and she wanted me to be on her Ph.D. committee. Okay, it's a topic that I'm interested in, and I've worked on it probably more than anybody else there, so there was just no way for them to say that I couldn't do it. Then the routine started. The first stage in the doctoral process is that the candidate has a meeting with a couple of faculty members and presents her proposal. Usually, two faculty members show up, that's about it. This time it was very different: they circulated a notice through the department saying that every faculty member had to show up and the reason was, *I* was going to be there, and they had to combat this baleful influence. So everybody showed up.

Well, the woman started presenting her dissertation proposal, and you could just see people turning pale. Somebody asked her, "What's your hypothesis?"—you're supposed to have a hypothesis—and it was that media coverage of South Africa is going to be influenced by corporate interests. People were practically passing out and falling out of windows. Then starts the critical analysis: "What's your methodology going to be? What tests are you going to use?" And gradually an apparatus was set up and a level of proof demanded that you just can't meet in the social sciences. It wasn't "I'm going to read the editorials and figure out what they say"—you had to count the words, and do all sorts of statistical nonsense, and so on. But she fought it through, she just continued fighting. They finally required so much junk in her thesis, so much irrelevant, phony social-scientific junk, numbers and charts and meaningless business that you could barely pick out the content from the morass of methodology. But she finally did make it through—just because she was willing to fight it out. Now, you know, you can do that—but it's tough. And some people really get killed.

INTRODUCTION TO CHAPTER 2

In "Rivers of Fire" Saltman and Goodman illustrate the ways that the oil and chemical industries are directly involved in producing school curricula that furthers the corporate agenda by envisioning nature, work, leisure, and life itself as ideally under corporate management. The chapter highlights the structuring absence in such curricula of the direct role these corporations play in global militarism, murderous U.S. led-foreign interventions, and environmental devastation. Focusing on BPAmoco and Monsanto and their actions in Colombia, this chapter expands the academic and public policy criticism of school commercialism beyond its more common focus on how students are made into a captive audience by advertisers to suggest that the corporate sector recognizes the importance of the classroom and curriculum in advancing the corporate agenda. It also challenges the extent to which some progressive educational methods have been appropriated for a neo-liberal agenda that advances violence.

CHAPTER 2

Rivers of Fire

BPAmoco's iMPACT on Education

KENNETH J. SALTMAN AND ROBIN TRUTH GOODMAN

SLICK!

This is a computer simulation of an oil spill at sea. Students must plan
and implement methods of dealing with an oil spill at sea. Designed for
use for individuals and groups, having two levels: beginner and expert.
This resource incorporates graphics, sound effects and a range of printed
materials . . . £20.00 . . . Add to Shopping Cart.

—BP Educational Services[1]

From the two sets of three colorful Amoco-branded wall posters to the
Amoco-branded curriculum box to the Amoco ads in the videos themselves,
Amoco's iMPACT middle school science curriculum provides this massive
multinational oil company with what advertisers refer to as multiple
"impressions" or viewing of the brand logo.[2] The curriculum is clearly
designed to promote and advertise Amoco to a "captive audience" in public
schools. Brightly mottled posters show Sesame Street–style cartoon characters riding roller coasters to learn physics, a lone cartoon diver encountering
a gigantic sea monster to learn biology, and an ominous black mountain
exploding with molten magma. These cartoons, with more rainbow-colors
than an oil slick, include scientific labels with arrows reminding kids that all
of this fun is educational. Amoco stamps its corporate logo on fun and
excitement, curiosity and exploration, education, nature, science, and work.
By rendering its red, white, and blue logo visible in school classrooms,
Amoco appears as a "responsible corporate citizen" supporting beleaguered
public schools with its corporate philanthropy. Not only does the corporate

Kenneth J. Saltman is an assistant professor in cultural foundation at DePaul University. He is the author of *Collateral Damage: Corporatizing Public Schools—A Threat
to Democracy* (Rowman and Little Field, 2001) and co-author of *Strangelove: Or
How We Learn to Stop Worrying and Love the Market* (Rowman & Littlefield,
2002).

Robin Truth Goodman is an assistant professor in the department of English at
Florida State University. She is the author of *Infertilities: Exploring Fictions of Barren
Bodies* (University of Minnesota Press, 2000) and co-author of *Strangelove: Or How
We Learn to Stop Worrying and Love the Market* (Rowman & Littlefield, 2002).

sector defund the public sector by evading its tax responsibility to such public goods as public schools, but the growing trend toward privatization, for-profit charter schools, magnet schools, and commercialization redefine the public schools as for private profit.[3] In reality, Amoco's use of the innocent-looking aesthetics of children's culture and its appeal to fun and child-like curiosity conceal the fact that this oil company is far from innocent of not only undermining the public sector in this country but of outright human rights violations, widespread environmental devastation, and the uprooting of indigenous communities globally.[4]

Like other corporate curricula, Amoco's sprightly lessons do more than provide entry for corporate advertisements into public space.[5] This curriculum serves a dual function. First, it functions to divert public attention from what Amoco is actually doing around the world. Second, it serves an ideological function, constructing a corporate-friendly worldview that defines youth identity and citizenship through consumption and nationality as the corporate interest rather than the public interest. Amoco's curriculum produces ideologies of consumerism that bolster its global corporate agenda, and it does so under the guise of disinterested scientific knowledge, benevolent technology, and innocent entertainment.

Separating the pedagogical from the political, Amoco's curriculum conceals how this corporation undermines democratic institutions such as public schooling and participates in the hindering of democracy and perpetration of human rights abuses and environmental destruction abroad. As Wharton economist Edward Herman and ColombiaWatch's Cecilia Zarate-Laun expose, the largest investor in Colombia, British Petroleum (BP, now BPAmoco), has not only created its own mercenary forces, but also imported British counterinsurgency professionals to train Colombians. BP gave its own intelligence reports to the Colombian military that used them to track and kill local "subversives." "Amnesty International and Human Rights Watch have documented numerous examples of collaboration between Colombian army units and brutal paramilitaries who are guilty of over 75 percent of the human rights violations that have been committed in Colombia's civil conflict."[6] The other oil companies in Colombia have also "cultivated the army and police and hired paramilitaries and foreign mercenaries to protect their oil pipelines."[7] BPAmoco's behavior overseas must be understood in the context of the relationship between the U.S. government's foreign policy and its support of the corporate sector. Though said to be specifically supporting Colombia's war on drugs and not its militarized counterinsurgency efforts pre-September 11, U.S. aid to Colombia (third highest amount of foreign military aid after Israel and Egypt) was initially earmarked for specific regions of the country such as the Amazon and Orinoco basins and the Putumayo region more largely, regions that happen to be the areas of influence of the rebel Revolutionary Armed Forces of Colombia (FARC). Exempting and supplying arms to an important segment of the drug trade suggests that, as with anticommunism in the past, the drug war rationale covers over the pursuit of larger objectives, which can be read from what the army and paramilitaries do—remove, kill, and silence the large segments of the rural population that stand in the way of the exploitations of Colombia's resources (by transnational corporations such as BPAmoco).[8]

Initially under the pretext of the drug war, and then additionally post-September 11 under the pretext of the war on terror, the U.S. government is funding Colombia's internal war against ideologically dissenting factions such as FARC (currently 18,000 strong) and the smaller National Liberation Army (ELN) (currently counting 3,000).[9] In June 2000, the U.S. Congress approved a $1.3 billion aid package to Colombia, including military training, helicopters, and intelligence. Even before September 11 the Bush administration escalated this package by $676 million to help Colombia and its neighbors in their war on drugs. This aid package has included a waiver of private contractor limits suggesting the deep interdependence of the business of oil and the business of war.[10]

Carla Anne Robbins of the *Wall Street Journal* reports that even though the United States has, for the past ten years, exercised caution in extending developmental aid to Colombia because of widespread allegations of human rights abuses, the Colombian government has managed to reassure Washington that its military equipment will only be used for antinarcotics maneuvers and not for counterinsurgency. Yet, as Justin Delacour of *Z-Net* has demonstrated, the Clinton administration was "remarkably resistant to conditions placed on the aid that require them to demonstrate that the Colombian government is vigorously rooting out complicity between the army and paramilitaries."[11] In fact, as Marc Cooper of *The Nation* remarks:

> Bill Clinton's State Department, with only hours left before the Bush transition, employed a loophole in the US aid package [Plan Colombia] and "voluntarily" decided to "skip" having to certify that the Colombian government has complied with US human rights demands attached to Plan Colombia legislation—specifically, suppression of the paramilitary death squads.[12]

The *Wall Street Journal* admits that unless the close ties between FARC and the drug trade are loosened, the United States stated intentions of bringing peace, political reform, and crop substitution to the region will surely fail. José Cuesta of the Citizens' Network for Peace in Colombia alleges, "The coca crops are nothing but a concrete response to the ravages caused by unrestrained free-market policies."[13] Washington has only committed 1 percent of the Plan Colombia aid package to crop substitution, and this means that *campesinos* will not be able to produce even at subsistence level without sustaining coca fields. "In general, a kilo of cocaine is sold at 1.5 to 1.7 million pesos (about $6,800–7,700) and net profit per hectare is 200,000 pesos (about $90). Comparatively speaking, a carga, which is about 100 kilos of corn, is sold for 30,000 pesos, and after paying the costs the peasant is left with only 10,000 pesos (about $4.50) per carga."[14] Even as the *Wall Street Journal* professes that the problem in FARC-controlled regions stems from drug trafficking; however, it also attributes the need for militarization to FARC's economic reforms, in particular their attempts to tax the corporate sector:

As conservatives were complaining that Bogotá was selling out to the Marx-ists [because of the Colombian government's agreement to negotiate a settle-ment with guerrillas], New York Stock Exchange Chairman Richard Grasso accepted an invitation to fly to the demilitarized zone to tutor the FARC on the joys of capitalism . . . [Carlos Antonio] Lozada [one of the FARC's negotiators] . . . explains that instead of indiscriminate kidnapping, the FARC's new Law 002 will levy a tax on anyone with more than $1 million in assets.[15]

The expansion of NAFTA into South America is being accompanied by the expansion of U.S. military presence, not only in Colombia, through the provision of military attack helicopters and counterinsurgency equipment for maneuvers nominally against trafficking, but also in Ecuador and El Salvador where bases are being built. This movement of capital through mili-tary expansion illustrates concretely *New York Times* foreign correspondent Thomas Freidman's thesis that "The hidden hand of the market will never work without the hidden fist—McDonald's cannot flourish without McDon-nell Douglas, the designer of the F-15. And the hidden fist that keeps the world safe for Silicon Valley's technologies is called the United States Army, Air Force, Navy, and Marine Corps."[16] This militarization opens the region to U.S. investment as it destroys the fields and livelihoods of poor peasants, using methods as brutal as those attributed to FARC. Alongside and contin-gent to militarization, education can work to open wider reaches for the neoliberal market. Wall Street's journey to the region demonstrates that investors understand how education in the "joys of capitalism" opens the way to corporate infiltration.[17] Clearly, the so-called war on drugs is in the business of an ideological production partly installed through the very processes of militarization.

This military intervention into the political situation in Colombia owes to the fact that the U.S. imports more oil from the region than it does from the Middle East (260,000 barrels from Colombia per day). Indeed, the claim that the administration was funding drug containment policies was hardly convincing when publicly funded treatment centers were radically cut from city, state, and federal budgets nationwide. In 1994, the White House commissioned the Rand Institution to research the most effective methods for controlling and reducing drugs. The Rand report found that treatment was 7 percent cheaper and more successful than domestic enforcement, 11 percent more than interdiction, and 23 percent more than source-country eradication policies, the policy embraced by this aid pack-age.[18] Clearly, therefore, the defunding of public support for treatment ultimately benefits the profit mongering of the private sector. This is why, unlike public advocates like Noam Chomsky and Ralph Nader, private corporations like BPAmoco support the militarization of Colombia's war on drugs:

[I]t's questionable whether or not it even qualifies as a drug policy at all. Several corporations whose interests have nothing to do with drug policy have been pushing the Colombia package from day one. Multinationals and U.S.–based weapons producers who are pushing the package include Occidental Petro-

leum Corp., Enron Corp., BP Amoco, Colgate-Palmolive Co., United Technologies Corp. and Bell Helicopter Textron Inc. Occidental Petroleum's strong
backing of the package derives from the fact that its extensive oil operations
in Colombia have been frequently sabotaged by guerrilla groups who object to
the terms of the agreement between the Colombian government and multinational oil corporations that operate in the country. Occidental Petroleum's Vice-
President Lawrence Meriage was even called to testify before the House
Government Reform Subcommittee on Drug Policy, leading observers to
wonder how oil executives suddenly qualified as drug policy experts.[19]

Ultimately, then, U.S. taxpayers are paying millions of dollars to protect
the oil pipelines of BPAmoco, Occidental Petroleum (a strong backer of Al
Gore's political career and presidential campaign), Shell, and Texaco—
companies that have spilled 1.7 million barrels of oil onto the soils and rivers
in the past twelve years. The Bush administration and inner circle is stocked
with former oil executives and members of chambers of commerce in countries being opened for oil exploitation (Bush, Jr., Bush, Sr., Cheney, Rice,
Armitage, Baker, etc.). At the same time, U.S. chemical companies Monsanto
and Dow are being enriched by U.S.-assisted spraying of their toxic herbi-
cides (*Roundup* and *Spike*) on coca and opium plants in Colombia:

> Monsanto's *Roundup*, which is the principal chemical being sprayed in Colom-
> bia to reduce the coca and poppy crops, contains phosphorus, which upon
> contact with water captures oxygen and destroys fish in lakes, lagoons, and
> marshes. Crop spraying affects food crops such as cassava, plantains, corn,
> and tropical fruits. Likewise, peasants exposed to the spray have reported cases
> of diarrhea, fever, muscle pain, and headaches attributed to their exposure to
> the chemical spray.[20]

Not only is this endangering the world's second-richest ecosystem (after
that of Brazil), but the same drugs evading eradication by the chemical sprays
(coca production is in fact on the rise) are being sold to the United States
with the profits being used to fund right-wing death squads and paramilitaries who work in the interests of the multinationals and the government
and to fund the left-wing guerrillas fighting against the government and the
multinationals.[21]

In short then, the same interests that are supporting drug trafficking are
also supporting multinational corporate expansion in the region. This is not
just a case of two blood-seeking powers—the government and the insur-
gency—fighting it out at the expense of the little guy, but rather an imperialist manipulation for economic and ideological control where corporations
are winning the conflict on both sides. The entire process of corporate expansion is militarized in combination with the drug trade. However, by omitting
any mention of the complex web of murder, pollution, and politics undergirding its quest for profit, Amoco lies to school kids by painting a picture
of science and education as innocent and free of their motivating forces—in
this case corporate greed. The Amoco curriculum is not simply about hiding
the insidious operations of the company abroad under sunny pictures of

smiling children playing happy games in pristine parks. The Amoco curriculum also constructs and naturalizes a worldview where public concerns are erased underneath the adventures of corporatism and the thrills of the consumer. Part of educating citizens in the "joys of capitalism" consists of, for instance, making the exploitation of other nations' natural environments, raw materials, and labor forces seem like affective friendships or even love affairs celebrated in joyous pictures of wondering gazes at the triumphs of technological mastery. These kinds of images stage a drama of corporate excellence that overrides any possible apprehension about how exactly such curricula are remaking public schooling itself as training ground for consumer armies:

> At the primary and secondary levels, the spoils of the public school system have long been coveted by "education entrepreneurs," touting the "discipline" of the marketplace over the "inefficiency" of the public realm, and normalizing the rhetoric of corporate management—the public as customer, education as competitive product, learning as efficiency tool. Remember Lamar Alexander's declaration, shortly before becoming Secretary of Education, that Burger King and Federal Express should set up schools to show how the private sector would run things? . . . While your local high school hasn't yet been bought out by McDonald's, many educators already use teaching aids and packets of materials, "donated" by companies, that are crammed with industry propaganda designed to instill product awareness among young consumers: lessons about the history of the potato chip, sponsored by the Snack Food Association, or literacy programs that reward students who reach monthly reading goals with Pizza Hut slices.[22]

While Amoco seduces school kids with the lure of fun knowledge, it is also actively engaging in practices that directly undermine the public. Domestically, as Amoco was distributing its "Rivers of Fire" curriculum in Chicago, it was creating real rivers of fire in Michigan and Missouri. In River Rouge, Michigan, the city was fighting to force Amoco to stop leaking explosive petroleum products into its sewer system.[23] City leaders worried that Amoco was re-creating the conditions for an explosion in 1982 that "set off fires and smaller explosions inside nearby sewer lines and blew out windows of buildings and cars."[24] While the *Rivers of Fire* video was being distributed in Chicago, in Sugar Creek, Missouri, families were forced to flee their homes as Amoco's cleanup of its decades-old ground, water, and air pollution forced contaminated air into the homes of local residents. The Chappell family, advised by the EPA to find alternative lodging, had begun an investigation into unusually high incidents of cancer in their neighborhood.[25] At the same time, BPAmoco pleaded guilty to felony charges in a case of illegal dumping of toxic chemicals.

> Alaska's North Slope is an environmentally sensitive area and BP's Endicott Island-drilling site sits on the Beaufort Sea, home to birds and marine life. Hundreds of 55-gallon barrels containing paint thinners, paints, oil and solvents were dumped, according to federal prosecutors.[26]

The conviction followed a sixteen-month-long legal battle in which BPAmoco denied knowledge of the dumping, despite the previous conviction of the same contractor on identical dumping charges. This pollution too had been going on for years.

Amoco produces this science curriculum in conjunction with Scholastic, Waste Management Inc., and Public Television and freely distributes it to the Chicago public schools. The overwhelming corporate interest in investing in this project is far from innocent, philanthropic, or charitable, as the curriculum participates in an overall corporate strategy of producing global corporate citizens and re-creating profit motives as moral values, or rather, tutoring the kids in the "joys of capitalism." As Alex Molnar has shown, Scholastic itself is one of the most aggressive and shameless cases of corralling youth into the consumer market:

> [Mark] Evans [a senior vice president of Scholastic, in his 1988 essay in *Advertising Age*] managed to paint a picture of noble purpose and business need combined in perfect harmony to advance the welfare of American students. Perhaps not wishing to seem too self-serving, he failed to mention that at the time he wrote his essay, Scholastic was in the process of establishing its educational marketing division and was looking for corporate clients. Early in his essay, Evans identified a few business-supported educational projects that, in his mind, illustrated how corporations, pursuing profits, and schools, trying to better educate their students, could work in tandem to advance the cause of social progress. Then he dispensed with the "good cop" fiction and came to the point: "More and more companies see education marketing as the most compelling, memorable and cost-effective way to build share of mind and market into the 21st century." Evans then set aside any pretense of high educational and social purpose when he chose a model for all to emulate. "Gillette is currently sponsoring a multi-media in-school program designed to introduce teenagers to their safety razors—building brand and product loyalties through classroom-centered, peer-powered lifestyle patterning."[27]

In conjunction with these company goals, the Amoco curriculum certainly shows how profits and market values are replacing social purpose in the education of citizens. The Amoco curriculum demonstrates how corporations are using schools to teach market values and make these values into common sense, even fashioning them as the basis of morality. Oil companies in particular, as David Cromwell points out, are using classroom curricula to spread propaganda that "modern civilization is dependent on the hydrocarbon business,"[28] as the popularization of this belief is essential to the survival of the industry. Specifically, as we detail in what follows, Amoco's curriculum envisions nature and knowledge, as well as work, education, and science, through the imaginary of corporate culture.

Nature

Each of the videos begins and ends with advertisements for Amoco. "Major funding for the New Explorers is provided by Amoco celebrating the adventure of scientific discovery for the year 2000 and beyond." This voice-over accompanies images of pristine nature: the moon, a bald eagle flying over a serene lake. The Amoco logo, in patriotic red, white, and blue, joins with the bald eagle in suggesting that the trademark could replace the U.S. flag. In the context of public school classrooms (replete with a U.S. flag hanging near the VCR), such mergings of these common tropes fashions the idea of national citizenship as corporate branding.

These framing advertisements present serene scenes of idealized yet decontextualized nature, labeled with the oil company logo and suggesting an alignment of ecological health and the Amoco corporation. The ad for Amoco is followed by a connected ad for Waste Management, "Helping the world dispose of its problems." Together these images and assuring voice-over present nature in a state of benevolent corporate management. The pristine horizon punctuated by a range of snow-capped mountains, pure colors, still lake waters, and soaring birds serves to Americanize the natural landscape further by placing the corporate logo in the spacious skies and mountain ranges of the beauty America sings. The pure air and stillness give a sense that time has stopped and that human hands have left nature's sublimity untouched and dazzling. The history of Waste Management reveals, of course, quite another story, and certainly the contention that Waste Management disposes of the world's problems is less credible than would be a contrary claim that it has created new ones. Founder and billionaire Wayne Huizenga, a hero of capitalist consolidation, mergers, and acquisitions, has come up time and again under allegations of unethical practices, illegal price-setting, stock bailings, and underworld corruption. Additionally, his profit motivations have proven far from environmentally astute, as he reneged on the waste-hauling industry's practices of breeding pigs to eat edible garbage when his own pigs developed special diseases not evident on the competitors' farms.[29] Though Huizenga has since sold the company, Waste Management has a stake in deregulating capital and finance as well as finding ways to avoid restrictive environmental legislation. The pedagogical intent here is to show nature, indeed, as self-regulating, able to revitalize and reproduce itself without human intervention or investments of any kind. The logo then serves to link the bountiful abundance and cleanliness of nature without controls to the advancement of clean, corporate, healthful capital.

The videos envision nature as not merely best served by corporate management but as an expression of corporate culture. *Rivers of Fire* opens with a drive through the jungle likened to that of a typical suburban commuter on his way to his desk job. "Except for the tropical foliage, [geologist Frank Truesdale's] routine looks like a typical suburban commute, but when he takes the first exit off the paved highway, we get a hint that he's not exactly on his way to a desk job in an office building." Frank's four-wheel-drive jostles down a dirt-paved road flanked on either side by lush vegetation. Corporations themselves thus come to seem part of nature.

Within the imaginary of the videos, nature appears alternately as dangerous and in need of control or as tamed suburban landscape. "If something goes wrong here," warns narrator and producer Bill Kurtis in *Dive Into Darkness*, "there's no easy escape to the surface. Since cave diving took hold in the 1960s, more than 300 people have died in caves in Florida, Mexico and the Caribbean alone." "Temporary loss of air supply, temporary disorientation, temporary loss of lights—those aren't reasons to die in a cave," admits one of the experts. "The reason people die in those situations is panic, perceived stress. That's what kills people." "But despite these risks," the video concludes, "not one of them [the divers] would turn back. This is not just a job for these divers. It's a mission. Like the original explorers in space, they had to send a person there to really know what's going on." *Rivers of Fire* presents scientists as adventurers, explorers, but also conquistadors driven to control an angry and unpredictable final frontier—namely, the earth itself about to spew forth burning deadly fluids. Bill Kurtis kneels before a stream of magma running into the ocean as he explains the danger. "In January of 1983," a voice-over begins, "the skies were just as blue on the big island of Hawaii, the beaches just as inviting as any other day. But thirty miles beneath the crater of Kilowaya, molten lava was rising." This narration is accompanied by ominous bassy music, invoking horror movie conventions as in *Jaws* when the monster is about to pounce. Continual video crosscuts intersperse the explosion of this deadly lava with shots of human technology—seismic equipment, which Kurtis explains, is necessary to watch and hence control the unpredictable earth. Lava flows "threaten homesites and other subdivisions that may be in its way." By framing nature as violent and in need of control by science and technology, *Rivers of Fire* naturalizes the role that the corporation, and here more specifically Amoco, plays in protecting citizens and property from the threat of nature. The technological instruments provide "a way to prevent lava from consuming those who live around the volcanoes."

In this case, the video does more than camouflage the real role that Amoco's science and technology play in threatening citizens and nature. It also denies the history of why the volcano observatory was established in the early twentieth century and by whom. The curriculum fails to mention that the observatory was initially funded by one of the five businesspeople who overthrew the indigenous Hawaiian government and installed a plutocracy. The observatory was designed not merely to study nature but to predict volcanic flows so that other foreign investors could be convinced that their investments in development projects and industry would not be destroyed by lava. In other words, the video presents, as disinterested study of nature, a history of economic and political imperialism. When Amoco and Scholastic describe their lessons as "An Amoco Expedition with the New Explorers," they are actively excluding the history of conquest that paved the way for today's seemingly disinterested measurement of nature. The establishment of the observatory was part of settling the frontier, annexing Hawaii, and continuing the westward expansion, which was part of an American history characterized by violence and exploitation and motivated by profit rather than a benevolent protection of citizens from an unruly nature:

> The entire history of this country has been driven by violence. The whole power structure and economic system was based essentially on the extermination of the native populations and the bringing of slaves. The Industrial Revo-

lution was based on cheap cotton, which wasn't kept cheap by market principles but by conquest. It was kept cheap by the use of land stolen from the
indigenous populations and then by the cheap labor of those exploited in slavery. The subsequent conquest of the West was also very brutal. After reaching
the end of the frontier, we just went on conquering more and more—the Philippines, Hawaii, Latin America, and so on. In fact, there is a continuous strain
of violence in U.S. military history from "Indian fighting" right up through
the war in Vietnam. The guys who were involved in "Indian fighting" are the
guys who went to the Philippines, where they carried out a massive slaughter;
and the same people who had just been tried for war crimes in the Philippines
went on to Haiti, where they carried out another slaughter. This goes right up
through Vietnam. If you look at the popular literature on Vietnam, it's full of
"We're chasing Indians."[30]

In the Amoco videos, nature, rather than technology, corporations, and
the capitalist economic system itself, appears to threaten families, consumption, and the innocent pleasures of beachcombing. Additionally, nature functions as an extension of the corporation, becomes plunderable, and
substitutes as the workspace. Such an understanding of nature as the work-
site serves well oil-drilling sponsor Amoco who also wants students to see
that nature is dangerous to civilization and in need of control, manipulation, and constant measurement by scientists. In "Dive Into Darkness" one
scientist reminds viewers that nature is being destroyed, "things are disap-
pearing so rapidly we need to document them."

Knowledge

The Amoco kit includes three videotapes, six colorful wall posters, teachers'
guides, and public relations instructions for teachers and gas station owners
to place promotional photos and stories about the "partnership" in local
newspapers. Amoco's curriculum suggests that education must be fun, exciting, exploratory, and meaningful to students. "I think it's important that
students see many things on the way home from school that they saw in the
classroom," explains one of the physics teachers. And the success of such
meaningful pedagogical practices is proven in the countless testimonies of
students who were never interested in science before now. "Any teacher can
go to college and get their degree and come in to teach and do all kinds of
chalk talk," one student observes. "But Mr. Hicks comes in and makes it all
fun. He basically loves every one of us. . . . We're a family and he teaches it
with love."

The Amoco curriculum draws on popularized notions of progressive
pedagogy to suggest that education should derive from experience, that
students be involved in "constructing" knowledge by participating in activities that are meaningful to them, and that learning must not disconnect
knowledge from the world. Another middle-level pedagogue, Nancy Atwell,
in her book *In the Middle*, professes to make learning meaningful by giving
kids more power to decide on curriculum and on what happens in the class-

room: "Together we'll enter the world of literature, become captivated, make connections to our lives, the world, and the world of other books, and find satisfaction."[31] Atwell, hailed in both the popular and educational presses as an educational innovator, emphasizes hands-on learning where kids take responsibility in deciding what the curriculum will be and formulate, in discussions with their classmates, the kinds of topics they will write about. Atwell contrasts this new way of teaching middle school with a more traditional teacher-centered methodology where kids' potentials for imagination and involvement are never tapped or developed. At the same time, however, she does not talk about how this freedom for educational experimentation functions to bolster the sense of privilege of her white private-school, suburban students, nor does she address how these methods are meant to train, precisely, those in control of the future means of production. For instance, given the classroom time to write poetry without being assigned specific topics, Atwell's student Joe writes about the emotions he experiences when alone in his bedroom, and Atwell comments, "When I read Joe's poem, I remembered my bedroom in my parents' house and the most complicated relationship I ever enjoyed with a physical space."[32] Atwell neglects to mention what kinds of students have their own bedroom, what are the politics of real estate that provide for these kinds of empty spaces, or what kinds of populations enjoy the privileges of solitude. For Atwell, "empowering" students means giving them a sense of confidence and personal power. Yet, Atwell has no sense of different levels of power, privilege, agency, and sense of entitlement experienced by different students in different social, economic, and cultural contexts. Atwell's kids are already in a class position to receive power. Atwell does not help her privileged students see their privileges as a part of a broader system that fails to extend basic social services to students elsewhere. Nor does she offer her students the tools for challenging oppressions, such as the maintenance of a highly unequal structure of educational resource allocation. Atwell, thus, embraces a highly individualized progressive *methodology* divorced from any social, political referent for more just social transformation. Likewise, Amoco's *Rock n' Roll Physics* shows conventional classroom physics lessons as the height of decontextualized, abstract, and boring education that fails by failing to engage students. A physics teacher drones on spewing formulas as students sleep, doodle, and play with chewing gum. Narrator Kurtis says, "This is no way to teach physics." Cut to the class riding on a roller coaster and Kurtis yells from the roller coaster, "Now this is the way to learn physics." As Atwell states, "Learning is more likely to happen when students like what they are doing,"[33] but there is no sense given here about what kinds of students get to experience such pleasures and under what circumstances, nor what kinds of political values, institutions, and configurations of power are being assumed and supported through such initiatives. Such pleasure is seldom innocent.

The use of adventure-thrill and high-speed derring-do in the Amoco curriculum keys in to a broader public discourse about the economy that promotes instability, fear, and physical trepidation as the goals of the good life. As the Amoco curriculum redefines the pursuit of knowledge as a dangerous game, *Time* and MTV both juxtapose high-risk sport with day trading and risky stock investment. Quitting jobs, starting businesses, and risky investment in the market are being likened to base-jumping, paragliding, mountain climbing, and other adventure sports. MTV shows bungee jumpers freaking out over whether or not to plunge while an e-trade advertisement contextualizes the situation in the lower right corner of the screen. Clearly, *Time* and MTV construct and romanticize the popular embrace of volatile and uncertain ventures. This could be viewed as simply a ploy to naturalize an increasingly unstable economy as an exciting challenge, which the brave can fearlessly negotiate. Job insecurity, an uncertain financial future, and growing inequalities in wealth and income appear as exciting obstacles to brave in the new economy. The economy metaphorizes as nature itself standing there as the tantalizing mountain to climb or jump off of in the Mountain Dew commercial. In other words, adventure sports are being used by corporate mass media to naturalize economic insecurity.

The notion of hands-on learning is indebted to contemporary progressive educational methodologies of constructivism grounded in Piagetian theory as well as the influence of the Deweyan tradition and the wrongful appropriation of Paulo Freire's criticism of banking education. "Education thus becomes," Freire maintains, "an act of depositing, in which the students are the depositories and the teacher is the depositor. Instead of communicating, the teacher issues communiqués and makes deposits which the students patiently receive, memorize, and repeat."[34] These progressive traditions share with the Amoco curriculum an insistence on the centrality of the learner, the need for a de-centering of teacher authority in the classroom, and the importance of knowledge that is meaningful as the basis for further learning. The Amoco curriculum seems progressive by appearing to take seriously the notion that education should be meaningful to students and that the classroom structure should not treat students as depositories for rarified teacher knowledge. However, like many wrong-headed liberal appropriations of Freire, the Amoco curriculum treats progressive educational ideals instrumentally, that is, strictly as methods to increase the likelihood that students will absorb knowledge of which the justifications for its teaching remain unquestioned.[35] In the case of the Amoco videos, this means that there are no questions raised as to why students should learn physics, whose interests are served by the teaching of this knowledge, what this knowledge is used for in the world, and at whose expense and to whose benefit. Hence, seemingly progressive methodologies are not theoretically justified and end up being just a more efficient delivery system for accepted knowledge about science.

The Amoco videos view nature as a resource. That is, nature appears as needing to be tamed and domesticated, brought within the control of scientific rationality represented in automatic machines drawing lines on graphs, making sense. Nature is out there waiting to be retrieved, transported back to laboratories equipped with state-of-the-art equipment for measurement and storage, named, and labeled for future research. "Imagine a place left on earth," says master of ceremonies Bill Kurtis introducing *Dive Into Darkness*, "that is virtually unexplored." The underwater cave Sagittarius in Sweetings Key of the Bahamas is, he continues, an "unstudied world waiting for . . . discovery."

However, the pursuit of knowledge here seems like an alibi. Scattered throughout the surfaces of these environmental niches, scientists find natural holes filled with energy sources: Jill Yaeger of Antioch University swims across blue holes brimming with blue bubbles. These blue holes, the voice-over explains, give off a strong force, which, when reversed by the tides, create twisting fields of force that sweep swimmers into tow without granting any path of escape or release. Searching for knowledge, the scientific exploration team is able to avoid such deep-sea traps. The energy fields themselves are resources to be used in the production of knowledge. Amoco which sponsors the videos do not think it worth mentioning that they themselves are in the business of exploiting energy fields as resources for production. Acquiring knowledge of nature as energy becomes a substitute, even a cover, for exploiting natural sources of energy for company profit. Collecting bits of natural knowledge becomes a safety valve, an antidote to the destruction that natural energy would cause if left unexplored and unexploited, and a compassionate rationale for expanding technocratic controls into foreign territories. Amoco's view of nature communicates that what is important to know about nature is how it can be used for human progress and profit. "Scientists believe that sharks may hold the secrets to important medical benefits for man," Dive Into Darkness informs students. "They're animals in need of protection and study." The video neglects to mention that human industry in the form of commercial fishing is the primary cause of the endangerment of sharks. Instead, "humanitarian" concerns serve to justify Yaeger's dives into darkness on a mission to bring back the newly discovered form of crustacia remipede to her research laboratory in Ohio. These animals need to be known about, named, labeled, and cataloged in order to construct a total knowledge of life, the videos suggest, and of evolution. In fact, the sea dives themselves are depicted as travels back through evolution, into the dark origins of life at the bottom of the sea, while the precarious return to the water's surface works as a triumphant enlightenment. However, what made the journey of discovery so successful turns out to be the successful retrieval of the remipede for scientific research, in other words, the collection and acquisition of resources. The videos translate activities of collecting into the ethical entertainment of learning, knowledge acquisition and accumulation. The idea that knowledge of nature needs to be whole and complete means here that mastery of nature leads to a greater variety of products. Also, nature is biding its evolutionary time, waiting to be brought to civilized places where it can be "taught to eat store-bought food," as Yaeger announces. Amoco does not allude to the ways nature might be destroyed when its products are extracted, nor to how nature and the ecosystem are not designed simply to be exploited for human instrumental use, or to how all nature is not passively waiting to be turned into products of consumption and objects of display.

Earthworms and Empires

Public Image: The corporate image of Monsanto as a responsible member of the business world genuinely concerned with the welfare of our environment will be adversely affected with increased publicity.

Sources of Contamination: Although there may be some soil and air contamination involved, by far the most critical problem at present is water contamination. . . . Our manufacturing facilities sewered a sizable quantity of PCB's in a year's time. . .

—Monsanto committee memo, 1969[36]

Amoco is not the only company using nature to teach kids the values and joys of capitalism. Under these types of curricula, nature is remade to express and reflect the social relations of capital, and thereby the unequal relations of capital are made to seem part of nature. A 2000–2001 exhibit titled "Underground Adventure," at Chicago's Field Museum of Natural History, for example, is a spectacular trip underneath the earth's surface to explore the wonders of the soil.[37] "You will never feel the same about the soil again," are the words that welcome you into Monsanto's "fun for the whole family" learning trek. On the other side of the video greeting room called the "base-camp" is Monsanto's magical shrinking machine, which makes all the critters around the visitors suddenly into towering monsters, gigantic plastic beetles, and bulging roots that would have made Kafka ogle and Gulliver shake his head. What is truly fantastic about the display, however, is not so much that Monsanto is hiding its own destruction of such fertility in the soil through its genetic manipulations or its annihilation of such critters through its production of insecticides such as Roundup or its own monopolistic stronghold of species' diversity by its horizontal control of agricultural products that create essential needs among farmers for its other exclusive products. Nor is it very surprising, after all, that Monsanto would not acknowledge, in this exhibit, its emissions of PCBs that contaminated much farming and breeding lands in West Anniston, Alabama, and caused cancer among much of the population there with the full and documented knowledge of the company itself as to the damage that PCBs cause.[38] Rather, what makes Monsanto's natural history lessons truly magical is precisely how the company manages to exhibit such unethical, unbalanced, and destructive capitalist practices as the way of nature, rather than of multinational corporations.

Monsanto's aims in its exhibit are clear from the moment the visitor enters. The first thing the visitor sees is a series of Plexiglas displays professing the importance of the soil in providing various consumer products. These are not just any consumer products, but rather major corporate trademarks. For example, one case displays an old pair of blue jeans with the glaring Gap label, while the sign reads: "Without soil, there would be no jeans. These jeans are made of cotton denim stitched together with cotton thread. Their blue color comes from indigo dye. Cotton and indigo come from plants that need soil to grow. No soil—no jeans." Next comes a basket of Coca-Cola cans piled on top of one another. The sign exclaims, "The aluminum in these cans has been recycled over and over again. But new aluminum starts out locked inside of soil in an ore called bauxite. No soil—no aluminum." The exhibit never admits what Monsanto or the other sponsors have at stake in displaying this particular constellation of goods, for example, Monsanto's production of NutraSweet artificial sweetener used in Diet Coke. "Without soil there would be no penicillin," the next sign triumphantly declares. The sign does not go on to explain Monsanto's investments in the pharmaceutical industry, nor how the consolidation of large pharmaceutical companies and their lobbying of protections for global intellectual property rights is making medicine less accessible throughout the world to those who need it most, but rather indicates how many lives are being saved because penicillin arises fruitfully from the soil.

Monsanto is clearly telling its young patrons that, just like the mall, the soil is rich in its offerings of fun and diverse things to wear and to buy, as if multinational products emerge straight out of the earth without involving people, labor, or social relations. In other words, Monsanto here seems to literalize the classical Marxist claim that naturalization erases the processes of production from the commodity. Nature is made to seem richly abundant of capitalist output, making invisible the inequalities inherent in the mass manufacturing of cotton or dye, or the injustices practiced in both Third and First World sweatshops where much of, for example, The Gap's merchandise is stitched together (often outsourced) by the poor, the exploited, and the marginalized, or when Coca-Cola's local parent-company Minute Maid employs child labor for low wages in Brazil. What is also not assessed is how such multinationals are involved in, say, polluting the very soil they are said to enrich by distributing nonbiodegradable and nonrecyclable litter, or dumping their excesses in Third World markets to keep prices high, thereby making such items not truly as widely accessible as their spontaneous soil generation would imply.

The first object the visitor sees after having been shrunken is a giant U.S. penny inscribed with the words, "In Soil We Trust." Indeed, the godhead capital lords over nature here. As well, Lincoln's prominent visage at the entrance invokes the authority of the state and American history to suggest an organic connection to capital growth here in the former prairieland of Chicago. More simply, first seeing a series of commodities that come from soil and then seeing money itself in the soil, the visitor is being told outright, "There is big money in the soil." To emphasize that the soil is naturally organized by the laws of capital, in the "Root Room," scientific labels mark uniform units of time along the branch of a tree, becoming farther and farther apart to demonstrate that the branch's rate of growth is accelerating. This celebration of unlimited accumulation and growth makes the project of capital seem driven by a natural propensity toward expansion, rather than, as William Greider points out, toward depletion and nonsustainability: "The nettlesome assertion," he writes, "that governing authorities did not wish to grasp [in 1992] was that rising affluence itself, at least as it was presently defined and achieved, faced finite limits. The global system, as it generated new wealth-producing activity, was hurtling toward a wall, an unidentified point in time when economic expansion would collectively collide with the physical capacity of the ecosystem."[39] In real terms, Monsanto's vision of unrelenting growth and monumentalized consumption can only be sacralized by forgetting the social costs of accelerated production, costs usually not accounted for on balance sheets, like "deforestation, desertification, urbanization and other activities that, so to speak, paved over the natural world"[40] as well as other costs attributed to the impoverishment of the places providing the raw materials, or to their domination by outside powers, like weakened institutions for justice, fiscal austerity, starvation wages, and diminished authority for taxing foreign businesses. Making capital bigger does not necessarily make the world better for most people. Moreover, the exhibit does not allude to the fact that Monsanto's own growth did not happen naturally at all. Rather, it resulted in part from a governmental action responding to pressures from big business interests: the passage of the 1996 Freedom to Farm Act, which was to phase out federal subsidies to farmers and thereby drive small farmers out of business. The legislation, however, did not work to stabilize prices nor to lessen the surpluses pushing prices up, but rather required an increase in government subsidies to farmers (from $16 billion in 1998 to $32 billion in 1999) as Congress enacted "emergency" relief measures. "Among the consequences," Greider concludes, "the capital-intensive treadmill for farmers sped up, and they became even more eager to embrace whatever innovation promised to boost returns. Just as farm prices were cratering, Monsanto and others began promoting genetically altered seeds for corn and soybeans with cost-cutting promises, and this new technology swept the landscape."[41]

Ideas about bigness and growth presented in the entryway set the standard, throughout the exhibit, for connecting consumption to the expansion of the good life promised by corporate growth. The individual museum-goer is supposed to identify with the bugs and critters and so with corporate greed, wanting to consume enough to fatten corporate bellies. Further down the path of exploration, a section is called, "Recycling Leftovers," where the sign reads: "Partnership or Parasite: Can You Tell Which Is Which?" The life-size panorama shows giant worms and bugs feasting on one another in a "feeding frenzy." Across the way stands a vending machine. The first item for selection in this vending machine explains, "millipede: decomposer" while the glass screen displays a package of decaying plants. The vending machine places the viewer into the same position of the feeding critters nearby, proving that nature is but another manifestation of the kind of consumption that vending machines offer when they sell junk food and soda. Critters seem to be selecting their nutrients in the same way that shoppers do, even as some of the selected nutrients cause death and decay to others. Like Amoco, Monsanto is presenting nature as consumer relations under corporate management.

This playful cartoonishness makes violence cute, and even as the bugs chew one another to death, nobody seems to get hurt and everybody equally seems to win organic improvements and benefits. Capital competition appears as a fearless game of destruction through consumption, like Time Warner–promoted Pokémon, making destructive competition fun rather than harmful as it was, for example to Karen McFarlane and her family in West Anniston:

[Karen] has PCBs in her body fat. According to tests done by a local doctor, Ryan's blood has nearly triple the level considered "typical" in the United States; for Tiffany, their 6-year-old, it's double. Nathan, 8, has severe developmental problems, and everyone in the family suffers from respiratory problems and the skin rashes associated with PCB exposure. Chris, Karen's 11-year-old son, who's home from school with an upset stomach and is splayed out on the couch, lifts his Panthers basketball T-shirt to reveal brownish-red blotches up the sides of his chest. "It smells like decaying flesh," Ryan warns. "Like it's rotten."[42]

Certainly for the McFarlanes, the soil where they grow their food and feed their livestock is not abundantly offering consumer items like clothes from The Gap, or giant smiling pennies, or the healthy promise of penicillin. Instead, the joyful critters happily participating in Anniston's consuming frenzy are increasing the McFarlanes' exposure to deadly PCBs as the contamination's rate of growth intensifies moving up the food chain. Not only are the McFarlanes and their neighbors now caught up in a litigation suit that will most likely take years before they see results, but it is also clear to them that the government would have more strictly scrutinized Monsanto if the contamination were happening in a wealthier and whiter area. As it eats away at the shrunken bugs and worms, Monsanto's drive for unlimited growth and profitability appears no longer as a cute and childish game nor an arcade governed by nature and its laws of free competition, but instead as excessive degradation and costs to powerless citizens with the stakes unfairly and quite unnaturally set against them.

In Monsanto's display of nature, natural organisms are not only consumers but they also compose the labor force. Certain critters are presented as looking for jobs, displaying their resumés, classifying their skills like "must work well with others in grazing and/or predatory relationship," "must be energetic and willing to work overtime," or "dis-assembly line worker." In case the point still is not clear, further along there is a tilted tank of soil with water pouring in, demonstrating the way water spreads through the earth. The tank is tagged, "The Trickle-Down Effect." Referencing Reagonomics, conservative procorporate economic language seems here to describe relations of nature, showing, as an established fact, how everybody benefits, grows, and nourishes when the top layers get moistened. As Donna Haraway notes about corporate-motivated representations of biotechnology and genetic fusion more generally, "The latent content is the graphic literalism that biology—life itself—is a capital-accumulation strategy in the simultaneously marvelous and ordinary domains of the New World Order, Inc. Specifically, natural kind becomes brand or trademark, a sign protecting intellectual property claims in business transactions."[43] As the visitor leaves the exhibit, famous quotes about the earth are painted across the wall facing a kaleidoscopic, holographic projection of the world. The globe is constituted by video images of trees and clouds merge into shots of tilled fields that, in turn, merge into housing developments. Consistent with multiple other displays, the video globe suggests a holistic endless cycle of nature within which the actions of clouds, trees, lightning, corporations, and consumers all play a role as redemptive forces of nature. Directly across from this the wall declares in bold letters, "Plowed ground smells like earthworms and empires."

Amoco's domination of nature as a resource, which the videos depict as benevolent and fun, clears the way for its domination and exploitation of peoples and nations, its violent bids to control Third World labor through militarization, and its wiping out of any local and more equitable terms of production. In other words, what the videos show as the healthy curiosity of scientists is, in reality, the violence of colonial conquest for capitalist acquisition, or the reduction of all value to money values and the simultaneous decimation of human values. Affirms David Harvey:

> This power asymmetry in social relations [between first and third world nations] ineluctably connects to the inequities in environmental relations in exactly the same way that the project to dominate nature necessarily entailed a project to dominate people. Excessive environmental degradation and costs, for example, can be visited upon the least powerful individuals or even nation states as environmental hazards in the workplace as well as in the community. Ozone concentrations in large cities in the United States affect the poor and "people of color" disproportionately and exposure to toxins in the workplace is class-conditioned. From this arises a conflation of the environmental and the social justice issues.[44]

Indeed, Amoco's treatment of nature models Amoco's treatment of the people who live in the areas surrounding the sites of exploration. The black people of Sweetings Key, Bahamas, do not seem to have gainful employment outside of waiting for the explorers to come and put them to work. Like the remipedes, they are sitting around waiting for the white scientists to put them to productive work. As picturesque backdrops, they stand by the boats, seemingly incomprehensive as the scientists explain the uses of the equipment to the video viewers. As they trek to the lake, the scientists seem overburdened with large and heavy tools for the dive, and Bill Kurtis explains that they have brought two of every piece of equipment in case of failings. The natives are therefore requisitioned to carry the heavy air tanks and gear on their backs, following the scientists through a wooded field in an image reminiscent of a typical colonial scene like the one Michael Taussig describes of Colombian Indians carrying Spaniards across the Andes: "The normal load for a porter was around 100 pounds, while some were known to have carried 200. Even with these weights they were said to climb the mountains with the greatest of ease and seldom to rest."[45] The relationship between the natives and the scientists in the Amoco video seems cordial but noncommunicative, as they silently do chores to their benefactors' bidding, expressing no will of their own or any sense of initiative outside of serving the needs and doing the tasks of the scientists. Though the natives in the Amoco video are indeed laboring, there is no sense of payment, contracts, organization, conflict, possibilities of worker self-interest, or of worker control over work conditions. Instead, the natives are rendered quasi-mechanical, instrumental, objectified, and vitally curious, mirrors of scientific wonder, proving that the scientists' curiosity is natural, primitive, and raw, the kernel of being human. The black men stare out over the waters, and the camera lingers over their profiled tense faces, creating suspense and worry about the scientists' welfare and safety in the dangerous waters. The bravery of the scientists in the pursuit of knowledge is made starkly visible as the natives sit by the water's edge, not knowing the treasures of discovery that the white establishment, in its superiority, values so highly.

What is the "iMPACT" of such colonialist portrayals being brought into the Chicago public schools that are disproportionately black and Hispanic? What are the videos teaching working-class students about their relationship to the white establishment and to science? The videos all begin with a message from a light-skinned black woman named Paula Banks who is an Amoco vice president. Banks, surrounded by countless antique and contemporary Amoco red-white-and-blue filling station signs, explains to young viewers that science should not only be educational but also fun and exciting. Distributed to largely nonwhite students in the Chicago public schools, the video suggests that alignment with the power of the corporation to control nature like the white scientists do, comes through a whitening. Aside from providing Amoco with a few solid minutes of advertising the logo, this prelude establishes the oil company as "multicultural" and hence offering a promise of potential employment to young nonwhite viewers. Absent here are the historical facts that domestically jobs above the level of service station "jockey" were not available to blacks during the time of the antique Amoco signs and despite the fact that globally the history of oil company exploration and production is the history of white imperialism and enrichment and black subjugation and impoverishment. This is, of course, aside from recent lawsuits against oil giants such as Amoco, Texaco, and others for the maintenance of corporate glass ceiling on promotions and racist harassment on the job, for their environmental exploitation of jungle lands inhabited by the indigenous people of Ecuador and elsewhere.[46]

More than this, the presence of a light-skinned black woman enters into a racial spectrum manifested in the videos that mirrors that of the skin-tone hierarchy of white supremacy. Race ranges from the dark-skinned primitive natives in the Bahamas to the light-skinned black Paula Banks to the white scientific explorers. The racial representations in the film position blacks as working with nature and a part of nature, while portraying whites as controlling, studying, and manipulative of nature. Dark-skinned black Frank Truesdale, a federal forestry worker and not an Amoco employee, the only nonwhite scientist in the videos, who works on the volcano itself is shown to be in a romantic relationship with a feminized moody earth. "Frank knows his volcano too well to relax," notes the voice-over. "He's seen all her moods. Serene beauty. Wonder. Anger." Unlike the white scientists, Truesdale appears to have an intimate relationship with anthropomorphized nature. "It was the beginning of a beautiful friendship," the voice-over narrates the history of Truesdale's career, "Frank and the volcano." This intimacy establishes him as closer to nature, elided with it. Frank is not the one you see operating the high-tech equipment, the machines, the large needles and measuring rods automatically drawing minute seismic changes on a graph. "These machines," the voice-over explicates, "could hear the volcano's heartbeat." Rather, Truesdale is the one out in the field, discovering and experiencing nature directly with a primitive metal stick that digs up the lava and a barrel of water that cools it for study. Truesdale's work shows him engulfed in nature and so part of it, distanced from technology that facelessly watches over him, overseeing his acquisitions and his labors while processing his collections of data reduced to numbers on a chart.

Neoliberalism envisions a world controlled by corporate power, where environmental and human rights as well as democracy are marginalized, if not completely annihilated, in the pursuit of power, profit, and growth. How does such a dystopian idea about the future become widely acceptable, even the only possibility imaginable? Currently, schools are often the ideological mechanisms where the values of international capitalist relations are being diffused. As Henry Giroux notes, "In this scenario, public education is replaced by the call for privately funded educational institutions or for school-business partnerships that can ignore civil rights, exclude students who are class and racially disenfranchised, and blur the lines between religion and state."[47] In other words, students are learning to see their interests coinciding with those of global capital, even and especially in those places where they are fundamentally at odds. Schools need to become, instead, places where students learn to renegotiate their relationships to corporate-sponsored ideologies and to formulate possibilities for oppositional political agency.

As Amoco and other corporate curricula continue to turn schooling into a propaganda ground for their own destructive interests, one solution is clearly to stop using them. Another is to provide teachers with resources for researching the agendas of the corporations that finance and distribute such products in public schools and museums so that the ideological functions of the curricula can be turned against themselves, and the corporations' global agendas will be shown as contextualized and centered within the curricula. In this way, students can be shown how their interests and worldviews actually differ from the way their interests and worldviews are constructed in the curricula. However, in the face of, for example, classroom overcrowding, the growing bureaucratization of teacher tasks and paperwork, and the cutting of public supports, equipment, programs, and infrastructures in schools, teachers are still prone and even sometimes propelled to use the preparation short-cuts that corporate curricula offer free of charge. Public actions like the anti–WTO and anti–World-Bank and IMF protests in Seattle and Washington D.C. provide important revelations about how corporations are operating against the public interest, are instrumental in perpetuating human rights and environmental abuses, are creating conditions for the exploitation of cheap labor abroad by destroying environmentally sustaining and economic infrastructures in already poor nations, and are weakening the institutions of democracy on a world level as capital gains power over civil governing. This type of counterhegemonic education of the public serves as a counterpoint to the seamlessly happy world ensconced in the pleasures of pure knowledge promised by Amoco and Monsanto and starts on the difficult, uphill path of demanding that corporations be held responsible for their crimes against nature and humanity. Simply teaching students to read critically cannot counter the adoption of global capitalist interests into school curricula. Additionally, the school needs to be revitalized as a public power that holds out against private interests. As in South Africa in the 1970s, schools need, therefore, to be linked to other battlegrounds fighting for democratic values and human liberation as well as to those popular forces now producing counterscenarios to the lie of disinterested satisfaction in a corporate-controlled public sphere.

Notes

1. BP Educational Services, available at www.bpes.com/default.asp.
2. Al Ries and Laura Ries, "The 22 Immutable Laws of Branding," *Harper Business* (1999).
3. For example, AOL Time Warner's weekly advertisement for all things corporate, *Time* magazine, informs readers that they should be principally concerned with Wall Street's profit from privatizing public schools rather than even mentioning the implications for democracy of turning over publicly funded institutions to be exploited by the corporate sector. John Greenwald, "School for Profit," *Time* (March 20, 2000), 56–57. For an extensive discussion of the dangers to democracy posed by public school privatization see Kenneth J. Saltman, *Collateral Damage: Corporatizing Public Schools—A Threat to Democracy* (Lanham, Md. and Boulder, Colo.: Rowman & Littlefield, 2000. See also, Henry A. Giroux, *Stealing Innocence: Youth, Corporate Power and the Politics of Culture* (New York: St. Martin's Press, 2000) and Alex Molnar, *Giving Kids the Business* (Boulder, CO: Westview, 1996).
4. For a discussion of the political use of childhood innocence, see Henry A. Giroux, *The Mouse that Roared: Disney and the End of Innocence* (Lanham, Md. and Boulder, Colo.: Rowman & Littlefield, 1999).
5. For an excellent analysis of this phenomenon in relation to the broader privatization of the public sector and of mass media, see Robert McChesney, *Rich Media, Poor Democracy* (Urbana: University of Illinois Press, 1999). David Cromwell notes that the oil industry, not merely a few companies, are engaged in funding and distributing pro-oil corporate curriculum ("Oil Propaganda Wars," *Z Magazine* (March 2000): 7–8.
6. Justin Delacour, "Human Rigths and Military Aid for Colombia: With 'Friends' Like the Senate Democrats, Who Needs Enemies?", available at www.lbbs.org/ZNETTOPnoanimation.html.
7. Edward Herman and Cecilia Zarate-Laun, "Globalization and Instability: The Case of Colombia," *Z-Net*, available www.lbbs.org/ZNETPOProanimation.html.
8. Ibid.
9. Marc Cooper, "Plan Colombia: Wrong Issue, Wrong Enemy, Wrong Country," *The Nation* (March 19, 2001): 14.
10. See Ken Silverstein's *Private Warriors* (New York: Verso, 2001) for an excellent illustration of the expansion of private militaries and their use by multinational corporations.
11. For an in-depth history of how U.S. drug eradication efforts in the region have helped to build up South and Central American intelligence operations which have routinely instituted torture and corruption, see Peter Dale Scott and Jonathan Marshall, *Cocaine Politics: Drugs, Armies, and the CIA in Central America*, 2nd ed. (Berkeley, Los Angeles, London: University of California Press, 1991, 1998). The authors here cite as an example the Peruvian agency SIN (National Intelligence Service), which was created by the CIA and whose agents were trained by the CIA. SIN was headed by the now-infamous Vladimiro Montecinos who was revealed as the terrorizing spook behind much of the corruption in Alberto Fujimori's regime. Though Montecino's acceptance of bribes became a mark of his immorality in a spectacle circulated in the international press in 2000, prompting Fujimori's resignation by fax from Japan, the same sort of outrage was never directed towards

what Scott and Marshall have documented as Montecino's undisputed ties to the drug cartels in Colombia and other places (x–xi).

12. Marc Cooper, "Plan Colombia," 14.
13. As cited in Marc Cooper, "Plan Colombia," 16.
14. Cecilia Zarate-Laun, "Introduction to the Putumayo: The U.S.-assisted war in Colombia," *Z-Net* (February 2001, available at www.lbbs.org/ZMag/articles/feb01laun.htm.
15. Carla Anne Robbins, "How Bogota Wooed Washington to Open New War on Cocaine," *Wall Street Journal* June 23, 2000, 1: A12. Not mentioned here is the proportion of now taxable large assets that are associated with the drug trade.
16. Thomas Freidman, *The Lexus and the Olive Tree* (New York: Farrar Straus Giroux, 1999), 309.
17. "Raul Reyes, commander of the FARC, met with Richard Grasso, chairman of the New York Stock Exchange, who explained to the guerrilla leader how markets worked. As the two figures embraced in this rebel-controlled area demilitarized by the government, Grasso told Reyes that Colombia would benefit from increased global investment and that he hoped that this meeting would mark the beginning of a new relationship between the FARC and the United States." As quoted uoted in Peter McLaren, *Che Guevara, Paulo Freire, and the Pedagogy of Revolution* (Lanham, Md. and Boulder, Colo.: Rowman & Littlefield, 2000), 70.
18. Delacour, Human Rights and Military Aid,"
19. Ibid.
20. Zarate-Laun, "Introduction to the Putumayo.
21. Cecilia Zarate-Laun, "Crossroads of War and Biodiversity: CIA, Cocaine, and Death Squads" by the Eco-Solidarity Working Group in *Covert Action Quarterly* (Fall–Winter, 1999): 16–17.
22. Andrew Ross, "The Mental Labor Problem," *Social Text 63* (Summer 2000): 1–31.
23. This wasn't the first time this particular river was made into a polluted site by oil-related industries. There's a history here. "Virulently antiunion employers, epitomized by Henry Ford, retained their own strikebreaking 'security forces.' During the Communist-led Ford Hunger March of unemployed workers in March 1932, Ford's men shot to death four workers at the gates of the huge River Rouge complex. After more than seventy thousand sympathizers attended the funeral march, Ford and other employers responded by purging and blacklisting thousands of suspected radicals from their plants." William M. Adler, *Molly's Job: A Story of Life and Work on the Global Assembly Line* (New York: Scribner, 2000), 104–105.
24. Steve Pardo, "River Rouge Fears Explosion: City Sues BP/Amoco in Effort to Clean Up Sewers and Avoid Repeat of 1988 Blast," *Detroit News* (November 30, 1999): D3.
25. Ibid.
26. Ibid.
27. Alex Molnar, *Giving Kids the Bu$iness: The Commercialization of America's School* (Boulder, Colo: Westview, 1996), 30–31.
28. David Cromwell, "Oil Propaganda Wars," *Z Magazine* (March 2000): 8.
29. Martin S. Fridson, *How to Be a Billionaire: Proven Strategies from the Titans of Wealth* (New York: John Wiley & Sons, 2000), 148–50. "Subpoenas and fines for harassment of competitors and price-fixing dogged Waste Management during its spectacular growth period. . . . [R]egulators and prosecutors relentlessly investigated Waste Management, inspired by previous revelations of organized crime's control of commercial waste hauling in southern New York and northern New Jersey. . . . Not only his business strategies, but also his financial practices generated criticism. Observers objected to the prices he paid in certain acquisitions, arguing that they exceeded industry norms. . . . Huizenga also had to endure the accusation that the companies he created through consolidation fared poorly after he left the scene. . . . Finally, critics lambasted Huizenga's practice of acquiring businesses for stock."
30. Noam Chomsky, "Breaking Free: The Transformative Power of Critical Pedagogy," edited by Pepi Leistyna and Stephen Sherblom, *Harvard Educational Review* (1996): 111.

31. Margaret Atwell, *In the Middle: New Understandings about Writing, Reading, and Learning* (Portsmouth, N.H.: Heinemann, 1998), 35.

32. Ibid., 52.

33. Ibid., 69.

34. Paulo Freire, *Pedagogy of the Oppressed*, trans. Myra Bergman Ramos (New York: Continuum, 1970, 1993), 53.

35. Amoco is hardly the first corporation to appropriate progressive methodology in a way that jettisons critical social transformation as an underlying ideal. Disney's Celebration, in Florida schools, exemplifies this corruption: see Giroux, *The Mouse that Roared*. As Donald Lazere has argued, "[m]any . . . Freireans . . . have failed to perceive that the political right has coopted their ideas to depict its own social camp, even in its most powerful, privileged, and prejudiced sectors, as meriting the same level of pluralistic encouragement of self-esteem and expression of feelings accorded the least privileged groups. Some such students expect teachers to make them feel good about being bigots, like Rush Limbaugh does—and some teachers . . . gladly comply." Donald Lazere, "Spellmeyer's Naive Populism," CCC 48 (May 1997): 291.

36. Nancy Beiles, "What Monsanto Knew," *The Nation* (May 20, 2000): 18–22.

37. Monsanto is the main sponsor of this exhibit. Other sponsors include ConAgra Foundation, National Science Foundation, the Fort James Foundation, Chicago Park District, Abbott Laboratories, Pfizer Foundation, Prince Charitable Trusts, Service/Master Company, Marion S. Searle/Searle Family Trust, and the Chicago Board of Trade Foundation.

38. " 'PCB is a persistent chemical which builds up in the environment. It, therefore, should not be allowed to escape . . .'—Monsanto, 1972" (Beiles, "What Monsanto Knew," 19).

39. William Greider, *One World, Ready or Not: The Manic Logic of Global Capitalism* (New York: Touchstone, 1997), 455.

40. Ibid., 456.

41. William Greider, "The Last Farm Crisis," *The Nation* (November 20, 2000): 15.

42. Beiles, "What Monsanto Knew," 19–20.

43. Donna J. Haraway, *Modest_Witness@Second_Millennium.FemaleMan_Meeets_OncoMouse: Feminism and Technsoscience* (New York and London: Routledge, 1997), 65–66.

44. David Harvey, *Justice, Nature and the Geography of Difference* (Malden, Mass. and Oxford, Eng.: Blackwell, 1996), 155.

45. Michael Taussig, *Shamanism, Colonialism, and the Wild Man: A Study in Terror and Healing* (Chicago and London: University of Chicago Press, 1987), 298.

46. Eyal Press, "Texaco on Trial," *The Nation* (May 31, 1999): 11–16.

47. Henry A. Giroux, "Cultural Studies and the Culture of Politics: Beyond Polemics and Cynicism" (forthcoming).

INTRODUCTION TO CHAPTER 3

Like the preceeding chapters, David Gabbard insists that the notion of education as enforcement provides us with far more than a metaphor that conveniently captures the essence of this latest period of educational reform. Uniquely, he draws upon two areas of academic specialization within the field of theology (ecclesiology and liturgy) to analyze how state-sponsored programs of compulsory schooling function as rituals that aid the state in performing that which it takes as its primary task—the enforcement of the market. The state, Gabbard contends, portrays itself as morally obligated to "help" meet everyone's universal "need" to be "incorporated" into the secular salvation of the market. In reality, however, such integration is not grounded in a universal need; it is compulsory. Therefore, it must be enforced.

CHAPTER 3

Education *IS* Enforcement!

The Centrality of Compulsory Schooling in Market Societies

DAVID A. GABBARD

Ken Saltman and I conceived this collection as an effort to shed light on recent initiatives within and around schools to enforce the population's obedience to corporatist ideals and its loyalty to the state. As evidenced by George W. Bush's post–September 11 call for our return to normalcy, chief beneficiaries and apologists of market societies typically conflate these two goals. Being good citizens, as Bush told us, means being good consumers—investing our energies in the production and consumption of goods and services from the market for "the good of our country."

Other contributing authors to this volume have done an excellent job of documenting some of the more significant efforts to strengthen the school's role in servicing this corporatist vision of citizenship. Some of them have also documented instances where the state has had to resort to more blatantly militaristic measures to contend with those sectors of the population most at-risk of failing their citizenship training—those who refuse or fail to recognize school as the only legitimate pathway to the secular salvation, which they can only find in the market. In my view, however, we should not regard either corporatism or militarism as recent features of education. I believe that Saltman's phrase "education as enforcement"[1] represents something far more than a convenient metaphor for capturing this latest era of perpetual school reform. "Education as enforcement" provides an apt literal description of the role of compulsory schooling in market societies. The modern nation-state has always taken the enforcement of a market society its primary task. Across its history, compulsory schooling has provided the state with an increasingly vital ritual for enforcing the market as the only permissible pattern of social organization. Moreover, instead of looking at education as *if* it were enforcement (that is, metaphorically), I contend that education actually *is* enforcement.

In stating this, I must clarify that I do recognize how some teachers and

David A. Gabbard is an associate professor in the Department of Curriculum and Instruction in the School of Education at East Carolina University. He is the author of *Silencing Ivan Illich: A Foucauldian Analysis of Intellectual Exclusion* (Austin & Winfield, 1993) and the editor of *Knowledge and Power in the Global Economy: Politics and the Rhetoric of School Reform* (Lawrence Erlbaum, 2000).

students frequently act in opposition to the general patterns of enforcement that surround them. We should encourage and support such practices, acknowledging the risks that resistance and refusal entail.

The Market, the State, and the Roots of Enforcement

As Karl Polanyi defines them, market societies such as our own differ from traditional societies in one primary regard: traditional societies embed their economic activities within their social relations.[2] Without romanticizing such societies, Polanyi describes how their concern for the general welfare of other individual members of the collective group, along with preserving their culturally determined patterns of social organization, places significant limits on the extent to which economic concerns could become a dominant force in individuals' lives and drive their thoughts and behaviors. The subsistence orientation of traditional cultures leads them to draw from their environment only what the group requires for its collective survival. Refuting the standard claim that the tendency to "barter and truck" represents a cross-cultural constant, Polanyi provides anthropological evidence to point out that trade with neighboring groups was limited and infrequent. Polanyi provides similar evidence to highlight the fact that individuals within traditional societies gain status from what they contribute to the collective effort. Hence, such societies place a premium on generosity. They never learn to equate status with individual economic gain or acquisitiveness.

In market societies, Polanyi contends, the situation is reversed. Rather than embedding the economy within social relations, market societies embed their social relations within the economy. Individual gain motivates productive activity; it is not what productive activity lends to the welfare of the group. Individuals derive status from how much gain they derive from market activity, not from what they contribute to the welfare of others. Acquisitiveness, even when performed in the name of providing for one's own family, places the ties of friendship and kinship under tremendous strain. As Juliet Schor describes in *The Overworked American*,[3] even in our age of labor-saving technologies, members of market societies are working longer hours than ever before, much to the neglect of familial and communal ties.

The centrality of compulsory schooling to the enforcement of a market society does not appear immediately obvious to us. To help us begin to appreciate this centrality, we should turn to the study of theology. For it is in the history of the Christian church, as Ivan Illich points out, that we find the origins of many of the ideas that helped the modern nation-state develop its mechanisms of enforcement.[4] First, within theology there is a field of study known as *ecclesiology*, which Illich describes as a precursor to sociology.[5] It concerns itself with the origin, development, and structure of that community known as the church. Legalistically defined, ecclesiology studies the *corporatization* of individuals into a single body—a more or less unified community. This community comes to include many more people than just the clergy and other church officials. In its idealized form, this community is "catholic." This idealization also defines its mission. The church seeks to incorporate *everyone* into its community.

Second, the field of ecclesiology contains its own areas of academic specialization. Central to our concerns, *liturgy* entails the study of how the church uses multiple series of rituals for socializing people to recognize and judge their status as members of the church. It studies the formation of what we commonly refer to as *conscience*—that internal court in which individuals judge themselves and their status as members of the church as determined by their degree of felt compliance with the norms and laws of the church. Taken together, ecclesiology and liturgy study the manner in which the church expands the size of its community by winning compliance through conscience and, thus, without revealing to people how their compliance is, in fact, compulsory due to the legal status of the norms covertly enforced through the rituals in which their participation is required. Though history abounds with examples of the church, in concert with the state bodies with which it colluded, resorting to overt militarism and violence to increase its membership and its power, many of these tactics were precisely that—last resorts. Overt imposition met with tremendous resistance and great resentment among its victims. The church came to understand that such reactions were counterproductive to the goal of compliance. Not only did conscience prove far more effective at winning compliance, it also made possible a more willful, even enthusiastic, compliance.

In order to effect the formation and exercise of conscience, the church had to present a benevolent image of itself to the world, an image that would define its institutional mission in terms of some universal moral imperative that the church had assumed responsibility for serving. But the church could not formulate such a moral imperative without first conceiving those whom it sought to incorporate into its community as lacking some quality that they could only acquire through this incorporatization. The "doctrine of original sin" provided the church the moral imperative that it needed. According to this doctrine, everyone is born constitutionally defective. They lack grace. Without grace, they cannot achieve eternal salvation. Instead, they will suffer eternal damnation.

The church, however, did not pretend to be able to provide people with grace itself, only the means for achieving it. People could only acquire those means through their incorporation into the church and through their subsequent participation in its rituals. Through their willful participation in these rituals, they would learn how to live their lives in compliance with the word of God. This was *the* path, and the *only* path, to grace and salvation. The word of God, however, was always interpreted and filtered by the church, and eventually transformed into church law as it sought to establish the Kingdom of Heaven here on earth. Hence, compliance with the word of God actually meant compliance with church law. And many of the rituals of the church, including and especially the mandate of yearly confession, sought to teach people to judge themselves and the status of their progression toward grace in terms of the degree of their compliance with that law. This marked the birth of conscience that would later become so crucial for the modern nation-state in developing the notion of citizenship.

Against this background, we can already gain some tentative insights into how the state uses compulsory schooling as a ritual for enforcing a market society. Ecclesiology leads us to consider, first, for whom does the state assume responsibility? On this matter, the language of globalization provides the most direct route to our answer. Every bit as "catholic" as the church, the state assumes responsibility for everyone. In its often self-proclaimed role in expanding and protecting markets, the state seeks to bring every living person in to the fold of the global market society. Long before the market society could be conceived in global terms, however, the early modern nation-states of western and northern Europe had to first concern themselves with bringing their domestic populations into this fold. Though seldom studied as such, the "enclosure movement" that began in England during the sixteenth century and later took root in other western and northern European countries ought to be regarded as a watershed moment in the historical unfolding of globalization. This movement transformed land, which had once been communally shared by peasant farmers to provide subsistence for local communities, into property for the production of commodities to be bought and sold on the market. Food ceased to exist as a communally grown and harvested source of sustenance. It became an economic value to be produced by wage-laborers for the profit of land "owners." But this new class of persons, the landowners, could only employ a limited number of laborers. And now that the land produced only large amounts of single cash crops, rather than a diversity of foods, the land could no longer support the same number of people as it had before. Thousands of people were pushed off the land and into the growing cities, which were experiencing the early stages of their own industrialization. Many of these displaced persons found themselves indigent, frequently ending up in work-houses and poor houses, if not prisons. Others migrated to overseas colonies in the Americas and elsewhere.

Not only did the state assist through its legalization of this movement, it also lent its military forces in putting down a sundry of peasant rebellions, most notably in England and Germany. Though it is beyond the scope of this chapter, the story of the market's decimation of the traditional societies of Europe represents an unwritten volume in the canon of multiculturalism. First in Europe, then throughout the rest of the world, the modern nation-state has always sought to impose the market society as the only legitimate mode of social organization. Any other pattern of social organization constitutes a threat and, therefore, must perish.

Just as the church formulated rituals to ensure compliance, the modern nation-state had to seek its own ritualistic means for incorporating people willingly and eagerly into compliance with the norms and laws of a market society. The state needed its own moral imperative for incorporating individuals into its ranks of citizens. While the "doctrine of original sin" provided the church with its moral imperative, one of the most fundamental laws of the market provided the state with the imperative it needed, namely, the law of scarcity. The law of scarcity defines the human condition and social conditions everywhere. Applied to the human condition, the law of scarcity proclaims that human wants are great (if not immeasurable), while their means for satisfying those wants are scarce. Only the market can provide those means—the means for achieving secular salvation, defined as the satisfaction of wants. But in order to access those means through participation in the market, one must possess something of value to exchange on the market. One must possess something akin to grace sought by those who identified with the church. The market's equivalent of grace is *use-value*.

The "doctrine of original sin" taught people to understand that they were born without grace, and that without grace they could not acquire eternal salvation. The "law of scarcity" teaches people to understand themselves as having been born without use-value. Without use-value, I have nothing to exchange on the market. Therefore, I have no means for satisfying my wants or achieving salvation in the secular world of a market society. In my raw state, like any resource, I possess no use-value. Also like any resource, however, I can be subjected to processes designed to make me useful. Again, however, the means for developing my use-value are scarce.

Ideally, given the utopian character of market fundamentalism that posits the market as the source of the satisfaction of *all* of my wants and needs, even the means for developing my use-value ought to be provided by the market. Unfortunately, the fundamentalist ideology of the market is fraught with contradictions. In order to pursue the development of my use-value within the market, I must first have use-value to exchange on the market in order to pay for the services through which my use-value can be developed. In an orthodox market society—a society devoid of any formal, regulatory state apparatus, only those, or those whose parents, who could afford to pay for such services would be able to access these particular means. Just as the market cannot provide for its own military power to enforce the conditions it has sought to impose throughout its history, first in Europe and then across most of the rest of the globe, this situation required state intervention. Whatever the market cannot provide for itself, the state must provide *for* it. In this case, what it called for was a ritual that would function to incorporate individuals into a market society, providing them with the means for cultivating their use-value in order that they might be able to find their own individual salvation in the market while contributing to the broader salvation that the market bestows upon the society as a whole. The state provided this ritual, of course, in the form of compulsory schooling.

Learning to *Need* School

I am not saying that everyone embraced this ritual from the moment that the state began legislating compulsory school laws. History almost always contradicts this degree of determinism. There *was* resistance to compulsory school laws. The creation of any new institution produces a problem of legitimatization, particularly when the state establishes laws requiring all future members of society to undergo the "treatment" that it provides. However, as the market society evolved from the nineteenth century to the present, the connections between compulsory schooling and the law have become less immediately discernable, helping to strengthen schooling's efficacy as a ritual for enforcing the market.

Two major features of the market society's evolution contributed heavily to the growing efficacy of schooling as a ritual of enforcement. First, and most obviously, the market began requiring educational credentials (diplomas, degrees, and certificates—testimonials to the degree to which a person's use-value had been developed) as a precondition of employment. To the degree that the market literally became people's only means for satisfying their wants and needs, these formal job requirements made compulsory school laws somewhat obsolete. Because the market itself began requiring participation in the ritual of schooling as a condition of employment, the connection between the compulsory nature of schooling, the state, and the law became less discernable. As a consequence, school could become viewed less in terms of being an institution that the state forced people to attend, and more in terms of an "opportunity" and, later, a "right" that the state granted to individuals, enabling them to meet the demands of the market.

Further blurring the connections between school, state, and law, this "opportunity" or "right" to participate in the ritual of schooling was cast in terms of a value—the value of education. Framed as a value and protected as a right, schooling came to fit into the logic of the market as something that could be acquired. In the vernacular of schooling, we have learned to say that we want our children to *get* an education, or to *receive* an education. Suddenly, something that had previously been treated as a process became a thing that one could possess. Befitting the market's logic of acquisitiveness, education devolved into a commodity, and the more of it that one consumes, as evidenced by the number of diplomas, degrees, and so forth, that one possesses, the more that person's use-value within the market grows. As a person's use-value to the market expands, so do the benefits that he or she can expect to derive from the deployment of that use-value in the market.

This brings us to the second major feature of the market society's evolution that contributed heavily to the growing efficacy of schooling as a ritual of enforcement. As industrial technologies allowed for higher rates of mass production, the number of commodities available on the market mushroomed to unprecedented levels. The net effect of this ongoing explosion of commodities, with newer commodities entering the market everyday, was to radically alter the picture of secular salvation in a market society. The intent of new commodities and the marketing that accompanies them is to induce new wants in people, to generate a sense that happiness stems from people's ability to satisfy their ever-expanding scope of wants. In the United States, we refer to this ever-expanding notion of secular salvation that equates "well-being" with "well-having" as "the American Dream." In its nationalistic implications, the idea of the American Dream not only strengthens the ability of the market to enforce people's compliance with its demands for consumption through the formation of conscience; it also associates that conscience with the idea of citizenship.

As Americans, or so the logic goes, we are supposed to collectively share and individually pursue this Dream. As citizens, we learn to view the pursuit of this Dream as a right, even a privilege as Americans. The church could not create rituals to determine for its parishioners the degree of grace they had achieved through their compliance with the word of God. Neither could the church offer individuals concrete evidence that compliance with its laws actually enabled people to achieve eternal salvation. The market, however, provides tangible means by which individuals can judge the amount of use-value that they have acquired and, consequently, the degree of secular salvation they have achieved. A market-driven conscience leads people to measure their level of individual compliance with the market—the degree to which they meet its demands, abide by its laws, and conform to its norms—by their patterns of consumption. It enables them to measure their own worth.

Compulsory schooling contributes to the enforcement of a market society by helping people establish their levels of expectations relative to their patterns of consumption. First, as previously described, I enter this world under the impress of the law of scarcity. I am born as a raw material without immediate use-value to the market. This condition poses a threat to me in a market society, for in a market society I need use-value to exchange on the market in order to meet all of my other needs. In a market society, my survival depends upon this exchange. Therefore, I learn to need use-value. Learning this need disguises the fact that the state *compels* me to attend school. Instead of learning that the state compels me to attend school, I learn to *need* school for my acquisition of use-value.

As a child of this contemporary age of mass media, mass production, and mass consumption, television advertising and the toy industry will have already taught me to associate my happiness with the consumption of market commodities. The American Dream will have already infected my sense of conscience whereby I judge myself by what and how much I own. School contributes to the formation of this conscience through the calculus of meritocracy. According to this accounting system, I must exhibit faith in the axiom that the number of years of schooling that I consume, multiplied by my level of performance/compliance as measured by my grades and standardized test scores that determine my placement within the hierarchy of the school's differentiated curriculum, will determine my use-value and, therefore, how much I can expect to gain from the market in exchange for the deployment of that use-value—my labor.

It should not surprise us, then, that the children who most fully comply with the demands of school in terms of their behavior as well as their performance come from families who have already achieved the American Dream. Those parents who have achieved this Dream will likely credit at least a portion of their success to the pastoral care of the school in developing their use-value and otherwise leading them into secular salvation. They will staunchly defend their children's "right to a good education," and reinforce in the minds of their children that school represents an opportunity to "make something of themselves," to "become somebody," implying that those who do not take advantage of this opportunity become, or remain, nothing and nobodies. Hence, these children learn to need school and to accept the benevolence of its intent. Internalizing this need, they comply with the school's regulation of their learning (what, how, and when). Those who demonstrate the highest degrees of compliance with the school's rules and values receive the highest levels of praise and affirmation from teachers. As an integral part of the formation of their conscience, their compliance defines them as "good students," and, therefore, as "good citizens." It earns them placement within the higher ability groups and higher curriculum tracks that will qualify them to consume yet more years of schooling and escalate their expectations of what market-based privileges their increased use-value will afford them.

Returning to the implication that those who do not take advantage of the educational opportunity that the benevolent state provides them become nothing and nobodies, not taking advantage of that opportunity implies a special form of noncompliance and, in some ways, a type of secular heresy. These "refuseniks" who make no effort to take advantage of this opportunity fail to demonstrate the requisite level of faith in the calculus of meritocracy. Consequently, they should learn to expect little or nothing from the market, since their non-compliance with this most basic of school norms does nothing to develop their use-value.

There are, of course, many other forms of noncompliance, including poor performance. While some children's poor performance may be attributable to what we might refer to in the vernacular of the market as deficits in their innate capacities to develop use-value, I believe that far more instances of poor performance stem from the inability or the refusal of some children to recognize the viability of schooling as the only path to secular salvation. These children tend to come from homes where the parents have failed to achieve the American Dream. Unlike their successful counterparts, these parents have less reason to communicate a pastoral image of a benevolent school to their children. In all likelihood, school pushed them to the margins for as long as they could be compelled to attend. Like themselves, their children have either failed or refused to internalize the norms of the school as their own. And everyone in school knows who the bad students/bad citizens are.

The trailer parks and shanties scattered across the desolate landscape here in rural eastern North Carolina are full of such parents and students. Because their lives bear so little resemblance to the American Dream, they are often held up by school-advocates and "good" parents as negative examples—living testimonials of what will happen to you unless you comply with the demands of school. Their noncompliance with those demands has condemned them to lives of secular damnation—that most dreaded of all conditions: poverty. Without developing the use-value that would enable them to contribute to the wealth of the market and the state, they never attain their full value as human beings.

The formal curriculum sends this message in its selection of whose lives are worthy of serious study in school. The study of history typically focuses on the lives and accomplishments of rich and powerful people who contributed something to the market society. It also focuses on the accomplishments of the generals who fight and win wars on behalf of those rich and powerful people who own and control the market. More recently, "little gray boxes" have been added to textbooks in order to highlight and give special acknowledgment to the contributions that women and "people of color" have made to the market and/or state power. Individuals who fought for the rights of their people to achieve equal access to the market and the equal educational opportunity in the schools that regulate and enforce it receive special attention. Those who have challenged the viability of the market as a mode of social organization receive no attention. Neither does the school afford the vast majority of children the opportunity to study the lives of people *like* themselves, much less the opportunity to study their *own* lives. The lives of people like themselves and the forces that shape those lives, it seems, are not worthy of study. This audible silence of the null curriculum further instills the economic worldview in the minds of its victims, teaching children that they should want to "become somebody," that they should want to "make something of themselves," meaning that they should strive to align their interests with those of the market and the state that enforces it. Until they do, they will remain nothing and nobodies.

Simply because these "refuseniks" have failed to internalize the norms of school does not mean that they have failed to internalize the norms of the market society. Most of them have internalized those norms of society's dominant institutions from the consumption of the messages of advertising. They, too, equate well-being with well-having. Unfortunately, they fail or refuse to recognize either the idea that they are born without use-value, the belief that this use-value can only be cultivated in school, or the notion that they must exchange this use-value on the market in order to satisfy all of the other wants and needs that the market society imputes to them. While they have internalized most if not all of these imputed wants and needs, their noncompliance with the demands of school forces them to seek to satisfy those wants and needs outside the official market. They seek the secular salvation of the American Dream through illegal means, creating their own markets for commodities not legally available in the traditional market. While many people typically adopt a self-righteous attitude toward these "criminals," viewing their noncompliance as a function of their having failed to internalize the values of the dominant society, I believe that precisely the opposite is true. The teenager who sells crack to elementary school children does not lie awake at night looking forward to ruining the lives of tomorrow's customers. Ruining people's lives does not motivate his or her decision to sell crack. "It's all about the Benjamins"—money: the means to satisfy imputed wants and needs. In keeping with the norms of our market society, morals and ethics should not be allowed to interfere with the individual's (or the corporation's) pursuit of the "bottom line." In this sense, the drug dealer is no more of a moral deviant than the people who ran Enron and WorldCom. Sadly, that teenager, if caught, will serve time in prison. The folks at Enron and WorldCom won't serve a day behind bars.

Likewise, compliance with the demands of school should not be taken as a sign that one holds a genuine enthusiasm for learning nor an insatiable hunger for education. The fact that compulsory schooling is actually counterproductive to learning and education mirrors the reality that a market society does not genuinely value education or learning. A market society generally looks upon the educated or the learned with a measure of suspicion, for their education or learning frequently leads them to challenge the legitimacy of market demands and reveals the myths and contradictions that the dominant institutions of such societies (i.e., the state and corporations) work to conceal. We can find other evidence of our market society's devaluing of education and learning in the responses given to those exceptionally "good students" who announce that they have chosen teaching as a career.

Many times their friends and family members respond to this announcement by saying: "But you're so smart, why do you want to be a teacher?" It is as if they expect schoolteachers to be of questionable intelligence. Of course, the real message here concerns the equating of intelligence with income. Smart people, as determined by school performance and the number of years spent consuming school, choose professions that earn large salaries.

We can cite still more evidence that compliance with the demands of school should not be confused with an enthusiasm for learning or education. For example, at some point in their maturation process, children learn to distinguish between life in school and life in the *real* world. Seldom, if ever, do the two collide. Seldom are children in school given the chance to learn from the real world or even *about* the real world in any meaningful sense. They must learn from packaged and planned curricula whose market value is determined, in part, by how noncontroversial they are. That is, in keeping with the market society's distrust of intellectuals, state textbook adoption agencies shy away from materials that might lead children to question the legitimacy of the market or the authority of state power. Consequently, as they advance through the school's system of graded promotions, even some of the "best" students learn to disvalue learning as dull and irrelevant drudgery that must be endured for the sake of getting to the next stage/grade level. At this point, school becomes counterproductive to the value that it professes to provide—learning. By the time these most compliant students reach higher education, they have adopted a very economically efficient attitude toward school. I can sense that on the first day of class when they sit and listen to me explain the syllabus, evaluating not what my class will provide them the opportunity to *learn*, but evaluating how much energy they will need to expend in order to receive what they have come for. And what they have come for is not learning. They have come to acquire/consume credit hours. They want to accumulate as many credit hours as they can as fast as they can. For once they collect enough of these credit hours, they can take them to the university's registrar's office and "cash" them in on a diploma. They fully understand, even without ever having been explicitly told, that in a market society the more school you consume, the more privilege you can expect to secure for yourself. An increase in the years spent consuming education amounts to an increase in one's use-value and a subsequent increase in what one can expect from the market in exchange for the deployment of that use-value.

Moreover, as a ritual through which the state enforces a market society, compulsory schooling *incorporates* people into that society by providing them with the opportunity to develop the use-value they would otherwise lack without school. Acquiring that use-value requires compliance with the demands of school and faith in its power to deliver them to the secular salvation known as the American Dream. Through the formation of their conscience, school teaches children to judge their own level of compliance and, in turn, establishes their expectations for what this compliance will produce for them—how much secular salvation they deserve. This is just as important for those who refuse to fully comply with school. If they fail to achieve the American Dream, they have only themselves to blame. School provided them with the opportunity to acquire the secular grace of use-value, but they either rejected it or never held enough potential for it in the first place. Hence, they deserve the secular damnation of poverty that they live, keeping in mind that community colleges and other school programs for reformed "refuseniks" offer them innumerable opportunities for redemption. Redemption is even made available to those whose lack of compliance led to their incarceration within the state's penal institutions. Again, the state is extremely "catholic" in the sense that it almost never ceases in its efforts to incorporate everyone into the market society.

Market Values

Thus far I have attempted to demonstrate how the ritual of compulsory schooling serves to assist the state in the enforcement of a market society. Owing to the inherent characteristics of this ritual that I have sketched out here, compulsory schooling could hardly be more corporatized and corporatizing than it is by design. Within this framework, I find no reason to be astonished by the current levels of corporate involvement in public schools. To this point, however, I have yet to establish the connections between corporatism and militarism that are so vital to Saltman's notion of "education as enforcement." In order to make those connections, I must refer to my earlier remark concerning the utopian character of market ideology. In shaping the conscience of individuals, state-sponsored, compulsory schooling socializes children to identify themselves, first and foremost, in nationalistic terms as Americans. Within this identity structure there comes a sense of privilege— the privilege of having been born or "naturalized" into a society that represents the very best of what any human civilization could ever possibly have to offer. At the most superficial level of analysis, the formal curriculum of compulsory schooling frames what is "very best" about America in jingoistic terms, celebrating its democratic form of government with all of the freedoms and rights that it affords its citizens. The school's hidden curriculum, however, frames those freedoms and rights primarily within the context of the market, not politics. Here the utopian character of market fundamentalism surfaces to define what is "very best" about America in terms of the "rights" and "opportunities" that the state affords individuals to pursue their own individual secular salvation. Again, through the formation of "consumer conscience," individuals learn to judge their own degree of salvation according to market standards. Given the total quantity and quality of goods and services currently made available through the market—the overall level of affluence that establishes the American market society as the historic and universal standard against which all other nations and societies pale in comparison, to what degree and for what duration must I comply with and consume schooling in order to cultivate the proper amount of use-value that will enable me to acquire a level of affluence comparable to that standard? Again, children must never learn to view their attendance at school as compulsory duty imposed on them by the state for the purpose of rendering themselves useful to the market as producers/consumers. They must recognize schooling in terms of the value of education and, therefore, as one of the first "opportunities," "rights," or "privileges" afforded to them by the benevolent state. As benevolent as the state might be, however, it offers no guarantee of secular salvation—only the "opportunity" to compete for it.

The corporatist dimensions of compulsory schooling focus on "incorporating" everyone into the same collective body of persons who share the values of the market and who equate those values with secular salvation—the American Dream. The militaristic dimensions of this ritual primarily reside in the structures that it creates for fostering competitive individualism. This begins with the commodification of education. Like territory, education becomes something that can be acquired. As I consume more education, I become more competitive within the labor market because I increase my use-value. In addition to the quantitative dimensions of this competition, there is also a qualitative aspect that is currently being intensified by the current wave of educational reform and its emphasis on high-stakes testing and curriculum tracking. Again, the level of students' compliance with the school's regulation of their learning is reflected in their performance on standardized tests as well as their grades. Just as the U.S. military used the original IQ tests to rank soldiers to determine which tasks they could most suitably be trained to perform, most state school systems are now using high-stakes to determine which curriculum tracks are best suited for which students. And these qualitatively differentiated curriculum tracks, of course, lead to different outcomes in terms of (1) students' future opportunities to consume more schooling, (2) students future opportunities to consume better quality education within the nation's hierarchy of institutions of higher education (i.e., 2-year college versus 4-year college, state institutions versus private Ivy League institutions), and thus (3) their future within the stratified income/occupational hierarchy of the labor market. In military terms, then, compulsory schooling assigns persons their rank relative to their future use-value as human resources.

As previously discussed, few students see much relevance in schooling as anything other than a vehicle for increasing their own individual use-values within the competitive, dog-eat-dog world and rat-race that constitutes their own individualistic pursuit of secular salvation within the market society—the American Dream. Since they find so little intrinsic value in school-compelled learning, the more compliant "good students" learn to perform chiefly for the sake of the grades and test scores that will grant them higher degrees of secular salvation later in life. But even this absurdity is not without its functionality. Insofar as the majority of future workers will likely find little intrinsic rewards in the jobs they will come to perform in the workplace, the relative meaninglessness of school provides a perfect "boot camp" for teaching them to accept alienation as an inevitable part of life. Submitting to the demands of school for the sake of grades and test scores, they receive a solid "basic training" for accepting the meaninglessness of work for the sake of a paycheck. One of the most essential lessons for learning to "thrive" within a market society is to eschew the search for meaning in either the development (education) or the expenditure (work) of one's use-value. Meaning, as perceived from within the conscience of the "good citizen," is found through the expenditure of one's earnings—in her or his patterns of consumption through which she or he judges her or his own status. Perhaps this helps to explain why so many people have learned to experience shopping as a form of therapy, though the psychological benefits may only be temporal.

In learning to view schooling as a vehicle for pursuing the American Dream, children also develop the spirit of acquisitiveness reflective of market-driven imperialism's incessant need for expansion that justifies its use of militaristic means for accomplishing that end. In this spirit, other persons become little more than a means to their own individual ends, things to be managed, manipulated, and otherwise exploited in their pursuit of that ever-evasive American Dream. The incapacity to find meaning in anything other than material acquisition diminishes their ability to establish and maintain meaningful relationships with others. In this sense, the market's degradation of the sustainability of biotic relationships within the natural environment parallels its degradation of the sustainability of our social relationships. Market societies define social life as a state of constant warfare between competitive individuals. Ironically, the inherent militarism of market societies is most obvious at the domestic level on the streets of America's impoverished inner cities where those persons of least value within the official market battle one another for control of the illegal markets that they create for satisfying the demands of their own consumer consciences. On those streets, the militarism of the market takes more literal forms, with rival gangs wearing "colors" (uniforms) and carrying automatic weapons to protect and expand their market share in order to increase their profits. In light of the relatively low level of affluence that either the minimum wage jobs available to them in the legal labor market or the state's welfare system would allow them to achieve, we can understand how the psychological demands of the consumer conscience (well-being = well-having) into which they are incorporated by the media as well as by schools push these people to take extreme measures in order to satisfy their learned acquisitiveness. Given America's standards of affluence—how much one must possess in order to feel as if she or he has achieved a relatively satisfactory degree of secular salvation, which choice would best enable a person to meet the demands of consumer conscience: Working at McDonald's or running cocaine for the drug lords?

I do not mean to suggest that we should overlook the moral ramifications of profiting from the proliferation of drug addition and violence. I only wish to point out the inherent militarism of the market society's corporatism that is so easily recognized in the social relations surrounding "black markets." These patterns, of course, are not new. They date back at least as far as the gangsters and mobsters of the Prohibition era. Furthermore, they do not differ significantly from what we might term the social relations of the global market societies. As I mentioned earlier, the state is every bit as "catholic" as the church. But the states of various market societies have only sought and continue to seek to incorporate everyone on the planet into the global market society because the utopian character of market fundamentalism allows for no alternative forms of social organization. In order to keep profits flowing and market share expanding, the market recognizes no borders. Everyone and everything must serve the market or suffer the consequences.

Education, Development, and the War Against Subsistence

It is useful to examine some of the rhetorical connections between the notion of "education" and "development" (in the sense of those efforts undertaken on the part of "developed nations"/market societies to assist Third World/"underdeveloped nations") to become more fully integrated into the "global economy" (as if the global economy were some natural phenomenon). To begin with, both education and international economic development have become synonymous with "progress." Although education has a history of conceptual evolution unto itself, its path has merged and congealed with that of "development" to produce one of the great and sacred certainties of our era, namely, a people's economic development proceeds in direct proportion to their level of educational achievement. Both education and economic development imply a process that is required for and leads inexorably to favorable change related to the improvement of people's means to meet their needs. In the rhetoric of U.S. educational reform discourse, education promises to effect this improvement by making the United States more competitive in the global marketplace and by integrating U.S. workers into the global economy's international labor market. Similarly, "development" offers the poor, underdeveloped nations of the world the assistance they "need" to join the more advancing nations in sharing the fruits of the international market system.

When limited to this context, development discourse originated from President Harry Truman's inauguration speech of January 20, 1949, when he spelled out his Point Four Program for stabilizing international relations in the aftermath of World War II. "The old imperialism—exploitation for foreign profit—has no place in our plans," Truman explained. "What we envisage is a program of development based on the concepts of democratic fair dealing."[6] At that particular moment, two-thirds of the world's population became *needy*, and Truman, at least rhetorically, committed the United States and the governments of other market societies to a system of world peace predicated on meeting the *needs* of that great majority so as to eliminate conflict among nations. Hence, the ultimate value of development rests, like education and the services of the institutional church as previously discussed, in the allegedly benevolent intentions of the nation-states of the world's wealthiest market societies to satisfy the needs of the world's poor in order to integrate them into a system of peacekeeping otherwise known as the "global economy."

Through development discourse, the nation-states of the rich, market societies that already enjoy the fruits of development adopt a benevolent and pastoral self-image for themselves and the international institutions that they have created (e.g., the World Bank, the International Monetary Fund) to serve the needs that they impute to undeveloped countries. As pastoral agents, the first *need* that these market societies must satisfy on behalf of the poor is *the need to be served* by the nation-states of those market societies and the extragovernmental agencies to whom they delegate their power, for their "development" services are compulsory for the satisfaction of all the other needs that underdeveloped people must be made to feel. Their services and their services alone will provide the "poor" nations of the world with the mean to achieve development—the secular salvation that comes from being successfully integrated into the market's peaceful kingdom of *pax œconomica*.

How can we ignore the bitter irony of identifying development as a program for world peace? The only peace to be found in the notion of *pax œconomica* is the peace between the nation-states of market societies as they cooperate in waging war against traditional, subsistence-based societies for the purpose of expanding the global reach of the market.

As I mentioned earlier, the history of this war against traditional societies began in Europe, as the early modern nation-states sought to integrate their own domestic populations into the market. In order to accomplish this feat, the economic sphere would first have to be disembedded from the social and cultural relations of those traditional European societies. Subsequently, those social and cultural relations would come to be embedded in the economic sphere, resulting in persons coming to understand their lives within the economy as holding primacy over their social and cultural relations. As market capitalism evolved over the course of Western history, economic growth and development presupposed "overcoming symbolic and moral 'obstacles,' . . . disposing of various inhibiting ideas such as myths, ceremonies, rituals, mutual aid, networks of solidarity and the like."[7] And to the extent that such notions as "myth," "ritual," and ceremony sound archaic to our modern ears, we can "hear" the success of the corporatist and militarist values of the market in overcoming the constraints of traditional culture.

As archaic as such ideas may sound to our modern ears, these attributes of traditional cultures helped to maintain certain social conditions from which we must learn in order to both diagnose and recover from the social and environmental illnesses generated by the destructive nature of the market. Ivan Illich, for example, contends that "all known traditional cultures," including those of pre-modern Europe, "can be conceived as meaningful configurations that have as their principal purpose the repression of those conditions under which scarcity could become dominant in social relations."[8] To do so, these subsistence-oriented societies limit their notion of human "needs" to that which is necessary to their community's survival. A people's needs take shape in relation to what natural forms of abundance they find in the commons and in relation to the social availability of means for drawing on that abundance.

Illich adopts the notion of the "vernacular" to characterize such needs and the activities that people pursue toward satisfying them. He argues that the word vernacular best expresses the sense in which these activities can be viewed as concrete responses to concrete conditions. Also, he points out that the Indo-Germanic root for "vernacular" suggests "rootedness" and "abode," whereas, in the Latin usage, *vernaculum*, it referred to that which was *homebread, homespun, homegrown*, or *homemade*. Vernacular activities, Illich claims, "are not motivated by thoughts of exchange," but rather they imply "autonomous non-market related action through which people satisfy everyday needs—the actions that by their own nature escape bureaucratic control, satisfying needs to which, in the very process, they give specific shape."[9]

By the time maintaining global economic hegemony required the nation-states of market societies to rely on the rhetorical services of what we now know as development discourse, observers recognized that the economic development of an underdeveloped people by themselves (pre-modern Europeans included) is not compatible with the maintenance of their traditional customs and mores. A break with the latter is prerequisite to economic progress. What is needed is a revolution in the totality of social, cultural, and religious institutions and habits, and thus in their psychological attitude, their philosophy and way of life. What is, therefore, required amounts in reality to social disorganization.[10]

Illich, along with Gustavo Esteva, believes that what triggers this revolutionary social disorganization requisite to economic progress is the imposition of that which traditional societies seek to repress—scarcity. As previously discussed, the market insists on scarcity as the defining characteristic of the human condition and, therefore, the universal condition of social life everywhere. Under the law of scarcity, human needs are no longer limited to the necessities for collective survival. This law transforms limited needs into unlimited *wants*. Although vernacular activities enabled members of traditional societies to obviate scarcity by providing for collective survival, market societies place conceptual limits on them, defining subsistence-oriented activities as incompatible with economic *growth* and *progress*. Those conceptual limits manifest themselves in the law of scarcity, which proclaims that "[human] wants are great, not to say infinite, whereas [their] means are limited though improvable."[11] Instead of limiting people's needs, as in traditional societies, market societies limit people's means to satisfy them.

It accomplishes this in a twofold sense. First, as just stated, the law of scarcity places conceptual limits on people's means to provide for their own needs. However, in presenting itself as the only path toward improving those means, the market also disvalues all other forms of social organization, deriding nonmarket activities and societies as "backward," "primitive," or just plain "underdeveloped." In producing this twofold scarcity of means, market society awards itself supreme status in a universal hierarchy of human needs. Access to the market constitutes everyone's most basic need. Without such access, their means for satisfying other needs remain forever limited. This, then, creates the need (among nonmarket, Third World, traditional societies) for development, offered by the wealthy, developed, market societies as the path to secular salvation that had previously been blocked by their "traditional customs and mores." Again, this form of salvation is incompatible with the maintenance of cultural traditions and other moral obstacles to market expansion. "Unhappiness and discontentment in the sense of wanting more than is obtainable at any moment is to be generated. The suffering and dislocation that may be caused in the process may be objectionable but it appears to be the price that has to be paid for economic development; the condition of economic progress."[12] Especially to the suffering and dislocated populations in the United States, where the market has already effected a modernization of poverty that produces a debilitating scarcity in the capacity of people to provide for their own needs, salvation requires the educational services of the state to "develop" their "use-value" as their only available means for both contributing to and accessing the market on which they have been rendered utterly dependent.

Even though Truman announced that "the old imperialism" had no place in America's plans for a new system of world peace, he never suggested that the concepts of "democratic fair dealing" that were to provide the basis of this new system included any nation's right to refuse integration into the global market society. Esteva points out how the "brutal and violent transformation" effected through market expansion, "first completed in Europe, was always associated with colonial domination in the rest of the world," where the market and colonization were synonymous. Herein lies the most painful irony of development discourse. In associating favorable change with the market, development discourse has liberated market expansion "from the negative connotations it had accumulated for two centuries, delinking development from colonialism."13

As many Native Americans and other indigenous peoples outside Western Europe could affirm from their own people's histories, the market has never been an option for the colonized. It has been imposed on them by the "developed" nations who conquered them. Sadly, the discourses of multiculturalism seldom acknowledge how the numerous vernacular cultures of Europe were similarly subjugated under the weight of the market. The market originated and continues as a war against cultural and social heterogeneity.

Like schooling, development constitutes a compulsory program for disciplining people into the habits and values of the market. The pastoral images of the institutions that deliver educational and development programs merely seek to convince people that the programs being imposed on them are for their own good, that they *need* those programs, and that they should willingly and appreciatively go along with the plans set down for them by others. Under vernacular conditions, people participate in fashioning the means by which their individual and collective needs are met. Compulsory schooling and compulsory development, on the other hand, fashion people to meet the needs of the market.

Once the thin veneer of deceit is lifted from the various development schemes that have evolved over the course of the past fifty years, as well as educational reform rhetoric since the 1980s, we recognize the familiar patterns of colonial domination. Development policies and practices merely represent a "kinder and gentler" approach to placing the peoples and resources of "undeveloped" nations in the service of the global market and the rich nations that manage and enforce it. Those people who might have other ideas about how the internal affairs of their countries should be arranged (e.g., Vietnam, Cuba, Honduras, El Salvador, Nicaragua) invite stern retribution from the global masters for their lack of humility and understanding.

Other forms of retribution await poor people in the United States who lack the humility and understanding to seek the development of their use-value offered to them under the conditions of compulsory schooling. In rejecting the opportunity to develop that use-value, they remove themselves from compliant and productive service to the market and its corporate directors within the state apparatus. Without use-value/market-value, the "uneducated" condemn themselves to the secular damnation of continued poverty, leading in many cases to eventual incarceration. But even those who sufficiently embrace the secular theology of schooling and tacitly agree to maximize their utility to the market have no guarantee that their "investments" in their education will reap "dividends." As real wages continue to decline and decent-paying jobs continue to dwindle, displaced workers are told to "go back to school" to update and upgrade their usefulness to the rich. Where school cannot guarantee secular salvation in the market, it can offer infinite opportunities for redemption.

In the final analysis, the economization of social space effected under the hidden corporatism and militarism of compulsory schooling transposes the relations of colonial domination typically associated with the international arena to the domestic scene. Despite the benevolent images that surround them, compulsory schools function to enforce a set of conditions where people have value only to the extent that they are useful and necessary to the market and the future goals of its directors. Those without such value are simply expendable.

Notes

1. Kenneth J. Saltman, *Collateral Damage: Corporatizing Public Schools—A Threat to Democracy* (Lanham, Md.: Rowman and Littlefield, 2000), x, 25–26, and 85.
2. Karl Polanyi, *The Great Transformation* (New York: Farrar and Rinehart, 1944), 57.
3. Juliet B. Schor, *The Overworked American: The Unexpected Decline of Leisure* (New York: Basic Books, 1991).
4. See David Cayley, "The Corruption of Christianity: Ivan Illich on Gospel, Church, and Society" Canadian Broadcasting Corporation Ideas Transcripts, January 2000.
5. David Cayley, *Ivan Illich in Conversation* (Concord, Ontario: Anansi Books, 1992), 65.
6. Harry S. Truman, Inaugural Address, January 20, 1949, in *Public Papers of the Presidents of the United States: Harry S. Truman: Containing the Public Messages, Speeches, and Statements of the President January 1 to December 31, 1949* (Washington, D.C.: Government Printing Office, 1964), 19.
7. Gérald Berthoud, "Market," in *The Development Dictionary: A Guide to Knowledge and Power*, ed. Wolfgang Sachs (Atlantic Highlands, N.J.: Zed Books, 1992), 72.
8. Ivan Illich, "The History of Homo Educandus," in *In the Mirror of the Past: Lectures and Addresses, 1978–1990* (New York: Marion Boyers, 1992), 117.
9. Ivan Illich, *Shadow Work* (New York: Marion Boyers, 1981), 57.
10. Berthoud, 72–73.
11. Gustavo Esteva, "Development," in *The Development Dictionary: A Guide to Knowledge and Power*, edited by Wolfgang Sachs (Atlantic Highlands, N.J.: Zed Books, 1992), 19.
12. Berthoud, "Market," 73.
13. Esteva, "Development," 17.

INTRODUCTION TO CHAPTER 4

Pauline Lipman's "Cracking Down" considers the relation between the global and the local, focusing on the racial nature of the discourse of discipline as it plays out concretely in Chicago public school policy and practice. Drawing on the work of global city theory, Lipman's chapter brings unique attention in this volume to the ways that disciplinary logic and language as an expression of neoliberal ideals creates a common sense that demands enforcement-oriented policies such as standardized testing, military public schools, and scripted curricula that defy more critical democratic forms of schooling and that perpetuate white privilege. Lipman's chapter illustrates the ways that the racialized rhetoric of enforcement is deployed in struggles over urban resources and the remaking of the urban space in the age of globalization.

CHAPTER 4

Cracking Down*

Chicago School Policy and the Regulation of Black and Latino Youth

PAULINE LIPMAN

Chicago's school accountability policies and centralized regulation of schools have become a model for urban school districts in the United States and a prototype of Bush's national education policy. Chicago's 1995 school reform law gave Chicago's Mayor Richard Daley control of the schools. Daley appointed his budget manager Paul Vallas to be CEO of Chicago public schools (CPS) and his chief of staff Gery Chico to head the CPS Board of Trustees. Promising efficiency, sound fiscal management, improved academic achievement, and equity, Vallas and Chico established a corporatist regime focused on accountability, high-stakes tests, standards, and centralized regulation of schools. As a result, thousands of primarily black and Latino youth have been retained in grade and sent to mandatory remedial programs and basic education transition high schools. Over one hundred elementary and high schools in black, Latino, and immigrant communities have been put on "probation" under strict central administration oversight.

CPS has also further stratified academic programs. New academically selective magnet schools and programs, mainly located in largely white upper-income and/or gentrifying neighborhoods, have been established alongside general high schools with limited offerings of advanced courses and new vocational academies, basic skills transitional high schools, the first two public military high schools in the United States, and an expansion of scripted direct instruction (DI)[1] in elementary schools—all attended primarily by African Americans and Latinos. (Not to be confused with direct teaching of specific skills and concepts, the DI schools are rooted in behaviorism and a deficit model of "economically disadvantaged" students.) There is also increased policing of youth through zero tolerance school discipline policies.

Pauline Lipman is an Associate Professor of Social and Cultural Foundations of Education at DePaul University, Chicago. Her research centers on the social context of education, race, and class inequality in schools, urban education, and critical policy analysis. She is the author of *Race, Class, and Power in School Restructuring* and *High Stakes Education: Inequality, Globalization, and Urban School Reform* (forthcoming), and articles in the *American Educational Research Journal*, *Cultural Logic*, *Urban Review*, and other journals.

*A substantially different version of this chapter appears in the journal *Race Ethnicity and Education*.

In this chapter, I examine Chicago's policies as a window on account-ability and militarization of urban U.S. schools. I argue that, in the name of equity and school improvement, Chicago's "reforms" concretely and symbol-ically "crack down" on African American and Latino youth who are seen as largely superfluous in Chicago's restructured, informational economy and dangerous in the racialized social landscape of the city. The policies are clearly linked to broader neoliberal and neoconservative discourses of indi-vidual responsibility and centralized regulation,[2] but my focus here is on ways in which the reforms are materially and symbolically linked to the regu-lation and control of black and Latino youth and their communities. While racial inequality, segregation, and injustice have been persistent realities throughout Chicago's history, I argue that racialized school policies have dangerous new ramifications in the context of the city's restructured econ-omy, gentrification and displacement of low-income communities of color, and its global-city agenda. I briefly examine the new common sense around these policies and argue for an alternative agenda for urban schools.

Framework, Methodology, and Data

Borrowing Grace's notion of critical policy scholarship,[3] my analysis of policy is theoretically and socioculturally situated and generative of social action. I link an empirical analysis of Chicago's educational policies with a political analysis of their genesis and social meaning.[4] I am interested in three aspects of policy: (1) regulations governing school organization, curriculum, and instruction, (2) policy as social practices of actors at all levels of the educational system,[5] and (3) policy texts and discourses as symbolic poli-tics[6] or "political and cultural performance."[7] In this sense, educational polices are part of a dominant system of social relations, framing what can be said or thought[8] and the social identities that are produced.[9]

Building on this framework, I examine education policy in the context of Chicago's new urban economy drive to become a global city, and a new geog-raphy of centrality and marginality along lines of race, ethnicity, and class. Drawing on critical race theory, my analysis "foregrounds race as an explanatory tool for the persistence of inequality."[10] My focus is the relation-ship of school policies to the cultural politics of race in the city.[11] Although official policy is contested at multiple levels, and school-level practices embody emergent and residual ideologies and past reforms, this complexity is beyond the scope of my discussion here.[12]

My analysis draws on interviews with school district administrators, a review of CPS quantitative data and policy documents as well as newspaper articles, studies of Chicago's changing demographics and economy, and publications of real estate, elite civic organizations, and city officials. I also draw on interviews with teachers, school administrators, and students and observations of classes, school activities, and meetings at four CPS elemen-tary schools between 1997 and 2001. I begin with the political-economic context of Chicago. Then I examine the role of accountability policies in the regulation of students, teachers, and communities. I go on to examine the ways in which these policies are a way of monitoring and controlling teachers, students, and communities of color. I focus on Chicago's military schools, which I argue are linked to a wider set of social policies that police and criminalize youth of color. I conclude by examining why the policies resonate with some families and communities and link this "good sense" with an alternative agenda for transforming urban schools.

The Chicago Context: Global City, Economic Restructuring, and the Politics of Race

Chicago school policies are unfolding in an increasingly racially and ethnically diverse and economically polarized city driven by processes of economic restructuring, globalization, and the displacement and containment of people of color. Under the regime of capitalist accumulation, "global cities" are command centers of global finance and production, the places where the organization and management of transnational capital accumulation and global production processes are concentrated.[13] With its concentration of sophisticated producer services, international markets, corporate headquarters, and its importance as a financial and tourist center, Chicago is vying for position as a "global city" alongside New York and Los Angeles in the United States.[14] In alliance with Chicago's business, financial, and real estate interests, Mayor Daley has consistently promoted the global city agenda. In his first mayoral campaign in 1989, Daley said, "I think you have to look at the financial markets—banking, service industry, the development of O'Hare field, tourism, trade. This is going to be an international city."[15]

As is typical of other major international cities, in Chicago globalization is producing "a new geography of centrality and marginality"[16] characterized by deepening inequality in salaries and wages, in housing, and in claims to public space. The face of Chicago has changed from a manufacturing city of "big shoulders" to a city of corporate headquarters, tourism, and gentrified neighborhoods alongside sweatshops, substandard housing, and isolated areas of deindustrialization and disinvestment. Established working-class and low-income communities are being supplanted by gentrified upscale housing, luxury shops, and hip leisure spots for high-paid professionals. Across the city, economic redevelopment in low-income areas has been sacrificed to renovation and development of the downtown area as a glamour zone of tourism, expensive restaurants and cultural venues, and luxury housing. This pattern is matched by the increasing social isolation of Latino and African American communities divested of city resources.[17] Through tax increment financing zones (TIFs),[18] the city has diverted millions in taxes earmarked for schools, libraries, and other public services to developers and real estate interests. Public housing, left to decay by decades of disinvestment and mismanagement, is rapidly being razed to clear the way for expensive new condominium and townhouse developments. Meanwhile, the former residents are dispersed and/or forced out of the city to impoverished suburbs or other socially isolated low-income areas.

Globalization and economic restructuring are also producing a highly stratified, economically polarized labor force through simultaneous upgrading, downgrading, and exclusion of labor.[19] In the Chicago metropolitan area, the shift from manufacturing to an informational and service economy has produced growth at both ends of the wage/salary scale, but the greatest job growth has come through the replacement of unionized manufacturing jobs with low-wage, low-skilled, primarily service jobs with less social protection than jobs in the recent past.[20] A contingent workforce of multi-task, part-time and temporary jobs without benefits is made up primarily of women, people of color, and immigrants, many of whom work two, three, even four part-time or temporary jobs. Others, even less fortunate, have been driven into the informal economy in order to survive.

The new economic inequalities are highly racialized. Disparity in wages between African Americans and Latinos, as compared with whites, is increasing;[21] and in 1999, Abu-Lughod reported that the Chicago metro area led all others in the economic disparity between whites and African Americans.[22] At the same time, large sections of the potential labor force, mainly African American and Latino youth, are largely excluded from the formal economy.[23] From the standpoint of capital and Chicago's political elites, many youth of color are not only superfluous in the labor force but potentially dangerous in a city designed to attract tourism and high-paid managers, technical workers, and business services at the core of the global economy. Processes of globalization, economic restructuring, and spatial isolation and dispersal converge with white racist ideology and structures of racial power and privilege to foster a cultural politics that pathologizes and criminalizes communities of color. These communities, especially black and Latino youth, have become the targets of stepped-up police occupation, harassment, and terror. The stark reality is that the future of a generation of young African American and Latino men and women is more likely to be in the bowels of the prison industrial complex than in the offices of Chicago's new informational and service economy.[24] Chicago school policies cannot be fully understood apart from these economic, social, and cultural processes.

Accountability and the Racialized Regulation of Schooling

CPS's accountability system gives central administrators the power to regulate many aspects of teaching and learning, professional development, school organization, and students' educational futures. However, in practice, this power is exercised differentially with quite different consequences in low-scoring schools serving low-income students of color than in schools in more affluent, white, middle-class communities. I draw on my data from four elementary schools—Grover, Westlawn, Brewer, and Farley[25]—to illustrate what this *selective* regulation of schooling means for students and teachers.

Four Schools: The Intersection of Race, Class, Power, and Accountability

Students at Grover and Westlawn are over 90 percent African American and low income. Grover is plagued by high teacher turnover and staffing by temporary and unqualified teachers. Westlawn has a more stable faculty and a reputation as one of the best schools serving a large cluster of housing projects. Brewer is over 90 percent Mexican–Mexican American and about 90 percent low income. It has a large bilingual, Spanish/English, program. Farley is a mixed income, multi-race school with a significant segment of professional parents, both white and African American. About 50 percent of Farley's students are African American and the remainder are white, Asian, and Latino. Farley has an established faculty, virtually all of whom have advanced degrees and are active professionally outside the school.

In 1996, Grover was one of the first schools to be placed on probation, and five years later less than 15 percent of students scored at or above national norms on the Iowa Test of Basic Skills (ITBS) in reading and less than 25 percent scored at or above national norms in math. Between 1997 and 2001, Westlawn raised its ITBS scores from below 25 percent of students at or above national norms to nearly 50 percent at or above national norms. In both Grover and Westlawn, the culture of the schools, although complex and contradictory, has become increasingly saturated with practices, language, and values shaped by performance on the ITBS, which is the basis for CPS accountability, and to a lesser extent on the Illinois State Achievement Test (ISAT). Concretely, this means teachers teach to specific test items/skills on which their students did poorly the previous year; teachers tend to reproduce the test content in the curriculum; and substitution of test preparation booklets (keyed to the ITBS and ISAT) for classroom texts is common. At key benchmark grades, one principal requires teachers to substitute test preparation materials for the standard curriculum for over one-quarter of the school year. At one school, teachers voted to use money earmarked for an arts program to purchase the test prep books. Teachers also focus on the mechanics of test-taking and strategies for selecting multiple choice answers. Even teachers who are highly critical of the emphasis on standardized tests feel obliged to do some test preparation given the serious repercussions for students and the pressures from their principals.[26] This practice can pay off. The inordinate focus on test preparation is a major factor in Westlawn's improving scores.

Acquiescence is partly the result of an accountability climate that is both coercive and normalized. Neoliberal, managerial discourse has so permeated public discussion about education in Chicago, and nationally, that other perspectives have been largely silenced. High-stakes testing and sanctions for failure are everywhere, necessary, normal, and inevitable. Despite some teachers' (private) opposition, "test prep" has become a taken-for-granted part of the curriculum. Passing the tests has come to be a publicly sanctioned purpose of schooling regardless of what other intrinsic, educational goals educators may hold. By the third year of my inquiries, some teachers seemed almost surprised that I would ask about a practice that had become so routine. They described test-taking as "a lifelong learning skill," and justified test practice in one grade as preparation for testing in the next grade, in high school, on the SAT, for a job at the post office, and for life in general. Also normalized (despite an undercurrent of moral outrage) is the widespread practice of educational triage. Students close to passing the ITBS are singled out for extra attention and tutoring, while those who are deemed to have little hope of passing and those certain to pass receive less attention.

Teachers, like the public in general, end up consenting to policies that deny agency to students and teachers alike and negate broader educational goals.

Although Brewer is less test-driven than Westlawn and Grover, efforts to encourage thoughtful, intellectually engaging instruction and bilingualism/biculturalism have been challenged by accountability policies. Although about 50 percent of Brewer students score at or above national norms on the ITBS, central authorities warned that Brewer might be forced to adopt district-mandated curricula if its scores dropped. This has narrowed the curriculum to some degree. For example, teachers dropped a conceptually grounded mathematics curriculum because it was not tightly linked to the ITBS. Some progressive teachers also struggle to maintain critical approaches to knowledge in the face of a test-driven culture that reinforces the authority of received information, memorization of facts, and simple right or wrong answers.

In contrast, at Farley, a school with a sizable proportion of middle-class and white students and an excellent academic reputation, most teachers, the principal, and, to some extent, parents, are openly opposed to the district's accountability agenda. In general, the school has a rich culture of literacy and students have opportunities to discuss ideas, defend their own opinions, and produce meaningful work (e.g., short stories, thoughtful essays). Though 70 percent to 80 percent score at or above national norms on the ITBS, the school cannot afford to ignore high-stakes tests. Yet, teachers fiercely hold on to a curriculum that they believe constitutes a "good education." For example, the third-grade teachers decided to reject CPS's formulaic writing curriculum in favor of approaches they believed developed fluent writers with their own voices. At the same time, Farley teachers are keenly aware that a significant drop in the school's test scores would have serious implications for the school and individual students, but they tend to clearly demarcate the regular curriculum from practice for the tests, and test practice is presented as an exercise, not a learning activity. Many teachers at Farley said they would leave and if necessary quit teaching altogether if Farley became dominated by the ITBS "like other schools."

The schools' different responses to district accountability are closely linked to past and present race and class advantages and the relative political power of their communities. They demonstrate that school policies that regulate and control compound the disempowerment of oppressed communities and that schools also reflect power differentials in the city. Farley's high test scores, a product of its middle-class and white advantages, and its location in a politically powerful professional community allow the school to avoid surveillance by district officials. The school, with a pro-active parent organization, partly composed of influential professionals, has a history of ignoring CPS mandates that preceded the 1995 reforms. Farley's middle-class core constituency and its affluent community have attracted a stable group of qualified teachers who typically see themselves as intellectuals and knowledgeable professionals. They make confident judgments about the Chicago academic standards, the merits of various tests, and research-based curricula and are supported by a principal who defends their professional competence and shields them from district mandates as much as possible.

The school also benefits from its close relationships with universities and involvement in university-sponsored curriculum development.

These advantages set Farley apart from Grover and Westlawn, both of which are in communities decimated by decades of disinvestment and now the demolition of public housing. Grover, in particular, exemplifies the inequity that plagues urban schools serving students of color. Until 1999, Grover had no playground, no all-day kindergarten, no science labs, no library. It had a long-term ineffectual principal, a teaching staff with little professional development beyond their original degrees, and no reading specialist. Although some of these deficiencies have been corrected by juggling funds, the school continues to have extremely high teacher turnover and a high proportion of noncertified teachers. Brewer, although also under threat of more direct control if its scores drop, has an energetic principal and an activist parent organization that has mobilized to challenge the board's retention policies. The community also has a history of fighting for bilingual education and for the rights of undocumented immigrants, and community organizations have been fighting against gentrification. This political activism and the school's strong community reputation provide some insurance against greater intervention by the district.

The four schools illustrate how current policies compound historical injustices. The histories and academic profiles of Grover and Westlawn are intricately connected with multiple forms of structurally and culturally rooted race and class subjugation and decades of educational inequity. Despite struggles by Latino and African American communities to improve their children's education, structural changes in the economy over the past thirty years have compounded race and class inequities. As deindustrialization and disinvestment have produced economic destitution, African American and Latino communities have been further undermined by demonization in the media and in public discourse. As a result, schools like Grover and Westlawn, located in very low-income African American communities in particular, are the schools with the fewest resources and least opportunity to make comprehensive, transformative changes, and their communities have the least political power. These are also the schools most subject to a narrow, test-driven curriculum at a time when the students in these schools urgently need an education that arms them with tools to analyze and critique the social inequalities enveloping their lives.

Districtwide Inequalities and Labor Force Demands

There is evidence that the pattern of narrowed curricula and test-driven instruction at Grover and Westlawn prevails across the system in schools serving low-income African American, and to some extent, Latino students. This is revealed by the demographics of schools emphasizing basic skills and those most pressed to improve test scores (probation schools, scripted direct instruction schools, transition high schools, and other remedial programs). Probation schools are overwhelming African American; a few are Latino or mixed African American and Latino, and very few white students are in schools on probation.[27] When CPS placed 109 schools on probation in 1996, the average poverty level of the 71 elementary probation schools was about 94 percent.[28] The 59 schools employing scripted direct instruction (personal communication, CPS Office of Accountability staff) follow the same demographic pattern as probation schools. The program is described by its staff as following a special education model. According to the information provided to teachers in scripted direct instruction schools,[29] the goal is to improve the "basic education of children from economically disadvantaged backgrounds."[30] Transition high schools, for over-age eighth graders who fail the ITBS, have a stripped down curriculum of reading, math, and world studies (no science, foreign language, or arts) geared to passing the ITBS in extremely sparse facilities.[31] A transition center teacher explained, "We try to boil the concepts down to the point where if they just pay attention, they will succeed."[32] Former Brewer students reported that their transition center English class had no discussion of literature but a steady stream of worksheets aligned with the standardized tests. The students facing this impoverished curriculum are mainly black and Latino. In 2000, an activist parent organization won a civil rights complaint against CPS for adverse discriminatory impact of the retention policy that placed black and Latino students disproportionately in transition high schools.[33] The same can be said for remedial after-school programs, which are part of the accountability system's "support" for failing students. These programs are aligned with ITBS preparation and target primarily low-income students of color.

To the extent that programs and schools follow a basic skills model, students in these contexts have fewer opportunities for critical thought, sustained intellectual engagement, or personally and socially meaningful work. As a Grover teacher said, "Suddenly the classroom is a place where you get better test scores, you learn to get better test scores instead of learning." In a reduplication of the racism that has pervaded CPS, these students are now bearing the brunt of a system that has historically failed to educate them. Clearly, a basic education for students who have historically been denied—and are thus most in need of—an enriched and intellectually rigorous program is hardly a solution to entrenched inequities. As Murrell argues, in relation to African American students, an emancipatory education is one that teaches children to think critically and act morally.[34] Schooling that is driven by standardized tests subverts critical thought and the sense of personal and social efficacy that is particularly important for African American and Latino students under conditions of intensifying race and class inequality. As Ladson-Billings notes: "If students are to be equipped to struggle against racism, they need excellent skills from the basics of reading, writing, and math, to understanding history, thinking critically, solving problems, and making decisions."[35]

Intended or not, a basic skills curriculum for African American and some Latino students coincides with the basic education requirements of low-wage service work in Chicago's new economy. Despite public perception that the new economy demands significantly upgraded skills for everyone,[36] in fact, many of the new, low-wage service jobs require basic literacies, the ability to follow directions, and accommodating dispositions toward work.[37] In 1998 the Commercial Club of Chicago (an organization of the city's financial, business, and civic elite) called for "ever-more-skilled employees" defined as people "who can, at the minimum, read instruction manuals, do basic math and communicate well."[38] Tough accountability measures certify that students who graduate from CPS will, at minimum, posses these skills. Good quality schools are also central to Chicago's drive to be a world-class city, and accountability, standards, and numerical measures of achievement are the language of quality. A 1998 Commercial Club report endorsed the mayor's school reforms and identified education for a skilled workforce as one of three top priorities to realize its vision of the Chicago area as a region of "knowledge, expertise, and economic opportunity."[39]

In addition to basic mathematical and print literacy, employers are particularly concerned with future workers' attitudes and "work ethic"—their reliability, trustworthiness, ability to take directions, and in the case of in-person service workers, a pleasant manner.[40] Theses concerns are highly racialized. A 1990 Commercial Club report noted that "minorities" in low-performing schools will become a greater part of the workforce and will need the new basic competencies. And, in the competition to become a global city, Moberg found that Chicago is at a disadvantage in attracting new firms because there is a widespread perception that Chicago's workforce is "ill-educated, untrained, and difficult to manage" and that this perception "especially affects the hiring of black men."[41] CPS's rigid accountability also signifies that schools are producing the disciplined identities business is demanding for the lower tiers of a highly racialized workforce.

Racialized Social Discipline

Vinson and Ross observe that accountability policies are a particularly insidious mode of social control that merges Foucault's notion of discipline as "spectacle" (the observation of the few by the many) and discipline as "surveillance" (the observation of the many by the few).[42] School probation, automatic retention, the publication and discussion of test scores in schools, and the constant media monitoring of test results constitute a public spectacle of failure. Students who fail are identified by assignment to remedial programs and grade retention. They are publicly humiliated by exclusion from eighth-grade graduation ceremonies and by assignment to transition high schools. Teachers and administrators, as well as students and their communities (overwhelming black and Latino), are publicly chastised by being placed on probation and under the authority of central administrators and outside agents contracted by the board to supervise and "help" them. At the same time, the policies promote a panoptic order of intense monitoring and surveillance. Central office administrators monitor principals, principals monitor teachers, teachers and staff monitor students and parents. It is important to be clear that this is not a policy that promotes engaged public attention to inequity in the system, nor is it a policy that encourages collective examination of the problems in schools. This is a process of powerful city and school officials holding up certain schools (and by extension, their communities) and students as public exemplars of failure without the democratic participation of communities to debate and act together with educators to improve their children's education. Despite the appearance of unilateral application of these policies, concretely, the schools under close scrutiny are in low-income communities of color. This is social discipline primarily directed to black and Latino students, schools, and communities.

Differentiated Schooling and the Construction of Student Identities

Disparities among the four elementary schools discussed here are reflective of Chicago's increasingly differentiated education. Despite the rhetoric of holding all students to high standards, high-stakes testing, grade retention, mandatory remedial summer school programs, and transition high schools are part of a two-tiered education system. On the one hand, a minority has access to new college prep magnet high schools and international baccalaureate programs alongside preexisting gifted and accelerated programs. The highly selective nature of these new programs and schools (at three of the six new magnets, only 3–5 percent of all students who applied and tested for admission were admitted, according to the Chicago *Sun Times*[43] and their disproportionate whiteness (Northside College Prep, for example, is majority white in a district with 89 percent students of color) means that only a small number of black and Latino students are admitted. On the other hand, the vast majority of students attend remedial programs and neighborhood schools with limited course offerings, uncertified and unprepared teachers, and high dropout rates.[44] The geographic location of academically advanced programs neatly corresponds to patterns of gentrification as school policy supports the drive to attract professionals and managers for the city's globalized economy.

While a minority of students are prepared with the cultural capital and educational experiences to become professionals and knowledge workers, actors in the informational economy, the majority, overwhelmingly students of color, are being prepared for skilled and unskilled low-wage sectors. Although academic tracking has a long history, as Ramon Flecha notes, "the prioritization of intellectual resources in the information society means that ... education ... is becoming an increasingly important criterion for determining who joins which [social] group."[45] This social selection is highly racialized. Moreover, students learn inside the social practices that constitute stratified educational experiences to take on a particular world view and master a particular identity with little opportunity for critical and reflective awareness.[46] The discourse of high-stakes tests teaches African American students at Grover and Westlawn that their own thinking has little value in the face of the authority of the "right answers" in the *Test Best* answer book. A discourse that eschews critical thought and demands acquiescence to received knowledge also teaches powerlessness.[47] Students in these schools are being immersed in very different dispositions toward knowledge and have fewer opportunities to practice independent thought and action than students at Farley. Although schools are only one site for young people to develop critical consciousness and agency, disparate school experiences provide them with quite different resources from which to do this. This is particularly significant in the face of increasing inequality and oppression.

The consequences of failing tests based on mastery of English and dominant discourses also demonstrate the high cost of assimilating the dominant language, knowledge, and dispositions. Students are being taught that their own experience, the language and culturally embedded meanings embraced by their families and communities, count for little in a school system governed by one-size-fits-all standards and the Iowa Test of Basic Skills. Brewer illustrates this point. New policies require students to take the ITBS in English after three years or less in bilingual education or English as Second Language (ESL) programs. Even teachers who grew up in Brewer's Mexican American community and are committed to bilingual/bicultural education are under great pressure to privilege the teaching of English. One of them explained, "We're not doing it [Spanish] justice. So it's sort of like, you know, again, let's put our beliefs aside, let's not think about 'it's great to be bilingual.' We can't practice what we believe." The severe consequences of failing the ITBS potently reinforce the supremacy of English and teach students to see their reality from the standpoint of the dominant group and its ideology. CPS standards for bilingual education also require that English language learners master behaviors characterized as "American." An administrator summarized the debilitating effects of this "cultural invasion":[48] "I can imagine feeling inadequate and thinking, 'God, if I want to be recognized or be anything, I'd better get rid of the Spanish and start getting on with the English. I mean that's what counts' . . . a feeling of inadequacy and what you have is not good enough."

A Pedagogy of Powerlessness

Accountability policies also undermine the agency of students, teachers, and communities. They shift the blame for school failure from the state to students who are in fact recipients of decades of substandard education and miseducation. As grade retention, summer school, transition high school, and low test scores are public markers of deficiency; they remind young people they are personally responsible. At Grover, some teachers post students' test scores from the previous year outside their door to shame them. And implications of deviance and individual responsibility reverberate in school leaders' warnings that, after all CPS has done, it is now "up to the students to work hard" if they want to pass. This lesson was echoed by eighth graders at Brewer who blamed themselves for failing the ITBS.[49] Of course students also resist these messages. Some Brewer students opted to drop out rather than face the demeaning prospect of attending the transition high school. However, in the schools I studied, there was an absence of critical analysis of high-stakes tests that might allow students to examine them from the perspective of race and class oppression and educational inequality.

Probation also demonstrates to the whole school community that it is powerless. It formalizes the subordination of teachers, principals, and local school councils to powerful superiors who scrutinize their actions and have the authority to regulate nearly every facet of the school (curricula, instructional approaches, school organization, professional development, educational programs, and plans for improvement). A teacher at Grover articulated the impotence she and her colleagues feel: "I don't think we have too much [control over what we can do in the classroom] because when you're on probation, it seems everybody wants to help you, everybody wants to tell you how to do things. You really don't have too much power or say-so in what goes on."

It is relevant that "probation" is also the language of the prison system, signaling the delinquency of schools in African American and some Latino communities, and by implication, the delinquency of students and families as well. It is this implied delinquency that justifies control and rectification. A Grover primary grade teacher summed up the implications, even for very young children, of the discursive connection between probation and the criminal justice system: "several of the kids know through the jail system what probation means. So you are connecting the jail system with the school and them hearing this word 'probation' and it becomes like a hammer just knocking them down, knocking them down."

While teachers and administrators at Grover and Westlawn (and to some extent Brewer) are closely monitored by probation managers, central office authorities, and district monitors, Farley's educators are relatively more free to pursue their own educational goals and processes precisely because they are under less surveillance for low test scores. Students at Farley also have more opportunities to practice making decisions about their own actions. In contrast, over the past four years teachers at Brewer have noticed a steady deterioration of opportunities for democratic participation in decision making. Farley's school culture clearly teaches students they have a degree of intellectual and personal agency that is quite different from that learned in the other three schools. I do not claim that more affluent and white schools necessarily promote critical approaches to knowledge. Nor do I want to negate powerful teaching against the grain at Grover, Westlawn, and Brewer, nor minimize problems at schools like Farley, particularly its racial disparities in the upper grades.[50] Despite these caveats, in general, students at Farley do have opportunities for critical thought and judgment that diverge from the overall narrowed curriculum and regimentation in the more test-driven schools, and Farley teachers certainly have more control over their own work.

In sum, accountability measures, basic skills curricula, retention, and probation are both an explicit means of regulating students and teachers and a pedagogy that teaches people to adopt subordinated identities. Policies that control African American and Latino students and their schools also under-mine the agency of their communities. Chicago's 1988 School Reform Act established the governance of local school councils (LSCs), made up of a majority of parents and community residents. Despite variation among schools, in its first years, the 1988 reform precipitated broad grassroots participation in school reform.[51] Recentralization, through the 1995 reform, has diluted the power of local communities across the city, but LSCs in probation schools have generally lost the most power as central office–appointed "probation managers" have superseded their authority. In some cases LSCs were dissolved altogether. High-stakes tests also determine much of the agenda of LSCs in schools in danger of probation. Thus, accountability has worked to negate the democratic participation of low-income communities of color in particular and has conveyed a public message that these communities are incompetent to govern their children's schools.

Racially coded "basic skills," scripted instruction, probation, and reconstitution of schools are part of a larger ensemble of social policies that control and police low-income communities of color. These policies are concretely and symbolically linked with interests of real estate developers and financial and political elites determined to make Chicago a center of tourism, upscale living, and a command center of global capital. Accountability standards discipline black and Latino youth who are "dangerous" in a city which brings together new gentrifiers and those disenfranchised, displaced, and pushed to the bottom of the new economy. As public housing is torn down and its residents dispersed to make way for new high-end townhouses, these racially coded policies justify the segregation and/or removal of blacks and Latinos much as the vocabulary of the "urban frontier" justifies gentrification and displacement in the name of "civilizing" urban neighborhoods.[52] School policies that discipline and regulate signify that those running the city are "taking it back" as a space of middle-class social stability and whiteness from dangerous "others," especially black youth.[53]

Military Schools and the Policing and Criminalization of Youth

Chicago's military schools are part of an ensemble of policies that criminalize and police youth of color and mark them as dangerous and deviant. These include CPS's zero tolerance discipline policy, which mandates automatic suspension and expulsion for specific offenses, Safe Schools, which segregate youth who have been involved in the criminal justice system, and Chicago's Anti-Gang Loitering Ordinance, which authorizes police to disperse groups in public places if police believe they are gang affiliated. Taken as a whole, these policies are part of a new process of racialized social control that is characterized by simultaneous inclusion and exclusion.

CPS has established two public military high schools and expanded military programs in middle schools and neighborhood high schools. Touting the regimentation of these schools, when the Chicago Military Academy opened, CPS Board of Trustees head Gery Chico said "It's a school based on rules and conduct. This is a very good thing."[54] Both the Chicago Military Academy and Carver Military High School are in black communities, and their enrollments are over 80 percent African American with the rest Latino. A partnership between CPS and the U.S. army, the Chicago Military Academy is led by military officers; teachers wear military uniforms and are called Captain. In addition to the CPS Uniform Discipline Code, parents and students must sign a contract agreeing to obey the military discipline code with its own set of punishments for infractions of school rules and failure to complete school work (e.g., students must do push-ups, run laps, scrub walls). Although administrators at one of the schools maintained that its purpose is not army recruitment, recruiters meet with all juniors and offer them the army admission test, which is administered in the school. Some students join the army and go through basic training before graduating high school. In fact, the selection process for admission to the school is a first screening to identify youth who will abide by military discipline. As evidence of this screening, administrators noted that few youth from a nearby housing project attend the school because they didn't seem to like "the military model" (personal communication, school administrator).

The schools teach competitive individualism and unquestioning obedience to a hierarchy of command embodied in the cadet system, which promotes those who exhibit the strongest military-oriented values and behaviors and show the greatest enthusiasm for military activities. Youth who advance to "colonel" lead daily military drills of students, inspect the "recruits" (new students), and exact obedience from those beneath them. Carver administrators extol the virtues of a system that requires youth to refuse to compromise military discipline for solidarity with other youth. A military officer at one of the schools explained, "You have to be kind of conceited, show off your skills. . . . There is no time for friends because if you have too many friends you can't lead. You can have friends but you have to do your job . . . if you are too close to people then you can't go against them if you have to as a commander." The schools respond to youth's desire for respect, responsibility, and leadership development, but shape these experiences as the exercise of authority over others. There is no place here for learning self-determination, collectivity, critical analysis of the world and one's place in it, or self-control for ethical ends. Rooted in the ideology of competitive individualism, the schools "help the kids who help themselves," as one school administrator put it.

Like probation and test drills, the ideological thrust of military schools is to publicly define African American and Latino youth as undisciplined. Despite Daley's claim that the military schools simply offer students "another option," the schools were established with much public fanfare in low-income African American communities—not white or middle-class communities. The media coverage of the schools' boot camp discipline commends them for bringing under control "dangerous" and " unruly" youth[55] and "at-risk" students, by exposing them to "order and discipline." Media accounts are filled with stories of failing and undisciplined youth who do not speak "proper English" and come from "dysfunctional" homes who have been transformed as a result of the military academies into young men and women who work hard in school, help out at home, respect adults, and even learn to speak "proper English." The schools are exemplars of a new "truth"—if schooling is going to work for urban youth of color, it will need to be highly regimented.

While these youth are being assimilated to a system of rules and authority, thousands of other youth like them are kicked out of school through zero tolerance discipline policies. Data collected by the Chicago youth activist organization, Generation Y, demonstrate that under Zero Tolerance students are being suspended primarily for minor, nonviolent infractions and attendance-related issues, and that targeting African Americans, in particular, has intensified under zero tolerance. In 1994, the year before zero tolerance began, African Americans made up 55 percent of CPS enrollment, but got 66 percent of suspensions and expulsions. In 1999–2000, African Americans were less than 53 percent of all CPS students, but received more than 73 percent of all suspensions and expulsions. While enrollment increased by only 665 students between 1999 and 2000, suspensions increased from 21,000 to nearly 37,000. "The biggest increases were among students of color, especially African American students—where the suspension rate increased from less than 7 percent up to 12 percent."[56] Expulsions have also surged, with African Americans the main target. According to *The Chicago Reporter* magazine, in 1995–1996 there were 80 expulsions; in 1998–99 there were 737 expulsions; African American students represented 73 percent of these although they were 53 percent of CPS enrollment.[57] This pattern of racial exclusion is reflected in the quarantining of youth involved in the criminal justice system in Safe Schools isolated from the general school population.

School policies parallel the containment and policing of African American and Latino youth in their neighborhoods. Chicago's 1992 Anti-Gang Loitering Ordinance, championed by Mayor Daley, allows police to round-up youth congregating in public places who are suspected of being in gangs. Between 1993 and 1995, the police arrested 43,000 people under the law[58] (a form of legalized police terror). Despite the determination that the law is unconstitutional, ongoing attempts to legalize harassment and street sweeps of youth continue to make it a powerful signifier that youth of color are dangerous and need to be locked up or removed from public space.

Military schools that single out some youth for their successful accommodation to a system of race and class discipline are simply the flip side of zero tolerance policies, Safe Schools, and the Anti-Gang Ordinance. Those newly disciplined by the army are explicitly defined by their difference from others like them who are, by implication, out of control and menacing. As a military officer at one of the academies put it, "*Our* gang colors are green, *our* gang is the army [emphases original]." The fact that military programs can turn these youth into models signifies that it is the youth (and their families and communities), not racism, not economic policies of disinvestment, not real estate developers, not demonization in the media that are responsible for their lack of a productive future. Molding these youth into obedient citizens justifies the demonization of others: "The partial nature of the process of racialization as criminalization may simultaneously allow the evolution of a symbolically more successful racialized fraction which serves publicly to rebuke the immiserated majority and divest white society of any responsibility for such immiseration."[59]

Conclusion: Constructing a New Common Sense

A critique of CPS policies should be juxtaposed with their resonance with some families, teachers, and administrators. This requires that we look not only at neoliberal ideology but also, in Gramsci's terms,[60] the "good sense" in the policies—their response to real problems and lived experience.[61] Support for CPS policies should be understood as a response to decades of educational failure, mismanagement, racial segregation, and perceptions of school violence. Like other big city school systems, Chicago has persistently failed to provide a decent education for low-income children of color. In 1990, Orfield summed up a situation that still prevails: "The great majority of black and Hispanic youths in metropolitan Chicago today attend schools that prepare them for neither college nor a decent job. Many are forced to live under circumstances unimaginable to middle-class suburban families."[62]

The good sense in CPS policies lies in the fact that, finally, school district leaders are taking decisive action. They are setting standards and holding schools, teachers, and students responsible for meeting them. They are refusing to simply promote kids to the next grade without teaching them. They are insisting that schools should be safe spaces. A number of teachers at Grover and Westlawn commented that teachers who had been little more than caretakers in the classroom were now, at least, forced to "teach something." My observations coincide with this assessment. There is more focus on instruction, more planning of lessons, more coherence in the curriculum than four years ago when I began studying the schools. Probation has also led to the replacement of a number of ineffectual principals, as at Grover. (Of course, this must be qualified by the critique of teaching and learning and educational discourse I have outlined.) CPS has narrowly defined education by standardized tests, but support for raising test scores is also rooted in the understanding that the pitifully low scores of many schools in African American and Latino communities are a marker of inequitable education. (Moreover, these tests are used as gatekeepers to academic high schools and college, especially for children of color). Having created social dislocation, impoverishment, and family stress through decades of disinvestment, deindustrialization, and racial oppression, capital and powerful political interests in Chicago now step in and offer centralized regulation and boot camp–style solutions. These solutions intersect with the urgency to improve urban schools and with racial profiling of African American and Latino youth, feeding the public perception that they require special forms of discipline, regulation, and control. Yet, military schools (billed as college prep) may be students' only alternative in a context in which there are very few opportunities for the vast majority to attend good, well-run high schools.

Indeed, the absence of a viable alternative liberatory educational discourse that concretely embraces the urgency to transform urban schools is at the heart of the current crisis in education policy. CPS leaders and the mayor have defined their policies as the only alternative to "the failed policies of the past." This argument holds sway because the failure of liberal education policies to address underlying issues of race, gender, and class inequality and oppression is not part of a national or local debate about education policy. Instead, neoliberalism is justified by the discourse of inevitability. As Bourdieu argues, "Everywhere we hear it said, all day long—and this is what gives the dominant discourse its strength—that there is nothing to put forward in opposition to the neoliberal view, that it has succeeded in presenting itself as self-evident, that there is no alternative."[63] Moreover, political and economic elites have skillfully rearticulated the struggle for equity to their neoliberal agenda. Accountability is framed in the language of equity and justice: all students and schools are evaluated by "the same test" and "held to the same standards"; the retention of thousands of students is "ending the injustice of social promotion." "Value legitimation" (giving people what has been promised) is replaced by "sense legitimation" as ". . . states, and/or dominant groups attempt to *change the very meaning* [emphasis original] of the sense of social needs into something that is very different."[64] Despite some school improvements (the value strategy), the thrust has been to shift discussions of equity to standards, accountability, and individual responsibility, negating historical and present race and class oppression.[65]

However, as Carlson argues, "because [recent basic skills and centralization] reforms have not addressed the roots of crisis in urban schools or countered the inequalities that generate conflict and resistance among various groups, 'basic skills' reforms are undermined by their own set of contradiction and crisis tendencies."[66] In the short run, they may raise test scores and legitimate the containment or exclusion of some youth, but these policies do not resolve underlying problems of equity, quality, and meaning in urban schools. They are hegemonic in the absence of an alternative discourse. Such a discourse will need to link the urgency to transform urban schools with goals of critical literacy and personal and social agency and pedagogies rooted in students sociopolitical realities and cultural identities. And clearly, the struggle for an alternative educational agenda must be understood as part of the larger project to reshape urban policy in the context of globalization.

Chicago exemplifies the law and order trend in Europe as well as the United States aimed at controlling the "enemy within" in the racially coded "inner city."[67] This is a response by the state to the new geography of centrality and marginality in cities defined by economic restructuring and globalization. On the one hand, these cities concentrate immense corporate and financial power, which has a commanding presence in the city landscape, extracts major financial concessions from city governments, and assembles a disproportionate population of highly privileged managers and professionals to run capitalist globalization functions. On the other hand, they also concentrate a growing population of immigrants along with other people of color whose low-paid labor is essential to the work of globalization but whose presence is devalorized and demonized and whose conditions of life produce growing despair. Although marginalized, Latino, African American, and immigrant "others" also exert a growing presence in the city through the politics of culture and identity and through their essential functions in the economy. They are poised to make their own claims on the city. Recent rebellions in Los Angeles, Cincinnati, and in Britain coupled with police-state conditions manifest this contention. This social dynamic is central to understanding educational policies and processes that discipline, criminalize, militarize, and exclude low-income urban youth of color and their communities.

In a post-September 11 world, racial profiling has gained new legitimacy and the police repression that has been standard practice in urban communities of color is now legitimated for the society at large. Democratic participation has become expendable and critique treasonous as the "war on terrorism" justifies authoritarianism and the suspension of democratic rights.

Fighting to win the battle of common sense over how our schools should be run, in whose interests, with whose participation, and to what ends has taken on new dimensions and new urgency. Liberatory educational discourse is part of a larger challenge to neoliberalism. It is also a refusal to accept a society in which the solution to perceived enemies (our children within or "demons" without) is cracking down.

Notes

1. The curriculum employs scripted lessons focused on discrete skills and one-right-answer responses. See Wesley Becker, "The Direct Instruction Model," *Journal of Direct Instruction*: 33:36 (Winter 1977).
2. See Michael W. Apple, *Educating the "Right" Way: Markets, Standards, God, and Inequality* (New York: RoutledgeFalmer, 2001); Nicholas C. Burbules and Carlos A. Torres, "Globalization and Education: An introduction," in *Globalization and Education: Critical Perspectives*, edited by Nicholas C. Burbules and Carlos A. Torres (New York: Routledge, 2000), 1–26; David Gillborn and Deborah Youdell, *Rationing Education: Policy, Practice, Reform, and Equity* (Buckingham: Open University Press, 2000); Pauline Lipman, "Bush's Education Plan, Globalization, and the Politics of Race," in *Cultural Logic 4*, no. 1. December 12, 2001), available at eserver.org/clogic/4–1/4–1.html and Kenneth. J. Saltman, *Collateral Damage: Corporatizing Public Schools—a Threat to Democracy* (Lanham, Md.: Rowman & Littlefield, 2000).
3. Gerald Grace, "Urban Education: Policy Science or Critical Scholarship," in *Education and the City: Theory, History and Contemporary Practice*, edited by Gerald Grace (London: Routledge and Kegan Paul, 1984), 3–59.
4. See Michael W. Apple, Review of "Devolution and Choice in Education," *Educational Researcher* 27, no. 6 (1998).
5. See Margaret Sutton and Bradley A. U. Levinson, eds., *Policy as Practice* (Westport, Conn.: Ablex, 2001).
6. See Joseph R. Gusfield, *The Symbolic Crusade*, 2nd ed. (Urbana, Il.: University of Illinois Press, 1986).
7. Mary L. Smith, Walter Heinecke, and Audrey Noble, "Assessment Policy and Political Spectacle," *Teachers College Record* 101 (2000): 157–91.
8. See Jenny Ozga, *Policy Research in Educational Settings* (Buckingham, Eng.: Open University Press, 2000).
9. See M. Foucault, *Discipline and Punish: The Birth of the Prison*, trans. Alan Sheridan.] (New York: Vintage Books, 1995 [1977]).
10. Gloria Ladson-Billings, "I Know Why This Doesn't Feel Empowering: A Critical Race Analysis of Critical Pedagogy," in *Mentoring the Mentor: A Critical Dialogue with Paulo Freire*, edited by P. Freire (New York: Peter Lang Publishing, 1997), 132.
11. See Stephen N. Haymes, *Race, Culture and the City* (Albany: State University of New York Press, 1995).
12. See Pauline Lipman, "The Politics of Chicago School Policy and Emerging Resistance," paper presented at the annual meeting of the American Education Research Association, Seattle (April 2001); and Pauline Lipman, *High Stakes Education: Inequality, Globalization, and Urban School Reform* (New York: Routledge, forthcoming).
13. Saskia Sassen, *Cities in a World Economy* (Thousand Oaks, Calif.: Pine Forge Press, 1994).
14. Janet L. Abu-Lughod, *New York, Chicago, Los Angeles: America's Global Cities* (Minneapolis: University of Minnesota Press, 1999).
15. Kim Phillips-Fein, "The Still-Industrial City: Why Cities Shouldn't Just Let Manufacturing Go," *American Prospect* (September–October, 1998): 28.

16. Saskia Sassen, *Globalization and Its Discontents* (New York: New Press, 1998), xxvi.

17. See John J. Betancur and Douglas C. Gills, "The Restructuring of Urban Relations," in *The Collaborative City: Opportunities and Struggles for Blacks and Latinos in U.S. Cities*, edited by J. J. Betancur and D. C. Gills (New York: Garland, 2000), 17–40.

18. A central tool of city government to facilitate this development strategy is tax increment financing zones or TIF's. Once an area is declared by the city to be "blighted," tax increments are diverted from schools, libraries, and other publicly funded services to subsidize infrastructure that facilitates development. For example, the North Loop TIF district is expected to produce $33 million annually for individual development projects and infrastructure to support development (Podmolik, Mary Ellen [1998]. Downtown Spreading Out as Residents Pour In. *Chicago Sun Times*, p. A20–21). Once declared a TIF zone, the city can also force owners to sell homes and businesses under the right of eminent domain, clearing the way for development.

19. Manuel Castells, *The Informational City* (London: Blackwell, 1989).

20. See Betancur and Gills, "The Restructuring of Urban Relations."

21. Ibid.

22. Abu-Lughod, *New York, Chicago, Los Angeles.*

23. See Sassen, *Cities in a World Economy.*

24. Christian Parenti, *Lockdown America: Police and Prisons in the Age of Crisis* (London: Verso, 1999).

25. To protect the anonymity of schools I have chosen not to disclose specific data that might identify them.

26. For similar findings, see Linda McNeil, *Contradictions of School Reform: Educational Costs of Standardized Testing* (New York: Routledge, 2000).

27. There are eighty-one schools on probation (fifty-two elementary and twenty-nine high schools). Of these eighty-one schools, sixty-one have a student population that is at least 98 percent black. Five schools have at least 84 percent "Hispanic" students, and most of the other students are identified as black. The remaining fifteen schools are mixed black and Hispanic. Seven of these fifteen schools with mixed populations have a student body that is at least 75 percent black. Only two schools on probation have 1 percent or over white students—one has 9.2 percent white students, the other 7 percent white students (CPS Office of Accountability, 2002).

28. PURE, Correlation of CPS Probation with Poverty Levels. Available from pureparents@pureparents.org/

29. The curriculum employs a strict hierarchy of skills and concepts (levels of lessons), and it employs scripted questions and scripted student responses that "leave(s) nothing to chance" (Kozloff, Martin A., Louis LaNunziata, James Cowardin [1999]. "Direct Instruction in Education" [online]. Wilmington, N.C., University of North Carolina at Wilmington [cited 22 August 2002]. Available at www.uncil.edu/people/kozloffm/diarticle.html. Lessons are "quick paced" with a single right answer which the whole group must master before the group can move on. The curriculum is based on a behaviorist model of learning, and there does not appear to be room for student interpretation of text, culturally specific content, or connections with students' experiences.

30. Wesley Becker, "The Direct Instruction Model."

31. See Elizabeth Duffrin, "Classes Revolve Around Test Prep," in *Catalyst* 10, no. 6 (1999): 9–11; and Elizabeth Duffrin, "Transition Centers: Services Praised, Instruction Questioned, Results Withheld," in *Catalyst* 10, no. 6 (1999): 4–8.

32. Duffrin, "Transition Centers," 6.

33. In 1998, the district ratio of African Americans to whites was 5:1, and the ratio of Latinos to whites was 3:1. However, in transition high schools for over-age eighth graders who failed the ITBS, the ratio of African Americans to whites was 27:1 and the ratio of Latinos to whites was 10:1.

34. Peter C. Murrell, "Digging Again the Family Wells: A Literacy Framework as

Emancipatory Pedagogy for African American Children," in *Mentoring the Mentor: A Critical Dialogue with Paulo Freire*, edited by Paulo Freire (New York: Peter Lang, 1997), 19–58.

35. Gloria Ladson-Billings, *Dreamkeepers: Successful Teachers of African American Students* (San Francisco: Jossey-Bass, 1994), 139.

36. National Center on Education and the Economy 1990. *America's Choice: High Skills or Low Wages*. Rochester, NY: Author.

37. Castells, Manuel. 1996. *The rise of the network society*. London: Blackwell.

38. Elmer W. Johnson (1995, November). *Chicago Metropolis 2020: Preparing Metropolitan Chicago for the 21st Century: Executive Summary*. Chicago: Commercial Club of Chicago.

39. Ibid., 3.

40. James P. Gee, Glenda Hull, and Colin Lankshear, *The New Work Order: Behind the Language of the New Capitalism* (Boulder, Colo: Westview Press, 1996).

41. Moberg, David. "Chicago: To Be or Not to Be a Global City." *World Policy Journal* 14 (1997): 71–86.

42. Vinson, Kevin D. and E. Wayne Ross. "Education and the New Disciplinarity: Surveillance, Spectacle, and the Case of SBER." *Cultural Logic* 41 (2001). [online] Winston-Salem, NC [cited] 11 November 2001] Available on the World Wide Web: (http://eserver.org/clogic/4-1/4-1.html)

43. Rosalind Rossi, "City's Toughest Prep Schools," *Chicago Sun Times*, A1–2, 2 April 2001.

44. The Chicago Consortium on Chicago School Research calculated the cohort dropout rate of CPS students followed from age thirteen to nineteen at 41.8 percent in 2000.

45. Ramon Flecha, "New Educational Inequalities," in *Critical Education in the New Information Age*, edited by M. Castells et al. (Lanham, Md.: Rowman & Littlefield, 1999), 46.

46. Gee, Hull, and Lankshear, *The New Work Order*.

47. See also Pauline Lipman, "The Politics of Chicago School Policy and Emerging Resistance," and Pauline Lipman and Eric Gutstein, "Undermining the Struggle for Equity: A Case Study of Chicago School Policy In a Latino/a School," in *Race, Gender, and Class*, 8, no. 2 (2001), 57–80.

48. Paulo Freire, *Pedagogy of the Oppressed* (New York: Continuum, 1992).

49. See Lipman and Gutstein, "Undermining the Struggle for Equity," 2001.

50. For a further discussion of these issues, see Pauline Lipman, *High Stakes Education*.

51. See Michael Katz, Michelle Fine, and Elaine Simon. "Poking Around: Outsiders View Chicago School Reform," *Teachers College Record* 99, no. 1 (1997): 117–57.

52. See Neil Smith, *The New Urban Frontier: Gentrification and the Revanchist City* (New York: Routledge, 1996).

53. See Stephen N. Haymes, *Race, Culture and the City* (Albany: State University of New York Press, 1995).

54. Quintanilla, Ray, "It's Not Just School It's an Adventure," (12 August 1999). *Chicago Tribune*, Sec. 1, pp. 1, 26.

55. Dirk Johnson, "High School at Attention," *Newsweek* (21 January 2002), available at http://www.msnbc.com/news/686928.asp?cp1=1.

56. Generation Y, "Right to Learn Campaign," *PURE* (12 January 2002), available at www.pureparents.org/pencil.html.

57. Brian J. Rogal, "Alternative Education: Segregation or Solution?" *Chicago Reporter* 304, no. 6–8 (2001): 10.

58. *Chicago Reporter* (September 1998). "High Court is the Final Chapter in Gang Ordinance Controversy" *Chicago Reporter* (5 May 2002), available at www.chicagoreporter.com/1998/09–98/0998court.htm.

59. Michael Keith, "From Punishment to Discipline? Racism, Racialization, and the Policing of Social Control," in *Racism, the City and the State*, edited by M. Cross and M. Keith (London: Routledge, 1993), 207.

60. Antonio Gramsci, *Selections from the Prison Notebooks*. Trans. and eds. Q. Hoare and G. N. Smith (New York: International Publishers, 1971).

61. See Apple, Review of "Devolution and Choice in Education."

62. Gary Orfield, "Wasted Talent, Threatened Future: Metropolitan Chicago's Human Capital and Illinois Public Policy," in *Creating Jobs, Creating Workers: Economic Development and Employment in Metropolitan Chicago*, edited by L. B. Joseph (Chicago: University of Chicago Center for Urban Research and Policy Studies, 1990), 131; see also ERASE Initiative *Facing the Consequences: An Examination of Racial Discrimination in U.S. Public Schools* (Oakland, Calif.: Applied Research Center, 2000); and Tammy Johnson, Jennifer E. Boyden, and William Pitz. *Racial Profiling and Punishment in U.S. Pubic Schools* (Oakland, Calif,: Applied Research Center, 2001).

63. Quoted in David Hursh, "Neoliberalism and the Control of Teachers, Students, and Learning," *Cultural Logic* 4, no. 1, 2001 (December 12, 2001) available at eserver.org/clogic/4–1/4–1.html.

64. Roger Dale quoted in Michael W. Apple, *Educating the "Right" Way*, 46.

65. William. F. Tate, "Critical Race Theory and Education: History, Theory, and Implications," in *Review of Research in Education*, edited by Michael W. Apple (Washington D.C.: American Educational Research Association, 1997), 195–247.

66. Dennis Carlson, "Education as a Political Issue: What's Missing in the Public Conversation about Education?," in *Thirteen Questions: Reframing Education's Conversation*, 2nd edited by Joe L. Kincheloe and Shirley R. Steinberg (New York: Peter Lang, 1996), 281.

67. Keith, "From Punishment to Discipline?"

INTRODUCTION TO CHAPTER 5

Following Lipman's analysis of enforcement-oriented school policies in the global city, Pepi Leistyna's chapter makes central the voices of youth who are the victims of these discipline-based social and school policies as well as the intensifying domestic militarization that is falling particularly hard on youth of color. As Leistyna's discussion and ethnographic study shows, schools are a component of the carceral response to the problems confronting youth—problems that derive in no small part from a corporate-controlled economy with corporate-enforced poverty, violence, racism, and despair. Part of what makes Leistyna's chapter unique to the volume is its focus on the insights and experiences of students most affected by education as enforcement.

CHAPTER 5

Facing Oppression

Youth Voices from the Front

PEPI LEISTYNA

As a member of a community leadership and social justice team in Boston, I was recently allowed to "tour" the Suffolk County House of Corrections. The visit began with a video that celebrated the philosophy and practice of "rehabilitation" of the prison, followed by a presentation from a controversial county sheriff who dismissed any critique of the United States' penitentiary system and his work therein, even when asked about the correlation between draconian cutbacks on programs to help inmates reacclimate on the outside and astronomical recidivism rates. This introductory section of the program day closed with two inmate panels, one with three women and the second with three men. These participants, who were obviously rigorously screened, color coordinated, and polished for our consumption, nervously spoke about how the local concept of "corrections" was helping them get back on their feet.

Our group did manage a bit of a coup when we were allowed to visit the male inmates in the "violence ward." Once we had entered this separate locked chamber, it was unexpected by the prison guards that were guiding us through this nightmare (with smiles on their faces and jokes to share) that we as individuals would begin to mix with the inmates while they walked about out of their cells as part of a brief respite from the other twenty-three long and useless hours of lockdown in predominantly three-bed, one-toilet cells no larger than an average walk-in closet.

What was immediately apparent about this depressing scene, though I had fully anticipated it, was that the overwhelming majority of inmates were racially subordinated—mostly African Americans and Latinos. Those who were white were marked as working poor by their teeth, tattoos, and speech,

Pepi Leistyna is an assistant professor in applied linguistics graduate studies at the University of Massachusetts–Boston, where he coordinates the research program and teaches courses in cultural studies, media analysis, and language acquisition. Speaking internationally on issues of democracy and education, a Fellow of the Education Policy Research Unit, and associate editor of the *Journal of English Linguistics*, Leistyna conceptualized and coedited the book *Breaking Free: The Transformative Power of Critical Pedagogy*, and he is the author of the books *Presence of Mind: Education and the Politics of Deception*, and *Defining and Designing Multiculturalism*.

let alone their stories. I had heard in the news of epidemic levels of illegal strip searches of women who are incarcerated in this prison, and even stories of rape of both sexes. Now I was actually hearing from inmates themselves about the frequent beatings that they endure from the predominantly white security staff.

When a member of our social justice team asked the sheriff about the actual racial makeup of prisoners and staff, he said that he was not sure of the exact numbers. He added (only after it had been pointed out) that he hadn't realized that the entire staff in the promotional materials we had been shown as part of our introduction to the prison was white—"I was not aware of this. . . . I've never seen this video before." Such disavowal is hard to swallow given that he is one of the main spokespersons throughout the footage.

Over 70 percent of prisoners in the United States are from non-European racial and ethnic backgrounds, and Suffolk County House of Corrections is no exception. African Americans make up the largest number of those entering prisons each year in the United States. As Loic Wacquant points out:

> The rate of incarceration for African Americans has soared to levels unknown in any other society and is higher now than the total incarceration rate in the Soviet Union at the zenith of the Gulag and in South Africa at the height of the anti-apartheid struggle. As of mid-1999, close to 800,000 black men were in custody in federal penitentiaries, state prisons, and county jails. . . . On any given day, upwards of one third of African-American men in their twenties find themselves behind bars, on probation, or on parole. And, at the core of the formerly industrial cities of the North, this proportion often exceeds two-thirds.[1]

What was equally upsetting about the Suffolk scene was that almost everyone in this stark environment was young. At thirty-eight, I felt like an old man in a sea of youth. But the concept of youth didn't connote a free-spirited, open-ended quest for future aspirations. On the contrary, the room was threadbare with despair, gloom, anger, silence, and pain. As one African American young man stated to me after I moved away from the prison guards and into the crowd:

> This isn't rehabilitation . . . just look around. These are young people locked up all day and night long, for what, for smoking a joint, or getting in a fistfight in the street! There's no education here, there's no preparation for a future, there's no room here for healing—there's just time, a waste of time. This place breeds anger and hostility. Just look around, this is an entire generation that's being thrown away like the day's garbage, only this "garbage" is profitable!

Prisons have been strategically used within the feudalism of today's capitalist social relations to lock up what's seen as superfluous populations that the powers that be have no immediate use for.[2] As Wacquant states, "the astounding upsurge in black incarceration in the past three decades results from the obsolescence of the ghetto as a device for caste control and the correlative need for a substitute apparatus for keeping (unskilled) African Americans in a subordinate and confined position—physically, socially, and symbolically."[3]

In addition to containment, where there's profit in what's increasingly turning into a privatized business endeavor, there's demand, and the prison population in the United States has consequently skyrocketed over 200 percent since 1980.[4] There are now over two million people in jail in the United States, and although we have only 5 percent of the world's population, we have 25 percent of its prisoners.[5] The United States surpassed Russia in the year 2000 and now has the world's highest incarceration rate. It's five to seventeen times higher than all other Western nations. By the close of the millennium, 6.3 million people were on probation, in jail or prison, or on parole in this country.

While the validity of these statistics is not in question in national discussions, there is great contestation as to why they exist. Conservatives endlessly wield racist and class-specific representations of violent groups that need to be contained. When young people are represented (as opposed to self-described) in the media, especially the poor and racially subordinated, they are overwhelmingly depicted as dangerous and untrustworthy. However, as Henry Giroux (1996) rebuts:

> Of course, what the dominant media do not talk about are the social conditions that are producing a new generation of youth steeped in despair, violence, crime, poverty, and apathy. For instance, to talk about Black crime without mentioning that the unemployment rate for Black youth exceeds 40 percent in many urban cities serves primarily to conceal a major cause of youth unrest. Or to talk about apathy among White youth without analyzing the junk culture, poverty, social disenfranchisement, drugs, lack of educational opportunity, and commodification that shape daily life removes responsibility from the social system that often sees youth as simply another market niche.[6]

Critical cultural workers and educators have been concerned with discrimination in employment and the judicial system and have provided important analyses of the high levels of incarceration and the correlation with unjust economic conditions, the dismantling of welfare, the driving down of wages, and the pursuit of neoliberalism and deregulation in the incessant search for cheaper labor outside the United States. It is axiomatic that poverty produces crime, and the United States continues to have the highest child poverty rate among major industrialized countries, along with huge levels of working poor who are relegated to living below the poverty line regardless of their employment.[7] In fact, one-in-five children, and one-in-four racially subordinated children, grows up in poverty in the United States.[8]

While all of these progressive arguments, which cogently connect incarceration with corporate class warfare and white supremacy, should be at the forefront of national attention, I emphasize in this chapter how institutions of public education in the United States are, in part, complicit in this corporate and hegemonic process—that there is an inextricable link between the astronomical numbers of racially subordinated and working-poor youth in prisons today and our system of schooling. The economic and political forces that shape public education—institutions that reflect the larger social order—do not make an effort to create culturally responsive, humanizing, and thus inviting public spaces where youth can achieve academically and come to voice about the historical, social, and economic forces that shape their lives. As Ken Saltman observes:

> Urban, largely nonwhite institutions do not even feign to prepare students for entree into the professional class, the class that carries out the orders of the ruling corporate-state elite. These schools contain students who have been deemed hopeless and have been consigned to institutional containment. Many urban schools function as the first level of containment while the second level, America's largest growing industry, the prison system, awaits them.[9]

Education is thus not concerned with infusing civic responsibility in preparation for public life; rather, it is about ensuring the dissemination of a particular market logic within which labor stratification is embraced and confirmed.[10] For those throw-away masses, a callous social infrastructure, constant exposure to harsh material and symbolic conditions both inside and outside of school, exclusionary and distorted curricula, and apathetic and abusive educator attitudes and pedagogies work to virtually ensure the self-fulfilling prophecy of youth deviance.

A Pedagogy of Neglect

Youth, especially the poor and racially subordinated, are far too often left out of drafting history, describing social realities, and debating educational policies and practices. In fact, conservatives have relentlessly worked to control public opinion and cut funds to dismantle participatory democratic spaces that nurture the possibility for coming to voice. Pertaining to public schools, Noam Chomsky elaborates:

> It starts in kindergarten: The school system tries to repress independence; it tries to teach obedience. Kids and other people are not induced to challenge and question, but the contrary. If you start questioning, you're a behavior problem or something like that; you've got to be disciplined. You're supposed to repeat, obey, follow orders.[11]

The newest waves of educational standardization across the nation, as being witnessed in the current federal government's *No Child Left Behind* policies and the English-only movements that are vigorously working nationally to dismantle bilingual education programs, are clearly intended to maintain this type of knowledge conformity.

Even in the apparently well-intentioned liberal calls to "empower" and "give voice" to students, young people are mostly heard about and rarely from. What many educators fail to realize is that even the most progressive and concerned pedagogue can't empower kids. On the contrary, it is both objectifying and patronizing to assume that cultural workers can simply tap any given child on the shoulder with a magical epistemological wand, abstracted from the critical process of active engagement and meaning making.

This critique also applies to the notion of "giving voice." It is presumptuous to claim to possess the ability to bequeath the power of expression. Since all people already have voices, often critical ones at that, the real challenge is for educators to be willing to create dialogical spaces where all of these lived experiences and worldviews can be heard. In other words, will teachers be able and willing to create the necessary self-empowering conditions that allow kids of all walks of life to explore, theorize, reveal, and act upon the truths behind the worlds that they inhabit? And, will teachers as ethnographers attempt to gather, so as to teach in a culturally responsive manner, information about the cultural capital—the literacies, sense of language, knowledge, learning and cognitive styles, and values and beliefs—that emerges out of the very violent material and symbolic conditions that many students are compelled to navigate on a daily basis?

This chapter makes use of the living personal narratives of a group of young people to expose what it is like to live in the city of Changeton for the most disenfranchised (as promised, all of the names of people and places in this study are pseudonyms).[12] The research sets out to capture testimonies that could reveal a great deal about the survivors and the sources of a historically based and ideologically produced set of social problems.

At the time this research was initiated, the city of Changeton's estimated population was: 74,449 white; 12,028 black; 1,589 Asian/Pacific Islander; 5,860 Latino/a; 269 Native American; and 4,453 designated "Other." In addition, there were more women than men, over thirteen thousand people living in poverty, and the annual crimes committed in the city totaled 6,895 with 1,156 acts of violence.

Of a total school enrollment of 14,015 students, 13.6 percent were Latino/a, 29.7 percent African American, 3.0 percent Asian American, and 53.2 percent white. One in every fourteen students in Changeton was limited-English proficient. Up to 53 percent of the elementary students enrolled in Changeton schools were receiving free or reduced-cost lunch.

Adding to the system's status of probation with the state because of its inability to effectively desegregate the schools, Changeton had high annual dropout rates, especially among racially subordinated and low-income youth. The high school lost nearly a tenth of its population the year that the interviews and research began, and the dropout rate for ninth graders was estimated at 12–14 percent. The retention rate (those held back) in high school was 11.5 percent. In addition, 13.5 percent of the students throughout the school system, overwhelmingly poor and racially subordinated boys and linguistic minorities, were in special education.

According to a desegregation report submitted to the school system's superintendent by an outside consulting group, the schools that are in the worst condition in the city are also the most racially imbalanced. It is in these schools that the bilingual education programs are predominantly housed and thus where the majority of linguistic-minority children reside. This is how the schools were described by the desegregation planning team "Most of the windows are in extremely poor condition—opaque . . . students have had to move to other classes or wear coats and gloves," they have "a very small book collection," "there is constant infiltration of water into corner classrooms and no ventilation system," "lighting in the classroom is extremely poor and needs to be completely replaced," "there are staff concerns regarding slightly elevated radon levels," "the playground is unsafe," "the faculty and students are unable to take full advantage of basic audiovisual instruction equipment because each classroom has just one duplex outlet near the classroom clock which leads to unsafe use of extension cords," "the library also serves for music instruction," "it lacks a gymnasium and functional office space," "students eat their lunch in the basement within fifty feet of the lavatories and boiler room."

The assessment team concluded that, in large part, Changeton school officials are "out of touch," and that the "Central Office is not perceived as providing the leadership the system needs, but rather, as creating barriers and protecting turf." According to the researchers, "We received multiple disturbing reports that there are teachers in the system who believe some children can't learn, who behave in ways that encourage truancy, and who discriminate against children of other different races or socioeconomic class." They noted that, "In the process of creating system-wide values, some schools could not agree on a value which embraced, honored, and respected diversity." As one teacher I personally interviewed exclaimed:

> The more that I think about this the angrier I get. You begin to understand why some of these kids, especially the black kids, get up and are violent: it's like water torture and they incessantly drip on you. At a certain point you've got to let it go—explode![13]

Within such an antagonistic environment, it should come as no surprise that, in droves, students have been expelled from Changeton schools on a daily basis. It was the high school principal's general attitude that with students "causing too many disruptions to stay in the regular day program" he had "little choice other than to put them in the streets." Experiencing firsthand the high rates of suspension and the permanent removal of some students from school, the outside research/desegregation team added in their report, "We were distressed that people identified the expulsion process as something that was working well in the system." Two progressive educators in the trenches in Changeton describe this very problem of suspension and expulsion that they face in their buildings:

> In a two-month period he [the principal] placed about thirty black students, and only two whites, in the In School Suspension Room. Most white students, especially those of the middle to upper middle class, are given a little lecture and returned to their rooms, while black students are kept in a closet for weeks for the same behaviors. Not only must the system subject those without sustainable power to an education that silences, but it must also recommend

the use of sedatives [Ritalin] to render students of subordinated backgrounds totally without voice.

They create progressive reforms that are never intended to succeed. The Haitian Bilingual Program was placed in an all white school in an attempt to appear on paper as though the school system was complying with the desegregation laws. They put this Haitian program in this all-White racist school. Imagine what it has been like for the Haitian kids and teachers—I mean, these black kids in a sea of white. There are no other minority people in the school except for this one health teacher. These kids are isolated, and the other students readily pick them on. Naturally, as anyone would, they react to such unwarranted abuse. Well guess what, the Haitian students are getting suspended from school all the time by an assistant principal who is a real S.O.B.

Instead of confronting such injustices, the powers that be in Changeton have maintained the system's education as enforcement agenda. Acting on such oppressive logic, according to a recent state audit, Changeton had used $300,000 in educational reform money for school police—three marked cars and eight male officers with powers of arrest who, during school emergencies, wear bulletproof vests and carry Glock pistols that shoot hollow bullets.

Youth(s) Coming to Voice

The type of critical pedagogy being proposed here is fundamentally concerned with student experience; it takes the problems and needs of the students themselves as the starting point. This suggests both confirming and legitimating the knowledge and experience through which students give meaning to their lives. Most obviously, this means replacing the authoritative discourse of imposition and recitation with a voice capable of speaking in one's own terms, a voice capable of listening, retelling, and challenging the very grounds of knowledge and power.[14]

After a number of conversations about my research with a friend who was at the time a team leader for a national organization's campaign in Changeton to help "at-risk" youth, I was invited to go to work with her on a regular basis and hang out with the young people that she had been supervising. Before my first visit, Liz told the group a bit about me and asked if it were okay with them that I be around. She said that they had voted and that the team members were "psyched" that I was coming, and that one in particular exclaimed, "We finally have a chance to speak out, and I've got a lot on my mind!"

Early in the morning, we all met in front of the Changeton Courthouse where the teams from the youth organization regularly hook up, exercise, and leave in two vans to do various projects around town. The group was predominantly black, Latino/a, and Cape Verdean. There were also a few whites, including a person with a disability, a young overweight woman, and a Gay young man. These were young people who had dropped out/been pushed out of school and, for many, were given the "choice" from the courts of working with the organization, going to boot camp, or getting locked up.

What these youth would eventually expose (as captured in the following dialogue) is a world full of crucial knowledge, a world that cannot be ignored if educators truly hope to engage in cultural politics and understand educational failure in Changeton and beyond. And yet, these are the very kids that people rarely, if ever, listen to. Rather than explore such subject positions as a source of vital knowledge, these urban poor in the United States are treated as a criminalized underclass that must be watched and contained.

One morning, we drove through the center of Changeton in the van and the group pointed out Main Street, where they said "the action goes down." The heart of the city has a very eerie feeling to it: there are literally dozens of boarded up homes that people have been forced to abandon because of financial difficulties. Many of the buildings have become crack dens or refuges for the homeless.

Passing the high school, there was a sudden burst of laughter that rang throughout the van when a local teacher was spotted in the street. After mocking him through the vehicle's windows, the group cynically reminisced about faculty that they had had. As I commented on the immense size of the building, Rhonda, a young black woman, turned to me and said, "The big school, you mean the prison. . . . Changeton high the big white lie!"

Continuing on our way, we drove through some of the housing projects. The team wanted me to see where many of them had grown up. In the first project, the nicest of the bunch, there were bits and pieces of garbage and ransacked rusty bicycles strewn all over the place. The long-since faded paint of the project was peeling off the walls and collecting in random piles in the bars that caged in the first-floor windows. As omnipresent shards of broken glass glittered on the pavement, much of the group talked about ways that they had escaped from the police (which they referred to as "Five-0") in this neighborhood.

While checking out another project, I asked the crew, "What's there to do around here?" There was an overwhelming chorus response, "Nothing!!" Rhonda elaborated:

> There are so many kids from eighteen down, and they have nothing to do but get in trouble . . . drugs, guns, and reputations, that's all we got! . . . Nothing to do but screw! . . . And school, well that's boring.

We returned to work in the park and after some long hours of painting in the hot spring sun I offered to take the team out to lunch. We ate, played some hoop, and then sat under a tree and began to talk. When I placed the tape recorder on the park bench, in the middle of the circle, one-by-one, each person pulled it intimately close to their mouths, to be sure that they would be heard.

Present on that day were: Roberto, an eighteen-year-old from Puerto Rico; Carlos, a twenty-year-old who described himself as Puerto Rican and half black; Dion, a twenty- year-old African American; Roland, an eighteen-year-old African American; Stevie, a twenty-year-old mix of white and Cape Verdean; Paul, a white seventeen-year-old; and Olavo, an eighteen-year-old Cape Verdean.

PEPI: How do you get out of the difficult situations that you're all in?

ROBERTO: Move if your parents got the money, if you've got parents.

DION: You gotta wanna help yourself if you want to get out of it!

STEVIE: You gotta have money!

DION: No man, it's not about money!

STEVIE: I'm sorry, you gotta have money. If you don't have money, how are you gonna get outta here?

OLAVO: There's no jobs out there!

CARLOS: The ghetto is everywhere, the hood ain't no joke and there's no way out.

PEPI: What about selling junk [drugs], a lot of people must sell junk to make money?

DION: Everybody been through that phase. We all pumped [sold] at one time, you know what I'm sayin. Either you fell into it or you were broke. I was both and got into it when I was fifteen.

PEPI: How old are most people when they get mixed up in this? (*There are a few responses:* "That age.," "Twelve." ...)

PEPI: How many of you have been busted, and for what? (*The entire group responds that they have been. Some of them, three or four times—for car theft, drugs, robbery, assault, etc. As one person from among the group answered,* "For everything!")

PAUL: Vandalism. I didn't do it, but I was there so I got arrested.

PEPI: All this stuff—robbing, violence, junking, having kids, leaving school—does that get you respect with the people that you're hanging with?

DION: You know what it is man, you wanna get a reputation. That's what it is. It's all about rep—give me the money and all that shit. They see you walkin out and they say "He's crazy y'all, I seen him the other day man, he went in the store and did dis and did dat!" You know what I'm sayin. That's all about rep, it's all about reputation!

PEPI: What's the rep for, making people afraid of you?

DION: Yeah, exactly!

STEVIE: I had my own mother's boyfriend afraid of me. He was a heroin addict, he used to shoot up heroin and stuff, right. He knew that if I sold him a twenty, or a bundle or something, and he didn't pay me when he got the money that I would kick his ass.

PEPI: He's living with your mom?

STEVIE: He was. It was kinda tuff on my mother cause one day I went down to see her and she was sleepin in the bed. There in the other room, he was dead on the ground. He shot up a bundle and shit and died. He had juss got out of detox and he shot up a whole bundle.

PEPI: Was he doing it to get high or did he just want out?

STEVIE: He did it cause he wanted to get high, but he wasn't sniffin, he was shootin—he was mainlinein. He shot up. . . . I went in there. I never seen a dead body until I went in there. He was all like blue. His whole body was blue. I woke up my mother and she was like, "What's the matter, what's the matter?" I said, "Stan is dead." She's like, "What!" She went in there and he was on the ground dead. He didn't have a pulse or nuttin. I checked his neck and his wrist, he didn't have a pulse or nuttin man, so I just called the ambulance and the police came. I'll never forget that man—that was shhh-hhh! I still think about that to, cause in a way I kinda think that I contributed to it. I mean, I didn't like him ... he was ok man, he used to give me money and stuff, you know. But, I just didn't like him in a way because he was doin that around my mother and shit.

PEPI: What about the cops, what are they like? (*Responses include:* "Pretty fucked!," "They suck man!," "Definitely suck!," "Pigs!" ...)

DION: Prejudice!! The system, it sucks man. You walkin on mainstreet right, I see you and you walkin and you stop to talk. You stand there for like five minutes and the drug gang, the police, come around and they arrest you—they charge you with trespassin.

PEPI: What if I came through, being white and all?

OLAVO: You white so they let you go, they ask you to move on. But if you black, we black and we talkin ... (*Dion jumps in*).

DION: They'd search you down man.

STEVIE: You [talking to me] look like a clean-cut, you know, clean-cut type of guy. At worst they'll think of you like someone that's buyin, so they just be like, get outta here, take a hike, or somethin. But someone like him (*points out Roland who is the darkest*), or even you dog (*pointing to Dion who is lighter skinned*).... They'd yell, "Open your mouth!" They'd make you take your shoes and socks off.... They'll lay trespassin charges on you.

CARLOS: Two cops took those kids from around here, one was thirteen and one was fifteen. They took em into an ally a little down from here and beat em down. They juss put them in the car, went down North Main Street, they brung em down to that ally, and they beat em up.

PEPI: Did the kids do anything about it—press charges?

CARLOS: Can't do anything about it.

STEVIE: Look at that dude that died in [names a city near by], that Puerto Rican dude. The cops threw him down the stairs. They had him in a choke hold and he went into a comma. Now he's dead!

OLAVO: There's another guy here who got killed Rodney King style.

STEVIE: I've got hit with a telephone book at the police station. They do that so it wouldn't leave no bruises. They put a telephone book up to my head and they hit me.... I got maced three times in one night. I wasn't resistin arrest, I was just layin there like that on the grass. He hit me three times and maced me. My friend too, who has asthma. He was in the back seat of the car and he couldn't breath because of the smell of the mace. I said to the cops, "My friend needs medical treatment!" I yelled, "My friend needs medical help, he can't breath!" I kinda started goin off, I was like kickin the window and stuff so I would get their attention. Instead, they stopped the car, opened the door, and sprayed us again!

PEPI: Are most of the police white, or is the force pretty mixed? (*The group says that the majority are white.*) What do you do with the money that you make on the streets? Is it to stay alive? Is it power? What is it?

STEVIE: I called it dirty money and I just blew it.

DION: Sneakers yo! You want sneakers, you want some gear, you know what I'm sayin.

OLAVO: Buy cars, buy clothes ...

DION: All the money I made, I smoked it all up! Yo cause when I was dealin I was like damn man what does this do man, they be comin back every ten minutes, you know what I'm sayin. It started from an oulee [a quantity of the drug]. I smoked a oulee, then two oulees went by, and then nigga, about three months later, I was like dis (*acts out a bony, deathly ill person*). (*The group laughs and one can hear,* "Exactly yo!") I was juss dried out yo. Dat shit ain't funny.

STEVIE: I never smoked coke!

PEPI: Ok, you're twelve to fifteen, where's the door out of all this?

STEVIE: You gotta change your environment, you gotta change your environment.

DION: I know, take it from me man, I was there yo. Before yo, if you woulda seen before, you ask everybody in outreach—I went there a few times man. All messed up man, real skinny, couldn't do, you know what I'm sayin. I wanted to help myself. I've been off it for a year now, since lass summer. I haven't touched it and I'm not gonna either yo! Cause I know where it'll take me yo! It won't take you nowhere—either six feet under or in jail. And you do a lotta shit, a lotta shit that you don't mean. I did a lotta stuff to a lotta people yo, and it hurts when I begin to think about it.

STEVIE: Tell me you don't have to change your environment!

DION: Of course, who you hang around with, who your boys are, who they really are! You gotta know who your boys are man. A friend isn't a person who comes up to you and says "Yo man, you lookin good, you look diesel man. Yo, I got this rock [chunk of coke/crack], you wanna go get high?" That's notta friend . . . after he juss said you look diesel and all dat—you lookin good so let's go get high.

PEPI: Who has family here, parents or whatever?

PAUL: I've got my mom, but my father doesn't live with us.

OLAVO: I live in [names a city in a bordering state].

PEPI: You drive all the way here for this program?

OLAVO: I made a deal with the judge, like I've gotta stay with the program until it ends. If not, I have to spend four months in boot camp.

CARLOS: Once you get outta there you'd be twice as worse.

PEPI: Where do you go to talk about these complications and problems? Is there anybody who listens?

PAUL: I got my mother.

CARLOS: My step-father. I wouldn't even bother my mother with my problems. She never understands. I go to my step-father who is more of a brother.

OLAVO: I've got my grandma.

DION: I can't talk to my mother. You can't talk to my mother yo! She be rippen ya know, she yells a lot. So I go there and take a shower and get some clean clothes. She be mad, and always say, "When you get to twenty years old, what you gonna do with yourself, I'm not gonna be here forever!" Which is true, you know, but after a while you get sick of it man, and you wanna be like, "I get sick a hearin you bitch all the time." But you can't say nothin—she put you in this world and she can take you out.

CARLOS: As soon as you go they want you back, as soon as you go . . .

STEVIE: My mother is still happy I left. I left when I was sixteen and she's still happy. Home was just a place you sleep at, if there's any food, which isn't often, you might have a sandwich or somethin, you know.

PEPI: At what age did most of you leave home? (*Most in their early to mid teens, but all have returned except for Stevie and Olavo.*)

CARLOS: I'm in and out all the time.

PEPI: How would you describe home, what is or was it?

DION: At that time, there was no home. You hang out on the block all night and pump, you know.

STEVIE: When you live with your mother, that's what I think of.

CARLOS: Right now, I live with my mother. Home is a place to eat and sleep. That's the only way I look at it. You can't even have a decent conversation without somebody startin a problem with you or somethin.

DION: You always get into a little beef wit your mother.

PEPI: But what are you yelling about? Is there yelling because you are in trouble a lot?

CARLOS: Cause you're tryin to say somethin and they don't wanna understand. They try to ignore it and think about it as when they were growin up— "Well when we were growing up we weren't doing those kinds of things. . . . You shouldn't be doing that!" That's not the point. The point is we're doin it now and we're tryin to get rid of it. How can we do that? They don't wanna understand that. That's why I moved out in the first place. I started livin on my own when I was fourteen. I just came back about lass year.

DION: I've got a single parent, my mother. We've gotten far being out here, you know what I'm sayin. Grew up in the projects on the east side. From there she got a section eight. Now we live in our own home. I mean, it ain't her house, but it's somethin man—it's better than being in the projects. The projects ain't as bad as it was man. Where you live now dog (*points out Carlos*), it ain't so bad as it was when I was livin there, it ain't nothin!

CARLOS: When I moved in there were shoot-outs every single night.

DION: That shit ain't nothin compared to when I lived there yo!

PEPI: Who's shooting who?

CARLOS: Different projects, different people (*the group begins to point out the turf and the gangs*).

ROBERTO: People mix in my project, but if you're from the outside, you're not welcome and you'll be in trouble. This town didn't use to be like this, it wasn't until the movies and shit. I mean I remember after the movie *Colors* [a hollywood film that romanticizes gang warfare] that this dividin of the city began. Now the east side fights the west . . . it's endless. You'll beat up one of their boys and they go after you with their boys, then it's guns, and the cops come three hours later to pick up anyone who is dead or hurt. Man, the playground we call the dead ground. Two sides lined up.

DION: That's cause a territory yo, survival of the fittest. . .

PEPI: If someone like myself comes into town and I don't know the territory, I don't know the boundaries . . . ?

PAUL: You'd get beat up.

CARLOS: You'd get fucked up!!

DION: I recently got beat up and they took my hat.

OLAVO: You couldn't walk with Nikes . . . they'd take them off your feet.

DION: That ain't nothin yo. Remember when eightball jackets come out. I got beat down for mine. I was walkin down Main Street and four mother fuckas jumped out of a car. They just took my jacket and all that yo.

PEPI: They want it cause it's quality goods?

DION: It's theirs, you know what I'm sayin. If they want it they gonna take it, they gonna take it from you. And it's not really that they wanna do it, it's the reputation that they wanna get when they jump out the car and beat you down. Then people be talkin, "Yo, nigga did that shit the other night, dude beat up homeboy the other night and took his shit dog." It's messed up ain't it (laughs).

PEPI: Anybody in a gang?

OLAVO: No, I was never in a gang.

DION: I was close.

CARLOS: I used to hang with a gang, but that's about it.

STEVIE: When we were young and shit, me and my friend Joe had a little clique. It wasn't like a gang, it was just a little clique. We had jackets and hats and shit. Now, most gangs follow teams, college teams like Duke and the Kings. But, I've never been a follower, I've never followed anybody. I'm not gonna be with a bunch a you know what. I mean, I got friends, but I'm not gonna like try to like hang out in a gang. To me that's kinda corny yo.

OLAVO: Yeah, now that you see.

CARLOS: When I used to pump, I used to juss hang on the corner with my boys. They weren't makin no money, they juss watchin my back, helpin me waste the money.

STEVIE: Yeah, that money is gonna be rollin in but, sooner or later, you're either gonna get . . . (Dion jumps in).

DION: Foggy, you're gonna fall, or you're gonna be six feet under. There's only three doors that you gotta watch out for: you gotta look out for the cop door, you gotta look out for the coffin door which closes and never opens . . .

PEPI: What about the rich people in Changeton. This city has some affluent sections. Do those people try to help the community at all?

STEVIE: Naw!! Especially not the mayor man. The mayor is a jerk and he's an asshole—you can quote me on that to because I think he is. He doesn't want to help. They wanted to have a free health clinic in the downtown, like for low-income people, and the mayor opposed it.

DION: He also didn't meet with the local religious leaders who were concerned about all the police violence and the racism.

STEVIE: Because he doesn't want to hear it. He's racist yo, he's racist! He's a basehead too (they all laugh). I sold him a joint the other day—I'm just teasin. He's a jerk though man, you know what I mean. He tries to act like a nice guy and everythin, but he ain't, he's racist. I mean, I never had to deal really with racism and shit, but I can tell he's racist!!

PEPI: If you're poor, even if you're white, are you in the same bind?

STEVIE: If you're white and you're poor, yeah man.

ROLAND: As long as there's niggas, there's always gonna be poor white trash. (The group has Roland repeat this statement.)

DION: It's true.

STEVIE: It is man. That's true. You know, cause I was a ghetto bastard.

PAUL: I was a ghetto bastard myself.

STEVIE: Runnin through the projects wit Fernandes kickers. Swear to god yo, my mom used to buy two for three dollar sneakers at Fernandes—I didn't care! You know, as long as I had a brand new pair of sneakers.

PEPI: Stevie and Paul are white, are they outcasts among other racial groups on the street?

DION: If you down then you down, you know what I'm sayin. It's not about white or black or nothin like dat. It's juss if you down wit da gang you down wit it. You gotta show them that yo, it's our gang and we're gonna go all out. If anybody try anything we beatin em down.

PEPI: How many of you have carried a piece? (*Three of them said that they have. Two say that they've been busted with one. From the back of the group comes, "Ahh, the guns and the knives." From beyond the park there is the haunting sound of a baby happily playing on the project grass.*)

CARLOS: At one point, I juss started sellin guns for a livin. Went to jail a couple times; moved to [names a city in the next state]; had a kid; got tired of sellin drugs out there; came back over here; went to jail again.

PEPI: Carlos, how old are you now?

CARLOS: Twenty. The only record that I'm proud to say I got was when I chased this dude with a hammer. He deserved it!

PAUL: I carry a knife.

STEVIE: I carried a piece, a piece of bubble gum. I never carried a gun, I never did.

DION: I like guns yo. I do, I like guns, ya know, shootin em. I don't like shootin at people. I've shot at people, but I didn't really wanna get em. It's juss like to sting em, you know what I mean.

PEPI: You hear about violence all the time around here . . .

STEVIE: I think that it's ridiculous, it's ridiculous!

PEPI: How many of you have been shot? (*A few speak up telling stories: one took a hit from a twenty-two, one got stabbed twice, and another talks about a bee-bee that is still stuck in his neck. Curious, the group touches the metal under his skin.*)

DION: Carlos, you got shot?

CARLOS: I still got the marks (*shows the group his scar*).

PEPI: How or why did you get shot?

CARLOS: No reason at all, juss at the wrong place at the wrong time. I didn't grow up in Changeton like everybody else here. I grew up in New York. And in New York if you're passin by and there's a shoot-out, there ain't no way you're gonna get outta there cause usually there's like at least five people shootin at the same time. That's life!

STEVIE: My ex-girlfriend stabbed me. I threw a bowl of potato salad on her head (*group laughs*). Swear to god I did, it was on one of my son's birthdays. I threw a bowl of potato salad on her head and she went crazy. She broke a bottle and stabbed me with it in my side—never forget it, it was a horrifyin experience (*group still laughing*).

DION: Never been shot, never been stabbed, knock on wood, but I have been hit with bottles. I got scars right here (*he begins to go over his bare body like a museum, pointing them out).* I got a scar here . . . I was hit wit a brick twice. I had seven stitches here, I got hit wit a bottle right here.

PEPI: If you walk on the street at night is somebody gonna fuck with you?

STEVIE: To be honest with you Pepi, to be honest with you, I don't like to go into the night man—I'm afraid man. I swear, I'm not jokin, I'm scared to walk out.

DION: Everybody wants to be somebody yo!

STEVIE: It juss seems like this is like a rough generation man.

PEPI: How many of you have dead friends from street violence? (*As I begin to count I realize that it's the entire group. They begin to talk about mutual friends that are dead.*)

DION: I've seen a lotta my friends die yo, not actually seen em die, but . . .

CARLOS: A lotta my friends were killed in drive-bys.

PEPI: Basically what you've got is poor kids killing poor kids. Does that make any sense? ("No!," *comes from among the group.*)

STEVIE: It's juss different now man. Like when I was a teenager, when I was fourteen, this shit first started happenin. Now man, damn! I can imagine what it's going to be like when my kids get older!

PEPI: You think that it's going to get worse before it gets better?

STEVIE: Hell yeah!

DION: It's gonna get worse yo!

OLAVO: The amount of people not gettin an education is getting worse.

DION: There's another friend (*names him*). I grew up with him in the east side, you know what I'm sayin, literally grew up with him. We was little kids growin up together you know. He was doin good. The only thing was that he was in a mix, you know, he was dealin drugs and all dat. They ended up killin him. I think it was jealousy yo.

STEVIE: He had a record contract.

CARLOS: That's the one who got shot in front of my house.

DION: He did talk a lot of shit yo. He used to show off a lot.

CARLOS: They got him.

DION: He used to live in the project yo.

CARLOS: He got shot right in front of my house.

DION: He got shot in his Benz yo, they shot him up.

CARLOS: That was like three o'clock in the mornin, somethin like that when I woke up to the blast.

DION: Drugs is a big problem with all this, but you cannot put a stop to the drugs that are comin into this country cause you know who's bringin the drugs in—the same people that claim they are tryin to get them out, they're the ones bringin it in.

STEVIE: The government's makin big money off of all of this.

DION: They're the ones bringin it in, all that CIA and all that shit. They're about makin money. The don't care. They only care about themselves. (*The group mentions a few local "reputable" people who have been known to be involved in drugs, including the Chief of Police who was eventually busted—"He was sniffin!"*) You know what, one of my cases got dropped in court because of that . . . because the evidence was tampered with.

OLAVO: So you don't know who's sellin drugs and who's dealin drugs in Changeton no more.

CARLOS: The way I look at it the cops are actually helpin. Like every single year there are more drug dealers, every year more and more dealers. Why, cause there's more and more crackheads. There's more people gettin into crack and other drugs so there's gonna be more dealers. If the police can't stop it, all they can do is profit from it.

DION: Every corner you got a liquor store.

STEVIE: And what do they sell, malt liquor—Saint Ives, Private Stock, OE [Old English] . . .

PAUL: You don't even need an I.D. to buy.

DION: It's true what he says. I'm not even twenty-one and I can buy, nobody gets carded.

CARLOS: I look like a little kid, but no problem.

OLAVO: Most of the liquor stores in Changeton, you just walk right in. (*The group begins to point out booze stores that sell to underage kids.*)

PEPI: Are the drugs and booze in schools? (*There is an enthusiastic group response:* "Oh yeah!" "Everywhere!" "They're all over the place!" "Shit yeah!") We were driving by the high school this morning and I said to Rhonda, "There's Changeton high." She responded, "You mean the prison . . . Changeton high the big white lie!" What is she talking about?

CARLOS: It's a joke cause that ain't no high school. The whole time I was there I got one book.

OLAVO: They dictate all the rules in the high school man.

STEVIE: It is a prison.

OLAVO: If you do something in the cafeteria, like you supposed to sit four on the table, and you sit five on the table, they'll grab you and give you three days suspension.

DION: Because you can't be sittin in a crowd like dat.

OLAVO: Like a prison man. That's why a lot of kids do stuff like that and they get suspended and then never go back to school. They changed all the rules in the high school man. I'm serious. I went there one day, there's one-ways everywhere man. You know how you walk around and there's like different marked buildings. It's all one way. You gotta go all the way around even if you just want to go straight ahead of you.

PEPI: Carlos just said a moment ago that while he was at the high school he only got one book . . .

STEVIE: Damn, teachers don't even care man, you know, teachers don't care! They juss makin their money, that's how they are. (*Among the group, there is expressed anger about the overall apathy.*)

CARLOS: They just let you hang with a paper and a pencil.

STEVIE: They care about their money man, and you always see em strikin for more and more money, but they aren't even doing shit for kids. It's obvious! Look it (*he looks around the group*), look at the drop out rate man. It's obvious! (*With a great deal of anger he shouts*) What the fuck man!!

DION: Big drop out rate yo, big drop out rate.

PEPI: Are the guidance counselors at school helpful? (*The group laughs and they hand out cigarettes to each other.*) So basically what you're saying is that you have no place to go, that you've got no one but yourself for the most part? (*There's a group* "Yup!")

STEVIE: I'm serious man. I hate that school, I hate the Changeton Public School System! Somebody oughta blow it up! They're a bunch of jerks man, I swear to god! You know what I notice Pepi, I noticed when I used to go to school, if the teachers knew you came from a nice like middle-class neighborhood, they'd treat you good. They give you special attention. But if they knew you came from the projects or somethin . . . (*Roland jumps in*).

ROLAND: If you black, the attitude is, "You dumb."

CARLOS: If you come from a bad neighborhood they make sure you never make it.

STEVIE: They think that you are a trouble maker.

DION: Automatically, automatically!

ROLAND: I was accused of a bomb scare that I didn't do. I was waiting in the principal's office for my advocate to show. I was juss sittin there waitin. After a while, I was like, I gotta go and I'm gonna go whether you say yes or no. Then she was like, "No wonder you have a funken tracker!" Well, she was like fat and ugly and everything, right, so I said, "It's no wonder you don't have a husband." She got pissed off and so I got suspended like my first week at Changeton high.

PEPI: When you say you're black and you get different treatment, what do you mean?

CARLOS: I had teachers that were so prejudice against Puerto Ricans and blacks, and I am both.

ROBERTO: I once threw a chair at a teacher who was racist against me and I made the front page—we've all made the papers.

OLAVO: They treat you different man. I had like three classes where I was the only nigga in the room. The teacher used to teach everybody in the class but me. I used to call her, "Can you explain this to me?" She used to like ignore me.

DION: You know, like explain it but not solidly. They just rush through it.

CARLOS: Because they think that we won't be able to make it anyway.

PEPI: They think that you won't be able to make it just by the way you look, they've had you before, they know something about you, or they just look at you with the attitude that you must be from the projects and come from a poor family?

DION: All of the above. Or, sometimes they read about you in the paper, you know what I'm sayin, for gettin arrested for somethin stupit. One time I got arrested for somethin stupit y'all, what was that shit, disturbin the peace I think it was. Man, half of Changeton knew dat shit. Everybody was like "Oh, you got arrested last night." Then I go to school and all the teachers are lookin at me like I murdered somebody or somethin. They make a big thang out of the littlest thangs.

PEPI: Do the teachers ever really try to talk with you and see what's up in your life—what's up in the street? (*There is a group chorus of* "No," Hell no!," "Nope.")

STEVIE: To be honest wit ya, I never had a cool teacher In my life. I grew up in Changeton and they've always been like kinda ignorant, or assholes.

DION: There was one teacher that I liked a lot (*he names him*). He'd be yellin at you yo, but he'd be teachin you no matter what you are.

PEPI: In the Changeton school system, how many of you had a black or Latino/a teacher? (*Only one person responds that they had a black teacher.*)

CARLOS: The only Latino was Mr. (*names him*).

OLAVO: I had two Cape Verdean teachers like when I first came from my country, cause I didn't know how to speak. I had a bilingual program.

PEPI: Outside of these classes, when you were in the hallway speaking Creole, did people give you shit?

OLAVO: Yeah, like students, they be like, "Why don't you speak English!" If I don't know how to say something in English, I gotta say it in Creole. If I'm talkin to my girl in Creole, you know what I'm sayin, I'm gonna talk in Creole.

PEPI: But, now that your English is strong, if you were in school, and the teacher was giving you a hard time for something, would you speak Creole—kind of a way to give shit back?

OLAVO: No, I wouldn't, and I don't think that other Creole speakers do.

CARLOS: I juss see it as, if teachers go out their way to make an ass out of you (*Dion chimes in with Carlos and together they say*), you go out of your way to make an ass outta dem.

PEPI: Do most teachers go out of their way to make an ass out of you?

STEVIE: They do, they kinda makin fun of you.

PEPI: You get in fights when you were in school?

STEVIE: I got in a lotta fights.

DION: Everybody into fights in school yo—Juss for a little walkin down the hallway and a little bump like dat.

CARLOS: Either that or you're wearin somethin that looks funny to them and they start cappin on you and you don't like that—you just gotta slammmm!

PEPI: Looking back on all this, if school were different, if it were to change so that you had a place where you could come in and express yourself and talk more about what's really happening in this community and in your lives—at least start there and then connect that to what's in the books and all the rest, would your response to education have been different? (*There is a group response of,* "Yeah.")

DION: Way different! It would be different cause you don't be hearin about reality. You don't even be hearin Afro-Americans in the history. You also don't be hearin about the Spanish. . . . They don't talk about what's goin on out there. They talkin the past. Alright, that's pass, you know what I'm sayin. Talk about now, we're in the future. Why don't you bring up the people that doin good for us now!! Those other people are dead, let dem rest in peace.

OLAVO: You gotta talk about what's going on right now.

PAUL: If you don't learn from history you're doomed to repeat it.

STEVIE: I like history, I like history man.

DION: I like history too, but they don't teach nothin. They don't teach you the real truth. Alright look, Thomas Edison, he invented the light, but who made it better? Who made the light better? A black man did yo! Did you hear about it? I read the black almanac yo, when I was in jail and there's a lotta thangs in there like who came up with all kinds of medicine. A black man came up with a lotta that shit yo! They don't teach you stuff like dat in school.

ROLAND: They tell you about the people who led the country, but they don't tell you about the people that built the country.

STEVIE: But you know what though, to sum it all up (*laughs*), no one here is an American except for the American Indians—they're the only true Americans.

DION: This is their land yo!

STEVIE: They had it took from em.

DION: Our so-called Americans took it from dem and now look at em—they ain't got no where to live.

ROLAND: They come over here for religion and freedom to do this and that right, but the people outside of them wanna do somethin different and they kill them or they just shut em off.

ROLAND: They just took it from em, took everythin and killed em off. It's a "I want what you got!" mentality. Kids on the streets do that nowadays and they are locked up and not celebrated—not that they should be. This whole country is a contradiction of itself.

PEPI: Most all of you have kids now, what are you going to tell your kids? What's your advice to any kid?

STEVIE: I wanna tell em to stay in school man, no matter how bad it is, juss do it, juss stay in school!

DION: Get through yo!

Challenging This Pedagogy of Entrapment

As vividly depicted throughout this dialogue, culture is not simply about food and fun, but rather, its production, distribution, and consumption is implicated in unequal and abusive relations of power that have produced and reproduced (via social policies, institutional practices and structures, and media efforts to manipulate the public) epidemic levels of unemployment and poverty, crime, police brutality, home and community disintegration, illiteracy, drug addiction, and public callousness. As Chomsky points out, the obvious effects of such sociohistorical conditions are "you get violence against children and violence by children."[15] And yet, despite all the national attention on violence and youth, and a growing body of literature in the social sciences documenting the unmet needs of so many young people in the United States, it is amazing how few links are made in the mainstream national and local debates in this country, between government, socially sanctioned, and educational policies and practices that have historically hurt children and their families, and the increasing violence involving kids.

Instead of blaming youth for the world that they are caught up in, but that they did not create, educators and other cultural workers desperately need to forge critical partnerships with them in order to analyze and confront the oppressive conditions and social formations that have inevitably manufactured and imposed a history of despair. Not only do students, like those in Changeton, readily express an interest in their own lives and what they are deeply connected to, but they also generate a great interest in education and the state of society if allowed to connect in substantive and politically influential ways to the very world around them.[16] When given the opportunity to speak, the youth in Changeton were more than willing and able to analyze whiteness, discrimination, institutional violence, and the commodification of culture and identity. They were also able to come up with solutions to problems in schools and the larger society.

The implication is not that what kids have to say should be taken at face value, but that educators romanticize their contributions and immediately implement their suggestions. Within a truly participatory democracy, a committed sign of respect and inclusion is that all voices be recognized, heard, and critically engaged for their theoretical insights and weaknesses, rather than simply affirmed. As Paulo Freire insists, "As active participants and real subjects, we can make history only when we are continually critical of our very lives."[17] This type of critical pedagogy demands a great deal of self-reflection about the ways in which subjectivities, desires, and actions are mobilized through social interaction and established systems of meaning and value.

What is being suggested here should not be misconstrued as an attempt to act as an apologist for the often-violent crimes that young people of all backgrounds do commit. Even the youth from Changeton held themselves (among others) accountable for their mistakes. Ways to appropriately deal with the immediacy of an actual crime—a thirteen-year-old that shoots someone—is to say the least an important topic for discussion; however, the point being emphasized here is that there is a serious need to look at and preemptively eliminate the ever-increasing macro conditions within which dehumanization and its consequential micro-violence are so prevalent. Addressing the commodification of identities within the logic of capital and popular culture, Chomsky, talking about an eleven-year-old who kills another child for a pair of sneakers (to the disbelief of the general population), states:

> Why not? We're telling this eleven-year-old through television, "You're not a real man unless you wear the sneakers that some basketball hero wears." And you also look around and see who gets ahead—the guys who play by the rules of "get for yourself as much as you can"—so, here's the easy way to do it. Kids notice everybody else is robbing too, including the guys in the rich penthouses, so why shouldn't they.[18]

The society as a whole needs to call into question the larger social formations and policies, which includes public schools, that have produced a culture of survival, materialism, and deviance—that "environment" that Stevie in the above dialogue talks about that needs to be changed.

Educators also need to develop the ability to differentiate pathology from acts of resistance, which are responses (though not always conscious) to domination—such as throwing chairs, evading the police, and developing reputations in order to survive by fear. Resistance is used to help individuals or groups deal with oppressive social conditions and injustice and needs to be rerouted so that it is connected to positive political projects of change.

In addition, from a more sociohistorical approach to understanding identity and human suffering, teachers can rupture and move beyond the inherently racist models that equate crime with the culture of particular racial groups—collective experiences abstracted from a history of antagonistic intergroup relations and abuses of power. They can also move beyond, without completely dismissing, psychological models that simply individualize and pathologize human behavior. Educators should be encouraged to work to understand and engage how the cognitive and psychological makeup of each person is a product of history and politics, and thus intimately affected by such oppressive ideologies as capitalism, racism, sexism, and heterosexism. As Bonny Norton Pierce argues, "We need a theory of social identity that integrates the learner and the learning context, and how relations of power in the social world affect social interaction between learners and teachers and among peers."[19]

It is only from a more inclusive, historically situated, and critical public debate that educators can better understand the complex roots of inequality and violence in this country, and thus better inform themselves of the current sociocultural context in which students live, as well as the tools they will need to become aware, active, and responsible citizens, and critical agents of change.

Perpetuating the myth of meritocracy, and promising to level the academic and employment playing fields with educational standards, conservatives have yet to clarify how their militaristic approach to public education, and privatization of public space, will address the material and symbolic violence and social turmoil revealed in this chapter. In fact, with the horrific outcomes of the Changeton State Comprehensive Assessment System (used in public schools)—in which, across the state, racially subordinated, linguistic-minority, and poor children overwhelmingly failed—the future of public education in the city is bleak. High school students who do not pass will not be allowed to graduate—they will instead be awarded a "certificate of attendance." In its first year of implementation, 42 percent of the grade-ten students in Changeton failed the English language arts section, 76 percent failed the math, and 58 percent failed in science and technology. With utter callousness, blaming the victims for their own victimization, one local teacher responded to these results by insisting that "The local gene pool in Changeton should be condemned!"

If educators truly wish to counter such an oppressive stance and become self-reflective agents of change, history must be embraced and engaged as a dialogue among multiple and contradicting voices, as they struggle within asymmetrical relations of power. Educators should work to not only include students in the developmental process of curricula in schools, but to help mobilize them into an organized political body (critical communities of struggle) so that they are able to voice their concerns and realize their own goals. This liberatory possibility is a far cry from the racist, classist, and hegemonic logic of those draconian policy makers and practitioners that engineer public schools into holding tanks that abuse and force young people into a life of survival in the streets, where they are quickly gobbled up by the insatiable and burgeoning prison industrial complex.

Notes

1. Loic Wacquant, "Deadly Symbiosis: Rethinking Race and Imprisonment in Twenty-first-century America," *Boston Review: A Political and Literary Forum* 27, no. 2 (April–May, 2002): 23.
2. See Margaret A. Bortner and Linda M. Williams, *Youth in Prison: We the People of Unit Four* (New York: Routledge, 1997); David Cole, *No Equal Justice: Race and Class in the American Criminal Justice System* (New York: New Press 2000); Angela Davis, *The Prison Industrial Complex* (Oakland, Calif.: AK Press, 2000); Joel Dyer, *The Perpetual Prisoner Machine: How America Profits from Crime* (Boulder, Colo.: Westview, 2001); Joy James, ed., *States of Confinement: Policing, Detention, and Prisons* (New York: Palgrave Macmillan, 2002).
3. Wacquant, "Deadly Symbiosis," 23.
4. It's important to note that as of 1998, 1.2 million prisoners were convicted of nonviolent crimes. In addition with the spreading of the three strikes law, people are going to jail for life for stealing golf clubs, food, etc. Mandatory minimums are also feeding this rapidly expanding industry. It is also crucial to acknowledge that in this rush to lock people up, about one-quarter of those people in prison in the United States are confined in local jails and state and federal prisons on drug charges. In federal prisons, drug offenders now comprise 59 percent of all inmates. In nine states, over 10 percent of the inmates were indicted on marijuana offenses, and over 50 percent of those convicted were on charges of possession. Very few of these prisoners are high-level drug traffickers. In 2000, according to the Office of National Drug Control Policy, "about two-thirds of the federal drug budget is allocated to interdiction, law enforcement and supply reduction efforts. One-third is allocated to prevention, treatment and demand reduction" (for all of the above statistics, see www.hrw.org/reports/2000/usa/Rcedrg00–03.htm).
5. Also see www.angelfire.com/rnb/y/majority.htm
6. Henry A. Giroux, *Stealing Innocence: Youth, Corporate Power, and the Politics of Culture* (New York: St. Martins Press, 2001), 85.
7. National Center for Children in Poverty (1999). Available at: cpmenet.columbia.edu/dept/nccp/cps99pr.html.
8. Chuck Collins, Chris Hartman, and Holly Sklar, "Divided Decade: Economic Disparity at the Century's Turn," *United for a Fair Economy* (December 15, 1999), Available at: www.ufenet.org/press/archive/1999/Divided_Decade/divided_decade.html last accessed August 25th, 2002.
9. Kenneth Saltman, *Collateral Damage: Corporatizing Public Schools—A Threat to Democracy* (Boulder, Colo.: Rowman & Littlefield, 2000), 86.
10. See Michael Apple, *Educating the "Right" Way: Markets, Standards, God, and Inequality* (New York: Routledge, 2001); Samuel Bowles and Herbert Gintis, *Schooling in Capitalist America: Educational Reform and the Contradictions of Economic Life* (New York: Basic Books, 1976); and Henry A. Giroux, *Stealing Innocence: Youth, Corporate Power, and the Politics of Culture* (New York: St. Martin's Press, 2001).
11. Noam Chomsky, Pepi Leistyna, and Stephen A. Sherblom, "Demystifying Democracy: A Dialogue with Noam Chomsky," in *Presence of Mind: Education and the Politics of Deception*, edited by Pepi Leistyna (Boulder, Colo.: Westview Press, 1999), 117.
12. The dialogue is a shorter version of the original.
13. All teacher interviews were part of the larger eight-year study that I conducted in Changeton. For detail on this study, see P. Leistyna. *Defining and Designing Multiculturalism: One School System's Efforts* (New York: SUNY Press, 2000).
14. Paulo Freire and Donaldo Macedo, *Literacy: Reading the Word and the World* (Westport, Conn.: Bergin and Garvey, 1987), 20.
15. Chomsky, Leistyna, and Sherblom, "Demystifying Democracy," 110.
16. Louise Cooper, "Youth Activists Fight Prop 21," *Against the Current* 86 XV, no. 2

(May–June, 2000); Elizabeth Martinez, "The New Youth Movement in California," *Z Magazine* (May 2000); and Jay MacLeod, "Bridging School and Street," *Journal of Negro Education* (1991).

17. Paulo Freire, *The Politics of Education: Culture, Power, and Liberation* (New York: Bergin and Garvey 1985), 199.

18. Chomsky, Leistyna, and Sherblom, "Demystifying Democracy," 112.

19. Bonny Norton-Pierce, "Social Identity, Investment, and Language Learning," *TESOL Quarterly*, 29, no. 1, (Spring 1993): 7.

INTRODUCTION TO CHAPTER 6

Enora Brown compares a discipline-oriented school of largely nonwhite working-class students with a nearby school of professional-class, predominantly white students to illuminate the ways that employment possibilities in the economy are very much tied to class and racial inequalities that are reproduced through public schooling. Building on the work of such reproduction theorists of schooling as Bourdieu, Althusser, Oakes, and others, this analysis considers how such economic changes as postindustrialism and automation, and political changes, such as domestic militarism are related to the demands for privatization and particular kinds of schooling for different segments of the population. The chapter is distinctive to this volume for its comparative approach, close attention to the relations between the structural demands of the economy and state and the imperatives of public schooling, and its focus on both class and racial privilege as well as subjugation, and the rise of automation as key elements of a sufficient analysis of education as enforcement.

CHAPTER 6

Freedom for Some, Discipline for "Others"

The Structure of Inequity in Education

ENORA R. BROWN

Lockdown is becoming the pervasive reality for working-class youth in public schools that resemble prisons or military camps rather than sites for learning and critical thought. In these schools, replete with metal detectors, armed guards, and periodic searches, poor youth, especially African American and other youth of color, are being subjected to increasing levels of physical and psychological surveillance, confinement, and regimentation. The physical restrictions imposed within the school walls are complemented by national policies and practices in education, such as school uniforms, more stringent, standardized forms of rote education, and JROTC, which signify the need for discipline, obedience, and conformity. This growing *culture of militarism* is being created/cultivated predominantly within grossly underfunded, tax-based schools of color in poor communities. Since youth identities in these communities are discursively constructed as under-achieving, violent-prone, education-aversive youth (i.e., the dregs of society, who are in need of discipline and restraint), the imposition and presence of enforcement policies to "civilize their untamed spirits" seems merited and natural.

Conversely, public schools for wealthy youth resemble *palatial edifices*, adorned with all of the resources that constitute sites for learning, critical inquiry, and fluid social interchange. These schools are located on spacious grounds and are equipped with state-of-the-art facilities in comfortable, resource-rich environs that encourage the freedom of mobility and thought to discover, problem-solve, and create. The physical breadth and expanse of these public schools for predominantly wealthy white youth are complemented by national policies, such as the privatization of public education, the standards movement (e.g., major overhaul of the Scholastic Aptitude Tests [SAT's]), and advanced math/science/technology curricula that signify inherited privilege and institutionalized entitlement and promote independent thought, analysis, and creativity. This *culture of privilege* is expanding within

Enora R. Brown is Associate Professor of Social and Cultural Foundations in Education at DePaul University. She has published articles on racial and class dimensions of human development in sociohistorical context. Her research in critical psychology includes discursive analyses of children's negotiations of power and educators' identity construction processes. Her academic work grows out of her long history of social service and activism.

schools that are brimming over with tax-based funds and supplemental resources from wealthy resident families. Since youth identities in these communities are discursively constructed as smart achievers and as the thoughtful professionals and cultured leaders of the future, the plentiful resources and relaxed, but rigorous learning environments seem to be the natural outgrowth of their self-directed, responsible, inquisitive, and creative spirits.

Polarized along social class and racial lines, public schools in poor, working-class and wealthy upper-class communities are *public* places whose fusion of space and experience are imbued with differential meanings[1] about the freedoms to which wealthy or poor youth are "entitled" and the consequent breadth of future life options that are available to them. These places constitute the physical space where particular social, economic, political, and psychic relationships are forged, nurtured, and contested. Public schools are sources of identity, constituted within webs of power relations that frame the choices and aspirations of youth. While the dominant discourse portrays these schools as the "natural" product of the values, capacities, and rights of residents in each community, it will be argued here that these schools are structurally embedded in, and historically constituted through, dynamic postindustrial, global economic, and political relationships. As such, the edifices *stand for/represent* a polarized and interdependent relationship between the upper class and the working class, the relative valuation of these classes in the dominant culture, and the "rightful" inherited identity positions of their youth in the existing social order. Shrouded in an ideology of individual choice, social Darwinism, and national unity, these schools reflect the intersubjective meanings created through the differential ways in which people live their lives in disparate communities.

This chapter will examine the differences between two public schools— Mountainview Township and Groundview Technical High Schools—as they manifest historical institutional inequities in the public education system, which are exacerbated and codified by current national policies (i.e., *corporate privatization and domestic militarization of schools*) and are reified and justified by current ideological formulations about the "nature" or essentialized identities of the youth in these different contexts. First, comparative portraits will be presented of the current *financial and material resources* available, the *curricular and pedagogical experiences* provided, and the *social relationships* fostered within the divergent school cultures. The significance of the observed differences and the dynamic interplay of these dimensions of the educational experience within each school will be discussed as they "validate" the meritocratic justification for inequity in education, and as they influence the futures that youth envision, the paths they "choose," and the stations in life that are readily available.

Second, the historic roots of these school differences will be examined through an analysis of the political struggles for public education for the exslaves that accompanied the ascendance of industrialization after the Civil War.[2] This analysis is based on the overarching premise that the disparate quality of education in wealthy–poor racialized schools is organically linked to the economy. It will provide insight into the structural reproduction and function of social class and racial inequities in education.[3] Further, this chapter will discuss the significance of *current economic crises*,[4] including the seismic shift that a burgeoning information technology and robotics are introducing into the national economy,[5] along with the wholesale movement of industrial capital to cheaper global markets,[6] and the *corresponding political repression* exercised through legislative and judicial policies and practices.[7] These developments in economic and political life have ushered in corresponding efforts to privatize public education and militarize schools in poor communities to support corporations' perennial search for new markets for profit and to thwart the inevitable resistance and rebellion of those displaced within a postindustrial economy. This analysis will posit the view that the introduction of robotics and gradual emergence of laborless production is creating a dramatic shift in the national/global economy that *requires* drastic changes in the state apparatus,[8] especially in public education, in order to support changes in the existing social order.

It is in this context that the dominant culture's ideological tools have intensified to justify the intensifying polarization of wealth, to scapegoat racial, and ethnic sectors of the population as sources of worsening economic and social conditions, and to redefine democracy as "individual, private choice," a first step in restructuring public education. This chapter will conclude by addressing the crucial role of critical pedagogy in educators' work to promote analytic understandings of the dynamics that undergird social inequity in education in order to guide our thinking and human agency in fostering social change.

Mountainview: Freedom to Become

Bourdieu posits that institutions' monopolized appropriation of and methodical failure to transfer cultural capital and other instruments necessary for success in the dominant culture will instantiate their exclusive ownership and that of the culture as a whole in hands of the ruling class.[9] Concordantly, Spears states that the rigorous quality of education at elite institutions prepares those students for their inherited leadership roles in society with concordant ideological underpinnings, and that the absence of comparable educational experiences for students at nonelite institutions mitigates against creativity and poor students' ideological investment in a critical examination of oppression that would challenge the existing social order and their position within it.[10] Mountainview Township High School exemplifies wealthy schools within an educational system that systematically transmits the instruments of appropriation to local affluent students, who are being prepared to inherit and fulfill leadership positions in the dominant culture.

The sprawling public high school campus of Mountainview Township High School is located in an affluent Chicago suburb. It is blanketed with a lush landscaped lawn that is adorned with winding tree-lined paths that lead to seven strategically placed, spacious, modern glass and stone buildings. The picturesque, well-maintained campus has a large track field and other sport-specific courts and athletic fields. It has an adjoining faculty-student parking lot that is within walking distance of the shopping district, replete with quaint shops, restaurants, and businesses. Mountainview is nestled near a commercial thoroughfare that connects local shoreline communities whose $500,000 to $1,000,000–plus homes are comfortably adjoined by wooded areas and jogging paths. This school campus is the site for the academic, cultural, athletic, social, and civic pursuits of over three thousand ninth-through twelfth-grade students in the adjacent wealthy communities.

Upon entering Mountainview High School, one is struck by the expansive marble hallways, lined with windowseats beneath large windows that over-look the campus grounds and allow natural light to bathe the art-lined hall-ways. Students, casually dressed in nondescript jeans and designer clothes, freely and comfortably walk through the hall, and perch on window ledges to read or engage in conversation with friends. Running slightly late for class, students are gently encouraged by staff to "Hurry along." They are unbur-dened by the threat of a detention slip and classroom doors are left ajar for their late arrival. Individual administrative offices are spacious, well-furnished, inviting spaces that support the ongoing work of the school and comfortably accommodate visitors. Classrooms are awash with natural light and equipped with advanced technology and audiovisual equipment. Plen-tiful seating is available for students and teachers to engage in flexibly arranged discussions and a myriad of learning experiences to a background of quiet music. What a conducive environment for learning, thinking, and creating with others. On this open campus, students freely eat and drink in class and go home for lunch.

The various wings of each building reflect the range of academic and cocurricular experiences from which students may design "majors" and interdisciplinary courses of study. In addition to the wing devoted exclu-sively to fine arts, other academic spaces include: state-of-the-art computers, science, technology, and language labs, a theater and performing arts depart-ment, student-run radio and cable television stations, music facilities, news bureau, multiple gymnasiums, swimming pool and accessories, dance studio, Nautilus exercise room and equipment, an expansive library housing thou-sands of volumes, a cuisine-plentiful lunchroom, a student lounge, and an art gallery. National and international trips provide rich off-site learning expe-riences for student interests in marine biology, geology, and family support for social/intellectual inquiry.

Mountainview resembles a small liberal arts college with over three hundred multilevel, discipline-based academic courses, including advanced placement, from which students fashion their schedules. Courses include: mathematics, speech and drama, modern/classical languages, technology education, business education, social work, social studies, music, science, multicultural studies, gourmet cooking, interior and graphic design. Soccer, lacrosse, polo, fencing, and field hockey are a few of the sports that comple-ment the usual array of athletic endeavors. In addition, there are over one hundred clubs and interest groups, from bridge to rugby and global exchange, from social service and AIDS coalition, to poetry, and cheerlead-ing. The range of academic and cocurricular experiences, along with a coun-selor for every twenty-two students undergirds the vision and actuality of a 95 percent college-bound student population.

Who inhabits this space called Mountainview? Almost 88 percent of the students are European American, about 9 percent are Asian American, less than 2 percent are Latino American, and less than 1 percent are African American. Almost 97 percent of the students graduate and less than 1 percent are from low-income families. About 93 percent of the teachers are European American, less than 3 percent Asian American, about 2 percent Latino, and approximately 1 percent African American. Eighty percent of the teachers have masters degrees and salaries average over $75,000. On the basis of local property taxes, over $15,000 is provided for each student.[11] For the youth in this community, Mountainview is *their space*, and hence *their place*. It is where *they* belong. The *socialized* choices, options, and freedoms that they experience and create in *their* school and community transmit and foster the creation of cultural capital that will prepare these youth to be the future CEOs, facile owners, and manipulators of emergent information technology, architects of public policy, and nimble consumers and promoters of "high culture." These youth expect material wealth from the profits of today and will step into *their* place, their future, in the world.

Groundview High: Discipline to Constrict

> The action of the school, whose effect is unequal among children from different classes, and whose success varies considerably among those upon whom it has an effect, tends to reinforce and to consecrate by its sanctions the initial inequalities.[12]

Educational institutions play a pivotal role in forging *aspirations* and structuring *choice* for youth through the daily actions and practices in schools that sanction and codify existent social and economic inequities. Groundview Technical High School exemplifies schools within an educational system that instantiates limited options for and validates the constricted vision of youth in this poor community. The aspirations of youth, both wealthy and poor, reflect their "internalization of objective probabilities" and inform their life choices (i.e., material expressions of their efforts to reach what is attainable).[13] Their "choices" are not those of "autonomous moral agents acting in an existential vacuum," but rather are created and exercised through the dynamic interplay of social, psychic, political, and economic forces.[14] As students at Groundview make sense of the dynamic interplay of forces evident in the school's physical environs, public school policies and practices, and their own lived experiences, they insightfully deduce the prospects for their future, for their survival.

Groundview Technical High School is located in a poor urban Chicago community twenty-five miles from Mountainview. Its grounds consist of an imposing, self-contained faded red brick four-story building, in considerable disrepair, with an adjoining, uninhabitable, concrete court. The school consumes an entire square block and is bracketed by trash-strewn patches of wilted grass and a variegated concrete sidewalk in a working-class community. The smokestack structure is barely distinguishable from the worn vacant public housing buildings that stand nearby, and blends in with the rugged deteriorating landscape and the ceaseless traffic and fumes of the adjoining busy intersections. This eighty-five-year-old building is the site for close to three thousand ninth- through twelfth-grade students in the surrounding crowded urban community. Like other neighborhoods on "this side of town," this community was intentionally cut off from the nearby commercial and residential areas by the strategic positioning of a racial barrier—one of the nation's largest interstate highways.

One is welcomed into the physical structure of Groundview in a manner quite different from that of Mountainview. Upon entering the heavy steel doors of the school's main entrance, one is immediately greeted by two armed policemen and metal detectors, whose presence is as imposing as the red brick, crumbling structure of the school. This reception typically generates considerable tension and wariness and does *not* have the "ring of freedom." Students clad in black and white uniforms are herded/filed into the school with their picture IDs and class schedule, and must pass through the metal detectors to ensure that there are no weapons on school grounds. Students must wear their IDs and class schedules around their necks throughout the day, so that they may be policed/monitored upon entry into the lunchroom and other school checkpoints. The drably painted, relatively bare walls lead down dimly lit, dingy hallways, whose overhead buzzing fluorescent lighting is compromised by some boarded-up windows and noticeable fixtures in disrepair. The deteriorating physical structure reveals the lack of attention and funds devoted to the condition of the school and its inhabitants.

Students are exhorted by guards not to linger in the hallways or exceed the four minutes allotted for them to move between classes. After the bell has rung, students are not permitted in the hallways without a written excuse, and tardiness is punishable by detention. The halls are for swift transitions to and from class or other destinations. Tarrying is not allowed. This social practice is enforced by the presence of guards in all of the corridors and by the absence of any space for students to comfortably congregate, to have a leisurely chat with friends, or to sit and read a book. The one place where students may congregate is in the lunchroom. The "closed campus policy" at Groundview prohibits students from leaving the school for lunch once they have entered in the morning. The policy is reinforced by the presence of metal detectors at all entrances and exits throughout the building and the pending threat of suspension if students fail to comply. Rules are made and strictly enforced, with the expectation that students will follow them to avoid sanction. After passing through this checkpoint, one arrives at the administrative office, a room of ample size with cramped, limited space for staff. Visitors who come to the school stand at a counter, sign in, and receive pleasant assistance from staff behind their desks. The classrooms and connecting corridors built for 2,500 students barely accommodate the 3,000 students enrolled.

There are no well-equipped academic spaces for students' interests or choice in various disciplines of study (e.g., the humanities or social sciences). There is a metal shop, a wood shop, and cosmetology room to prepare students for particular skilled trades. There is a locked room full of wood-shop and carpentry equipment in the school, but it is inaccessible to students, since staff members are not available to operate the equipment. There is one gymnasium and one computer in the sparcely-volumed library, which is often locked, as are student bathrooms. There is no theater, music area, pool, or exercise equipment, no science equipment and few books to share during class. The State of Illinois's required courses are available in the areas of English, history, mathematics, some sciences, and a few courses for elective credits to fulfill graduation requirements. The absence of current texts, equipment, or operative library for students' learning is synchronous with their "skilled" preparation for work, if any, in marginal service industries.

In the classrooms, students are seated at old desks and in some classes, as many as twenty-five students are crammed around four small tables. Few classes are fueled with engaging conversation between students and teacher. Most students are "busied" to the point of obvious boredom with ditto sheets or scripted lessons for recall and rote comprehension and are often engaged by teachers with directives and discordant communications. Frustration, disdain, contempt, and helplessness are apparent. Over two hundred students are assigned to a school counselor and few students are college-bound.

In contrast to Mountainview's fine arts wing or technology lab, Ground-view in recent years has created a separate and distinct wing that is devoted to the Junior Reserve Office Training Corp (JROTC). It is a privileged space, inhabitable only by those who are enrolled, and is increasingly becoming a major component of the school's emergent curriculum and character as a site of military discipline. The JROTC hallways are adorned with military memorabilia, pictures of generals, scenes from past wars, and traditional patriotic images and symbols. This wing is equipped with many up-to-date computers and ample space for students to study. Students are allowed to move freely from place to place and to make choices about courses of study. Imbued with hopes for further education, these youth are being prepared to enter the disciplined ranks of the armed forces and to serve on the front lines of this nation's international skirmishes.

Who inhabits this space called Groundview? One hundred percent of the students are African American, over 93 percent are from low-income fami-lies, and less than 50 percent of the students graduate from high school. Forty-five percent of the teachers are European American, 40 percent African American, 11 percent Latino, 2 percent Asian American, and almost 3 percent Native American. Forty-five percent of the teachers have masters degrees and salaries average $50,000, one-half and one-third less that those at Mountainview, respectively. Students at Groundview receive half of the financial investment per student that students at Mountainview receive. On the basis of the property taxes in this community, $7,800 is spent on each student to ensure his or her place and space in the social order and the contin-uation of a well-oiled tracking system of inequity.[15]

For the youth in this part of the city, one gets the sense that they are *contained, confined, restricted,* and *monitored* in a space that *does not* feel like *their place*. There is no sense of ownership. It is where they are, but not where they belong. The paltry curriculum, physical restrictions, closed options, structure, discipline, control, and order, imposed "for their own good"[16] in prison-like schools, are preparing them for a place, at the lowest rung of the job market, in jail, or in chronic/permanent unemployment.

Curricular Preparation for the Future: Business or Military?

The differences between the two Chicago area high schools are stark. The disparate financial and material resources, curricular and pedagogical experiences, and physical and social environs create different cultures or webs of meaning that are constitutive of particular social identity positions in society. Of particular interest are the *new* curricular offerings at each school. The burgeoning JROTC, vocational curricula at Groundview and expansive college- and business-prep, academic curricula at Mountainview are indicative of the social identities that are being forged for these youth and the proscribed future positions as adults in society for which they are being prepared.

 · At Mountainview, the extensive new programs of study are in electronics, robotics, digital and laser technology, computer science and programming, globalization, culture and Eastern languages. These cutting-edge areas of inquiry complement long-standing curricula in business (e.g., the economy, stockmarket, politics), engineering, interdisciplinary studies, advanced math, and science, and are burgeoning disciplines that will thrive on the knowledge constructed in the twenty-first century. These programs of study will support the profound and rapid economic shift from industrialization to robotics and electronic/information technology in a global market,[17] reinforce the digital divide, and secure the social class position of these students as they are prepared for leadership in business and the political, economic, and cultural centers worldwide. The school provides the opportunity for these students to produce and appreciate various forms of popular culture (e.g., videos, film, literature, music, drama), and to study the cultural meanings that are being negotiated around the globe. Armed with "technical knowledge" and cultural understanding, students at this elite public institution are being socialized to be arbiters of corporate capital. Their cultural capital will "confirm . . . their monopoly of the instruments of appropriation of the dominant culture and thus their monopoly of the culture."[18] Students at Mountainview have the most to gain from the continuation of the current social order.

JROTC is the "privileged" field of study at Groundview. Military enlistment is being marketed heavily in poor communities, especially those of color. Under the guise of enhancing students' educational opportunities, JROTC promises a less than glorious, uplifting future for these youth. JROTC takes $50,000 per year from each school budget, substitutes some important academic subjects for JROTC courses, and may hire teachers that are not certified in the subjects they teach.[19] With current efforts to privatize public education, the corporatization of the educational curriculum (i.e., courses of study tailored to corporate interests and profit) is being realized.[20] While JROTC is promoted as a program that will afford poor youth a career, a "way out," the Veterans Administration reports that veterans earn less than non-veterans, and that one-third are homeless and 20 percent are in prison.[21] Though 54 percent of the nation's JROTC participants and 50 percent of the front line troops of the military are people of color, few are likely to receive technical training and are thus more likely to be unemployed when they get out.[22] So much for the army motto: "Be all that you can be."

The proliferation of JROTC programs and the presence of military schools in Chicago reflects the current surge of militarism in poor communities, especially those that are African American and Latino. Students at Groundview and other working-class communities are being channeled into the military to protect the global interests of corporate capital and the future CEOs from Mountainview. As former Secretary of Defense Dick Cheney stated, "The reason to have a military is to be prepared to fight and win wars. That is our basic fundamental mission. The military is not a social welfare agency. It's not a job program."[23] Retired Rear General Eugene J. Carroll, deputy director of the Center for Defense Information states, "It is appalling that the Pentagon is selling a military training program as a remedy for intractable social and economic problems in inner cities. Surely, its real motive is to inculcate a positive attitude toward military service at a very early age, thus creating a storehouse of potential recruits."[24]

The nationwide declination of troop strength and pending war over oil in the Middle East has prompted massive efforts to recruit from certain communities. The armed forces have added $1.5 million to their $95 million advertising budget to recruit youth enlistees. Though humor-laced advertisements for students and parents encourage youth to stay in school so that they may enter the army,[25] youth from the nation's Groundviews are not responding to this call to the military as enthusiastically as anticipated. To mask the marginal success of recruitment efforts, New York State's Army National Guard's systematically inflated troop strength figures in the 1990s.[26] For the first time since the Vietnam War, the Pentagon has extended active duty for 15,000 reserve troops from twelve months to two years, jeopardizing enlistees' salaries and employment stability.[27]

The marketing of JROTC programs in poor African American and Latino communities comes at a time when major changes in the nationally administered, standardized Scholastic Aptitude Test are under way. By 2005, the SATs will be overhauled to include a writing exam, grammar questions, a critical reading exam in history, the humanities, science, and so forth, and an extended math exam based on advanced math covered in three years of high school. Ostensibly, these changes will better align exams with the 97 percent of college-bound students that take higher-level math.[28] They will also structurally exclude Groundview students, whose school is on probation, provides scripted instruction, and has a graduation rate below 50 percent, and will fuel the adage: "College isn't for everyone." The SAT overhaul and an addition of $8–12 to the $26 registration fee will affect school curricula and systemically constrict the already narrow band of high school students who will be able to afford or be adequately prepared to take the SAT exam or attend college.[29]

There is little question about which students are being tracked to become CEOs in business and which are being tracked to *serve and protect* corporate capital's interests in the military. The systematic implementation of such grossly unequal new programs of study adds new meaning to the idea of "choice" and reveals the powerful role of schools in reproducing and normalizing existent social class inequities. The divergent qualities of "freedom" and "constraint" at the two schools reflect interdependent, carefully maintained socialization processes necessary for students' future positions in society.[30] While dominant culture ideology champions the aspirations and accomplishments of youth as products of individual will, family values, and personal vision, it masks the powerful role of social, economic, and political forces in codifying and justifying the hierarchical positions occupied by youth across social class and racial lines.

While some from Groundview may "make it" in spite of the odds and are to be lauded for overcoming the obstacles, this portrait does not lend itself to a celebration of resilience and does not discount the many heroic and subtle forms of resistance exercised by marginalized youth to create new possibilities. Neither do these portraits suggest that social and economic relationships are unidirectional, deterministically creating mindless drones that blindly assume their stations in life. Rather, these portraits were designed to unequivocally render visible the pervasive, *evolving* structure of inequity, privilege, and discrimination in education that has unjustly benefited/ damaged youth and to critique an educational system that prohibits success for the many and enables success for very few.

The disparities between Mountainview and Groundview are not new to public education, but may be traced back to the mid-nineteenth century. In 1857, African American leaders fought against the gross difference between the $16 spent on each white student in schools, which were "splendid, almost palatial edifices, with manifold comforts, conveniences, and elegancies," and the lone penny spent on African American students, whose school buildings were "dark and cheerless" in "environs full of vice and filth."[31] Similarly, Kozol's poignant accounts in 1991 document the funding-based *structural continuity of inequity* in education for white, wealthy youth and working-class youth of color.[32] Race and class disparities in public education historically have been linked to the oppression of the working poor and the economic interests of industrial and corporate capital. As the driving needs of the capital have changed and economic relations have shifted with technological innovation, there have been related changes in the state apparatus and political infrastructure that are manifested in public education. The following sections will examine some continuities and discontinuities in the fundamental relationship between major shifts in the economic social order and relations of production (i.e., rise of the industrial economy and the information-driven economy), that have been accompanied by repressive political measures and have ushered in requisite changes in public education.

Historical Roots and Significance of the Difference

The current inequities and related injustices in public education are deeply rooted in the sociohistorical, economic, and political structures of this country and serve an indispensable social function in maintaining and perpetuating the social order. *Industrialization created an economic necessity for universal public education*, which in turn, has been both an instrument of oppression and the maintenance of a two-tiered system in this country and a tool of liberation for democracy. In *The Education of Blacks in the South, 1860–1935*, Anderson examines the inextricable link between late nineteenth- and early twentieth-century industrialization and mass schooling as a "means to produce efficient and contented labor and as a socialization process to instill in black and white children an acceptance of the southern racial hierarchy"[33] and the pivotal role of racial division in maintaining the burgeoning Northern industrial capitalists' control over white striking workers. For wealthy whites, universal public education would promote social stability, production efficiency, and economic prosperity.

Ex-slaves were the first native Southerners to struggle for universal, state-supported public education in the *classical liberal tradition*, in defense of emancipation and against the planters' regime.[34] However, "white architects of black education," a contingent of Northern and Southern white entrepreneurs, social scientists, and philanthropists, crafted a special form of *industrial education* for blacks to substitute older, cruder methods of socialization, coercion, and control and to support the demand for an efficient, organized agricultural sector to supplement the emergent industrial nation's trade with England.[35] The "architects" advocacy and financial support for an industrial education for blacks and classical liberal education for whites afforded marginal material and psychological privilege to white workers (i.e., racial privilege would compensate for their social class disadvantage). This stratified public education would address the educational and ideological needs of a growing industrial society, while subjugating black and white laborers in relation to the owners of wealth. William Baldwin, Northern philanthropist and universal public education advocate, states:

> The potential economic value of the Negro population properly educated is infinite and incalculable. . . . Time has proven that he is best fitted to perform the heavy labor. . . . This will permit the southern white laborer to perform the more expert labor, and to leave the fields, the mines, and the simpler trades for the Negro.[36]

> The union of white labor, well organized, will raise the wages beyond a reasonable point, and then the battle will be fought, and the Negro will be put in at a less wage, and the labor union will either have to come down in wages, or Negro labor will be employed.[37]

> Except in the rarest of instances, I am bitterly opposed to the so-called higher education of Negroes.[38]

Baldwin's and other advocates' financial support for public education was contingent on a brand of industrial education for blacks (i.e., Hampton-Tuskegee Idea), that was not equivalent to higher education for whites, and would divide the working poor in the interests of the burgeoning industrial capitalists.[39] These conditions informed the structure, social practices, and justificatory ideology of emergent separate, unequal education, and reflect Bourdieu and Passeron's analysis that the "neutral" face of public education, as social equalizer, conceals its dynamic contribution to the reproduction of class structure, with its attendant privileges and relations of power.[40] W. E. B. DuBois, noted African American scholar and advocate, understood both the emancipatory possibilities of public education and enslaving function of race-class stratified education. Thus, he vigorously opposed the limited goal of industrial or classical education and argued for higher education that would promote blacks' strident moves toward equality and not compromise the working poor.[41]

While support for universal public education was integral to the ongoing struggle for democracy, the architects' economic motives were neither noble nor altruistic, and dovetailed with those of Southern white planters who opposed public education. Though the opponents relied on "illiterate, exploited agricultural laborers" and feared that education would fuel workers' economic and political aspirations, both agreed on black disfranchisement, segregation, and economic subordination.[42] During reconstruction, the architects "ignored" opponents' funding of widespread vigilante violence by the Ku Klux Klan and other terrorist groups to force freedmen and freedwomen back to slave status, to secure a wedge between them and poor whites, and to reestablish the rule of white slave-owning oligarchy.[43] The architects and opponents of public education strove to protect the economic interests of the wealthy through both legal and extralegal forms of coercion. In concert, the industrial education "for" and the reign of terror against blacks served to maintain the social and economic order.

This legacy of race-class inequity reveals *structural and ideological continuities* between past practices and the current relationship between Groundview Technical and Mountainview Township High Schools. First, Groundview's curricula resembles the industrial education model designed for ex-slaves, which prepares poor African American youth to take on the "simpler trades." The "higher education" is reserved for the white propertied class at Mountainview to prepare them with expertise for leadership. In addition, the bifurcated forms of public education and the divergent cultural capital afforded different race-class groupings mitigate against current fears that education will "inflate workers' economic and political aspirations." While the "nonelite" education at Groundview does not encourage poor African American youth to document or question their oppression, the transmission of power and privilege at Mountainview fosters students' investment in the existing social order. Third, the ascendant culture of militarism in poor schools of color hearkens back to the legal and extralegal forms of coercion used by the early advocates and opponents of public education, imbued with the warning, "Stay in your place." The surveillance, confinement, discipline, and systemic violence in poor schools is reminiscent of earlier efforts to deter freedmen's and freed women's resistance to forced labor and their struggle for the freedoms afforded whites.

There is continuity. What prevails is a two-tiered educational system maintained by systemic efforts to quell the stirrings of poor youth of color. While today's postindustrial economic and political configurations do not mirror those that existed during the post–Civil War days of the late nineteenth century, the fundamental disparity between the wealthy and the poor characterizes current relationships within global capitalism.[44] There is discontinuity. The ascendance of an information-based, electronics-driven postindustrial economy has ushered in a new era that is reshaping the political and educational landscape, creating more pronounced forms of structural inequity and attendant forms of repression.

The Economy and the State

The rise of industrial capitalism laid the foundation for structural inequities in universal public education. In this postindustrial era, what economic and political conditions are structuring, altering, or dismantling public education? Do current inequities in education and the cultures of militarism and privilege, in turn, serve certain economic interests? These questions flow from the premise of a fundamental, synergistic relationship between *the economy and the state*. The *base* (i.e., social relations and the tools, skills, technology that constitute the process of production to meet human needs), is both reflected in and protected, organized, and strengthened by a corresponding *superstructure* (i.e., political state apparatus or societal laws, institutions, and ideological formations).[45] While some have disavowed the validity of this structural relationship on the basis of economic determinism or the exclusion of human agency, this perspective, even in the postindustrial era, provides a lens through which complex, often contradictory processes of social life may be understood. While Engels did posit the economic necessity of societal development, he discussed the base and superstructure as a dynamic, *bidirectional*, and interdependent relationship between the economy and the state and emphasized the inherent, indispensable role of humans in shaping history.[46]

Complementarily, Althusser's treatise on the state apparatus highlights the interdependent roles of ideology and repression within the superstructure. The Repressive State Apparatus (RSA) (i.e., the government, administration, army, police, courts, and prisons) and Ideological State Apparatus (ISA) (i.e., religious, educational, family, legal, political, trade union, communications, and cultural) function to maintain and support capitalist relations of production. While the RSA and ISA function primarily by repression and ideology, respectively, each contains elements of the other (i.e., the RSA can function ideologically, the ISA repressively).[47] In mature capitalism, the educational ideological system is the dominant apparatus within the ISA. "Thus . . . Schools . . . use suitable methods of punishment, expulsion, selection, etc., to 'discipline' not only their shepherds, but also their flocks."[48] The theoretical constructs, base and superstructure, and repressive and ideological arms of the state apparatus are valuable analytical tools for examining the dynamic, nonlinear processes that constitute societal change. The next sections address the emergence of automation and corresponding rise of domestic militarism as profound changes in base and superstructure that contextualize the privatization of public education and militarization in schools bolstering structural inequity.

From Industrial Production to Automation and Robotics

The introduction of new technologies under certain conditions precipitates qualitative leaps in the scale of production and gradually changes the nature of social and political life.[49] The innovation of the steam engine and electric motor in the late 1800s launched the Industrial Revolution, transforming society from an agricultural to financial industrial economy.[50] Electromechanics enabled the creation of *labor-saving devices* for efficient, routinized, mass production that far exceeded the limits imposed by the manual labor of the individual artisan, cottage industry, or chattel slavery. The mechanization of Southern agriculture and centralization of large-scale, assembly-line production severely disrupted agrarian life and forced laborers to migrate to the nation's cities. The social nature of production in industry reconfigured the nation's economy, transferring its hub from declining rural to thriving urban financial centers.[51]

Just as electromechanics forged the ascendance of industrial capitalist production, so has the emergence of microelectronic technology catalyzed the digital revolution, forging a postindustrial, information-driven economy. The invention of the microchip in 1971 harkened the incipient overthrow of the reign of electromechanics in industrial production, transforming an economy based on mechanical labor to an information-driven global economy based on automation and robotics.[52] Microchips could record and play back human activity in small, affordable computers, eclipsing the labor-saving devices of industrialization, with the epochal introduction of *labor-replacing devices*.[53] Replete with the cumulative knowledge, skills, and efforts of human activity, computers, robotics, digital telecommunications, and biotechnology can create, manage, and monitor goods and services for human consumption and survival.

The automation of production is precipitating an unprecedented reorganization of society and permanently altering the forms and nature of work, as robotics and the independent commodification of information and knowledge are replacing the sale of labor power and decentering human activity in the productive process. Some project that the perpetual production of innovation (i.e.,"new knowledge for making goods")[54] and cyber factories, consisting of a "web of intelligent machines," will be the source of profit, and shift the role of humans to more autonomous, decentralized, supervisory functions.[55] With the further bifurcation of manual and intellectual work, hierarchies of knowledge production occupations are anticipated. High/low paid technical/professional workers may increasingly design, compose, and alter instructions for machines, as others' intellectual work (e.g., engineers, architects), is deskilled through computer software.

Laborless production is permeating every aspect of economic life (e.g., agriculture, medicine, law, construction, automobile, steel, and wood production, telecommunications, commodities trading, education, transportation, retail, clerical work, space travel, oceanography, government agencies, social services, insurance, libraries, computer programming, and so forth).[56] Internet shopping by manufacturers for raw materials is affecting supply and demand, pricing, marketing, inflation and global labor markets.[57] Computerized systems allow technicians in the U.S. to control production in low-wage shops abroad. Tasks may be performed well beyond human capacity.

In mining, computer-operated systems command/monitor the excavation of over one hundred tons of coal an hour by massive whirling drills, the production of an army of shovels, drills, and trucks, and the transport of 240 tons of rock by one truck and driver, with prospects for fully operated coal mines via satellite. These and other advancements in the steel and automotive industries have increased profits and reduced the workforce by 21 percent since 1997.[58]

In agriculture, computerized controllers and navigation systems provide precision farming via satellites to pinpoint specific fertilizer, pesticide, and water needs of crops. Digitalized infrared photography identifies problem areas undetectable by the human eye, resulting in earlier, targeted diagnosis and treatment of produce. Increasingly, $160,000 robotic sanitized cow milking systems are being used by large farmer/owners, who anticipate major profits from 10–15 percent increases in production and decreases in the number of hired farm workers.[59]

Nanotechnology (the science of molecule-sized devices) is revolutionizing medicine, computing, and food supplies, through small machines that grab and rearrange individual atoms.[60] Nanomedicine has produced a DNA computer, which in the future will provide noninvasive surgery, detect and destroy disease-causing agents, and synthesize drug treatment, through the ingestion of nanobots.[61] Nanofood supplies will synthesize food molecularly and, in the right hands, *could* prevent starvation and clean up toxic waste on an atomic level.[62] IBM's data-storage technology holds the equivalent of two hundred CD-ROM's on a postage stamp-sized surface, and projections for nanocomputing are supercomputers the size of a drop of water.[63] The miniaturization of electronics has created far-reaching possibilities for humans to meet their needs. However, contention surrounds this domain (e.g., genetic engineering) as patents threaten to privatize knowledge for profit or egregious violations of human dignity, which retards progress in medical science that is vital to the improvement of the human condition.[64]

The military's well-funded, aggressive pursuit of large, top-down automation has produced robots that are central to "DDD" work (i.e., "Duty, Dull, and Dangerous" tasks), including spy satellite surveillance and scout-search-destroy missions. Unmanned cars, planes, trucks, cruise missiles, and "smart bombs" perform many functions in robotic war via computer-operated systems. Robotocists have produced protein-based solar connected combat helmets, which mimic the surrounding environment and are difficult to detect electronically, and exoskeletons, which are prosthetic suits that carry soldiers' weapons and supplies. Robotunas support efforts to create swift submarines and do research on the ocean deep. Prospects for robots that "think and walk" range from domestic service to law enforcement and military combat.[65] The notion of Robocop is not far-fetched.

Technological developments have had a profound effect on the global economy and are pivotal in the unending cycle of economic crises inherent to capitalism. As international corporations introduce labor-replacing devices, "downsize," and export factories to cheaper labor markets to maximize profits, blue- and white-collar workers are expunged from the workplace. From 1960–92, workers employed in the steel industry declined from 600,000 to less than 200,000; half of the jobs in the auto industry were lost; machine tools/electrical machinery decreased by 40 percent.[66] In 1982, 1,287,000 jobs were lost to plant closings and layoffs, augmented in 1987 with merger-induced layoffs in banking.[67] Steadily, average unemployment has risen, from 4.9 percent between 1956–73, to 7.2 percent between

1974–87, and poverty in 1994 had not been as high since 1961.[68] Increasingly, workers are relegated to temporary, part-time, or contractual jobs without benefits, disguising the 12 percent unemployment rate and swelling the ranks of the "working poor" and permanently unemployed.[69]

As consumers worldwide are less able to buy goods, corporations increase layoffs and technological innovations to cut costs, and thrust the impoverished abroad further into slave-like subsistence. The cycle of massive overproduction and underconsumption of commodities, competitive capital expansion/consolidation, and structural unemployment, endemic to capitalism, is exacerbated and accelerated by automated laborless production. Polarized redistribution of the nation's wealth results, from 1967–92, in the wealthiest white families' incomes increasing twenty-fold, and the poorest black families' incomes decreasing fortyfold.[70] The full impact of corporate efforts to mask years of declining profits (e.g., Enron, Tyco, WorldCom scandals, and ensuing bankruptcies), unprecedented layoffs, and continual automation of the workplace, has yet to be seen.

Under these conditions of plenty, the livelihood and survival of many are at stake. Some blame technology for the unbridled propulsion toward the "end of work," for distorted and unethical uses of technology, and for "the declining significance of humans." These critics overlook the profound contribution that human innovation makes to humanity, if used as an instrument for human need, rather than for private profit.

Under these conditions, the financial arbiters of global capital scapegoat the disenfranchised as the cause of the crisis. They seek new methods of control, new forms for the state apparatus to accommodate the changing economic relations, and new ways to stem the rising tide of disillusionment and resistance that the "grotesque international inequities of wealth" produce. Hence, domestic militarism, armed with its ideological weapons, arises to sustain the social order.

Domestic Militarization

> The state apparatus . . . i.e. the police, the courts, the prisons; but also the army . . . intervenes directly as a supplementary repressive force in the last instance.[71]

> The Repressive State Apparatus functions massively and predominantly *by repression* (including physical repression), while functioning secondarily by ideology. . . . The Ideological State Apparatuses function massively and predominantly *by ideology*, but they also function secondarily by repression, even if ultimately . . . this is very attenuated and concealed, even symbolic.[72]

In *Lockdown America: Police and Prisons in the Age of Crisis,* Parenti provides an insightful historical analysis of the successive wave of repressive legislative, political, and institutional measures, adopted from 1968 to the 1990s, that were coterminous with the wave of economic crises and reflect the dual function of the state through ideology and force. The mid-1960s were characterized by social activism in factories, schools, and communities, and urban rebellions following the civil rights and anti–Vietnam war movement.[73] Simultaneously, drugs were invidiously infused in the military in Vietnam and in urban communities, serving to narcotize emergent restlessness and disillusion. Though the government instituted many ameliorative, short-lived social programs, the emergent ideological shift to *law and order* was pronounced, sustained preparation for ensuing repressive measures. This shift culminated in the 1968 Omnibus Crime Control and Safe Streets Act, initiating the erosion of civil liberties (e.g., wiretapping and dilution of Miranda Rights), and $3.55 billion for the Law Enforcement Assistance Administration (LEAA) in 1970 to bolster local and state police training and equipment.[74] Through the SAs' twin arms—ideology and force—the law and order campaign and passage of repressive legislative measures reasserted social control over social reform.

With the advent of microelectronics and exodus of factories and local businesses from thriving urban centers in the 1970s and 1980s, deindustrialization, unemployment, and competition from cheap labor abroad grew, putting labor unions in jeopardy. In 1979, a frontal attack on unions was made with the aggressive, divisive firing of eleven thousand striking air traffic controllers, wage freeze, and deregulation of the industry. This chastening, repressive move within the ISA against organized labor and rhetorical blame for rising costs and fewer jobs on unions, along with Reagan's incisive tax cuts for the wealthy, positioned the government solidly behind corporate interests. From 1965–92, a group of manufacturers moved 1,800 plants to Mexico, employing 500,000 workers, and from 1980–85, close to 2.3 million jobs were lost forever.[75] Thus, the bargaining position of labor and the right to strike were simultaneously compromised for workers, and the state reestablished the primacy of corporate control.

Illegal drug use and sale escalated in declining cities, as class polarization, white flight, and the concentration of urban poverty among people of color grew. Increased violence, local rivalries for profits from the drug economy, and thousands of arrests were symptomatic of rampant unemployment and desperation. This social and economic deterioration swole the ranks of the cast-off populations, deemed "social junk" (e.g., addicts and mentally ill) and "social dynamite" (e.g., displaced workers). Parenti argues that the growing "surplus population" had to be contained or subjugated through brute force to destabilize a potentially rebellious, cast-off population of displaced workers and to mask the illusory health of the national economy.[76] Conditions were ripe to scapegoat the "racial other," one of the state's indispensable ideological weapons of deflection. Through the discourse in popular culture and other venues, "inner" cities became synonymous with violence, drugs, and African American and Latino youth, which served as "proof" of the inefficacy of social programs. This view ideologically presaged the roll-back of the social programs of the 1970s and "a new wave of criminal justice crackdown."[77] Though "crime control" was marginally related to crime, it was presented as a means to contain the "dangerous classes" and accompanied the simultaneous resurgence of vigilante organizations, and extra-legal terror.[78]

As part of the war on drugs, the 1984 Comprehensive Crime Control Act sanctioned the denial of bail and federal parole and increased the fines.[79] The Anti-Drug Abuse Act of 1986 and 1998 imposed higher sentences on the use of crack cocaine (cheaper and more prevalent in communities of color) than on cocaine power (more expensive and prevalent in white upscale communities), and sanctioned the death penalty for tag-alongs in drug-related felonies and (un)intentional killings.[80] These "legal" measures institutionalized inequity in the judicial system's sentencing and imprisonment processes and the disproportionate incarceration of poor people of color. They masked the prevalence of drug use in affluent, white communities, contributed to the demonization of African Americans and Latinos, which provided ideological justification for increased state repression, violence, and containment in these communities (e.g., police brutality, racial profiling). As the legislative arm of the ISA legalized inequity, the RSA's court system forced incarceration based on race and class, and in turn, reaffirmed demonizing, scapegoating discourses within the ISA.

The ideological and repressive aspects of domestic militarism have surfaced primarily through the legal, judicial, and law enforcement apparatuses of the state. The institutionally sanctioned militarization of public housing in Chicago, designed to be massive intern/containment centers in impoverished communities, was new terrain for the state, bringing surveillance and law enforcement to the homes of the poor. Though allocated funds for building upkeep were diverted for years from residents, resources for containment and surveillance appeared rapidly (i.e., security, ID cards, metal detectors, police, electronic surveillance, and "Clean Sweeps").[81] Though the history of fiscal mismanagement contributed to the rapid deterioration of the buildings, it was ascribed to residents' criminality, uncleanliness, and disregard for property. This justified the need for residential imprisonment and paved the way for the needed demolition of public highrises, but brought about massive displacement of successive generations of permanently unemployed people of color. The repressive and ideological arms of the state have been unrelenting in implementing domestic militarism and have hit those on the bottom of the economic rung the hardest. The successive array of legislative and law enforcement measures serve as a defense against the resistance of the "surplus populations" and the devastating social ills that result from inadequate means to live. They paved the way for the state's reliance on more stringent repressive apparatuses—the prison system and the military.

The massive expansion of the prison-industrial complex, a lucrative entity, is at the center of domestic militarism and corporate privatization of public services. As the criminalization of the poor escalates, the prison industry is housing the cast-offs, employing the unemployed in cities devastated by deindustrialization, and creating profits for private corporations. Based on third-grade reading scores, the projected needs for prison construction are increasingly daily. The prison population has doubled since 1978, running 15 percent over capacity, due to the imprisonment of "offenders" who historically have received alternative sentences.[82] The current annual budget is over $25 billion, far exceeding that of welfare, 1 percent of the GNP.[83] Consistent with the pattern of structural inequity, of the 6.6 million people in prisons, 63 percent are African American, 25 percent is Latino.[84] They are incarcerated with adult inmates 12–25 times more often than are white youth.[85] Arrests are increasing for illegal drug use and driving under the influence of alcohol, signaling the shrinking life options and demoralizing efforts to "ease the pain."

The prison system plays a clear role in the discipline and forced containment of inmates, exercised through cell life, prison guards, SWAT commandos, and violence. Its ideological function surfaces by examining the prison system's role in the provision of free labor, enabled by the Federal Prison Industries Enhancement Act (PIE) of 1979.[86] In this era of economic retrenchment, the captive prison population is a prime source of free/cheap labor, legitimated by their "need for rehabilitation." Though private corporations have taken advantage of prison labor, it has been unprofitable, due to limited space, threat of law suits, public relations concerns about prison-made products, the imposition of prison procedures on the work process, and poor quality of work due to prisoners' resistance.[87] Though prison labor is not profitable, the repressive function that prisons serve is complemented by their ideological function of reassuring the public that the "wayward and morally depraved" are being rehabilitated, that their tax dollars are being efficiently used, and that they are safe from the "dangerous classes." The removal of libraries, educational programs, and exercise rooms from prisons signals a return of the view that prisons are for retribution and punishment, not for rehabilitation of society's cast-offs. The domestic militarism escalates with the unprecedented extension of surveillance and the military into civilian life.

The tragic events of September 11 have forever changed life in the United States and its relationship to the international community, economically and politically. The economy was further wounded, as exemplified in the airline industry, and American confidence in the market waned as further layoffs occurred. The personal and national vulnerability created on that day has forged national unity and a pervasive underlying current of fear. The threat of terrorism in the midst of a deepening recession contributed to the invocation of Operation TIPS (Terrorism Information and Prevention System) to establish networks of public workers, "worker corps," to report "any suspicious activities" observed. Now neighbors and civilian workers will serve as an auxiliary arm of the state.[88] In an effort to further stem the tide of terrorism, plans are under way to revamp the Posse Comitatus Act of 1898, which severely restricted the military's right to participate in domestic defense.[89] The overhaul of this Act will allow the military to act as a law enforcement body within the nation's borders. Visions of tanks in the nation's streets are not far-fetched, and the threatened loss of civil liberties embodied in the sweeping terms of the legislation has evoked outcries from the American population to *preserve democracy in order to defend it.*

Ideology and Repression in Education

The rise in domestic militarism that is reflected in legislation, the criminal justice system, the military, and institutional policies, and that functions dually through ideology and force, complements the economic restructuring and deepening crisis of the world economy. As such, it provides the context for commensurate shifts in education. There has been a glaring reversal in government policy in providing or guaranteeing services that were once considered entitlements and requisite supports for a decent quality of life. Health care, education, welfare, social security, and other social programs that supported the maintenance of the workers' capacity to work are being replaced by programs of control or being subjected to corporate privatization. The public face of welfare-to-work, managed care in medicine, and educational vouchers belie less noble intentions than efforts to improve self-sufficiency, curtail insurance abuse, or enhance individual choice.

This significant shift signals the SA's "response" to the economic crisis and new conditions of laborless production.[90] By cutting costs in social programs, and more importantly by divesting in the livelihood and survival of the masses of working people, the state is supporting the consolidation of corporate capital. Plagued by declining profits and the redundancy of labor in production, privatization provides an excellent opportunity for financiers to commodify public spheres of services, including public education. More insidious, however, is the idea that with increasing automation, the maintenance of workers, who are irrelevant to the production process and creation of the nation's wealth, is no longer a priority. The general population and the cast-offs in the economy bear the brunt of these developments. In this context, the dismantling of public education becomes an "economic necessity" for the arbiters of power.

The neoliberal promotion of "market" choice, repositions individual/private rights over the common good in order to justify corporate privatization and school vouchers. The promotion of "market choice" is cojoined with the drive toward standardization as the means to regulate variations in the educational marketplace (i.e., the quality of schools from which to choose and the quality of education provided for students).[91] Ostensibly, corporate privatization will promote equity and increase accountability, flexibility, and local control for failing schools through competition and the efficient use of resources, and standardized testing will even the playing field. In fact, *privatization redirects public funds for private accumulation*. It allows the government to abdicate its social responsibility to educate youth, and reduces education to a privately owned commodity of corporations, whose consumers are students, subject to the fluctuations of the market (i.e., the financial resource needs of their sponsors). "Schoolchoice" and the imposition of a national curriculum and standardized testing will exacerbate existing inequities hidden in the structures of public education.

The construction of "choice" as the property of autonomous moral agents is far from reality in its conception and execution. Students' use of vouchers at their school of choice is a fallacy, as efforts to implement the Leave No Child Behind Act (NCLB) Act of 2001 illustrate. Frustrated parents, boards of education, and policymakers are chafing under a plan that cannot work. There are insufficient transfer schools to serve the 3.5 million students in failing schools.[92] In Illinois, of the 124,000 eligible students, 1,200 were granted transfers.[93] The geographic distance between differential property tax–based schools precludes travel for most students in poor communities, and some magnet schools and others have "chosen" not to accept school transfers or have set preclusive standards for student admittance. While some poor and middle-income students may use vouchers to attend religious or adjacent community schools, or escape the "inner city," the overwhelming demand for and obstacles to voucher use in "good" schools are prohibitive. However, the wealthy may use vouchers, money from the public sector's poorly funded schools, to subsidize their private education. Disguised as an entitlement for all, vouchers and other forms of "choice" will benefit very few.

The surge of militarism in schools mirrors the national trend toward domestic militarism. True to form, the poor are targeted, especially those of color, who are expendable in the workforce. While Ph.D.s are being hired to teach wealthy youth, Troops to Teachers is preparing retired military personnel on a "fast track" for certification in education administration, to provide "leadership" and structure in "at-risk" schools. While specialized magnet schools are being built in cities for some, disciplinary schools are being constructed for others. The CEO of Philadelphia Public Schools, Paul Vallas, is contracting $7 million with private firms to create alternative disciplinary schools for "violent" youth, and to set up widespread Saturday detention, in-school suspension, and community service for nonviolent disruptive youth.[94] These programs to end bad behavior after one infraction further demonize urban youth as guilty offenders and institutionally serve as "halfway" houses to jail, contributing to the fivefold (500 percent) increase in African American men's incarceration in the past twenty years, versus a mere 23 percent increase in their college enrollment.[95]

As evidenced at Groundview, the presence of metal detectors and police for student protection not only contains the "dangerous classes," but prepares them for their proscribed place in the new economy—prison or the military. The culture of militarism and pronounced presence of force in schools supports Althusser's notion that both repression and ideology are operative within the ISA, as each arm of the state, containing elements of the other, is used as necessary to support or push forward the existing social order. Expulsion, punishment, selection, and discipline complement the ideological function of schools. This overt repression is accompanied by a defunct curriculum and inadequate resources that deprive youth of their human desire to think, explore, and create. It conveys a powerful ideological message to the students and the broader culture: "This is your worth." The absence of resources seems to "fit" the essential qualities of the youth and justifies the institutional inequity.

The repressive and ideological aspects of the culture of militarism support the renegotiation of boundaries for Groundview youths' anticipated role in a postindustrial society. At Mountainview, the ideological aspects of the culture of privilege are not supplemented by force, but are complemented by proscriptive practices and policies that socialize students "to be free" to fulfill their complementary role in the emergent economy, as the privileged.[96] As such the policies and practices in the educational system play a vital role in the maintenance and in the restructuring of society.

Conclusion

Every society is really governed by hidden laws, by unspoken but profound assumptions on the part of the people, and ours is no exception. . . . The time has come, God knows, for us to examine ourselves, but we can only do this if we are willing to free ourselves of the myth of America and try to find out what is really happening here.[97]

The restructuring of a postindustrial economy is well under way, accompanied by the emergence of domestic materialism throughout society. This process is also evident in education with the privatization of public education and introduction of militarism to poor schools. On the one hand, the present examination paints a bleak picture of increased polarization between the poor and wealthy, declining schools, and efforts by the state to protect corporate capital's interests through ideology and force. On the other hand, it addresses the powerful dual historical role of education as a site of struggle, in both maintaining structural inequities in society and in promoting major changes in economic, social, and political lives. Education has both enslaving and emancipatory possibilities, especially during this period of economic restructuring and rapid change in our social life, and may, in turn, forge new ways of thinking about social life.

Educators have a crucial role to play in countering the domestic militarism and privatization in schools and society at large, both ideologically and practically. It is incumbent upon educators to examine, wrestle with, and strive to understand the historically embedded, social, economic, ideological, and political realities that exist, so that our efforts to promote change will be well-guided. By examining the motive forces of the economy, the state, and social life in all of its forms, we may arrive at critical analyses to guide our strivings for an educational system and quality of life across race and class that disrupt structural inequity and affirm our basic humanity. In this sense, education across multiple contexts is *a key*—a vehicle in the informed process of change.

Most important, we must challenge the corrosive ideologies and institutional practices that constrain the possibilities for youth, by changing the objective probabilities before them. Toward this end, we must struggle to preserve democracy and to ensure a quality education for all youth across racial and class lines. We must strive to create schools and other sites of learning that nurture the natural strivings of youth/humans to explore, think, inquire, discover, create, and innovate. Central to this work is our role in providing a forum for students to critically examine their immediate realities and the broader questions that have bearing on their lives through multiple texts. Our struggle *against inequity* requires thoughtful examination in educational contexts that will contribute to the preparation of successive educators' participation in the *struggle for humanity*.

Notes

A substantially different version of this chapter appeared in *The School Field: International Journal of Theory and Research in Education*, XII (3/4), Autumn 2001, p. 91–109.

1. Robert Friedland, "Space, Place, and Modernity," *A Journal of Reviews: Contemporary Sociology* 21, no. 1 (1992): 8–36.
2. James Anderson, *The Education of Blacks in the South*, 1860–1935 (Chapel Hill, N.C.: University of North Carolina Press, 1988).
3. Pierre Bourdieu, "Cultural Reproduction in Education, Society, and Culture," in J. Karabel and H. Halsey, *Power and Ideology in Education*, edited by (London: Sage, 1977).
4. Michael Apple and Christopher Jenks, "American Realities: Poverty, Economy, and Education," in *Cultural Politics and Education*, edited by M. Apple (New York: Teachers College Press, 1996); Christian Parenti, *Lockdown America* (New York: Verso, 1999); Jim Davis, Thomas Hirschl, and Michael Stack, eds., *Cutting Edge: Technology, Information, Capitalism, and Social Revolution* (New York: Verso, 1997).
5. Davis, Hirschl, and Stack, *Cutting Edge*.
6. Richard Appelbaum, "Multiculturalism and Flexibility: Some New Directions in Global Capitalism," in *Mapping Multiculturalism*, edited by Avery F. Gordon and Christopher Newfield (Minneapolis, Minn.: University of Minnesota Press, 1996).
7. Parenti, *Lockdown America*.
8. Louis Althusser, *Lenin and Philosophy and Other Essays* (New York: Monthly Review Press, 1971).
9. Bourdieu, *Cultural Reproduction*, 494.
10. Arthur Spears, "Race and Ideology: An Introduction," in *Race and Ideology: Language, Symbolism and Popular Culture* (Detroit: Wayne State University Press, 1999), 42.
11. Illinois State Board of Education Report Card, 2000 (isbe.net).
12. Bourdieu, *Cultural Reproduction*, 493.
13. Jay MacLeod, *Ain't No Makin' It: Aspirations in a Low-income Neighborhood* (Boulder, Colo.: Westview Press, 1987), 19.
14. Michael Dyson, "Growing Up Under Fire: Boyz N the Hood and the Agony of the Black Man in America," *Tikkun* 6, no. 5 (November–December 1991): 74–78.
15. Illinois State Board of Education Report Card, 2000.
16. Alice Miller, *For Your Own Good: Hidden Cruelty in Child-Rearing and the Roots of Violence* (New York: Doubleday, 1983).
17. Guglielmo Carchedi, "High-Tech Hype: Promises and Realities of Technology in the Twenty-first Century," in *Cutting Edge: Technology, Information, Capitalism, and Social Revolution*, edited by Jim Davis, Thomas Hirschl and Michael Stack (New York: Verso, 1997), 73–86.
18. Bourdieu, *Cultural Reproduction*, 494.
19. "Military Industrial: JROTC Is a Recruiting Program for Dead-End Military Jobs," available at www.schoolsnotjails.com (March 29, 2001): 1.
20. Kenneth J. Saltman, *Collateral Damage: Corporatizing Public Schools—A Threat to Democracy* (Lanham, Md.: Rowman & Littlefield, 2000), x.
21. "Military Industrial," 2.
22. Ibid., 2.
23. "Military Industrial," 1.
24. Ibid., 3.
25. Allison Fass, "Advertising: The Army Is Helping to Pay for a 'Stay in School' Campaign," *New York Times* (June 25, 2002): C6.
26. Richard Perez-Pena, "Report Says Enrollment in Guard Was Inflated," *New York Times* (June 29, 2002), A13.
27. Dave Moniz, "15,000 Reserves to Serve 2nd Year: Longest Call-Ups Since Vietnam," *USA Today* (August 26, 2002): 2.
28. Tamar Lewin, "College Board Announces an Overhaul for the SAT," *New York Times* (June 28, 2002): A1; Sean Cavanagh, "Overhauled SAT Could Shake Up School Curricula," *Education Week* (July 10, 2002).
29. Ibid., 3.
30. Noam Chomsky, "Intellectuals and Social Change," in *Understanding Power: The*

Indispensable Chomsky, edited by Peter Mitchell and John Schoeffel (New York: New Press, 2002), 236.

31. Linda Darling-Hammond, "Inequality and Access to Knowledge," in *Handbook of Research on Multicultural Education*, edited by James A. Banks and Cherry A. Banks (New York: Macmillan), 466 (citing D. Tyack, *The One Best System*).

32. Jonathan Kozol, *Savage Inequalities: Children in America's Schools* (New York: Harper Perennial).

33. Anderson, *The Education of Blacks*, 27.

34. Ibid., 4–8.

35. Ibid., 89.

36. Baldwin quoted in Anderson, 1988, 82.

37. Ibid., 91.

38. Ibid., 247.

39. Ibid., 33–78. Anderson examines the origins of this particular form of industrial education and the controversy that surfaced between W. E. B. DuBois and Booker T. Washington, and Northern philanthropists and Southern planters.

40. Pierre Bourdieu and Jean-Claude Passeron, *Reproduction in Education, Society, and Culture*, 2nd ed. (London: Sage, 1970).

41. W. E. B. DuBois, "Does the Negro Need Separate Schools," *Journal of Negro Education* 4 (July 1935): 328–35.

42. Anderson, *The Education of Blacks in the South*, 81.

43. Howard Zinn, *A People's History of the United States* (New York: Harper Perennial, 1980), 198.

44. Apple and Zenk, "American Realities: Poverty, Economy, and Education," 71.

45. Althusser, *Lenin and Philosophy*, 137–42.

46. Frederick Engels, "Letter to Joseph Bloch," (September 21, 1890): 12–14.

47. Althusser, *Lenin and Philosophy*, 142–143.

48. Ibid., 145.

49. Thomas Hirschl, "Structural Unemployment and the Qualitative Transformation of Capitalism," in *Cutting Edge: Technology, Information, Capitalism, and Social Revolution*, edited by Jim Davis, Thomas Hirschl, and Michael Stack (New York: Verso, 1997), 157–74.

50. Ibid., 158.

51. Guns, Germs, and Steel Jared, *Diamond, Guns, Germs, and Steel* (New York: W. W. Norton, 1999).

52. Hirschl, "Structural Unemployment" 159.

53. Jim Davis and Michael Stack, "The Digital Advantage," in Davis, Hirschl, and Stack, *Cutting Edge: Technology, Information, Capitalism, and Social Revolution*, edited by Jim Davis, Thomas Hirschl, and Michael Stack (New York: Verso, 1997, 121–44.

54. Tessa Morris-Suzuki, Robots and Capitalism, in *Cutting Edge: Technology, Information, Capitalism, and Social Revolution*, edited by Jim Davis, Thomas Hirschl, and Michael Stack (New York: Verso, 1997, 13–28.

55. "The Cyber Factory: A Web of Intelligent Machines," available at www.global-technoscan.com, 1–5.

56. Ibid.

57. Michael Casey, "Internet Changes the Face of Supply and Demand," *Wall Street Journal*, (October 18, 1999): A4, 3Q.

58. Michael M. Phillips, "Business of Mining Gets a Lot Less Basic," *New York Times* (March 18, 1997)" B13.

59. Marc Levy, "Robots Do the Milking On Some Farms," *Associated Press*, March 1, 2002.

60. Jesse Berst, "What's Next: Nanotechnology Promises Big Changes by Getting Small," (August 2, 2000), available at www.zdnet.com/anchordesk.

61. Patricia Reaney, "Scientists Build Tiny Computer from DNA," *India News: World* (November 22, 2001).

62. Ibid.

63. Ibid.

64. Jonathan King, "The Biotechnology Revolution: Self-Replicating Factories and the Ownership of Life Forms," in *Cutting Edge: Technology, Information, Capitalism, and Social Revolution*, edited by Jim Davis, Thomas Hirschl, and Michael Stack (New York: Verso, 1997, 145–56.
65. The Science Channel, "Technology Circuit: The Digital Domain," June 25, 2002.
66. Stanley Aronowitz and William DiFazio, *The Jobless Future: Sci-Tech and the Dogma of Work* (Minneapolis: University of Minnesota Press, 1994), 48.
67. Ibid., 2.
68. Hirschl, "Structural Unemployment," 161; Davis and Stack, "The Digital Advantage," 137.
69. Hirschl, 2.
70. Apple and Zenk, "American Realities," 72–73. In 1992, 80 percent of people were earning less than half the national income, and 20 percent of the wealthiest had almost 50 percent.
71. Althusser, 137.
72. Ibid., 145.
73. Parenti, *Lockdown America*, 4.
74. Ibid., 8–11.
75. Ibid., 42.
76. Ibid., 45.
77. Ibid., 44.
78. Noam Chomsky, *Rogue States: The Rule of Force in World Affairs* (Cambridge, Mass.: Southend Press, 2000), 153.
79. Parenti, *Lockdown America*, 50
80. Ibid., 57–61.
81. Ibid., 59.
82. David B. Kopel, "Prison Blues: How America's Foolish Sentencing Policies Endanger Public Safety," *Policy Analysis* 208 (May 17, 1994), available at www.cato.org/pubs/pas/pa-208.html. "Race and Incarceration in the United States: Human Rights Watch Press Backgrounder" (February 27, 2002), 1–3, www.hrw.org/backgrounder/usa/race.
83. Ibid., Kopel, 4.
84. Fox Butterfield, "Study Finds Big Increase in Black Men as Inmates since 1980," *New York Times* (August 28, 2002), available at www.hrw.org/backgrounder/usa/race, 1; Jonathan D. Salant, "6.6 Million Under Nation's Correctional System," *Florida Times-Union* (August 26, 2002), 1.
85. Butterfield, "Study Finds Big Increase," 1.
86. Parenti, *Lockdown America*, 230.
87. Ibid., 233–35.
88. Adam Clymer, "Security and Liberty: Worker Corps to be Formed to Report Odd Activity," *New York Times* (July 25, 2002).
89. Eliabeth Becker, "Bush Seeks to Review Military's Home Role," *Chicago Tribune* (July 16, 2002): 1; Tribune News Services, "Ridge Calls for Study of Military's Home Role," *Chicago Tribune*, 22 July 2002, np.
90. Hirschl, "Structural Unemployment," 168.
91. Michael Apple, *Educating the "Right" Way: Markets, Standards, God, and Inequality* (New York: Routledge, 2001) 75.
92. Stephanie Banchero and Michael Martinez, "Federal School Reform Stumbles: Confusion Reigns Over Choice Plan," *Chicago Tribune* (August 28, 2002): 1.
93. Diana Jean Schemo, "Few Exercise New Right to Leave Failing Schools," *New York Times* (August 28, 2002), 1.
94. Susan Snyder, "Vallas: No Shuffling of Violent Students," *Philadelphia Inquirer* (August 22, 2002): 1.
95. Butterfield, 1.
96. Chomsky, *Intellectuals and Social Change*, 236–237.
97. Baldwin, 1961/1989, p. 11.

INTRODUCTION TO CHAPTER 7

Following Pepi Leistyna's chapter, in which oppressed youth in a Massa-chusetts city recognize that their oppression is the historical inheritance of a colonial project that began with the decimation of Native Americans, and following Enora Brown's chapter, which lays out the production of systemic racial and class privilege through the economy and culture of different schools systems, Don Trent Jacobs's chapter "A Warning and Solution from Indian Country" offers a discussion of the ways that the project of colonial genocide continues today through the federal government's attempts to steal Native lands for corporate use, to maintain poverty, and to continue destruc-tive cultural impositions. Jacobs's chapter uniquely highlights both the main-tenance of the colonial legacy of violence and the ways that militarization and corporatization are operating in these particular rural contexts.

CHAPTER 7

Forceful Hegemony

A Warning and a Solution from Indian Country

DON TRENT JACOBS
(Cherokee/Creek/Scots-Irish)

Some pilots from NASA were practicing moonwalking maneuvers on the similarly contoured landscape of the Navajo reservation. A Navajo elder told a bilingual boy to ask what they were up to.

"We are training for a trip to the moon," one astronaut replied.

The elder nodded at the boy's translation, and then told him to ask if he could send a message up with them to the moon. The astronauts, seeing a PR opportunity in such a collaboration, agreed to do so. The old man wrote a note in Navajo and gave it to them, but neither the elder nor any other Navajos would tell the pilots what the note said. Anxious to know, the astronauts paid someone to interpret the message. It read:

"Be careful. These guys have come to take away your land, your freedom and your children."

On May 29–30, 2001, I presented at the International Conference on Militarism in Education in Israel. Educators from a number of countries described schools that infuse a military presence into educational programs. They documented ways that hegemony, serving the interests of an elite few, colors curriculum and marches to military drums that enforce it. A few examples offered included:

- Teaching children how to make dog tags and paint camouflage on their faces;
- Hiring retired military personnel to serve as authoritarian teachers and administrators;
- Hanging posters that boast about service to country and warn against conscientious objectors;
- Using textbooks that encourage military service upon graduation from high school.

Don Trent Jacobs is an associate professor at Northern Arizona University in Flagstaff and a faculty member at Fielding Graduate Institute. From 1998–2001 he served as Dean of the Education Department at Oglala Lakota College. He holds doctorates in health psychology and curriculum and instruction. He is the author of ten books, including *The Bum's Rush: The Selling of Environmental Backlash*; *Primal Awareness: A True Story of Survival, Awakening and Transformation with the Raramuri Shamans of Mexico*; and *Teaching Virtues: Building Character Across the Curriculum*. Don Jacobs has been a marine corp pilot, a rodeo cowboy, a firefighter/EMT, an old-time stride piano player, a sport psychologist, and a professor.

Such things might be expected from the Middle Eastern countries represented at the conference, but what of Western societies like the United States? As an ex-marine officer of the Vietnam era, I know about corporate influence on government and military policies. As an educator, I am concerned when I hear the U.S. Secretary of Education saying that teachers are tools in the war against terrorism, or when I see oil company–sponsored textbooks that teach third graders that there is no global warming problem. My gravest awareness, however, of the U.S. government's increasing use of some form of "forceful hegemony" relates to its policies in Indian country, especially on American Indian reservations. What is happening there should be a warning to all of us, while the continuing resistance to it by some groups can exemplify possible solutions.

Before addressing educational issues of forceful hegemony in indigenous cultures, let's briefly consider how governments from around the world use military might against the sovereignty of indigenous populations to enhance state and corporate interests. For example, the culture of the U'wa people of Colombia is currently being threatened by oil drilling. A military patch depicting a man with a rifle standing next to an oil rig is worn on the right shoulder of every soldier that protects oil installations in Colombia. The same thing is happening to the indigenous democracy in Cauca. In both cases U.S. support of right-wing Colombian military is involved in crushing social structures that are unwilling to buy into the market economy's distorted values.

The Raramuri Simarone people of central Mexico are another example closer to home. They have chosen to live in remote caves deep in Copper Canyon rather than adopt western cultural values. Yet, efforts to protect their land from development and lumbering are thwarted by military intervention. Moreover, with the illicit support of corrupt government military troops, indirectly supported by the United States, drug mobsters violently are forcing the Natives into extinction.

Even in the heart of the United States, force is used against indigenous sovereignty. One example relates to what happen to the White Plume family on South Dakota's Pine Ridge Indian Reservation. The White Plume family's efforts to support itself with a hemp farm was halted in an early morning raid by dozens of FBI and Drug Enforcement Agency troopers armed with AK-47s.[1] Without any warning or involvement of the sovereign Lakota nation, whose laws support the growing of industrial-grade hemp, the intruders destroyed the entire crop, ending their hope for ecological economic development in this impoverished region.

Pine Ridge has been no stranger to contemporary U.S. militarism. In the 1970s, the FBI and DEA joined with corrupt tribal leaders to crush antigovernment protests in the reservation town of Wounded Knee. Leonard Peltier, a scapegoat of this conflict and a man considered by Amnesty International to be a political prisoner, remains in prison in spite overwhelming evidence for his innocence. Consider also the peaceful protest marches on the reservation every Saturday. In an effort to close down a border-town liquor store built on land that mysteriously is no longer in reservation boundaries and that is responsible for contributing to the plague of alcoholism on the reservation (and somehow related to the unresolved murder of several Lakota men), a dozen or so people, mostly elders, women, and children, walk from Pine Ridge to the White Clay liquor store, stopping four times along the way to pray. Each time more than a dozen heavily armed police officers line the streets and position themselves on rooftops as if prepared to ambush a company of soldiers!

Native people around the world not only have resources that corporations want for one form of profit or the other but they also have a worldview that challenges the fundamental ideas about capitalism that have been drummed into Western minds. Military action against indigenous people is thus a form of hegemony designed to keep growing Indian populations, with their different views about materialism, spirituality and ecology, in check. Such colonizing is also a part of formal schooling, and here is where American Indian education offers both a clear example of a tragedy unfolding in all American schools, but also possibilities for a solution.

Up until the past two decades, Indian children were taken away from their parents and forced into Western culture's school systems. Their hair was cut off and their mouths were washed out with soap if they spoke their native language. They were beat if they misbehaved. They were forced to wear uniforms. Under threat of punishment, they were not allowed to participate in their spiritual ceremonies and were forced to learn Christian orthodoxy.

Today the enforcing effects of the corporate/government powers in schools are more subtle but equally powerful. They are found in

- The curriculum;
- High-stakes standardized testing mandates;
- Neoconservative character education movement;
- Federal Bureau of Indian Affairs mentality;
- Non-Indian teachers;
- Blood quantum policies;
- Authoritarian pedagogy;
- Encouragement of military service as a "way out";
- Military teachers and administrators;
- Decreasing boundaries and exodus of students;
- Religious conversion;
- State exemptions;
- Western medical and psychological approaches.

In each of these arenas briefly described below, consider how "education as enforcement" in Indian education might correlate with similar problems in public education throughout American schools.

The Curriculum

State standardized curriculum supports an agenda that continues to ignore oppressive historical and contemporary interpretations of reality. For example, in a course on "The First Americans" taught in a social studies class for sixth graders at a reservation school, Davy Crockett and Daniel Boone were presented as "the first Americans"!

Of course, one of the more egregious examples is how Christopher Columbus is still regarded in elementary textbooks.[2] Consider the words of Jeffrey Hart, the Distinguished Professor of English at Dartmouth University and senior editor of *The National Review*, a magazine influential in current U.S. government policy making decisions. He says, "Columbus was a genuine hero of history and of the human spirit. To denigrate him is to denigrate what is worthy in human history and in us all."[3]

How else does curriculum in Indian schools continue forceful hegemony? Are complete understandings about the cause of wars encouraged? Are issues relating to social justice and American violations of civil rights really covered? How seriously do schools teach about ecological sustainability and the urgency the crises currently faces? What about authentic multicultural perspectives?

There is much we can learn from understanding both the curriculum in Indian schools that American Indians are forced to learn and how some people resist it. A letter written by an anonymous American in 1744 to the educators at William and Mary College offers a perspective that may be equally pertinent today:

> We know that you highly esteem the kind of learning taught in those colleges, that the maintenance of our young men, while with you, would be very expensive to you. We are convinced that you mean to do us good by your proposal; and we thank you heartily. But you, who are wise, must not take it amiss if our ideas of education happen not to be the same as yours. We have had some experience of it. Several of our young people were formerly brought up at the colleges of the northern provinces; they were instructed in all your subjects; but when they came back to us, they were bad runners, ignorant of every means of living, neither fit for hunters nor counselors, they were totally good for nothing.
>
> We are however, not the less oblig'd by your kind offer, tho' we decline accepting it; and to show our grateful sense of it, if the gentlemen of Virginia will send us a dozen of their sons, we will take care of their education, instruct them in all we know, and make men of them.[4]

Notice how respectful this letter is of those whose values seemed misplaced by the writer(s). As necessary as it is for us to pull our collective heads out of the sand to observe the problems brought to us by a worldview that is overly materialistic, authoritarian, corporatized, and militarized, it is also vital to engage with those who have bought into these things respectfully and with understanding. (The following should be considered with this in mind.)

High-Stakes Standardized Testing

According to President George Bush's new education program, "Leave No Child Behind," any school that does not achieve significant improvement in standardized test scores will be punished by the removal of federal and state dollars from that school. American Indians score the lowest on such tests than any other population. Notwithstanding the fact that the tests illustrate an approach to teaching and learning that stifles creative and critical thinking, the tests themselves are biased to non-Indian students. The requirements for schools to play this game add to the continuing colonization of the Indian children while testing companies head for the bank, and the problem goes way beyond Indian reservation boundaries.

Neoconservative Character Education

President Bush has proposed $25 million for character education programs throughout the United States and the push for such programs on high-crime Indian reservations is significant. Unfortunately, these programs tend to be extensions of conservative ideology and are more about compliance to authority than good character. Reflection on character as it relates to ecological issues, social justice, wealth equity problems, democratic ideals and authentic virtues such as generosity (considered to be the highest form of courage by American Indians) is minimal in many of the popular character education programs. Character education in American schools, which for thousands of years emphasized such authentic virtues, now implements an agenda designed to replace them with learned obedience to the values of the state.[5] And of course this is happening in many American schools as well.

BIA Mentality

Reservation schools are largely under the influence of the Bureau of Indian Affairs (BIA). Infamous for its anti-Indian history, even today money for education is wasted, innovative practices are either ignored or suppressed, and children become cogs in the bureaucratic machinery of an agency that has historically been more dangerous to sovereignty and health than helpful. In their book on Indian education, Vine Deloria and Daniel Wildcat point out that the BIA system encourages a continuing line of recycled "Indian" educators who have been indoctrinated by dominant assimilation policies.[6] (What bureaucracies such as school boards that are similar to the BIA influence the public schools in general?)

Non-Indian Teachers

Nearly 70 percent of the teachers on Native American reservations are non-Indian teachers. Although many are wonderful, caring people, more than a few actually are prejudiced against Indian people and their ways. When this happens, the "hidden curriculum" of assimilation is not so hidden. Certification standards require that teachers must be graduates from teacher training programs that serve the state and do little to honor Native values and learning styles. (In most public schools teachers do not reflect the diverse cultural values of the students in the classroom. How wonderful it would be if each student's culture could at least be honored if not learned throughout the school year. Instead, U.S. schools are moving toward "America first" and "English only" prescriptions.)

Blood Quantum Policies

Government monies for educational institutions relate to tribal membership and tribal membership relates to blood quantum. The federal BIA controls federal dollars that are based on blood quantum. The genocidal potential of such policies is devastating because the only way to ensure sufficient blood quantum is to marry from within the tribe. This is getting harder to do without marrying close relatives. But for people in abject poverty, marrying a first cousin is preferable to losing funding, and many of our students go to school as a way to earn money. (How "white" does one have to be to receive certain "benefits" in most American schools?)

Authoritarian Pedagogy

Indigenous people see authority in terms of personal experience and reflection in light of the spiritual awareness that all things are related.[7] Authoritarian pedagogy goes against the very nature of Native learning styles. Based on this factor alone, it should not surprise anyone that Indian student drop out rates on the reservation are higher than any other population group. (And what is happening outside of Indian schooling that reflects a problem with overly authoritarian structures? Is critical, creative thinking encouraged or stifled?)

Military Recruitment

American Indians are proud of their veterans because of the traditional values of bravery and fortitude, so children are likely candidates for U.S. armed forces recruitment campaigns. Recruiters tell young people the military is a way out of reservation poverty. They promise that young men may return home for special spiritual ceremonies like the sun dance. When this promise cannot be kept, young men go AWOL and wind up either court-marshaled for desertion or become fugitives. (The war on terrorism is now bringing such "recruitment" policies into all schools.) Consider President Bush's "No Child Left Behind" legislation. Buried deep within it is Section 9528, which grants the Pentagon access to directories with student names, addresses, and phone numbers so that they may be more easily contacted and recruited for military service.

Military Teachers and Administrators

As is happening in other countries, the United States has passed initiatives to encourage retired military personal to move into administrative and teaching positions throughout the nation's schools in order to meet the increasing demand for teachers and administrators. This is especially focused onto Indian schools but may be a concern nationwide. Militaristic discipline in schools can continue an oppressive, authoritarian perspective that can stifle critical challenges to hegemony.

Decreasing Boundaries

Most American Indian reservations are rampant with poverty. The federal government, in violation of treaty rights, is continually confiscating land through one legal maneuver or another. The land usually goes to corporations who rape valuable resources. Non-Indian ranchers often move boundary lines to encroach on Indian lands. For example, even as I write this Navajo people are being forced off their lands with threat of imprisonment if they do not relocate so Peabody Coal can continue to mine in selected areas.

Religious Conversion

In direct contradiction of the First Amendment establishment clause about separation of church and state, the U.S. government contracted with churches to help destroy Indian identity. Missionaries were provided with federal funds to educate Indian children. Today, religious conversion continues to be a force in private Indian schools that smothers cultural values and a spirituality that has existed for thousands of years. (Current Supreme Court decisions about vouchers show how this approach to hegemony has already moved off reservations and into the mainstream educational system.)

State Exemption

States have been given permission by the federal government to regulate Indian education, but states have withheld public services to Native Americans because of their special relation with the federal government. States utilize the Native population census to increase their share of federal funds for public services. The secretary of the Interior assesses fees for various services that benefit Indian people, even though the monies given relate to federal bonds or other legal obligations. (This kind of fraudulent connection between corporations and government has been common in Indian country for many years; however, corporate influence in public schools across the nation that influence everything from curriculum to the kinds of soft drinks children consume is increasing.)

Western Medical and Psychological Approaches

American Indians are generally forced to consume Western medicine and psychological services to the exclusion of more traditional alternatives that honor different assumptions about disease and healing. This is not dissimilar from mandatory vaccinations and other possible iatrogenic phenomenon that are forced upon non-Indian children.

The Solution

In spite of genocidal policies of forced hegemony in Indian country, some tribes have managed to maintain their cultural values. It may be that those who have succeeded have done so because of a worldview that is a necessary counter to enforced hegemony.

Until educational systems modify their essential worldview with one more in harmony with that of traditional indigenous tribes, such as those of America's first nation peoples, schools will continue to erode, not sustain, democracy.

I am not saying that any race, culture, religion, or ideology is better than any other. All people of any race or culture are subject to living according to unhealthy assumptions. However, if we study the outcomes of their respective worldviews, I believe that traditional indigenous perspectives, such as those held by North American Indian tribes, have proven healthier for the common good than those that have driven more dominant cultures for the past two thousand years. Consider the American Indian perspectives below and contrast them with the dominant worldview that now drives educational policy.[8,5] The traditional American Indian paradigm:

- Sees genuine democracy as being about equal rights for all members of the democratic community, not just for property owners.
- Focuses on cooperative systems, not predominantly about competition and "winning."
- Emphasizes the common good for life's intricate interconnections, not the accumulation of individual material gain or authoritarian power.
- Assumes that children are inherently sacred, not bad or relatively incompetent.
- Believes that women are great models for moral strength.
- Sees reflection on personal experience in light of spiritual awareness, not religious dogma, as the source of authority, rather than external authority figures or institutions as being absolute.
- Emphasizes intrinsic motivation to meet universal principles of right, rather than external rewards and punishments for the motivation to do good.
- Reflects an awareness that all things are related, people as well as rocks, trees, rivers, and animals.
- Leads to a world of joyful relationships, not to a culture based on fear.
- Is about balance and is not inclined toward conveniences that lead to wholesale conditions of personal and ecological disease or poor health.
- Says that spirituality is guided by the great mystery, rather than by orthodoxy that claims exclusive knowledge about God or that allows one group to force conversion on another.

All cultures have similar universal principles somewhere in their memory, but too many have forgotten them, allowing power politics and propaganda to create new belief systems or apathy that allow us to tolerate schools as vehicles for enforcement. Oppression from the dominant culture continues in many forms, most notably in our education systems. Yet there is hope if enough of us reform our schools in accordance with the universal path to harmony, which our indigenous brothers and sisters from around the world still remember in their hearts.

Ohiyesa, a Dakota Indian from South Dakota who was the first American Indian to earn a medical degree from Boston University back in 1890, once asked, "Is there not something worthy of perpetuation in our Indian spirit of democracy, where Earth, our mother, was free to all, and no one sought to impoverish or enslave his neighbor?"[9,6] I believe all of us, in our hearts, know the answer to his question. It is time now to act.

Notes

1. Don Jacobs, "Dance of Deception" in *Mother Jones on Line*, available at www.motherjones.com/reality_check/pineridge_contradiction.html on July 7, 2002.
2. This view is often taught in American schools today and sometimes even on Indian reservations. In 1492, Columbus sailed the ocean blue, then he "discovered" America, is how it goes. Seldom do students learn about his return voyage in 1493 with an invasion force of seventeen ships and his orchestration of an extermination of the Native population in the Caribbean islands that reduced about 8 million people down to 100,000 within seven years and down to only two hundred individuals within fifty years. Of course, within the next one hundred years, 100 million more of America's first nation's people would be killed by disease and violence. This also is not a favorite subject in American classrooms, but certainly gives pause for the adoration of Columbus.
3. Quoted in Ward Churchill, A *Little Matter of Genocide* (San Francisco: City Lights Books, 1997), 44.
4. T. C. McLuhan, *Touch the Earth* (New York: Outerbridge and Dienstfray, 1971), 57.
5. Don Trent Jacobs, *Teaching Virtues: Building Character Across the Curriculum.* (Lanham, Md.: Scarecrow Press, 2001).
6. Vine Deloria, Jr. and Daniel Wildcat, *Power and Place: Indian Education in America* (Golden, Colo.: Fulcrum, 2001).
7. Don Trent Jacobs, *Primal Awareness* (Rochester, Vt.: Inner Traditions International, 1998).
8. Don Trent Jacobs, "The Indigenous Worldview as a Prerequisite for Effective Civic Learning in Higher Education" Volume 2, 2002. *Journal of College Values*, available at www.collegevalues.org (July 7, 2002); see also *Teaching Virtues*.
9. Alexander Charles Eastman, "The Ways of the Spirit," in *The Wisdom of the Native* Americans, edited by Kent Nerburn (Novato, Calif.: New World Library, 1999), p. 115.

INTRODUCTION TO CHAPTER 8

In this chapter Berlowitz and Long discuss the history and role of Junior Reserve Officer Training Corps programs as one of the central methods of recruiting students into military service. The chapter highlights that in addition to recruiting, these programs serve a pedagogical function of teaching all students which values and dispositions are of social worth. As well, the chapter addresses the racial dynamics of JROTC programs as they prey on youth of color to create a military that is racially hierarchical and puts soldiers of color at greater risk—most often preparing them to go to war for White commanders against other nations of color.

CHAPTER 8

The Proliferation of JROTC

Educational Reform or Militarization

MARVIN J. BERLOWITZ AND NATHAN A. LONG

The primary objective of Junior Reserve Reserve Officer Training Corps (JROTC) is to serve as a vehicle of military recruitment. There have been some attempts to deny this and portray JROTC as a viable contribution to educational reform. However, the events of September 11 have created a climate that glorifies and provides legitimacy and a necessity for the objective of recruitment. The resurgence of Reagan's objective to destroy the evil empire, including the remnants of socialism in North Korea and Cuba; in addition to George W. Bush's offensive against significant portions of the Arab world, including Libya, Iran, and Iraq, will necessitate simultaneously opening multiple military fronts around the world.

The recent worldwide decline of socialism has given rise to a resurgence of conservative ideology, which takes the position that the economics of free enterprise constitute the only viable road to social and economic development. Any semblance of the welfare state in the form of social programs, regulation, or economic safety nets is seen as extraneous at best and an unwarranted obstacle at worst. The most rapid deregulation and privatization of social and economic institutions is the order of the day. This global movement has come to be known as neoliberal ideology.

Neoliberal policies and legislations have dramatically impacted the most vulnerable of the world's children, impoverishing them and often leading to their violent conscription into sweatshops, the sex industry, and the armed forces. In more developed nations such as the United States, the violent economic conscription of impoverished children into the armed forces is more indirect. Johan Galtung coined the term "structural violence" to describe the indirect violence that arranges institutions so that they systematically discriminate against specific groups; such discrimination is legitimated by dehumanizing ideologies such as racism.

Marvin J. Berlowitz is a professor in the Department of Educational Foundations in the College of Education at the University of Cincinnati, where he also serves as the Director of the Urban Center for Peace Education and Research (UCPER).

Nathan A. Long is currently a doctoral student in the Department of Educational Foundations at the University of Cincinnati. He also is a Melman Fellow with the Institute for Policy Studies in Washington, D.C., and assistant director for the Urban Center for Peace Education and Research at the University of Cincinnati.

The incorporation and proliferation of JROTC as part of the current U.S. educational reform movement constitutes a form of structural violence that employs economic coercion and deception to conscript disproportionate numbers of African Americans and other racially oppressed groups into the U.S. military.

A Brief History of JROTC

Since its inception, the U.S. government has strategized the military indoctrination of its youth for the purpose of preparedness and recruitment. The first official movement to implement training in military and democratic processes began with President George Washington, who, as early as 1789, had sought support for a "national university." It was Washington's philosophy that such an institution would enforce the ideals of democracy and the need to protect America's borders from foreign assaults against the free republic—both intellectually and militarily. The idea never fully materialized, due, in large part, to poor financial planning and lack of public support.

The concept of training youth to better serve America eventually came to fruition when Thomas Jefferson and the U.S. Congress founded West Point Military Academy (known more commonly as the U.S. Military Academy). Born out of concern that military officers were undereducated and lacking in skills that would benefit American forces in time of conflict, West Point Military Academy sought to rectify these issues via institutional military education. Over the next two centuries the country witnessed expansion ranging from the merchant marine, naval, coast guard, and air force academies to state preparatory academies, anchoring themselves throughout America effectively establishing military education as part of the American way of life.

The passage of the 1862 Morrill Act allowed for several million acres of public land to be set aside for the construction of land grant colleges and universities, and mandated that military instruction account for a portion of each new college or university's curriculum (including drill, military history, tactics and strategies).[1] Over time, this would set the framework for Senior and Junior Reserve Officer Training Corps within public educational settings.

However, the American public, most notably in the antebellum South, typically perceived both the academies, but more often the military establishment, with skepticism. Many citizens, still reeling from the rancor of the Civil War, found the idea of a federal standing militia unsettling. Standing militias and military training were sometimes viewed as "dangerous," even unconstitutional, and threatening to civilians' rights should a corrupt government seize control (it is interesting to note the irony of Southern concern over civil rights). This skepticism, alongside the growing isolationist tendencies of the American public, forced the government to impede growth with relation to increases in military-proposed aims.

Near the turn of the century (1898), the Spanish American War prompted some shift in attitude. America's military performance was scattered, often haphazard. Military officials, including "Rough Rider" Theodore Roosevelt, exhorted deep concern over American troops' preparedness. This concern (bordering on hysteria) led to eighteen years of political confrontation between pacifist and preparedness activists. For the first few years of the twentieth century, the preparedness advocates were gaining some momentum, claiming that if America was to remain a prominent force in world affairs and continue protecting its people from foreign attack, strengthening military processes was critical, including the training of young men in military process.[2] However, Woodrow Wilson's election to the presidency struck a severe blow to preparedness rhetoric. Wilson, tied to Southern ideals, knew very well the concerns many had about a strong, standing military in addition to his general repulsion to war.[3] Instead, he advocated for America to be an influence abroad as a neutral power. His approach stemmed from economic as well as political motivations. His stance was increasingly powerful in light of the fact that American industry was able to cater to various European nations, increasing profits and economic stability for the United States.

The arrival of World War I in 1914 drastically affected the pacifistic leanings of President Wilson, causing him to gradually reverse his philosophy. Though not yet immersed in war, over the next two years, several members of the Wilson administration, most notably General Leonard Wood, began voicing opposition to antipreparedness activists. Wood believed that if America was drawn into a war with Europe or was attacked, the military forces would be rendered useless. He began a national campaign to discredit the neutrality movement, sounding alarms to Americans that the military was indeed unprepared for any war or defense of its borders. Wood continued to implement military training camps for youth and spoke at numerous colleges and universities in an attempt to generate support for his preparedness platform.[4] He eventually received support from corporate executives and clubs devoted to the military in addition to the National Education Association, which advocated military discipline and training as relevant to a young American male's education.

The success of the camps, which enrolled hundreds of young men in the first year, coupled with the attacks against American merchant ships, the sinking of the Lusitania, and the economic "stickiness" confounding American "neutrality," prompted further (though strained) support from Congress and Wilson himself. As a result, on June 3, 1916, the most comprehensive congressional act for military reorganization in history was passed, known as the National Defense Act.[5] Among many other components of the act (including strengthening of the army, reorganization of the National Guard, and strengthening the Department of War's powers), the legislation established the Senior and Junior Reserve Officers' Training Corps. The original conception envisioned JROTC as the feeding element to ROTC. Though its impact was minimal at the onset, its objectives to establish an educated reserve officer commission were clear. Arthur Coumbe and Lee Harford, in *U.S. Army Cadet Command: The 10 Year History* noted JROTC units "required a minimum of three hours per week of instruction in military instruction over a period of three years. Any JROTC graduate who completed this course of military instruction was authorized a certificate for a reserve commission, to be honored at age 21."[6] Schools shared the financial burden with the federal government, including texts, weapons, uniforms, and the like.

JROTC did not initially enjoy either the popular or institutional support that it does today. Even the efficacy of the program in serving its alleged purposes has always been questionable. In fact, numerous military and political officials questioned its viability from the moment the National Defense Act was ratified. Increasing criticism surrounding recruitment and JROTC's drain on military resources were persistently voiced. In 1917, a report from the Bureau of Education, reviewed international efforts to train youth, and espoused the position that such training enhances military preparedness and operations.[7] It may be assumed that this act was attempting to reinforce the viability of JROTC by addressing the concerns raised by the Corps' critics. Yet as a result of the war effort and the mounting criticism, both Senior and Junior ROTC programs were temporarily dismantled, leaving approximately thirty units in operation nationally.

JROTC did not hold a strong grasp on the secondary schools until 1964 when President John F. Kennedy signed Public Law 88–647, commonly known as the ROTC Revitalization Act. This strengthened the amount of resources for the JROTC even though many of JROTC's detractors drew concern out of the fact that it accomplished very little in terms of viable recruiting outcomes. The Revitalization Act of 1964 proved critical, however, as Robert McNamara (secretary of Defense) and military officials redirected JROTC to be more aligned with recruitment and enlistment processes. Hence, JROTC units "between School Year 1963–1964 and School Year 1973–1974 . . . grew from 294 to 646 units, while enrollment increased from 74,421 to 110,839."[8] From this period through the early 1990s, JROTC enjoyed expansion and reform with support from presidents and congressional representatives. President Gerald Ford expanded JROTC from 1,200 to 1,600 units and President George H. W. Bush signed the next initiative to increase the JROTC to 2,900 units. Bush's drive toward expansion resulted from a successful new initiative titled "Operation Capital," which targeted inner city urban schools in Washington, D.C. for JROTC units. "Today I'm . . . doubling the size of our Junior ROTC program . . . we're going to expand it (from 1500) to 2900 schools . . . [JROTC is] a great program that boosts high schools completion rates, reduces drug use, raises self-esteem, and gets these kids firmly on the right track."[9]

Bush's proposed expansion was further buoyed by a memorandum issued from General Colin Powell in reference to Operation Capital. Powell emphasized that "[JROTC should have] particular emphasis . . . where drugs, gangs and juvenile delinquency flourish."[10]

Hence, the military retooled and billed the Junior ROTC operation as a means for providing leadership and development programs to at-risk youth. General Colin Powell solidified this stance by supporting Operation Capital, with its large successes, proliferate nationwide. Thus the push for JROTC units in every school was made and for all intents and purposes has succeeded. It is important to stress that JROTC on the surface states that its mission is not to recruit for the military, but to "motivate and develop young people." In 1999, President Bill Clinton expanded the units to over 3,500;

and, as of September 20, 2001, Congress passed a reappropriations bill for the National Defense Act, with full executive branch support, for lifting the caps entirely.[11]

Structural Violence as Economic Conscription

The recent globalization of the U.S. economy has resulted in dramatic structural changes. It has been transformed from a primarily industrial economy to one dominated by information technology and service. Dramatic increases in wealth and productivity have benefited a wealthy minority, but have led to a decline of the middle class and an intensification of the economic disparities between the very wealthy and the very poor. Current educational reform movements in the U.S. have concentrated upon preparing the U.S. to engage in more successful global competition, as typified in the Nation at Risk Report. In so doing, the focus on "urban education" which was so central to the "War on Poverty" of the 1960s has been omitted from the current agenda of reform. Not coincidentally, it is precisely in the population of urban school children where we find the highest concentration of poverty and racially oppressed groups.

Almost half a century after the landmark *Brown* decision which mandated an end to racial segregation and unequal opportunity in U.S. public schools, the majority of urban school children still attend racially segregated schools where inequities in funding and facilities preclude their viable participation in an economy dominated by the current scientific and technological revolution. For these children, the economics of racism so exacerbate the growing disparities between the wealthiest sector of the population and the poor that the latter have been referred to by some social scientists as the urban "underclass." And neoliberal ideology merely contributes to these economic disparities by making the privatization of public schools their central focus for educational reform.

The advocates of JROTC, who are endeavoring to transform their schools into military academies, target these "urban underclass" school children for recruitment. Defense Department guidelines for JROTC specifically seek "the less affluent large urban schools" and populations who are "at-risk." These children are trapped by a form of economic conscription referred to as the "push-pull phenomenon," in which they are pushed by poverty and the economics of racism and pulled by the promise of military benefits.[12] Once enrolled in JROTC, they are locked in by JROTC requirements, which are so time consuming that they preclude most college preparatory courses. The JROTC further channels these students by enticing them with a menu of "watered down" academic courses. Their function in the new global economy will be to serve as cannon fodder in the proliferation of "limited wars" waged against those forces that might interfere with U.S. protection and expansion of the free market.

The current approach of our federal government to the growing impoverishment of urban underclass youth is to institute the most draconian welfare reform in the brief history of the welfare system. Families are being deprived of even the most meager welfare benefits and sent forth to compete in a labor market that is infinitely more demanding than that of the industrial economy where even school dropouts could find viable long-term employment. Now they are being asked to enter this competition in a climate where the most severe austerity and drives for privatization are dismantling their public schools.

In response to the impoverishment of these families the Pentagon lavishes money on its campaign to proliferate JROTC. According to the *Washington Post*, in the past decade, their JROTC budget has more than doubled from $76 million to $156 million.[13] The most recent budgetary estimates from Army Cadet Command and the Department of Defense indicated monies for fiscal year 2001 show an increase in $7 million from the previous year amounting to $108 million. In addition, Congress approved an additional $65 million from reserve coffers for a total of $173 million. The number of JROTC high schools has risen from 1,464 to 2,267, with a 32 percent increase in enrollment bringing the number of adolescents enrolled to 310,358.[14] The most recent defense authorization bill (June 5th, 2001) called for the lifting of all caps on JROTC expansion, giving the Corps a green light for expansion into the secondary school system. Finally, it is crucial to understand the potential relationship between the above-mentioned statistics and military recruitment efforts. Over the past decade, the military experienced one of the largest draw-downs since the implementation of the National Defense Act. This severely cut recruitment efforts and budgets. A recent Rand research study of recruitment trends depicts the recruiting conundrum as sizable and potentially detrimental to enlistment needs due to the aforementioned draw-downs, budget cuts, and the lack of good recruiters and recruiter training. The study cites the need for more aggressive recruitment of those in high school (reaching students at an earlier age). One could assume the JROTC with its expansive budget and proliferation of units is perhaps the military's best response to its "recruiting crisis" as the program targets efforts toward first- and second-year high school students. Louis Caldera, Secretary of the Army during the Clinton administration, cited in his 2000 Report on the Army (ironically under the heading of "Meeting the Recruitment and Retention Challenge") that "the [JROTC] program may help motivate young Americans toward military service ... [JROTC] will inform young Americans about the opportunities available in the military while providing a positive influence during the high school years."[15] Army Cadet Command, while attempting to maintain its "veil of secrecy" over its real intentions toward recruitment, states in an internal presentation by Colonel Carlos Glover, JROTC director, that the main objective is to "Recruit quality prospects, retain quality cadets to commission, and sustain the force."[16] No matter how resolute the military elite remains about JROTC as a "nonrecruitment" source, the evidence points to recruitment as the main goal and primary benefit of the program.

In a surrealistic Horatio Algier extravaganza, General Colin Powell, an African American, has been cast as the Pentagon's Pied Piper of JROTC recruitment. The strategy appears promising as the proportion of African American cadets recently exceeded 54 percent. As for Latino immigrants, the federal government is unequivocal about waiving the requirement of a high school diploma as a condition for admission into the army, while continuing to vacillate in its support of the bilingual programs so critical to their academic development.[17]

Exploring the Claims of Military Recruitment: Myths versus Realities

Duplicity has always been standard operating procedure for military recruiters. There are at least four major deceptions central to the proliferation of JROTC. The first two of these deceptions are embodied in the assertion that JROTC will contribute to a reduction of violence and drug abuse in the public schools and enhance educational attainment and academic success. After the Los Angeles riots in 1991, Colin Powell contributed to this myth by claiming that the armed forces could provide an alternative, leading to a reduction of drug trafficking and gang activity. But then as the deception unfolds, the Pentagon assures itself the appearance of success by excluding many of the very students it claims to help. JROTC requirements include a minimum grade point average of "C" for admission and no prior history of behavior problems.[18] Furthermore, the image of the Pentagon as a role model for violence reduction requires the suspension of logic. The Pentagon institutionalizes the centrality of violence as a mode of conflict resolution. The JROTC specifically raises mixed messages to new levels, as the study of weapons, marksmanship, and membership in the National Rifle Association (NRA) are central to its curriculum in school systems attempting to enforce zero tolerance policies regarding the possession of weapons.

It is interesting to note that despite the abundant knowledge base, research, and programs committed to the nonviolent resolution of conflict and violence prevention, the federal government has chosen the militarization of public high schools as its priority. This policy decision was certainly not grounded in research and evaluation. A search of the social science databases revealed 157 studies on the efficacy of conflict resolution and violence prevention programs. Although results varied, this body of data tended to support the notion that conflict resolution and violence prevention programs have some measurable effect in reducing the level of violence in schools and improving school climate and academic achievement. A similar search, which included the Government Publications Office (GPO), revealed only four studies on JROTC. These studies focused upon JROTC objectives relating to "leadership skills" training. There was no accountability for JROTC's other claims of success because none of the studies included any school-based outcomes, such as a reduction of violence or drug abuse in schools, improved school climate, or measures of academic achievement or educational attainment.[19]

If we acknowledge the ability of JROTC to impart leadership skills, we must also take note of the fact that skilled leadership does not ensure constructive outcomes. Adolf Hitler, Charles Manson, and Al Capone serve as excellent examples of highly skilled leaders. Manuals dealing with leadership emphasize "following the orders of those above you" as the central element of leadership. History has demonstrated that the confusion of authoritarianism with leadership facilitates atrocities such as the Nazi death camps and the infamous massacre of the Mylai villagers in Vietnam. The Pentagon blithely ignores such connections in their JROTC history textbooks.

The Central Committee of Conscientious Objectors (CCCO–Western Region) has gathered relevant anecdotal evidence from newspapers. They found evidence to substantiate the claim that the institutionalization and glorification of violence in JROTC actually contributes to violence among its students. The following is a sample of these incidents:[20]

1. In Detroit, Michigan, a JROTC squad leader at Cooley High School reportedly formed a gang called the Fenkell Mafia Killers. The squad leader personally shot and wounded one person. Police say that on September 26, 1994, she ordered "a hit" at school in which a student was shot twice in the thigh.

2. Members of a Long Beach, California, JROTC unit formed a gang called the Ace of Spades (based on a special forces unit in Vietnam known for leaving cards on people they killed), went on crime sprees (including vandalizing a gay bar), then murdered Alex Giraldo, age sixteen, one of their members who they believed was talking with the police.

3. A year later, also in Long Beach, in August 1993, a member of the JROTC drill team scheduled to be the commander of this unit was arrested and charged, along with a former member of the JROTC program, with kidnapping and murdering an elementary school crossing guard.

4. In Arizona, Jonathan Doody, a seventeen-year-old ROTC enthusiast, murdered nine residents of a Buddhist temple. He was wearing military fatigues as he committed the crime.

5. In Clifton, New Jersey, one member of the Sea Cadets, a navy program for high school youths, conspired with his gang to murder, execution style, another member of the Sea Cadets.

6. In South San Diego County, JROTC students dressed in camouflage fatigues led "war games" in which they attacked and robbed immigrants coming across the border from Mexico.

7. On February 22, 1994, three JROTC cadets at Balboa High School in San Francisco were physically assaulted by the rest of the drill under the orders of the senior commander. One student suffered a punctured eardrum. The three have filed a suit. A secret city attorney's report, leaked to a reporter, revealed a five-plus year tradition of hazing, including, "a drill team initiation in which cadets jumped their victims, stripped off their clothes and paddled them with their hands and with a wooden slab from a broken desk. The investigation also found that members of the Balboa high drill team commonly beat fellow cadets as punishment."

8. An anonymous student in JROTC at a second San Francisco high school, Wilson, has admitted to taking part in a hazing at that school in 1991.

9. At Lowell, a third school with JROTC in San Francisco, the student paper reported "friendly" hazing is a tradition there too.

10. In Houston, Texas, in May of 1993, despite similar problems in previous years, the assembled drill teams were ordered to stand in formation in the

hot sun. Over fifty students were overcome with dizziness and/or fainted. Twenty-six students were hospitalized.

11. The most recent incident occurred in April 2001, involving an eighteen-year-old JROTC cadet from New Bedford, Massachusetts. He was charged after police found a small arsenal of explosives and machine gun bullets in his home. Ironically, he appeared in district court wearing the army shirt and pants issued by the JROTC.[21]

While the generalizability of these incidents might be questioned, these, along with the other evidence cited, seriously call into question the militarization of our high schools as a national priority.

The third deception of JROTC recruitment is the notion that such training enhances employability. Proponents of JROTC appeal to the popular belief that the military service increases employability by increasing discipline and by developing skills transferable to the civilian labor market.

Available evidence indicates that this argument is as weak as the first two. Among Vietnam-era African Americans, both veterans and nonveterans had a 9 percent rate of unemployment in contrast to a rate of 4.3 percent for whites.[22] In a longitudinal study of more recent cohorts, funded by the assistant secretary of Defense, it was reported that only 12.4 percent of male veterans and 5.0 percent of males who left the military reported any use of occupational skills acquired in the military in their postmilitary employment. However, their data on males who never served in the military revealed higher degrees of labor force participation and higher income. It comes as no surprise that the military terminated funding for the study in 1984.[23]

The fourth deception of JROTC recruitment perpetuates the myth that the armed forces are a sanctuary from the racist abuses prevalent in civilian life. Using General Colin Powell as their African American spokesperson, the Department of Defense has attempted to make the case that the military is a meritocratic sanctuary for those seeking refuge from the patterns of racist discrimination in civilian life. Despite the military's claim to be an equal opportunity employer, people of color currently constitute 32 percent of enlisted personnel while only 13 percent are officers.[24] The rates of conviction in court-martials, less than honorable discharges, and incarceration in military prisons are more than triple for people of color.[25] Thus patterns of racist discrimination in the military are comparable to the civilian criminal justice system. It should come as no surprise that a society in which racist patterns of structural violence are central would replicate these patterns in its military. Perhaps the myth of a meritocratic military is the cruelest hoax.

The most horrific and even genocidal manifestation of racism in the military is signified by the disparities in combat casualties. This is compounded by the prospect that U.S. imperialism pits people of color in disproportionate numbers in this country in mortal combat with people of color around the world. Dr. Martin Luther King, Jr. captured the essence of the intersection of an economic conscription at home and disparities in combat casualties in a statement aired by a Canadian radio station, opposing the war in Vietnam:

It was sending the sons, brothers, and husbands of the poor to fight and die and in extraordinarily higher proportions relative to the rest of the population. We were taking black young men who had been crippled by our society and sending them eight thousand miles away to guarantee liberties in Southeast Asia, which they had not found in southwest Georgia and east Harlem. And so we have been faced with the cruel irony of watching Negro and white boys on TV screens as they kill and die together for a nation that has been unable to seat them together in the same schools.[26]

In an information paper by the Department of the Army titled "Blacks in the Vietnam Conflict," cited in Binkin, it was reported that between 1961 and 1966 the casualty rate for African Americans was 20.1 percent. The proportion of African Americans in the general population during this period was only 10 percent and in the armed forces it was 13.7 percent.[27]

In his last Southern Christian Leadership Conference (SCLC) presidential address, Dr. Martin Luther King made the following demographic observations:

When we view the negative experiences of life, the Negro has a double share. There are twice as many unemployed. The rate of infant mortality among Negroes is double that of whites and there are twice as many Negroes dying in Vietnam as whites in proportion to their size in the population.[28]

Patterns of participation in the Gulf War reveal that the trend to disproportionately subject African Americans to the perils of combat is accelerating. Out of a general population of 12.4 percent, they were 30 percent of the troops in the Gulf. African American participation in the army was 29.1 percent, in the marine corps 16.9 percent, in the navy 21.3 percent, and in the air force 13.5 percent.[29]

The Gulf War was heralded as ushering in a new era of high technology warfare, which was limited in duration and U.S. combat casualties. And of course it was portrayed as a decisive "victory" for President Bush and future leaders of the New World Order. But revelations by the Czechoslovakian military and a protracted struggle by U.S. veterans' groups with the Congress and the Veterans Administration have revealed the unprecedented horrors collectively labeled as the Gulf War Syndrome. The survivors of the Gulf War and future "victories" can look forward to incurable lesions covering their bodies, disabling chronic cancer, headaches, vision loss, and a legacy of birth defects for their children.[30] Given the trends discussed, it is likely that people of color will suffer these horrors in disproportionate numbers.

Conclusion

As stated earlier, conscription in developed nations such as the United States takes the form of structural violence with racism as central to its self-perpetuation. It is therefore imperative that the lack of racial diversity in peace organizations be overcome if they are to be effective in their struggles against conscription. And the strategy for overcoming this lack of diversity must be multifaceted. The concept of positive peace, which recognizes the dialectical relationship between the struggle for social justice and the struggle for peace must replace concepts of negative peace, which define peace, merely as the absence of violence.

In his analysis of the shortcomings of socialist as well as trade Union organizations, William Z. Foster called for a struggle against white chauvinism, which would lead to a greater acceptance of leadership from people of color. Peace organizations must also accept a significantly increased leadership from people of color. Peace researchers and peace organizations must begin to study and celebrate the contributions of peace leaders such as Mary Church Terrell, Coretta Scott King, Diane Nash, Bayard Rustin, Ralph Bunche, and James Farmer with the same enthusiasm as they extend to Dr. Martin Luther King, Jr. Peace can never be achieved "in a white skin while the black is branded."

Notes

1. Russell Weigley, *History of the United States Army* (Bloomington: Indiana University Press, 1984), 282.
2. Ibid., 342–54.
3. Ibid., 378–80.
4. Ibid., 342–54.
5. *The United States Statutes at Large* (Washington, D.C. Government Printing Office) (39), 191–94.
6. Arthur Coumbe and Lee Harford, *U.S. Army Cadet Command: The 10 Year History* (Washington, D.C.: Government Printing Office, 1996), 258.
7. W.S. Jeswein, *Military Training of Youths of School Age in Foreign Countries*, Report prepared for Bureau of Education, Bulletin 17, No. 25 (Washington, D.C.: Government Printing Office, 1917).
8. Coumbe and Harford, *U.S. Army Cadet Command*, 261.
9. President George H. W. Bush, Speech to Lincoln Technical Institute Students, August 24, 1992.
10. Coumbe and Harford, *U.S. Army Cadet Command*, 276.
11. Congressional Record, House, National Defense Authorization Act for Fiscal Year 2002 (147:123), (Washington, D.C.: Congressional Record, September 20, 2001), sec. 538.
12. Marvin J. Berlowitz, "Racism and Conscription in JROTC," *Peace Review* 12, no. 3 (2000): 394.
13. Coleman McCarthy, "ROTC and the Three Rs: A Bad Mix," *Washington Post* (April 18, 1995): C9.
14. Ibid.
15. Louis Caldera. "Report of the Secretary of the Army," available at www.dtic.mil/execsec/adr2000/army.html (December 13, 2000).
16. Col. Carlos R. Glover. "Junior ROTC: Forging Leaders and Citizens," available at www.acc.mil (December 10, 2001).
17. Catherine Lutz and Leslie Bartlett, *Making Soldiers in the Public Schools: An Analysis of the JROTC Curriculum* (Philadelphia: American Friends Service Committee, 1995), 6.
18. Ibid., 12.
19. Daniel Kmitta, "Effects of JROTC Programs: Negative Evidence," University of Cincinnati, unpublished paper presented at the second annual International Education Conference (1994), 1.

20. These incidents were compiled by the Central Committee for Conscientious Objectors (CCCO) Western Region located at 655 Sutter Street, San Francisco, CA 94102. The (CCCO) provided the following primary sources:

   1. *Detroit News* 9/28/94
   2. *Press Telegram* 6/18/92, 6/21/92, 8/5/92; *LA Times* 6/22/92
   3. *LA Times* 8/11/93
   4. *Morning Call* 5/17/93
   5. *New York Times* 2/15/94
   6. *LA Times* 2/24/90, 4/26/90, 10/3/90
   7. *San Francisco Examiner* 3/4/94, 3/5/94, 3/9/94, 4/6/94, 10/9/94, 10/30/94
   8. *San Francisco Chronicle* 3/5/94, 4/6/94, 6/16/94, 10/10/94; *San Francisco Independent* 3/11/94, 3/22/94
   9. *San Francisco Guardian* 3/9/94, 6/15/94; *San Francisco Weekly* 3/9/94, 5/4/94, 5/18/94; *Washington Eagle* 4/94
   10. *Bay Area Reporter* 6/30/94; *Philadelphia News* 10/14/94; *Sentinel* 9/28/94

21. Megan Tench, "On the Defensive JROTC Says it Teaches Discipline, Critics Say Violence," *Boston Globe* (April 13, 2001), B1.
22. Sharon R. Cohaney, "Employment and Unemployment Among Vietnam Era Veterans," *Monthly Labor Review* 113, no. 4 (1990): 22–29.
23. Stephen L. Magnum and David E. Ball, *Military Service, Occupational Training, and Labor Market Outcomes* (Columbus: Center for Human Resources Research of the Ohio State University, 1986).
24. Judy Rohrer, "JROTC Expansion: The Defense Department's Plan for the Public Education," *Z Magazine* (June 1994): 36.
25. Martin Binkin and Mark Eitelberg, *Blacks and the Military* (Washington, D.C.: Brookings Institution, 1982), 170.
26. Martin Luther King, Jr., "A Trumpet of Conscience" in *A Testament of Hope: The Essential Writings of Martin Luther King Jr.*, edited by Melvin J. Washington (San Francisco: Harper and Row Publishers, 1986), 635.
27. Martin Binkin and Mark Eitelberg, *Blacks and the Military* (Washington, D.C.: Brookings Institution, 1982), 76.
28. Martin Luther King, Jr., *A Testament of Hope: The Essential Writings of Martin Luther King Jr.*, edited by Melvin J. Washington (San Francisco: Harper and Row Publishers, 1986), 245.
29. Marc Crawford, "Fighting Wars Abroad," *Emerge Magazine* (April 1991): 16.
30. Gregory Jaynes, "Walking Wounded," *Esquire Magazine* (May 1994): 70–75.

INTRODUCTION TO CHAPTER 9

Haggith Gor's chapter explains the extent of militarism in Israeli education. This chapter is the only one in the volume that does not focus on schooling in the U.S. context. However, her chapter relates directly to the U.S. in a number of ways. First, the distortions of history and the ideological dimensions of the curriculum that celebrate power and violence and frame peace and understanding as impossible ideals are very familiar in U.S. schools and culture. Second, Gor elaborates on the way that the Holocaust, as both a collective identity-forming event and as an ideology, informs the militaristic form of schooling in Israel. To any reader in the United States, the events of September 11, though not in any way comparable to the Holocaust, can be understood for how they too are naturalizing violence and forming the basis for ideologies of survival-justified brands of aggression. As she suggests in the end of her chapter the United States attack on Afghanistan has the same logic as the Israeli onslaught against Palestinian civilians. Third, Gor suggests an important parallel regarding her insight that the ideological uses of the Holocaust obscure global interests such as the arms industry, which plays a major role in the Israel Palestinian conflict. The same can be said of the U.S. war on terrorism which obscures global interests, such as oil, that play a central role in the intensified U.S. aggression. Finally, Israel is a U.S. client-state that allows the United States to project power in the region. Israel's hypermilitarism owes to United States military and financial largesse. Israel is the largest recipient of U.S. economic aid—about $3 billion a year. Israel has also been a conduit to arm nations around the world, including apartheid South Africa, with U.S. weapons.

CHAPTER 9

Education for War in Israel

Preparing Children to Accept War as a Natural Factor of Life

HAGGITH GOR

After the Oslo agreements, a wave of peace education initiatives swept Israeli schools. The ministry of Education declared peace as 1994's central theme in schools, and every school was obligated to address the subject in various ways. A visitor to any school that year would see white cardboard doves, olive branches, and children's poems decorating the walls. Cynically, we called it the "Year of the Dove." Most schools addressed the topic superficially, teaching of Peace as a utopian dream we all strive for, detached from the realistic issues of the conflict, ignoring Palestinian culture, language, human rights, human diversity or social justice. Dealing with the topic of peace did not change any substantial attitude in our education system.

Following Yitzhak Rabin's assassination in 1995, schools reacted by designing a memorial corner in each classroom for Rabin, and by holding memorial services on November 4. Most of the physical space dedicated to Rabin's memorial, including the content of the memorial ceremonies, stressed his heroic military career. His steps toward peace, which were controversial in Israeli society and served as an alleged reason for his murder, were played down in the commemoration of Rabin as a leader. Thus the legend of the man fit into the militaristic education that characterizes our education system.[1]

It would be misleading to discuss education for peace in Israel without an understanding of the social-political setup that laid deep-rooted foundations of militaristic education—cleverly integrated into the infrastructure of our schools and hardly noticed by the majority. Understanding the sociopolitical backbone of Israeli education, which is by substance an education for war, is necessary, in my opinion, in order to acquire an ability to change and bring about a transformation on the grassroots level. Any attempt to apply peace education otherwise would be reversed, the same way that Rabin's commemoration became a worship and admiration for his military career and legend.

We need a better recognition and understanding of today's militaristic

Haggith Gor is the head of the Center of Critical Pedagogy, Kibbutzim College of Education. She is the author of different curricula in peace education, human rights, and gender equality. She is also an academic consultant for several social justice educational projects.

education. A militaristic education constructs thinking and emotional readiness to accept the use of power as answers to political problems.[2] It teaches the individual to dismiss its effects on her or his personal life and view it as a natural, normal, and even healthy course of life. Without a critical analysis of the education for war that occurred in the mainstream Israeli education system, a significant change is not likely to takes place.

I see a correlation between education for war and the psychology of power and powerlessness that governs our lives. In Israel, children are psychologically prepared for war in a variety of ways. The message transmitted through the teaching of holidays, literature, history, and the Bible, even through ceremonies in schools is that power represents the only option that guarantees life. What is at stake is our physical survival; it is a question of the survival of the fittest. There is no alternative. One has to be strong, powerful, and ready for war. It is a message that perpetuates and strengthens our victim mentality. War is just, because we were dragged into it, because we are its victims, much in the same way as we were victims of the Holocaust.[3]

As a result of our collective trauma, our education system prepares children for war, albeit perhaps unconsciously and unwittingly. The message it sends, often strengthened by education at home, provides the rational and emotional justifications for fighting. It prepares boys for personal sacrifice; for the sake of the collective, it prepares girls to serve the boys—soldiers—bearing children and sending them to the army. It is intimately linked to the confusion we Jews suffer from, in the shadow of the Holocaust, between power and powerlessness.

The analysis of how education in Israel constructs a culture that accepts militaristic solutions to policy issues is an analysis of my own education. I was born and grew up within this culture and accepted it until my early adulthood. My father immigrated to what was then Palestine in 1936, while it was still under British rule. His middle-class Austrian family had a clear, realistic grasp of the future rise of fascism in Germany and decided to carry out their Zionist belief and emigrate from Austria. On arriving here he volunteered for the local British police force, into which many young Jews enlisted in order to receive paramilitary training. Later on, he volunteered for the Jewish Brigade of the British army, deployed to combat the German forces in northern Italy. The next stage of his military career took him to the Haganah—the Jewish underground active prior to establishment of the Jewish state—and to the Palmach—the most prominent combat units of the Haganah. After the State of Israel was founded and the Israel Defense Force established, he became a lieutenant colonel. I grew up on his heroic stories. As a young girl I felt cheated by the fact that I wasn't born a boy and by the fact that I'd missed out on the "courageous battles." The growth of my critical consciousness and my realization of the deep militarization of Israeli education was a slow and painful process of severing integral parts of myself.

The message I got at home from my father acknowledging the importance of military power is one that is transmitted already at kindergarten level in Israel's education system. Cognitive and emotional messages, such as "we must be strong and united, because in the absence of unity, we risk the danger of annihilation," are common. The implicit motif that there are only victims ("The whole world is against us," "Everyone is out to destroy us") and heroes is widespread and perceived as a "natural" given truth. The exercise of power serves, therefore, as an appropriate response to the feeling of powerlessness. Military option becomes a logical answer to problems. Observance of human rights is not presented as a potential answer to the persecution suffered by the Jews. Our education system offers no middle ground, only black and white solutions of victor and vanquished. It portrays the Jews' conflict with the Arabs as a zero sum game in which what is good for one is necessarily evil for the other.[4]

The teaching of Jewish holidays, a focal point from preschool level, revolves around myths of heroism and evokes strong feelings. Hanukkah, the Festival of Lights, for example, commemorates the revolt of the Jews against Greek rule in 167 B.C.. The uprising broke out after decades of Greek control, in response to the coercion of the Hellenic religion upon the Jews. Children in kindergarten are taught that the Greeks persecuted us, only to be defeated by the heroic Jewish Maccabees. The emphasis is on strong identification with the power of the Maccabees who defeated the evil Greeks. A great deal of dramatic play in kindergarten centers on the Sons of the Maccabees who rebelled and were brave fighters. The boys are assigned the role of the heroic warriors; the girls make *latkes* and support them. Their role as the sacrificing mothers bearing their heroic pain graciously are transmitted through the "Hanna and Seven Sons" story. (According to the legend, she watched her sons being executed in front of her, but refused to bow down to a statue and save their lives this way.) Instead of stressing the universal message of freedom of religion, there is an emphasis on the importance of Jewish nationalism, of power, and the strength of the Maccabees.

Purim, the festival of costumes in a carnival-like atmosphere, commemorates a biblical story, which took place in ancient Persia. King Achasverosh, under the influence of one of his advisers, ordered the destruction of the Jews. It is important to note that nationalistic ideas and chauvinist concepts are transmitted together by assigning girls and women to their traditional inferior place in society. Vashti, the first beautiful queen of Achasverosh, was sent away from the palace because she dared to say "no" to her king. The message girls get through the way the story is being told is strong and clear. "Be obedient to your king or else you would be driven out of the palace. And with no king to serve, your life is not a worthy life." In addition, Ester, the chosen beautiful queen after Vashti's expulsion, saved her people (the Jews) by using her sexuality to influence King Achasverosh. Protecting the Jewish collective justifies every act, even the one that goes through the king's bed. As I mentioned nationalism and chauvinism go hand in hand.[5]

In Purim the emphasis is on the persecution of Jews ("the goodies"), by Haman and his cronies (the "baddies"). The universal message of negation of autocracies, or rejection of discrimination of ethnic minorities, that stems out of this story is not transmitted in our education system. On Independence Day, children are taught that Arabs wanted to throw us into the sea and that the armies of all seven Arab states surrounding us invaded Israel. The day is celebrated in kindergarten as a military holiday. Kids visit military camps and teachers display flags of various military corps. Children hear heroic tales from the War of Liberation and send gifts to our soldiers. Instead of celebrating the establishment of a democratic state, which, in its Declaration of Independence, enshrines equal rights—without regard to race, sex, and religion—they bow down to power. Boys are taught to admire the soldiers and identify with them; they are encouraged to develop fantasies of being fighter pilots, tank drivers, or submarine commanders. Girls are encouraged to mail sweets to the front and wait for their hero soldiers to return from the army. They are expected to give unconditional support.[6]

In some of the kindergartens the celebration theme was admiration to the army: "the teacher parades the children dressed in what seemed like IDF uniform and march them to and fro as they call out 'left, right left,' and 'attention!' or 'at ease!' The military parade was accompanied by children singing at the top of their lungs: 'Soldiers of Israel, march on and stay on guard, both day and night.' At another kindergarten, in a small town near Tel-Aviv, the graduation ceremony included storming targets with [toy] swords. There too the children recited texts about being fighters in the service of the state of Israel."[7]

The emotional imprinting at a very early age, prior to the development of critical faculties, makes it highly unlikely that at a later age, children will express doubts, ask questions or reexamine what has been drilled into them. The list of unquestioned concepts engraved into the children's minds from early age is simple and clear: admiration of the army and its power, simplisticly dichotomous, look at the national reality of denomination of the Arabs as enemies, assigned roles of boys as heroic soldiers and girls as patient accepting mothers/wives who iron uniforms with love and devotion.

In higher classes, national history is taught from a Jewish-Zionist perspective. This school of thought perceives anti-Semitism as the major element linking Israel to other nations. Our view of history relates to two thousand years of anti-Semitism, during which different oppressors plotted against us. Rational "facts" are added in history lessons to the emotional, experiential knowledge derived at a younger age. History is a continuum of plots against Jews in different countries, resulting from anti-Semitism; the expulsion from Spain in the Middle Ages, the Chemelnitzky riots, and so forth.[8] Then there is the story of Massada, where Jewish zealots, fortressed on Mount Massada, slaughtered their wives and children, and then committed suicide themselves, so as not to fall into the hands of the Romans. The story has become a myth about an unflinching stand against the enemy, a symbol of power and heroism. The pronouncement of "Massada shall never fall again" has taken on added significance in relation to the establishment of the State of Israel and its victories in the wars against the Arabs: pride and independence are worth more than life itself.

Consistently, through the study of history, we are defined from without, by the way others view us (by anti-Semitism), rather than from within, through our own perceptions and values. While the historic narrative learned may have made sense at earlier times, ignoring other narratives in our days does not serve in understanding of the Other and getting closer to peace. Our education system presents the Israeli Arab conflict as a war that was inflicted on us by the Arab rejection of peace. Other perspectives, explanations that contain complexity of interests and viewpoints, do not penetrate schools.

Clearly, the message absorbed already at a young age is particularistic and not universal; the Jews are faced by an enemy, not conditions under which the likelihood of persecution might be diminished. Events are related in terms of what was done to the Jews as Jews, rather than the Jews as a minority. We embrace strength and power rather then humanism; we adopt the emotional rather than the rational. The messages lack self-criticism and reappraisal. They are gleaned from one perspective only, one historiography that students must accept as absolute truth, leaving no room for other lines of thought.

The history textbooks and curriculum taught in high school went through major changes since 1975. It enabled more autonomy to teachers; it included variations in teaching-learning methods and realization that goals should be determined by the discipline structure. Yet the contents were geared toward the consensual Zionist narrative. The new curriculum preserved the Zionist ethos of the new Israeli Jew and thus the old perspective remained untouched. In spite of the declared recognition in the necessities of pluralism, the Other was not included in the hegemonic story.[9]

Changes in the academy led to the publishing of two new modern history textbooks in the 1990s, one by the Ministry of Education curriculum department and another by history scholar Eyal Nave.[10] These two textbooks attempted to include the Palestinian perspective of the 1948 war. They threaten the official right story and received a very harsh critique, which caused a "political storm." The heated public debate reached the education committee in Parliament and resulted in a reluctance of schools to use it. The new minister of Education Limor Livnat, upon her entrance to the ministry, banned the new textbook written by the curriculum department of the Ministry and ordered it to be shredded.[11] Thus she signaled a clear message to the schools that any deviation from the hegemonic national story would not be tolerated, the "official right" version of history must be taught with no exceptions.[12]

Thus the attempt to present some of the criticism of the new historians and develop an inquiring mind in the young learners failed. The possibility of looking, for example, at the Zionist movement in the context of European colonialist background where it started, was concealed as illegitimate in the political atmosphere of 2000. The ability of the Israeli academy for a critical look at the orientalism,[13] which characterized the Zionist movement, was not allowed to be taught to high school students.

The Holocaust plays a central role in the continuum of events and provides evidence of the role of the Jews as history's victims of anti-Semitism.[14] The Holocaust symbolizes the epitome of the Jewish feeling of powerlessness. It created the myth of the Jews "who went like sheep to the slaughter." The teaching of the Holocaust also provides incisive proof of the thesis of power: we suffered it all because we had no state. The myth was of weakness and powerlessness vs. the myth of power; "they went like sheep to slaughter" versus "had the State of Israel existed, everything would have been different." In the acquired mind-set, it is preferable to be a perpetrator than a victim: "Never again will we be victims." It was hammered forcefully into my head as a child. My mother experienced adolescence under Nazi rule, in the course of World War II. Her mother survived Auschwitz, while she herself was a fugitive, moving from one hiding place to another throughout the war. I grew up listening to a recurring argument between my mother and father. He was critical of the Jews who failed to rebel against the Nazis, "they went like sheep to the slaughter," he repeated the common saying, while she insisted that his view was an arrogant, uncomprehending judgment. It hurt her and made her cry. He was in fact expressing a belief that organizing and becoming an army was a solution to the Jews' helplessness. Such a belief is at the core of the pervasive militarization of education in Israel. As a young girl I experienced a split—rationally, I agreed with Dad; emotionally, I sided with Mom. One of the effective structures underpinning patriarchy is the higher credibility assigned to (supposedly male) rational thought and devaluing emotions.

The conviction that physical survival is at stake serves as a justification for everything our army does. Although Hitler did not succeed in physically annihilating the Jewish people, he did win, insofar as he instilled in us the perpetual fear of physical destruction and ingrained a psychology of survival that is infinitely more about the physical aspects of that survival than about its nature and quality. In the shadow of the Holocaust, the Jewish people find it difficult to walk the line between power and powerlessness, or as former Israeli Foreign Minister Abba Eban has so aptly put it, "To distinguish between the psychology of our vulnerability and the reality of our power." The trauma of total powerlessness, which we experienced as individuals and as a people, led us to heightened anxiety about loss of control, feelings strengthened by our education system.

During the Holocaust we were the vanquished. We will never let that happen again. The existence of options other than victims and perpetrators is not a part of our mind-set. The possibility that there are other ways of protecting ourselves (peace, for example) does not exist in our consciousness and does not therefore appear in our curricula. For most Jews, the State of Israel is the only answer to the Holocaust. The Arabs became, knowingly and unknowingly, surrogates that symbolize the powers out to destroy us (including the Nazis).[15] Consequently, the justification for fighting them becomes clear. The history of our wars with the Arabs is taught in that manner. The chronology, beginning with 1945, is taught as military history;[16] battles are enumerated and justifications for wars found. Other facets, such as the cultural, economic, or social, are hardly dealt with. The central motif is clear, even bordering on the simplistic: the Jews must successfully defend themselves against their Arab aggressors.

History presented from this perspective serves to justify war and prepare the boys, intellectually and emotionally, "to die for the sake of our country," and the girls, to support them in this endeavor. There is emotional identification with the need for war; after all, "we have no alternative." After years of learning from history that only wars can deliver us from death, the thought that a particular war may not be essential, or that there is another way of solving a conflict, is not presented as an option for discussion. The collective identity of first-, second-, and third-generation Holocaust survivors[17] makes it difficult for many of us to make the distinction between the feelings of victimization that emerged from the Holocaust and those emanating from our present reality.

To take one example, in Jewish-Arab encounters, Israeli Palestinians talk about the suffering they have undergone as a result of the conflict, but the Jews talk about the Holocaust. The Jews have a need to show that their victimization was greater.[18] In a situation where no distinction is made between our past victimization and our present reality, every act of terror or war takes on the significance of plots against the Jews as Jews. The logical conclusion: the struggle against the enemy is a struggle unto the death, which justifies every action, regardless of price—curfews imposed upon an entire population, the violation of human rights, or hostile public opinion.

Our concern with physical survival is rooted in reality. There were periods in history in which our physical survival was endangered, both as individuals and as a people. Yet, many of our responses to the present-day reality stem from unresolved issues of the past. The intensity of feelings aroused by the Holocaust, even if repressed, runs deep.[19]

It has been several years since our physical survival was at stake. Yet, we haven't adapted the perspective through which we educate our children to that changing reality. The State of Israel's very foundation is built on powerlessness. Our education system tries to turn out Israelis who are not powerless as a collective; Israelis who won't "go to the slaughter like sheep." It is a system that does not teach its young people about tools nations need to survive in today's world. Fear of physical annihilation runs deep and is in many cases genuine, yet it originally comes from an inner reality. It also serves now as a manipulative mechanism of control in the education system. This way, the education system is engaged in an undifferentiated repetition compulsion, as we catapult our children into a viscous cycle of self-fulfilling militaristic prophecies.

It is difficult for us to rid ourselves of our self-perception as victims, deeply imprinted as it is in the psychology of the second-generation Holocaust survivors in Israel. It serves to justify and emotionally convince people to continue to fight. Jewish soldiers are fighting not only for themselves here and now. They are also fighting for the Jews who were annihilated in the concentration camps, devoid of the ability to fight back.

These messages are transmitted in the teaching of the Holocaust in a way that makes for a deep emotional impression. Critical self-examination is needed to allow us to distinguish between our psychology of vulnerability resulting from the trauma of the Holocaust and present-day reality.

The way Holocaust is viewed helps to conceal understanding of the global interests that play a major role in the Israeli Palestinian conflict, the interests of the arms manufacturing for example. Israel is a vibrant active test field of a new weapons. We serve as guinea pigs for American and European arms industry. By ensuring a perception that wars with the Palestinian are inevitable, the global arms industry gets its guarantee that Israeli youth will not question their interests before enlisting and risking their lives.

Education at home and in school unwittingly helps create a hermetically sealed rationale that facilitates the sacrifice of a son, or a partner, a rationale supported by social pressure. Jews who are forced to send their children into the army may well have to pay a very heavy price, the price of life. Such sacrifice evokes traumatic memories of the Holocaust, memories of a terrible loss. That is why we are in need of an ordered worldview, grounded in well-established beliefs in the justice of our ways. How otherwise could we justify the immense sacrifices involved? The justifications must necessarily be stronger than the innate need to protect our children. We need a well-thoughtout strategy in order for that to happen, one applied to the very young, so as to reach a level of bluntness necessary for the sacrifice we have to make. Such a system is constructed during a child's schooling, covering his cognitive, emotional, and motor domains. It uses social pressures, both of the peer group and of the adult world.

Home and school are well synchronized in this effort. The education system uses diverse means and directions: history, trips, holidays, the Bible, and literature. It works in accordance with all the effective educational rules. It is consistent and hard to question. A critical approach and the raising of doubts can undermine it. But these do not go past the school's gates.

The history learned is one of absolute truths: a closed book with no room for criticism or doubts. It does not call for questions, such as who wrote it. Or, what were the interests of the presenter? Or, are there perhaps, other histories, other narratives as well? Children in Israel are educated with a simplistic view of reality, a view that sees only black and white, just and unjust, right and wrong. It is a view that strengthens the need to fight. The absence of peace necessarily means war. There is no middle ground.

Yet, Israel's ability to understand the limits of power is the key to a change of the message supporting war and national power, which the education system transmits.

When Prime Minister Rabin announced that peace had been reaced with made an enemy and that the PLO is the only Palestinian partner with whom we can make peace, activists of human rights education were joking that he took this phrase out of our teachers guide of peace education. Yet education did not become a negotiable subject for any group discussing the peace agreement. Among the teams negotiating the different aspects of peace, an education team has not been established to introduce the necessary changes in the psychology of war education. Prime Minister Rabin's handshake with PLO leader Yasir Arafat created, for the first time, an alternative to the dichotomous view that sees only a winner and a loser. That handshake opened an option hitherto unknown in our psychological repertoire. It stirs up fears and anxieties even among the left in Israel, among people who, for decades, fought for peace. The bullet that killed Rabin was taken from the same education arsenal of the victim psychology.

Over ten years later, most of the public in Israel is convinced again that we have no partners for peace, that we have done everything we could to obtain peace and the Palestinian rejected our genuine and sincere efforts. Over ten years later Israel's Prime Minister Ariel Sharon, like his predecessor Ehud Barak, (both ex-generals), doesn't find it difficult to convince the Israeli public that the state terror inflicted by the Israeli army on the Palestinians in the occupied territories is an inevitable defense war, and the Palestinian terror attack on civilians is part of their plan to annihilate the State of Israel. A majority of Israeli's were raised and educated with this historical interpretation as a sole narrative. Breaking away from it, examining other possible narratives, means defying the militaristic consensual education.[20]

After September 11 many Israelis felt that "Americans will better understand us, now they will understand what it means to live under terror and will know that the military force applied on Palestinians civilians in the West Bank and Gaza is a 'no choice' war with an enemy who understands only power." The lesson of the Holocaust and the lesson of the suicide bombing and terror attacks are the same; in this mind-set, we have to react with power, and we have to crush the enemy, the same way that the American's attacks on Afghan civilian is justified as a reaction to September 11. No other alternative is possible. It is a strong position that overpowers all other ways of thinking.

Notes

1. Vered Vinizky-Sarusi, "The Commemoration of a Violent Narrative: Rabin's Memorial Ceremonies in Schools," in *Militarism and Education*, edited by Haggith Gor (Tel Aviv: Babel, 2003).
2. Peter Kraska and Victor Kappeler (1997) "Militarism is a set of beliefs and values that stress the use of force and domination as appropriate means to solve problems and gain political power," Militarizing American Police: The Rise and Normalization of Paramilitary Units" *Social Problems*, February 1997, vol. 44, no. 1, 1–16.
3. Avner Ben Amos, ed., History, Identity and Memory, Past Images in Israeli Education, School of Education, Israel Polack's unit for sociology of education and community, Tel Aviv University, 2002.
4. Rela Mazali and Haggith Gor, "Man, Woman, War and Peace," *Panim, Quarterly for Society, Culture and Education* (Summer 2001).
5. Haggith Gor, "Purim Scroll," *Davar Aher* 38 (March 1995).
6. Haggith Gor and Rela Mazali, "Militarism in Israeli Education," *Mifnae*.
7. Aviv Lavie, *Up on the Jungle Gym, Charge! Ha'aretz* (June 28, 2002).
8. Ruth Firer, *Agents of the Zionist Education* (Tel Aviv: Hakibutz Hameuchad, 1985).
9. Avner Ben Amos, "Impossible Pluralism," *History of European Ideas* 18, no. 1 (January 1994): 267–76.
10. Eyal Nave, "The 20th Century," Tel Aviv: Sifre Tel Aviv, 1999; Dan Yakobi and Nava Dekel, eds. *World of Changes, History for 9th Grade* (Jerusalem: Ministry of Education).
11. Rally, Sa'ar, "Livnat Decided to Ban the History Textbook: World of Changes" Haartz, 13.3.2001.
12. Eyal Nave, Ester Yogev, *Histories: Toward a Dialogue with the Israeli Past* (Tel Aviv: Babel, 2002).
13. Edward Said, *Orientalism* (Tel Aviv: Am Oved, 2000).
14. Keren Nili, "Influences of Public Opinion and Holocaust Research on Teaching of the Holocaust in High Schools and Informal Education in Israel between 1948–1981," Hebrew University, Jerusalem, 1985.
15. Phillip Lopate, "A Distance from the Holocaust, Resistance to the Holocaust," *Tikun* (May–June 1989).
16. Eli Podeh, *The Israel-Arab Conflict in the History and Civic Textbooks, 1953–1995*, 1997,
17. Avner Ben Amos, ed., *History, Identity and Memory, Past Images in Israeli Education*, School of Education, Israel Polack's unit for Sociology of Education and community, Tel Aviv University, 2002.

18. Haggith Gor and Rela Mazali, "Reflections on Encounter Groups of Jews and Palestinians from Israel," Research Report to the Ford Foundation, April 1998.

19. Refael Yoel, ed. *Concealed Memory and Unconcealed Memory, Holocaust Conciseness* (Tel Aviv: Ministry of Education, 1998).

20. "To fight militarism we must resist the socialization and brainwashing in our culture that teaches passive acceptance of violence in daily life that teaches us we can eliminate violence with violence." hooks, "Feminism and Militarism: A Comment" in *Women Studies Quarterly* 23 (fall/winter 1995) 58–64.

INTRODUCTION TO CHAPTER 10

Julie Webber's chapter focuses on the reformulation of U.S. foreign policy in the form of the Bush administration's expansion of military force doctrine as its representation participates in the broader culture of violence informing school violence and school security in the U.S. Webber explains how the increasingly singular response to school violence of zero tolerance fails to address the causes of school violence that are part of a broader attempt to squelch more democratic forms of schooling that could avert such violence. As Webber puts it, "the environment in which education takes place (by no means limited to the school site, but reflecting the school's absorption into the political environment that houses it) determines the ways in which student resistance takes place. Central to understanding this impact on schools is the impact of foreign policy and militarization on domestic populations."

CHAPTER 10

Post-Columbine Reflections on Youth Violence as a (Trans)National Movement

JULIE WEBBER

We have already seen—in Afghanistan and elsewhere—that domestic unrest and conflict in weak states is one of the factors that create an environment conducive to terrorism. More importantly, demographic trends tell us that the world's poorest and most politically unstable regions—which include parts of the Middle East and Sub-Saharan Africa—will have the largest youth populations in the world over the next two decades and beyond. Most of these countries will lack the economic institutions or resources to effectively integrate these youth into society.

—"Worldwide Threat—Converging Dangers in a Post 9/11 World," Testimony of Director of Central Intelligence George J. Tenet Before the Senate Select Committee on Intelligence

The "Columbine event" crashed into our collective present on April 20, 1999, and to add further aspects of incomprehensibility to the event, the authors chose Adolf Hitler's birthday to symbolize their rage at the students at Columbine High School in Littleton, Colorado. This event marked the trauma of school shootings in so serious a way that it took school violence outside the intelligible boundaries in which it had been previously contained; further, the choice of date identified the event with fascism. In the years preceding Columbine, the hermeneutic bandages provided by experts neutralized the effects of prior shooting events. Focusing on the specific themes raised by the means of violence, they exploited the obvious features (violent film, guns, psychiatric disorder), ignoring the role that schools and society might play in provoking violence. The public was able to contain its anxiety/hysteria by ingesting these explanations and managed to separate the experiences of those traumatized communities from ones that might take place closer to home. The media interpretations managed these events for the viewer by containing them to precise determinants/precipitants for indicators of school violence. After Columbine, the school became the locus of intervention, but when the critical gaze turned inward, it wasn't the school that was examined, it was the student body.

Julie Webber is assistant professor of politics and government at Illinois State University. Her research focuses on the intersection of politics and education, especially theories of violence in education. She is the author of *Failure to Hold: The Politics of School Violence* (Rowman & Littlefield, 2003).

Post-Columbine, the wound was continually torn open by episodic witnessing rituals (such as *See You at the Pole*) throughout the country or scare campaigns promoted by the antigun lobby; these forms of collective renewal were largely confined to the special interest groups that sponsored them. The boldest example of this has been the campaign suggested by Senator Jessie Helms and subsequently written into the Juvenile Justice Bill, to have the Ten Commandments posted in schools.[1] The Family Research Council has extended this campaign, encouraging positive role models (lawmakers, teachers, and so forth) to post them in their offices. In the fall of 1997, students recruited into prayer circles following the shooting at West Paducah, Kentucky, were not primarily concerned with witnessing the shooting events in an effort to prevent their occurrence in the future. Nor were they speaking out to "work through" their emotional implications, but rather to witness the presence of God in their lives to others. This witnessing is significantly different from the type that would take place following Columbine. Instead of witnessing as an exercise of persuasion (persuading students to bring God "back" into the schools, to feel his presence in their lives, to serve as missionaries for the Christian cause) the post-Columbine testimonies mirrored the event, shattering the public's defenses. Columbine ruptured the boundary between public mourning and civility demonstrating the fragile separation of church and state, faith and politics.[2] No longer able to get the necessary "pathos of distance" from school violence, the public began talking, incessantly.[3]

What is ignored in most interpretations of youth violence is their interconnectedness to the media and the polity; that is, how violent youth across the globe have, in the absence of what Mary Kaldor calls a "forward-looking political project," engaged in violence, becoming increasingly militarized and justifying their violence by resorting to nostalgic images of past political movements they have not lived through or experienced.[4] This chapter discusses the ways in which public indifference to global affairs and passive militarism have contributed to the transformation of social relations within the United States. Further, it uses the public's reaction to school violence as an instructive example of how the popular mind-set equates containment strategies of the cold war with effective public policy measures in a theoretically democratic society. While nonstop media attention has characterized the post-traumatic stages of Columbine era as a means of healing, more aggressive forms of preventive medicine have been favored to deal with the threat of repetition elsewhere. Within schools, any and all available means to contain student violence have been implemented without regard for the difficulty it may cause students and how it may possibly contribute to future violent episodes. We can see how this new trend in youth mobilization for violence that is backward-looking and largely imaginary surfaces in the Columbine shooting. Thus, the third, and perhaps most important concern is to make the connection, however fragile, between student disposition toward militarization and U.S. foreign policy objectives. (Indeed, even the teachers and administrators are "collateral damage" from the point of view of the student shooters—they're aiming at *students en masse*.) By favoring epiphenomenal sources of motive such as predatory culture, violent masculinity, guns, video games, pornography, biology, and psychiatric illness, the "experts" have ignored the material evidence of the shootings. The fact is that shootings take place at school, against classmates in areas that are not beholden to the formal curriculum. I aim to show that the environment in which education takes place (by no means limited to the school site, but reflecting the school's absorption into the political environment that houses it) determines the ways in which student resistance takes place. Central to understanding this impact on schools is the impact of foreign policy and militarization on domestic populations. For the form that this resistance takes is scripted by the militarized culture in the United States. By examining several texts that look at the connections between foreign policy and domestic civil practices we shall see the precise extent to which acting as an "American" is an outcome of foreign policy endeavors abroad and the military readiness necessary to carry out U.S. foreign policy objectives, specifically through a reorganized military based on fourth-generation warfare aided by liberal capitalist exploitation of every available resource from outer space to ideas about daily life.[5] What was (and is) needed is a new way of looking at the hidden curriculum in the context of the changes in foreign and domestic policy pre- and post- September 11, one that applies new concepts to a radically altered form of hidden curriculum; one not tethered to the nation-state conceived of as an empirical entity with stable values and interests attached to it (e.g., nationalism), but a shifting concept of political allegiance that is semiotically driven by mediated events.

Borrowing a much/over/badly used term from foreign policy analysts, containment is said to have been first used by George Kennan in 1947 to "start" the cold war,[6] and expanded upon by American studies scholars more recently to describe the containment of schools by corporations within U.S. society.[7] There are a number of other uses of the term containment, but this chapter will briefly outline a very specific form of containment that is used to seemingly pacify domestic populations, especially student populations, because they are not only potential fodder for the war machine, but they are the next generation of militarists, whose dispositions need to be effectively shaped to continue to justify future militarism and therefore support administrations that favor the military information complex. First, it is necessary to outline and discuss three important terms in relation to education as "enforcement" where the narrative of containment is most effective: the domestic analogy, the so-called RMA (Revolution in Military Affairs), and militarization.

Domestic Analogy

The domestic analogy is found in a famous realist school text by Hans Morgenthau called *Politics among Nations*. Morgenthau argues that relations between nations are different from relations between individuals within a society. This difference is owing to the peculiar arrangement of power in each sphere: in the domestic sphere, there is law, and in the international sphere, there is none (anarchy, which simply means the absence of a sovereign). The argument works like this: domestic factors do not (and should not) pollute U.S. foreign policy because they obscure the analyst's ability to read the balance of power in the international realm and figure out where and when intervention is necessary. The analogy upon which this imperative rests is the smallest domestic group shared by most societies, the family (not individual). According to realist logic, humans have always (and will always) organized themselves in groups for the purposes of conflict, and the group is to be protected from outside forces, but the composition of the group itself and the relations between its members are said to be largely unimportant. Of course, imbedded in this assumption is the idea that the internal aspects of the group are unimportant because they are cohesive and relatively peaceful compared to the bellicosity coming from other groups outside the family unit.[8] During the cold war, subversive and national liberation movements around the world discovered the flaw in this assumption: domestic populations can be turned against one another in foreign wars for which most of the citizens in the imperial nation-state—read the United States—do not see the value of supporting the war, economically and in terms of loss of human life on both sides of the conflict. All the weaker, or insurgent groups have to do is extend the war and not lose.[9] When the Bush administration and Defense establishment make arguments to revamp relations between Congress and the executive branch, the reorganization of the military structure and command and the increase in budget devoted to national defense, they argue that it is to fight "asymmetric conflicts." Asymmetrical warfare is simply another name for the strategy of guerrilla fighters and national liberation movements, only now it has been broadened to include terrorist attacks and groups that do not claim to "liberate" a named people or a land.[10] Yes, this is Vietnam all over again, but with some notable exceptions. It is necessary first to understand how and why the U.S. military has conceptualized the post–cold war era in this particular way.

> Here we are in the year 2002, fighting the first war of the 21st century, and the horse cavalry was back and being used, but being used in previously unimaginable ways. It showed that a revolution in military affairs is about more than building new high tech weapons, though that is certainly a part of it. It's also about *new ways of thinking*, and new ways of fighting.
>
> —Defense Secretary Donald Rumsfeld, "21st Century Transformation of US Armed Forces," National Defense University, January 31, 2002.

The new strategy of military thought that accompanies the response to asymmetric warfare is the "revolution in military affairs" as Donald Rumsfeld has consistently argued in public speeches. This revolution is severely debated by scholars, policy analysts, and the defense establishment as to whether it's really a revolution, if it's feasible or affordable, a genuinely new approach to warfare or simply another means to spend taxpayer dollars. What is no longer in debate post-September 11 is whether it will be implemented; the Bush administration has gone forward with the technological, strategic, and financial means necessary to implement the revolution (it's a bit like Lenin's reformation of Marx's theory of capitalist revolution: a chain is only as strong as its weakest link). Although it must be said that the Clinton administration laid much of the groundwork for this revolution to take place by supporting the deregulation of the communications industry and allowing independent firms to militarize space without censure.[11]

Thus, what the RMA intends to accomplish is an overhauling of the US military ground forces, its strategic command and sources of intelligence. This revolution does not aim to transform the military in light of the changing nature of conflict around the globe caused by economic disparity and globalization, but rather is intended to increase the United State's comparative advantage in military technology in order to maintain stability in regions around the globe through monitoring and surveillance technologies. This increased advantage from "above" operates like a global panopticon, allowing the United States to eliminate potential asymmetric threats posed by groups that oppose globalization in its present form. Why would the United States do this? Well, before markets can be created the areas on which firms have set their sites must be stabilized.

The most important trend inaugurated by the RMA that the Bush administration's neorealist policy will institute is to transform social relations within the United States and perhaps abroad. The success of RMA will depend on U.S. citizens' willingness to pay for it with budgets already increased over 20 percent for military spending alone. This willingness will also depend on the media's ability to influence citizens to support high military expenditures at the expense of other social welfare items, such as public schools and subsidies. This support to overcome the public divisiveness, which military spending in the absence of a clear threat poses, depends on two things: the success of militarizing the U.S. population and the necessary threats to sustain this militarization. This process will transform social relations within the United States and abroad by changing the nature of gender relations through the valorization of war technology and concepts of duty and sacrifice, and will disproportionately affect racial and class lines by coloring threats and prompting widespread austerity measures in a shrinking U.S. marketplace. This will also disproportionately affect gender relations as we witness an ongoing retrograde movement to put women back in the domestic space, or contain them as necessary to go forward with militarization. Examples of this gender retro movement range from U.S. popular culture to justifications for waging war in Afghanistan.[12] A recent television show demonstrates the split between the RMA and the effects of an increasing militarization of the U.S. mind-set. If you're wondering why *Meet the Folks* is a popular television show, ask yourself how the original film *Meet the Parents* was so horribly misinterpreted by the media: a newly retired CIA agent monitors, interrogates, and tortures his proto-son-in-law and by the end of the film asks *him* for his hand in marriage! Dragging his militarized mind into the domestic space, the father played by Robert de Niro is a caricature of a bygone cold war era, not a model for each and every American father to emulate as the new television show presents him. What makes Americans now imagine that they are CIA agents who should interrogate other Americans?

Militarization

Populations worldwide will need to favor militarization on an increasing scale for the RMA to be successful. The nature of this militarization is less about old cold war ideas of "us" versus "them" that are clearly stated and explicated by ideologies, but about fearing the other in any form. This new disposition toward a war (on four fronts as the Bush administration is now conceptualizing it, instead of two) does not depend on national unity. The schools had previously supplied the state with its national component; the group cohesiveness that sustained the competition of the cold war. This explains why both republicans and democrats are like-minded concerning school vouchers and the disintegration of public schooling. Previously, the school was a citizen-building institution that formed nationalism in people at an early and impressionable age. It built the "nation" part of the nation-state. As is often noted by critical IR theorists, the sovereign nation-state is a relatively new concept and is often conceptualized as the vehicle for the goals and progressive claims of the Enlightenment.[13] This newness should alert scholars and activists to the instability of the entity that it designates: the populations, territories and nationalisms that are assumed to follow from its logical premise. So, if we are to think about foreign policy, especially U.S. foreign policy, as a stable or fixed policy that is backed by the national will or interest, then, given the newness of both the United States and the concept, we have grounds for sufficient speculation. Further, I would note that at the outset of the cold war theorists had already pointed out the precariousness of assuming a stable "national interest" in foreign policy decision making.[14] Likewise, other scholars have pointed out that even the term foreign was not associated with national policy until Bentham coined the term and its actual use by states trailed long after that.[15] In short, the nation-state is new and national unity has already been undermined by globalization since at least the 1970s. The government does not need national unity to continue the process of war-making; it only needs for the domestic population to become militarized and it can do without the schools in this process. Key is understanding how this militarization will be continued and maintained (for it has already been achieved).

According to Michael Mann, we must at least "define militarism in a way that makes it at least potentially separate from states" and he goes on to define it this way, "Militarism is the persistent use of organized military violence in the pursuit of social goals."[16] The only change that has occurred post–cold war in terms of militarization is that the organization of violence has changed; it is no longer fought through nation-states, but through groups whose allegiances constantly shift and change according to resources and capital. Fortunately for military planners, there is a perfect symmetry between capitalist growth and militarization as they both locate productive allegiance in the individual. All that is necessary to continue support for militarization is to make the individual afraid of potential threats in civilian life. Worldwide, 80 percent of casualties in military excursions are civilian, occurring in the poorest parts of the world, which, as George Tenet's quote shows, also have the greatest youth populations and the smallest economies. And yet, if we look at the percentage of fear aroused in populations, we would have to say that the United States has quite possibly the greatest share. Arguably, this is because of the September 11 attacks; however, the United States has been deprived of terror relative to other states in Western Europe, Great Britain, and Asia.[17]

Essentially, what I am arguing is that this new home-grown militarization is the result of the emotional damage done to U.S. populations during the cold war who are now freed from an identifiable enemy, but are encouraged to police themselves for the sake of security. Following the cold war, populations, primarily in the United States, have become inundated with the ideas of militarization with no clear-cut military objective that would base its claims on the national interest (Waco, Oklahoma City, school shootings, workplace shootings).[18] A clearly *detached* military disposition is what is responsible for this mentality.[19] This mentality is detached because of the need for U.S. citizens to view themselves as individuals; that is, as "clearly delimited social agents" responsible for their own security, which is transformed into bodily and emotional integrity. By viewing themselves as separate (and vulnerable), citizens take on the policing of themselves. As Mary Kaldor has noted, private security in the United States now outnumbers the police by two to one, and, in the absence of clear threats, we can only be fearing ourselves. As Tom Ridge urges Americans to fear, police, and snitch on one another, we can see that he took a page out of the book of school violence. Homeland Security is designed to root out terrorists in our midst, but it is more likely to expose the ordinary idiosyncrasies of citizens to one another in a moral outrage the likes of which have not been seen since the McCarthy era. As Osama Bin Laden continues to elude U.S. intelligence the media must keep hope alive that he will be found and punished, as U.S. allies abandon support for a war on terror they sense is less about September 11 than the intervention strategies of a falling empire. And, finally as globalization marches on, by which I mean our unending support for ideologies of competition and valorization of information technologies and ill-advised labor exploitation worldwide, youth with nothing to do will find salvation in picking up arms and fighting wars that contribute nothing to global progress.[20] Global youth movements will increase, it's a demographic fact; but whether or not they are militarized is up to those who govern the world and the people who support them. Finally, we will continue to witness youth violence in the United States, not because the youth are "evil," but because the culture that nourishes them is uncivil and increasingly militant with more and more competitive attitudes and less and less prospects for future progress.

We should view school violence as an effect of the extension of foreign policy no matter how far the signifying chain extends into the public sphere. In a globalized world, we cannot afford to think of the public school as a site for nation-building and consensus modeled on old cold war paradigms. Recent literature has shown the school is less a citizen-building institution than a site for corporate exploitation, training individuals to think of themselves as consumers in a marketplace who need to compete against one another and fear the unknown.

My intervention into this discussion has been to argue that not only do states formulate and use foreign policy to reinforce their sovereignty; and to extend their sovereignty in the United States or simulate that it is really there.[21] States also use it as a basis for their domestic policy; this is what Kennan attributes to the Soviet Union at the start of the cold war. The conceptual apparatus of foreign policy comes to frame whatever domestic crisis the United States is currently experiencing. Arguably, the United States' former policy of containment toward the Soviet Bloc was the basis for domestic policy with regard to militant movements within the United States. This is demonstrated in the case of the United States following the cold war. In the absence of a dominant international paradigm on which to base foreign policy, the United States (and scholars of U.S. foreign policy) struggled to find a model for decision making based on the balance of power status of the international system (Was it bipolar, unipolar, multipolar, hegemonic, or an empire in decline?). As one paradigm waxed then waned, the executive office of the United States began to focus on the inside while trying to maintain a fragile "hold" on the aleatory outside. Without a coherent policy the United States foundered in its diplomatic missions and military interventions (Somalia, Bosnia, Dayton Accords, financial crises in Southeast Asia) the only clear-cut victory was in 1992, when President Bush forged a bombing campaign against the Iraqi invasion of Kuwait only to find it was liberating less than a nation-state as the recognized government was able, thanks to the virtual age of technology, to flee the territory with all the national wealth.[22] This era has been referred to as the era of "recline" in which all foreign policy endeavors failed but also failed to provoke political imagination, ushering in the "end of history" (Fukuyama) when all other states were to follow the United States's path to development and history was said to remain forever launched on the same boring liberal capitalist path.[23] September 11 changed all of that as those asked to follow the path resisted.

Containment as Domestic Foreign Policy

Education was an issue largely ignored by the federal government during the cold war, except at the outset when school curriculum was encouraged to compete with that of the Soviet Union (e.g., *Sputnik* and the space race) in the late 1950s. However, once the cold war had officially ended, education once again became a rhetorical issue in presidential debates. Goals 2000, as a means for helping U.S. students compete in international markets was an important tool in this debate. Finally, the repeated failure of the United States to master any foreign policy endeavor was compensated for by containing the inside (e.g., student identity). Although one among many identities that were policed during the cold war era (the political identities of the left-leaning, women as housewives, men as wage-earners and soldiers, and so forth) the student identity has always been the most important for the national security state because it needs a militarized population to support its wars, and most important, a reserve army of labor to fight them, even if in the United States this means "above the ground" through satellite technologies and unmanned aircraft.

Containment

It is an undeniable privilege of every man to prove himself right in the thesis that the world is his enemy; for if he reiterates it frequently enough and makes it the background of his conduct he is bound eventually to be right.

—Mr. X, "The Sources of Soviet Conduct"

Educational researchers frequently reference the events of the cold war between the United States and the Soviet Union as determinants of curriculum development. For example, allusions to *Sputnik* as the watershed event in U.S. education often bring with them accusations that the space race reoriented the curriculum to overrepresent certain subject areas—math and science. Alongside this curricular change, a significant amount of shaming took place in which educators were criticized for dropping the ball in the competition between the two superpowers. The metaphors of the cold war were very important rhetorical devices used to motivate and at times coerce educational scholars and practitioners into dropping their own educational standards in favor of those inspired by U.S. foreign policy. This occurred even when such remarks were as unabashedly condescending as Reagan's proud assertion that teachers were "clerks for the empire."

Even though the cold war is over, its policies still operate in the minds of U.S. policymakers, especially those who have been called on to address the problem of school violence. In the aftermath of the Columbine shootings, the media debated which level of the government should intervene to assess and recommend policies to prevent further student violence. The overwhelming response was that the federal government should address the problem immediately. President Clinton called on Attorney General Janet Reno to work out the prosecutorial options presented by the shooting (i.e., whether or not the case could try anyone and, if so, at the federal level). Congress put aside regular business to formulate a Juvenile Justice Bill that would effectively dismantle the juvenile justice systems operating at the state level. No longer content with panel sessions discussing student violence hosted by the first lady and Carolyn McCarthy (D–New York), the public invited the federal government to enact large-scale policies that would be designed to prevent further violence. Meanwhile, this focused attention obliged school administrators to take under advisement the policy initiatives recommended by the federal government. Part of this initiative demanded that schools look to exemplars of school security such as Boston public schools and those systems that had already adopted surveillance strategies.

Perhaps it is an effect of policy lag; that is, that foreign policy during the U.S. reign as international hegemon operated at such an existential level that it became part of its national identity. This claim implies that the United States doesn't know itself, as such, without containing resistance to an opposition. The influences that formerly presented themselves as capitalist contradictions are now signified as systemic "glitches." Now that the cold war was over and capitalist logic operated as uncontested victor, there was nothing more to do, as Baudrillard said, than perfect the model.[24] Part of this model was and still is the perfect citizen-consumer, disciplined and quieted by consumer comforts. This disposition is molded by the hidden curriculum of the schools. When the media pundits call upon every American to support the war on terror they are asking them not to support an identifiable way of life that has a coherent political philosophy and value system behind it, but the right to consume without disruption by outside forces, even if they are suffering for our consumer habits. Either old cold war policy, the one recommended by Kennan, or the one actually pursued by Paul Nitze's Department of Defense conformed to a policy of containment similar to that practiced in the schools as a response to the "threat" of violence posed by shootings. The object of the policies is to never trust or consult the policy object directly, but to slowly and deliberately locate it and shut it down, forcing it to conform to the dominant ordering principle of society (e.g., herd mentality and vigilante justice) or, as I have argued here, a version of world order that imagines others as accessories to U.S. desires, including student populations.

Outside determines inside or, rather, is used to determine elections on the inside as well as increase output of certain markets as in Pentagon capitalism. "Foreign policy is a specific sort of boundary producing performance," writes David Campbell, and it uses the outside, the concept of the "foreign" or "different," to realize its (the state's) identity.25 But I wish to go further here and argue that not only does foreign policy serve this boundary policing function, but it also serves domestic populations a heavy dose of hyperidentified nationalism that targets individuals and is exacerbated by the social effects of market competition and militarization. As the shootings at Columbine High School were taking place, media pundits moved between shots of students falling out of broken windows to coverage of the United States-led bombing of Kosovo. Moreover, mediated examples of masculinity circulate almost without value during this crisis as one masculine marker is exchanged for another in an economy of desire completely detached from any gendered regime of intelligibility.26

In schools whose communities and workers find overt security measures distasteful or harsh, programs designed to target nonconformist student behavior are becoming popular. Marketed as the "humanitarian" alternative, conflict management programs in which monitoring and surveillance of behavior are significant features of violence prevention are designed to mediate problems between students whose anger interferes with school functioning. Not only are students asked to conform to the rigid disciplinary concerns of the school administration through conflict management programs, but they are also asked to snitch on one another. What is so insidious about this ideological alternative is that it is justified as protectionism with the intention of looking after the welfare of those nonconformists. For their own good, school administrators reward peer reporting. Students in the new "leadership" programs report students whose behavior, dress, and extracurricular performance deviates from the (invisible) norm of the school. Most disturbing, however, is the revelation that medicated students are routinely monitored to ensure that they do not lapse in taking their antidepressants. This might not be so disturbing if studies were not reporting 25 percent of the student population on medicine for depression. Yet, as a school administrator claims, the situation is under control now that the normal students are cooperating with the disciplinary apparatus. As she is quoted as saying of the peer reporting, it "gives us 130 pairs of eyes."[27] This same response would later characterize the release of terrorist pictures to the public by the government asking citizens to identify and help find potential terrorists lurking in our midst.

Other forms of monitoring not popularly associated with security technology are more easily adopted yet infringe on student rights. Policies like dress codes prevent students from wearing clothing that could conceal weapons or demonstrate consumer preferences. Also, the banning of backpacks or the adoption of a clear-backpacks-only policy limit student confidence and trust. These forms of discipline are the most popular because they, unlike metal detectors and body searches, do not resemble prison security procedures. Yet, these forms of monitoring and control do slowly chip away at the confidence students have and the trust they feel for one another contributing to the overall militarization of the domestic population of the United States. Specifically, these disciplinary procedures act as subtle forms of fear-based indoctrination. It doesn't matter how indirectly offensive the procedures may be (certainly the cold war was indirectly offensive; primarily defensive), they still undermine the public trust necessary to develop the skills students need to cultivate to live and participate in a healthy democracy. Further, these measures also exist outside of public schools in places of business where employees are forced to carry clear purses, as the assumption is they might steal the merchandise. As Lipshutz underscores, the "insecurity dilemma," a generalized and pervasive sense of fear with no identifiable source, has promoted active citizen participation in monitoring and surveillance throughout the public sphere, and it is these affective responses that animate reactions to crime, tragedy, and violence. Instead of asking, in a serious way, how these measures might affect the development[28] of student's democratic skills, they are enacted in the name of safety and protection. Security has become the only response to school violence, but it will never solve the problem. Meanwhile, a generation will grow up as if they were inmates in a prison, not citizens in a free society.

Notes

1. For more on this, see William Chaloupka, *Everybody Knows: Cynicism in America* (Minneapolis: University of Minnesota Press, 1999). As he writes in response to the "values remedy" to political cynicism, "Believers insist that a smothering layer of values will help reconcile democracy's necessary noise, its many codes and strident voices, with the ongoing need for clear national focus and policies. The problem is that values talk provides an opening for resentful and cynical backlashes that corrupt institutions, including those institutions the believer endorses, such as education and journalism" (p. 23).

2. The media's relentless portrayal of the battle between the parents of slain students and those who would publicly support the salvation of the perpetrators' souls was played out with crosses built and placed on a hill overlooking the school site.

3. See Friedrich Nietzsche, *On the Genealogy of Morals. Ecce Homo*, trans. W. Kauf-

mann (New York: Vintage, 1967 [1887]) for the pathos of distance. This term may be read as similar to Jacques Lacan's ethical claim that one maintains a necessary distance from the object of desire.

4. Mary Kaldor, *Old and New Wars* (Palo Alto, Calif.: Stanford University Press, 1999), 7.

5. Donald Rumsfeld, on transforming the Department of Defense, is informative here, "We must promote a more entrepreneurial approach to developing military capabilities, one that encourages people, all people, to be proactive and not reactive, to behave somewhat less like bureaucrats and more like venture capitalists; one that does not wait for threats to emerge and be 'validated,' but rather anticipates them before they emerge and develops new capabilities that can dissuade and deter those nascent threats," available at www.defenselink.mil/speeches/2002/s20020131-secdef.html, p. 8.

6. There is much debate surrounding the origins of the cold war. In fact, it is now a cottage industry. See Ernest May *Interpreting NSC-68* (Cambridge: Harvard, 1993), the Cold War Museum Project, and any book by revisionist historian John Lewis Gaddis.

7. Alan Nadel, *Containment Culture: American Narratives, Postmodernism and the Atomic Age* (Chapel Hill, N.C.: Duke University Press, 1995) and Kenneth J. Saltman, *Collateral Damage: Corporatizing Public Schools—A Threat to Democracy* (Lanham, Md.: Rowman & Littlefield, 2000) (respectively).

8. Feminist critics have called attention to the fact the border is not stable because the domestic sphere is not the "safe" zone Morgenthau needs it to be in order to have an unstable outside. Further, the actual domestic space that Morgenthau uses as an analogy, the family, is problematic because this space is not safe or conflict-free either See J. Ann Tickner Gender, "International Relations" in *Women and War*, edited by Jean Bethke Elstain (New York: Basic, 1987). U.S. society has operated as if the inside should be (and is) stable with relatively little democratic discussion of the matter.

9. See Andrew J. R. Mack, "Why Big Nations Lose Small Wars: The Politics of Asymmetric Conflict," *World Politics* 27, no. 2 (1975): 175–200.

10. As Mary Kaldor has argued, the difference between "old" and "new" wars and our ability to apprehend their significance to the people fighting them is that new wars are driven by economic and political vacuums in poor, developing countries whose leaders use nostalgia for the past to gain allegiance to fighting causes. The difference between terrorist groups and rebel factions now she argues, is that they no longer aim to capture the "hearts and minds" of people but capitalize on their fear and hatred for the other. Kaldor, *Old and New Wars*.

11. See Jack Hitt, "The Coming Space War," *New York Times Magazine* (August 5, 2001). Hitt's most important analysis is of the deregulation of space for independent corporations and the explanation of how this was a way for the U.S. government to avoid violating the 1967 Outer Space Treaty, which explicitly states that space cannot be used by governments for military purposes; however, corporations who wish to use it for commercial exploitation through satellite technology, which is the basis for fourth generation warfare, can rent it to governments for military purposes.

12. See Joan Wallach Scott, "Feminist Reverberations," keynote address at Twelfth Berkshire Conference on the History of Women, June 7, 2002, Storrs, Connecticut, available at berksconference.org/programs/scott.htm (July 16, 2002). This speech will appear in *Differences* 13, no. 3 (February 2003).

13. Arguably, the state, as a legal term, predates the Enlightenment by over one hundred years, but politically and most important, ontologically, the realization of Enlightenment according to Hegel took place through the vehicle of the modern state.

14. Arnold Wolfers, " 'National Security' as an Ambiguous Symbol," *Political Science Quarterly* 67 (1952): 481–502.

15. David Campbell, *Writing Security: U.S. Foreign Policy and the Politics of Identity* (Minneapolis: University of Minnesota, 1992), 42.

16. Quoted in Ronnie D. Lipschutz, *After Authority* (New York: Suny, 2000), 175.

17. Andrew J. Bacewich, "Terrorizing the Truth," *Foreign Policy* 125 (August 2001): 74–75. The numbers are up in Asia, but there were zero in North America prior to September 11, with the next highest rates going to Africa, Latin America, and far behind in Western Europe.

18. And yet, we see it elsewhere, the increasing militarization of youth in the global south whose only access to economic security is to join mercenary armies or be sold into prostitution or slavery, in school shootings in northern europe such as the Netherlands and Germany as well as the European enclaves of South Africa, the incorporation of young women into the armed forces as the means for achieving upward mobility, but most important, gender equality, the use of rape as a war strategy, the inclusion of native women in militant liberation movements in Mexico also as a means for escaping previously accepted gendered roles, the influence of JROTC in schools all over the United States, and the incentives offered for continued participation in the national security state, and so on. See Cynthia Enloe, *Maneuvers* (Berkeley: University of California Press, 2000). Enloe speculates that the reason the United States refuses to sign the UN Convention on the Rights of the Child (or even begin the process of ratifying it) is because they would have to dismantle the JROTC program, which provides that children cannot be recruited for military purposes.

19. For a more theoretical discussion of this process see the classic by Georges Bataille, "The Psychological Structure of Fascism," in *Visions of Excess Selected Writings, 1927–1939*, edited, introduced, and trans. by Allan Stoekl (Minneapolis: University of Minnesota Press, 1993).

20. For an explanation of this ideology, "globalism" see Manfred B. Steger, *Globalism* (Lanham, Md.: Rowman & Littlefield, 2001).

21. Cynthia Weber, *Simulating Sovereignty* (London: Cambridge, 1993).

22. Timothy W. Luke "The Discipline of Security Studies and the Codes of Containment: Learning From Kuwait," *Alternatives*16 (1994): 315–44. Enloe 2000, 12–14; 242–44. For an example of the tropes deployed during the Gulf War, see Avital Ronell, "Support Our Tropes" in *Rhetorical Republic: Governing Representations in American Politics*, edited by Frederick Dolan and Thomas L. Dumm (Amherst: University of Massachusetts Press, 1993).

23. Arthur Kroker and Michael A. Weinstein, *Data Trash: The Theory of the Virtual Class* (New York: St. Martin's, 1993).

24. Jean Baudrillard, *The Perfect Crime*, trans. Chris Turner (New York: Verso, 1996).

25. Campbell, *Writing Security*, 69.

26. R. W. Connell, *The Men and the Boys* (Berkeley and Los Angeles: University of California Press, 2000), p. 150–55.

27. "A Week in the Life of a High School: What It's *Really* Like Since Columbine," *Time* (October 25, 1999): 75.

28. Ronnie D. Lipschutz, *After Authority* (New York: SUNY, 2001).

INTRODUCTION TO CHAPTER 11

To assist teachers in teaching to the standards, we have developed curriculum frameworks, programs of study, and curriculum models with daily lessons. These materials are based on training models designed by the Military Command and General Staff Council. . . . Increasingly, we have built collaborative relationships with the private sector.

—Paul Vallas, former "CEO" of Chicago Public Schools and current "CEO" of Philadelphia Public Schools.

Sheila Landers Macrine's chapter considers how the rhetoric of enforcement informs the educational reform debates in the Pennsylvania state seizure of the Philadelphia schools and subsequent transfer to largely private for-profit management companies such as the Edison Schools. Macrine's chapter highlights the relationship of disciplinary rhetoric to privatization reforms that assault the public sector. Her chapter uniquely centers on the youth, teachers, and administrators who have resisted the state and corporate sector in Philadelphia and the teachers and administrators who oppose this form of corporatization that is guided by disciplinary language and logic.

CHAPTER 11

Imprisoning Minds

The Violence of Neoliberal Education or "I Am Not for Sale!"

SHEILA LANDERS MACRINE

> Ain't it funny how the factory's doors close
> Round the time that the school doors close
> Round the time that the doors of the jail cells
> Open up to greet you—like the reaper
> —Rage Against the Machine, "Ashes in the Fall"

Over the past few years, the Philadelphia school district has been under siege from the blight of poverty to threats of take-over. Under-resourced and abandoned by state and federal monies, the school district has hobbled along. Then in December 2001, the state of Pennsylvania seized control of the city's schools and practically put them on the auction block. Yet, the state had no intention of running the schools. They are following the Bush administration's embrace of proposals to privatize education and open public schools to the market. The state had plans to sell off the management of schools to the highest bidder. In an unambiguous transfer of public monies to private hands, the state replaces the management and organization of public institutions like schools, hospitals, and even prisons with the ever-encompassing neoliberal model of corporate management. The case of the Philadelphia schools is another example of public institutions under attack.

As many for-profit and some nonprofit school management companies applied to run clusters of Philadelphia's low-performing schools, the newly state-appointed School Reform Commission (SRC) awarded Edison Schools Inc., the country's leading for-profit manager of public schools, a six-year, $101 million contract to run forty-five of the city's neediest schools in partnership with community groups. There are two smaller management corporations that will be contracted with also, Victory and Beacon Academies. The hope here is that corporate management methods can do a better job of running Philadelphia's schools. When classes began in the 2002 school year, the district launched the biggest experiment to date in creating the largest-scale privatization of a school system in the country.

Sheila Landers Macrine focuses her research on the intersections of critical education, psychology, and special education. She teaches in the school of education at St. Joseph's University in Philadelphia.

H. Christopher Whittle, founder and CEO of Edison, reports that his plan consists of opportunities for all—students, teachers, parents, school districts, governments, and especially their corporate investors. On Tuesday, May 14, 2002, Edison Schools Inc. (NASDAQ: EDSN), the nation's leading private manager of public schools, reported net revenues for the quarter ending March 31, 2002, of $121.9 million compared to $92.8 million[1] a year ago, an increase of 31 percent. Gross site contribution for the quarter increased to $21.7 million from $18.1 million[2] for the same period the previous year.

Just months into the state takeover, major chunks of the state's vision of school reform are having profound and turbulent effects on the Philadelphia school district. To date, these measures have caused more turmoil (school walkouts, hundreds of teacher resignations and transfer requests, lawsuits, and other protests) than any concrete educational change. As this chapter goes to press, Edison is embroiled in a series of inter-related scandals over accounting, test-score reporting, and questionable financial practices that have driven down share price and raised questions about the for-profit schooling.

Beyond the specific case of Edison, my concern is the way that neoliberal educational policy making has infiltrated education reform and harmed teachers, students, and administrators. These ideologies move to silence and strip teachers of their decision-making role and view students as potential consumers to be trained in brand loyalty. Additionally, an increasingly corporatized model of educational leadership rewards administrators for embracing the corporate model that abstracts questions of efficacy from equity and the broader purpose of schooling. In no small part owing to the corporate mass-mediated discussion of education on the corporate model, administrators are entrenched in a corporate mentality of cutting costs, accountability defined strictly through "outcomes," high-stakes testing, and standardized test performances and hence fail to grasp the necessity in a democratic society for students to develop as thinkers and for education to be understood as a process of self- and social edification rather than merely as an outcome.

In this chapter I discuss the results of neoliberal reform in Philadelphia. I utilize interviews with Philadelphia teachers, administrators, and students about how the privatization of their school district is affecting their lives. I show how these corporate ideologies reinvent schools through discipline-oriented reforms that threaten the possibility of remaking public education as an endeavor ideally engaged in preparing students for democratic participation and renewal. Corporate reforms also threaten the possibility of teaching as an intellectual undertaking toward the end of more just social transformation.

The Take-Over

I have been a professor at a mid-sized university in Philadelphia for seven years, and I have had many dealings with the school district. I have volunteered in numerous ways, as other professors around the city have, to help with curriculum development and to promote more school district/university partnerships. Some of the schools that I worked in did not even have paper and pencils. With the federal push for inclusive education, the district had to move on to inclusion of special education students in regular classes. Yet, the teachers did not have copies of children's IEP (Individualized Education Plan), which is in violation of the State Compliance Law. The special education law is stringent, going so far as to hold teachers personally responsible for not implementing IEPs or not having them available to the tune of being sued up to $10,000 personally. Most of the teachers who I spoke to said that they had no idea where the IEPs were and thought that perhaps they were locked up somewhere. So, yes there were problems in the Philadelphia schools.

Philadelphia school district has always had its share of wonderfully dedicated teachers. Some teachers come into school at 6:30 A.M. to build literature clubs and to share great books with their students. The students do their best in an impoverished school system that the state capital had forgotten about. Most are there to learn with no books or supplies, and with asbestos walls and ceilings falling in on them. They remain impoverished, abandoned, and dejected. It is imperative to consider neoliberal school reform in relation to the bleak future promised by the undermining of the social safety net and the real opportunities awaiting youth after they leave Philadelphia schools. Unfortunately, the continuation of current models not only marginalizes nondominant groups but also perpetuates class, race, and gender differences that serve the profit imperatives of a postindustrial economy. Ultimately, neoliberalism serves to justify an educational system that enhances the emerging American economy of service managers, franchise workers, entrepreneurs, and venture capitalists that sit on a huge underclass of burger wrappers and security guards, certainly not what the "promise of a literate" society intended.[3]

Enter Edison, Christopher Whittle, media entrepreneur and founder of Whittle Communications, who has a history with education. He created the controversial Channel One in-school news program designed to make students into a captive audience for the program's advertising of junk food and other consumer goods. In 1991, he introduced the Edison Project. His plan was to build one thousand new, for-profit schools, two hundred of them within five years, at a projected cost of $2.5 billion. Over the next four years, Edison invested $44 million from private investors into research and development. Whittle tapped former Yale University president Benno Schmidt in 1992 to lead a group of educators and businesspeople and spent the year developing the Edison school curriculum.

Several lawsuits have now been filed, which, if successful, may prevent the implementation of the plan. A majority of city council members and several advocacy groups have filed suit in federal court in an attempt to overturn the state take-over. They contend that the take-over violates residents' constitutional rights. They also announced plans to seek a preliminary injunction that could bring the most pressing business of the state-run school district to a halt by the end of March 2002. Employee unions and other groups have filed two lawsuits that are pending in state court. One challenges the constitutionality of the take-over; the other seeks to prevent an educational management firm from doing business with the city, citing a conflict of interest.

Schools in the United States and elsewhere are now set within the logic of a market system where devolved budgets, calls for reform, and corporate raiding of school systems have set the framework for the corporatizing of education. In the following section I interview teachers about their experiences with the privatization reforms in Philadelphia.

The Teachers

Within the model of enforcement, teachers are increasingly directed by districts and school administrators to focus on raising test scores rather than teaching for understanding or, in the long tradition of Dewey, Gramsci, Giroux, and other progressive educators, as an intellectual activity fostering democratic social transformation.

Teachers have many concerns about the outcomes of the reforms. One of the cuts being considered in this "cost cutting–profit making experiment" is to cut libraries and librarians.

> *Teacher C:* And I don't understand why you're going to think of depriving the children of this school of a library and a librarian. With all of the concern about early literacy and lack of literacy practices the last thing to cut is the libraries. We have no books in the class rooms now they are taking the last resource that we have. . . . Unbelievable.

State Departments of Education increasingly intrude into the lives of teachers and teacher educators through more and more regulations. These regulations are manifest through technical methods such as accounting, compliance to mandates, and auditing. Regulation occurs through technical means of standards, testing, and measuring.

Recently a former graduate student of mine (Teacher A) told me that she was leaving the Philadelphia school district. She told me that she wants to teach in Philadelphia public schools, but no longer can.

> *Teacher A:* You know that Governor Ridge sold this school District down the river to Edison even before he left office. He never had any respect for teachers . . . you know (that) when he said that you could put any non-certified person in the classrooms, which he did . . . and then he turns around and complains about low-test scores.

In August 1, 2001, Governor Tom Ridge (former PA governor and now Secretary of Homeland Security) selected Edison Schools—the nation's largest private manager of public schools—to lead an intensive two-month review of the Philadelphia school district's educational and fiscal management. "Edison Schools knows what it takes to produce better educational results for children, and they know how to do it within a budget," Ridge, a republican, commissioned Edison to conduct a $2.7 million study of the district, which became the basis for the plan ultimately put forward by his successor, now Pennsylvania Governor Schweiker. Ridge said, "This will not be just another audit of the district's books. This will be an expert, performance-based management analysis, such as Philadelphia's schools have never seen before. It is designed, not to point fingers, but to suggest fresh ideas and inno-vative perspectives for the district—ideas and perspectives that will be fully grounded in the tough day-to-day realities of managing and improving a struggling urban school district."4

> *Teacher B:* Teachers are fleeing the school district. You know that everyone knows that problems exist and many even doubt the severity of those prob-lems. I am resigning too [she sighs]. I wrote that in my letter to my principal and the chancellor of the district told them that, "should the many adminis-trators, politicos and bureaucrats who sit in their ivory towers in cluster offices, union halls and City Hall fashioning solutions for mass consumption deign to ask teachers and students who labor without paper and pencils in schools polluted with asbestos and lead for their opinion and perspectives, they just might hear the truth and find the beginning of the path toward the light. But they don't. And they won't, until the system stops rewarding lies and decep-tion. They won't until our so-called leaders are no longer permitted to tread upon the spirit and hopes of the children as they greedily grab for more power, perks and favorable opinion polls."

Teachers are protesting angrily. Not only are they being replaced, but the ones who stay are going to be under the gun to cut costs. Some teachers report that they were forced to replace art and music with test-taking drills last year. There's a lot of pent-up anger. Teachers know that education is not just about taking tests.

> *Teacher B:* These tests are culturally biased and they do not measure the bright lights that I see in my kids' eyes. Or do they measure the knowledge that my students have and continue to garner?

> *Teacher E:* I am a guidance counselor here for the past four years and I was a teacher for the past twenty-six years; so, I have worked for the district (Philadelphia) for the past thirty years. I am also a product of this school system. That said I am putting in for early retirement at the end of this school year. I have worked hard to help my students achieve, both in the classroom and in the guidance office. I am leaving because I simply cannot take what is happening to the school district. I feel that I am not valued as a hard-working professional, by the district, the city or the state. [Tears well up in her eyes.] No one has bothered to ask the opinion of the front-liners, the teachers, those working in the schools everyday, trying to give students the best education possible. It is obvious that our opinion is not wanted. So for reasons too numerous to list, I will not be back here when school opens in September. I wish the best for the students, parents, and teachers that are remaining, but frankly, all I see happening is the worst. And I refuse to be a

part of shortchanging students at the same time building someone else's stock portfolio.

Teacher D: What about the sixth-grade material? We don't have sixth-grade material. We have nothing to start these children with. We also have no teachers coming back because we have a revolving door of educational staff.

These women and men who have dedicated their lives to teaching in the inner city are being silenced, written off, and replaced by inexperienced teachers. The Philadelphia school district is facing a huge teacher shortage in the fall as hundreds of teachers retire, resign, or transfer, and the pool of qualified applicants dries up as a result of the hodge-podge of so-called reforms being inflicted on city schools. According to the Pennsylvania Federation of Teachers, "This has the makings of a major disaster for the children of Philadelphia when schools open come September," Ted Kirsch said, "and the School Reform Commission only has itself to blame. Its single-minded pursuit of this risky experiment with privatization is costing Philadelphia many of its best and most experienced certified teachers."[5]

School district figures show 416 teachers filed by April 15 to retire or resign on June 30, up from 290 the previous year. Approximately 720 employees filed voluntary transfer requests by May 17, many of them from schools that will be reconstituted, turned into charter schools or handed over to private management. Last year, 369 employees had requested transfers as of May 17. Of the 720 transfer requests, 200 came from apprentice and literacy intern teachers at targeted schools, and the district said it is in the process of returning those requests because only appointed teachers with three years of building seniority are eligible for voluntary transfers.[6]

"All told, the District begins the hiring process with nearly 800 teaching positions vacant," Kirsch said. "And we expect even more resignations by next fall, when teachers who are applying for jobs in neighboring school districts are snapped up. Thousands of Philadelphia children will likely begin the new school year without a certified teacher to welcome them back to school, and everyone knows that you can't raise test scores without caring, compassionate and qualified teachers."[7]

Arlene Kempin, Pennsylvania Federation of Teachers (PFT) personnel officer, said a fourth-year teacher at one of the schools targeted for private management resigned. She said:

He said, that with the turmoil surrounding the privatization of public schools and the blatant lack of respect for teachers, he just can't take anymore, and he's getting out. If the School Reform Commission's goal is to provide a qualified, certified teacher in every classroom, it won't succeed by throwing schools into chaos and stripping teachers of their right to workplaces that are free from harassment and arbitrary, unfair and capricious treatment. When you combine the number of resignations, terminations and existing 100 to 200 classroom teacher vacancies, you're looking at 850 teaching positions that will have to be filled this summer, and that's before the suburban districts siphon off more certified teachers.

The Administrators

Philadelphia is also losing its administrators. Another former graduate student who is a current administrator spoke about being one. He told me that he knows that he doesn't fit the model type administrator that corporate America is looking for.

> People are going back to the classrooms . . . they are giving up administration, there is no way that they [administrators] are going to be displaced after putting in so many years in the district. There is no way that our present administrators are going to stay here under a Gestapo regime! Edison is going to come in like the Queen of Hearts and it's off with their heads . . . they have no mercy and don't care to have any discussions. I can tell you, folks are shaking in their boots!

One administrator said that, "Philadelphia Public School is not going to be in the business of replacing failing public schools with failing privatized schools. It is going to be accountability through controlling teachers through threats." The hiring of former accountant and former CEO of the Chicago public schools Paul Vallas to Philadelphia is specifically geared for such strong-arm tactics. Vallas has a record of precisely such control through such tactics as threatening to fire teachers, dissolve schools, and "reconstitute schools" (move teachers around to other schools suffering disinvestments) when they do not make the scores. Vallas, arriving in Philadelphia, has "declared war" on low achievement (achievement of course being defined through test scores).

The Students—Fighting Back

To the surprise of many adults, student activism is alive and well in Philadelphia—in the form of elementary and high school students. It is the Philadelphia public school students who have been leaders of opposition to the state taking over the schools, according to Aldustus Jordan, a student reporter for the *Notebook*, an independent local school newspaper. On April 17, 2002, members of the Philadelphia student union actually staged a series of street protests including a student walkout, a sit-in, and a nonviolent block-ade of the school district administrative offices in protest over the privatization of schools.

Student activism, like these examples have shown, can inspire adults to take action as well. It has been said that the students from the Philadelphia student union and Youth United for Change have often been ahead of adults in getting the facts, seeking out information, demanding answers and even engaging in nonviolent civil disobedience. Students in groups like Philadelphia Student Union, Youth United for Change, and Asian Americans United have demonstrated, marched, independently organized students, held educational forums, and spoken out about the type of education they desire. They have, on two occasions, blocked entry to the district's main offices in protest to the privatization of schools.

One of two students that I spoke with was a junior at the local high school. She told me that the students (mostly of color) are feeling like they are being traded like slaves to the highest bidder to improve profits for big corporations. Unfortunately, members of the Philadelphia student union, fending for themselves in court on April 19, 2003, face a lawsuit from the school district and possible fines of up to $50,000 for blockading the district administrative offices. Two days earlier about twenty-five students had slept overnight in front of the building and blocked all of the entrances by early morning. This was to protest the SRC meeting scheduled to take place later that day and where the SRC was expected to announce its plans for the privatization and other dramatic management changes to seventy Philadelphia schools.

Although the SRC moved their meeting the District still got an injunction to force students to move away from the buildings entrances. On April 24, 2001, Albert J. Snite, Jr. issued an injunction, valid until August 2002, that orders all protesters to stay seven feet away from the building's entrances and prevents protesters from hanging signs on buildings. The school district did not stop there and reserved the right to sue adults involved with the protests for $200,000, the amount it says the school district lost when employees could not report for work.

A high school student and member of the Philadelphia student union named Sara wrote this poem on Philadelphia schools titled, "I Am Not for Sale!"

> 2.7 million dollars down the drain,
> But we could've told you we were in pain,
> But you called up this for profit corporation,
> That betters the schools through process of illumination,
> These Edison people are already in debt,
> So we have price tags till their demands are met,
> This is no way to treat adults of tomorrow,
> Philly's school funding is a pitiful sorrow,
> The plight of our schools would make even Snow White turn pale,
>> So say it now ... I am not for sale!
>> I'm not for sale!

> I want a textbook from the nineteen-nineties,
> It should be a right, but we're still askin' pretty please,
> Don't I deserve a proper education?

> Some say that Edison has helped some schools,
> But those people can be mistaken for the fools,
> Because in a school that Edison has backed,
> 14 out of 15 students kicked out are black,
> Edison's school in San Fran I warned ya',
> IS one of the worst scoring schools in California,
> Does this sound like the answer we need?
> These Whittle executives are wrapped up in their greed,
> I don't need these rich white males ...
>> So say it now ... I am not for sale!
>> I'm not for sale!

The state slaps on what they think is an answer,
But you're giving us problems like tumourous cancer,
You'll sit coiled up in your bittersweet satisfaction,
But remember state:
>To every action there is a reaction!
We are students we are young and proud,
We are smart, energetic, bossy, and loud,
Who better than us to know what we need,
And (Gov.) Sweiker up yours because I can obviously read,
So we are young willing and able,
We will fight back with all the cards on the table,
It's the adults that walk over us that we'll nail,
>So scream it loud ... I AM NOT ... FOR SALE!
Not a dirty school and civil rights violations
What did I do to be put in this mess?
I have a swipe card around my neck, and you tell me
>How to dress,
These are no ways to run our schools,
We are people with needs, not money earning tools,
At this rate I'm never going to Yale,
>So say it now I'm not ... for sale!
>I'm not for sale!

>—Sara Davidson, student at Central High
>School, Philadelphia, 2002

Sara, the author of this poem, is not the only young person who is transforming the bitter experience with Edison, and more generally the state and the private sector, into the basis for rejuvenated public action. Various organization such as Research for Action, ACORN, Parents Advocating School Accountability, as well as numerous students have responded to the ways that instead of getting resources they are getting rules. The lesson to be taken from these activists is that the struggle to strengthen public schools as part of an effort to bolster the public sector is central to the work of making a more democratic society that puts people over profit.

Notes

1. Revenues for 2001 reflect the reclassification of approximately $6.8 million.
2. Prior year third-quarter amounts have been restated to reduce the loss from operations by $0.6 million for losses, primarily related to two school contracts, that should have been recorded in the first quarter of 2001.
3. Patrick Shannon, *Becoming Political, Too: New Readings and Writings in the Politics of Literacy Education* (Portsmouth, NH: Heinemann, 1989), available at: www.heinemann.com/shared/authors/302.asp
4. Arlene Kempin, "Major Teacher Shortage Looms: Record Numbers Retire, Resign, Transfer," *The Reporter: A Publication of the Pennsylvania Federation of Teachers*, June 2002. Available at: www.pft.org/archrept0602/p2.html
5. Ibid.
6. Ibid.
7. Edison Schools Corporation Press Release, August 1, 2001.

INTRODUCTION TO CHAPTER 12

Ron Scapp's "Taking Command" discusses what Peter McLaren has termed "predatory culture" as an outgrowth of a capitalist economy and a threat to democratic education. Scapp shows how predatory culture plays out through educational policy resulting in the proliferation of military and corporate values. Scapp suggests that teachers and administrators can challenge predatory culture in their own locales through the practice of critical pedagogy. His analysis points to the need for the reformulation of democratic education that links with broader movements to challenge a capitalist economy as the root of predatory culture.

CHAPTER 12

Taking Command

The Pathology of Identity and Agency in Predatory Culture

RON SCAPP

... the adaptive person is person as object, adaptation representing at
most a weak form of self-defense.

—Paulo Freire,
Education for Critical Consciousness

There is not one of these aspects—not the least operation, the least industrial or financial mechanism—that does not reveal the insanity of the
capitalist machine and the pathological character of its rationality: not
at all a false rationality, but a true rationality of this pathological state,
this insanity ...

—Gilles Deleuze and Felix Guattari,
Anti-Oedipus: Capitalism and Schizophrenia

The rejuvenated relationship between education and the military and corporate sector of the United States has recently become more pronounced despite
the Enron and WorldCom debacles and the lingering concerns over national
security since September 11. Just consider the growing number of Americans putting stock in the revitalized practice of regarding military and corporate institutions as hallmarks of achievement and success, embracing them
as welcomed models for guiding the transformation of the nation's public
schools. Evidence of this trend can be readily identified in: (1) the renewed
popularity of Junior Reserve Officer Training Corps (JROTC); (2) the expansion of the Edison project, the for-profit education company now running
charter schools in over twenty states; (3) the widespread and enthusiastic
support for President Bush's national initiative to recruit military personnel
and businesspeople to fill administrative and teaching posts at the elementary
and secondary levels; and (4) the increasing number of "nonprofit" colleges
and universities following the for-profit, University of Phoenix model of
marketing a no-frills education specifically for consumers on the run. From
preschool-K to graduate school, those in charge are turning with greater
frequency to the values, strategies, and organizational structure of the mili-

Ron Scapp is director of the graduate program in urban and multicultural education,
College of Mount Saint Vincent. He is the author of *Teaching Values* (Routledge,
2003).

tary and corporations to rescue education and, in so doing, "leave no child (read consumer) behind."

Politicians, administrators, teachers, parents, and students alike rightly seek better and safer teaching and learning environments. The question is, however, why have so many people turned to the military and corporate sector to improve schools? Why have discipline, order, accountability, efficiency, and cost cutting become the guideposts for transforming schools and not traditional democratic concerns such as interest in social justice, equality, and the fostering of a critically minded citizenry? In other words, why has *education* apparently been abandoned in favor of "taking command" of the lives of students and teachers as well as the schools they inhabit?

In what follows, I argue that the reason why taking command is so dependent on military and corporate perspectives and values is due to the existential circumstances arising from what Peter McLaren has identified as "predatory culture," a culture that continues to flourish and dominate virtually every aspect of American public policy.

In his powerful indictment of both the militarization and the corporatization of public schools titled *Collateral Damage: Corporatizing Public Schools–A Threat to Democracy*, Kenneth J. Saltman persuasively argues that part of the reason for the current emphasis on education reform can be traced to the fact that in the United States today

> [t]he omnipresent language and logic of the market works to redefine the public sphere as one more opportunity for profit. Within the current neoliberal order, business ideals of competition, accountability, and efficiency eclipse democratic concerns with the development of a critical citizenry and institutions that foster social justice and equality.[1]

With this kind of language and logic dominating the debate over the public sphere, including the debate over school reform, comes the recasting and the reproducing, if you will, of students, and citizens generally, as *only* consumers whose rights to consume must be safeguarded from any and all threats, including the very sort of "disruptive" questioning that genuine education engenders and encourages.

As Saltman goes on to note,

> [t]he triumph of market language imposes a singular vision of the future and singular set of values—namely, faith in capitalism. When this happens there is nothing left to discuss. Authority becomes unquestionable, and dissent, the lifeblood of democracy, appears as disruption and threat. The only question is how to enforce this faith in the market. *Education becomes a matter of enforcement.*[2] [emphasis added]

Efforts to transform schools in this context quickly become efforts to control and direct. Enforcement substitutes for administrating; managing and disciplining replace teaching. Saltman bluntly states that

[t]he emphasis on discipline includes tightened curricular constraints such as federally, state-, and locally mandated curriculum guidelines, and more standardized curricula geared toward the reduction of teaching as an intellectual endeavor. In the current climate, top-down constraints surpass even the most traditionally stifling, instrumentalizing controls on teacher work. We are beyond the era of Frederick Taylor and into a whole new realm of anti-critical, thought-squelching tactics.[3]

Education is abandoned in favor of law and order as defined by the language and logic of the market, that is, the continued smooth and repetitive flow of production and consumption. Inevitably, students and teachers find themselves being assaulted by the systematic dismantling and disciplining of—the taking command of—their lives resulting from privatization efforts to transform schools, namely efforts to downsize, if not destroy, government support of public education and public services generally. This assault becomes all the more immediate and concrete due to the subsequent militarization of the public sphere, which occurs, disingenuously, in the name of ensuring safety at destabilized schools—ensuring, one suspects, the safety of investments made in the newly established "education market," and by extension the safety of capital at work anywhere around the globe.

Maintaining "this faith in the market," as Saltman encapsulates it, demands the enforcement of what Henry A. Giroux identifies as "the ideology of corporate culture." In short, transforming schools becomes part of the larger process of promoting and protecting American values, part of the defense against what the religious and political right claim is a two-pronged evil corrupting our nation: moral relativism and social welfare. One consequence of the enforcement and maintenance of this ideology is the proliferation of what Peter McLaren describes as "predatory culture." He explains that

[i]n predatory culture identity is fashioned mainly and often violently around the excesses of marketing and consumption and the natural social relations of post-industrial capitalism. . . . Predatory culture is the left-over detritus of bourgeois culture stripped of its arrogant pretense to civility and cultural lyricism and replaced by a stark obsession with power fed by the voraciousness of capitalism's global voyage.[4]

In such a culture, education finds itself engulfed by the desires and fears of those struggling to take command of the moral destiny of our nation, of those McLaren declares, to be obsessed "with power fed by the voraciousness of capitalism's global voyage." Under such conditions, education quickly becomes merely the enforcement of values dogmatically defined and defended by those who pledge allegiance, first and foremost, to profit and security—by those not necessarily committed to democracy.

One could further argue that predatory culture is in fact the birthchild of the "community" most committed to profit and security—the religious and political right—a community generously described as antagonistic toward the public sphere. As Herbert I. Schiller pointedly notes in his *Culture Inc.: The Corporate Takeover of Public Expression,*

> [t]hough evident in many measures adopted by Congress before 1980, *it was the Reagan administration's policy to gut the public sector.* The huge tax reductions in 1981–82, accompanied by the staggering increase in military expenditures, created the mountainous deficits of the 1980s—a trillion dollars of debt piled up in eight years. In the face of these unprecedented deficits, the deep cuts that were made in social and public expenditures were made to seem unavoidable. *This, in fact, was the intention of the policy from its inception.*[5] [emphasis added]

The birth of predatory culture, then, is to be viewed as inextricably linked to policies promoted and sustained by the community who hoisted Reagan onto the presidential stage and onto a bully pulpit, aggressively and illegitimately (if not illegally) constricting government's role in and support of public services such as health care and education, and substituting a rhetoric of national identity and pride for much-needed resources. Criticizing the initiation and enforcement of this nationalistic cultural identity, Stanley Aronowitz and Henry A. Giroux argue in their *Postmodern Education: Politics, Culture and Social Criticism,* that

> [s]ince the second term of the Reagan administration, the debate on education has taken a new turn. Now, as before, the tone is principally set by the right, but its position has been radically altered. The importance of linking educational reform to the needs of big business has continued to influence the debate, while demands that schools provide the skills necessary for domestic production and expanding capital abroad have slowly given way to an overriding emphasis on schools as sites of cultural production. The emphasis on cultural production can be seen in current attempts to address the issue of cultural literacy, in the development of national curriculum boards, and in reform initiatives bent on providing students with the language, knowledge, and values necessary to preserve the essential traditions of Western civilization.[6]

With this turn people got pulled away from the concrete needs of students and teachers and pulled into the culture wars. The right was, and remains, able to claim a moral high ground by distorting the education debate, by distracting all involved with demands for "standards," "accountability," and a cultural literacy à la E. D. Hirsch.

The right's new vision for America was Reagan's dream of a brighter tomorrow, "a new morning" as it was framed. But it was a new day predicated on the necessity of a whole community *buying into the dream* and seeing itself as the only community with the appropriate values and abilities for envisioning and establishing a better day ahead. Those taking command of and participating in America's moral and political destiny correctly saw themselves as "privileged" members of a *right-minded community.* In his insightful book, *Community: Seeking Safety in an Insecure World,* Zygmunt Bauman warns, however, that

[t]here is a price to be paid for the privilege of "being in a community"—and it is inoffensive or even invisible only as long as the community *stays in the dream*. The price is paid in the currency of freedom . . ."[7] [emphasis added]

Of course, Reagan and his community began to erode the public sphere in the very name of freedom (read free enterprise). Reagan's mantra of deregulation and Congress's implementation of it via a costly stimulation package to benefit private industry (namely, tax cutting to the nth degree) gave birth to predatory culture and its correlate: the desire for ever-greater security from the now "freed" and out-of-control market.

With deregulation Americans were charged with the excitement of unlimited consumption and the responsibility of making it on their own. This double charge resulted in a schizo-culture: Americans were now driven by the desire for what they did not have, but also were filled with anxiety concerning their future, what they did not know. In deregulated America one was promised freedom, but, in fact, forced to submit to the dynamics of a volatile and unpredictable market. The future was open-ended and unclear, and an uneasiness settled in just as the government-sponsored free-for-all began. And "[a]midst uncertainty and insecurity," Bauman observes, "discipline (or rather, submission to the 'there is no alternative' condition) is self-propelling and self-reproducing and needs no foreman or corporals to supervise its constantly replenished supplies."[8] The deregulatory policies liberating and enabling capital to be invested, moved, and removed from the market with speed and little, if any, supervision engendered not a self-disciplining corporate and military milieu but rather an out-of-control predatory culture. Our culture became driven by forces too tempting for too many people not to dream about or desire: *the freedom to consume beyond our means*. Nevertheless, it also became a culture paradoxically obsessed with and worried about wealth and security, a culture desperately submitting to the dynamics of propelling and reproducing itself based on the uncertainty and insecurity of a "free market."

At a moment in U.S. history when those elected to government were busy dismantling it, more Americans than not were busy *buying* into the dream. Down came the barriers to doing business, down came the Berlin Wall, but down too came the quality of life for the average citizen, who like the government itself, was *charging* her or his way through the dream. And as the debilitating debt grew, so too did the fallacious domain of predatory culture. This, McLaren claims, is because

[p]redatory culture is the great deceiver. It marks the ascendancy of the dehydrated imagination that has lost its capacity *to dream otherwise*. It is the culture of eroticized victims and decaffeinated revolutionaries. We are all its sons and daughters. The capitalist fear that fuels predatory culture is made to function at the world level through the installation of necessary crises, both monetary and social. Computers have become the new entrepreneurs of history while their users have been reduced to scraps of figurative machinery, partial subjects in the rag-and-bone shop of predatory culture, manichean allegories of "us" against "them," of "self" against "other." The social, the cultural and the human has been subsumed within capital.[9] [emphasis added]

The turmoil, the "necessary" monetary and social crises encountered because of *dreaming only this way and not otherwise,* as McLaren laments, fuels the construction of subjectivities that appear unwilling or unable to pull themselves out from the alienating spiral set in motion by the gyrating forces of greed and fear. Yet it is from within this whirlwind of predatory confusion, desire, and anxiety that all too many Americans today seek to reorder and reform their lives, such as they have come to hope their lives might have been (the lure of winning the lottery, or cashing in on Wall Street continue to self-propel and self-reproduce).

As complicated or even contradictory as it may sound, predatory culture is simultaneously deregulating itself in a state of maniacal exuberance while frantically seeking to control its own excesses—*now* becomes a time of placing and removing limits and restrictions on fragmented and overdrawn lives, lives contemporaneously moving closer to and further away from dearly held "core values." This is the psycho-socioeconomic suction propelling the transformation of everything, including education. Everything is beyond overextended and is hyperextended, and *now* is the moment to reconstitute, reconstruct, and reclaim the order of things. And who better to take command than the very sources of the maintenance of the dream of riches and protection? Who better to turn to in order to save us from our enemies, from ourselves? Who better than the military and corporations that rendered us predatory in the first place? Who better than those who created and defended dreaming beyond our means? The turn, therefore, is reflexive. It is, in fact, as Deleuze and Guattari unironically suggest, a *pathologically rational* return!

The result is that today we find ourselves in the midst of a reform movement pathologically seeking the input of those who have sent so many spiraling out of control. Many in this pathology "rationally" return to the military because of its reputation for preparing for crises with discipline, integrity, and courage. Many similarly return to corporations for their expertise regarding competitiveness, (fiscal) responsibility, and quality (control). Understandably, but wrongly, many return to both because of their "proven" track records of success and their histories of "excellence." They return to them, so their argument goes, because only the military and corporations can transform education, only they can bring back discipline, accountability, and efficiency, only they can save us (from what they have created: predatory culture).

The fact that many Americans, too many, are still blinded by the bright promise of the dream—of a better tomorrow predicated upon a better yesteryear—is perhaps part of the explanation. America evidently still longs for a past it never had, for a present that does not exist and for a future that, at best, is unlikely to come to fruition unless something radical takes place. McLaren dramatically summarizes this state of affairs in the following way:

> Now we are living in the future anterior in which we are discovering that we have a profound nostalgia for a moment that has yet to take place, even in the imagination. We have arrived at the cusp of an absent present era of unspeakable horrors and unnamable pleasures. Democracy is becoming less the motor

force in our daily lives, its pedigree of innocence having long been exposed as the posture of the shameless knave. We have given up the search for an all-embracing, undifferentiated and transcendental conception of democratic justice. We now desire not justice but *accessibility*. We demand that everything be made accessible to us, including the past, present and future—at a single moment's notice. Humanism has failed to restrict the bourgeois citizen's desire for power. Power disguised as liberation has become deputized by the logic of exploitation that drives market forces. Imperialism is the name of this power.[10] [emphasis added]

In such a state of longing and desire, of wanting, here and now, what has been produced and consumed by others, many find themselves turning away from the hope and promise driven by genuine democratic reverie, and instead moving toward *that which is there to be had* (cell phones, SUVs, PalmPilots, among the many other products that are and represent power)—if only one could gain *access to all of it*. Access to the things themselves becomes as important, if not more important, than the things themselves. After all, the things themselves come and go, are in and out of vogue, but *access to that which is there to be had*, whatever it might have been, is and will someday be, becomes the quintessential index of power itself, of being and identity in predatory culture: *access is agency*.

Too many Americans want a share in what is there to be had—to be shareholders. Thus they turn themselves back toward the mechanism that began the repetitive process of production and consumption, of consumption and more consumption, of consumption and identification, of inevitably becoming what Giroux calls "consuming subjects." Their desire becomes not just to have that which is there to be had, but to become that which is there to be had because their mode of being in the world has become confused and distorted—"pathologically rational." They understand themselves *to be only* what they have, what they own, what they have access to; this is what their existential value becomes in predatory culture. This is the reason for the continuous acts of consumption and the insatiable desire for accessibility. In predatory culture, identity is as fleeting as the things consumed, and so is one's agency along with it. One's value, therefore, is more than merely tied to the objects one consumes, in predatory culture without them one is nothing. Without them one becomes unrecognizable, nonexistent, and inert, as it were, because one's identity and agency are perversely integrated and enmeshed in the very things one consumes (one is identified and gains agency, and, in turn, identifies and acknowledges the agency of others by a system of signifiers synonymous with contemporary social status: Nike, Gap, Armani, Rolex, and so on; *you are what you have access to*).

Assessing the existential import of such subjectivity Saltman wonders,

[i]s this the culmination and limit of consumerism when individuals do not merely desire commodities but desire to be desired as commodities? We don't just want these sacred things. We want to be them. We want to be desired as they are desired, consumed as they are consumed, coveted, sought after, prized, elevated, and endlessly reproduced such that we approach the interminable

infinity of the almighty (God/commodity). This is the central problem of consumer culture. It produces desire in the service of assimilation, homogeneity, the abandonment of individual uniqueness; it tends toward massification, undifferentiation, brutal acriticality, and docility.[11] [emphasis added]

This is why so many pathologically return to the military and corporations for support and guidance. These are the systems, the forces behind establishing, securing and enforcing the very consumerism that is now a globalizing enterprise—a totalizing enterprise—an enterprise that has thus far controlled and directed school reform as part of, what McLaren calls, "the voraciousness of capitalism's global voyage." Thus the desire to take command of schools is part of the pathology of predatory culture because such desire is merely reactionary, adaptive as Freire claims and "at most a weak form of self-defense."

The current popular approach to school reform is one generated from within the confusing and disorienting existential fog of predatory culture, a haze that distorts one's identity and agency, one's democratic sense of self, and one's ability to enact Freire's call to embrace "education as the practice of freedom." We must move beyond the pathology of identity and agency as determined by predatory culture and beyond the consequent "pedagogy of pathology" taking command of school reform. We must continue looking toward the "pedagogy of hope" that Paulo Freire, Henry A. Giroux, and Donaldo Macedo offer as a strategy for reclaiming education as a meaningful process facilitating critical consciousness, a process that allows for the possibility of values not controlled by "market forces" alone to reemerge. As bell hooks urges, we must

> open our minds and hearts so that we can know beyond the boundaries of what is acceptable, so that we can think and rethink, so that we can create new visions, [we must] celebrate teaching that enables transgressions—a movement against and beyond boundaries. It is that movement which makes education the practice of freedom.[12]

We must continue the movement beyond the boundaries of predatory culture, toward justice, democracy and freedom. We must continue to move with faith in education and hope for the future. We must continue the movement "against and beyond" the boundaries of those taking command.

Notes

1. Kenneth J. Saltman, *Collateral Damage: Corporatizing Public Schools—A Threat to Democracy* (New York and Oxford: Rowman & Littlefield Publishers, 2000), ix.
2. Ibid., x.
3. Ibid., 80.
4. Peter McLaren, *Critical Pedagogy and Predatory Culture: Oppositional Politics in a Postmodern Era* (New York and London: Routledge, 1995), 2.
5. Herbert I. Schiller, *Culture Inc.: The Corporate Takeover of Public Expression* (Oxford: Oxford University Press, 1989), 66.

6. Stanley Aronowitz and Henry A. Giroux, *Postmodern Education: Politics, Culture and Social Criticism* (Minneapolis: University of Minnesota Press, 1991), 24.
7. Zygmunt Bauman, *Community: Seeking Safety in an Insecure World* (Cambridge: Polity Press, 2001), 4.
8. Ibid., 42.
9. McLaren, *Critical Pedagogy and Predatory Culure*, 2.
10. Ibid., 172.
11. Saltman, *Collateral Damage*, 69.
12. bell hooks, *Teaching to Transgress: Education as the Practice of Freedom* (New York and London: Routledge, 1994), 12.

INTRODUCTION TO CHAPTER 13

Sandra Jackson's chapter provides a broad overview of the intersecting metaphors of war and business as they have informed the educational reform debates in the U.S. context. Her discussion focuses on the landmark "A Nation at Risk" report in comparison to its legacy—the Bush administration's "No Child Left Behind" report. This chapter illustrates the significance of language as a form of cultural politics in the public struggles to enact educational reform. The chapter also, unique to the volume, considers how the conservative backlash against multiculturalism relates to enforcement-oriented reform reports. She situates these reports within domestic and international/material and cultural struggles and highlights the key questions of justice that these reports strategically erase from consideration in their discussion of educational reform.

CHAPTER 13

Commentary on the Rhetoric of Reform

A Twenty-Year Retrospective

SANDRA JACKSON

The Legacy of "A Nation at Risk"

Educational policies in the United States have been integrally related to social and economic policies, with domestic and foreign interests linked inextricably. During the twentieth century, education and schooling in the United States have functioned to increase efficiency of work and labor, select and channel individuals within differential education and training programs according to national manpower needs, and sort them into desired slots in the labor force. Testing and measurement of intelligence, skills, and abilities have been the instruments of this sorting and ranking, which has taken place within a discourse of education purported to serve citizens in enhancing their individual development and individual interests, as if they were autonomous and disconnected from any national agenda. From a competing perspective, in an overview of post-1950s phases in national public policy regarding education in the United States, Spring has identified the following uses of schools: to end poverty in the 1960s; to establish law and order and end unemployment in the 1970s; and to solve problems of international trade in the 1980s.[1] Beginning with the mid-1940s, he argues that military, corporate, scientific, and political leaders have struggled to have the federal government play a decided role in shaping educational policies, which were rooted in "containing communism and protecting the interests of American corporate expansion into foreign markets."[2] With the demise of the former Soviet Union, the impetus to dominate the global market remains, and schools in the United States have a mission to produce a workforce and future leaders to further consolidate power.

Today for the United States in the realm of public policy, matters that relate to the public good, social welfare and social services are the subject of

Sandra Jackson is professor of women's studies at DePaul University in Chicago. Her published works include the following co-edited books: *Talking Back and Acting Out: Women Negotiating the Media Across Cultures*; *I've Got a Story to Tell: Identity and Place in the Academy*; and *Beyond Comfort Zones: Confronting the Politics of Privilege as Educators*. She is currently working on a book of essays on race and gender in academe.

intense debate, often contentious, regarding what is good for the nation and its citizens. Education, particularly that of children and youth, is at the heart of polemical exchanges among different constituencies, especially those who desire a greater federal investment and commitment to efficiency, and those desiring greater state and local autonomy, also in the name of excellence. The question I pose is, in whose interests and who will benefit from the propositions?

In response to the launch of *Sputnik* (1957), with the United States in the race to be number one globally, nationally there was a massive infusion of money to enhance the curriculum of high schools, with greater emphasis on math and the sciences as well as foreign language instruction. This same appeal to be number one was the impetus for the report, A Nation at Risk (1983), commissioned by Terrell Bell, secretary of Education under President Ronald Reagan as well as No Child Left Behind (2001) by President George W. Bush. Though the language and tenor of these two reports are different, I will argue that the underlying assumptions and arguments are the same: to make an apparent case for change, while proclaiming broad social benefits for everyone, which will in reality sustain the status quo because the matters of structural barriers to equity in opportunity—access as well as outcomes, go unacknowledged and thus unaddressed, unexamined, and hence undisturbed in perpetuating inequalities.

The militaristic and nationalistic language of A Nation at Risk served as a clarion call, sounding an alarm that the United States could no longer take its position of worldwide preeminence for granted. Whenever I reread this document, I hear bugles resounding and the drum corps beating in the background, summoning us to march as if going to war. Indeed, the very premise of the report is that the nation will soon be under siege with the dust blown or kicked in our faces if we do not act now. Consider the following quote from A Nation at Risk: "If an unfriendly foreign power had attempted to impose on America the mediocre educational performance that exists today, we might well have viewed it as an act of war." This sixty-three-page report proposed sweeping changes for American high schools, colleges, and universities, private and public, which would ostensibly reinstate the United States to the position of number one, first among the most developed nations of the world.

The language is one of economic and military competition and the specter of losing ground in the face of powerful foreign countries whose economic engines are propelling them to success: Japan, South Korea, and Germany, singled out as primary targets engendering angst. The underlying logic of the report is that America's economic crisis is primarily a symptom of the failure of public education. The effect of focusing upon schools as the locus of deep-seated problems in the United States is to turn public attention away from economic and social policies and practices that undermine job security of American workers and send thousands into poverty, unemployment, under-employment, and financial ruin.

While A Nation at Risk asserts that no nation approaches the United States in terms of the preparation of youth completing high school and going on to higher education, it claims that we have fallen behind.[3] To remedy these symptoms of desuetude, antidotes in the form of standards, accountability, pluralism, competition, and choice are proposed. Bush's No Child Left Behind plan is rooted in the same kind of reasoning, outlined in ten sections: Achieving Excellence through High Standards and Accountability; Improving Literacy by Putting Reading First; Improving Teacher Quality; Improving Math and Science Instruction; Moving Limited English Proficient Students to English Fluency; Promoting Parental Options and Innovative Programs; Encouraging Safe Schools for the Twenty-First Century; Enhancing Education through Technology; Providing Impact Aid; and Encouraging Freedom and Accountability. Except for allusion to literacy and reading skills among inner-city fourth graders, there is virtually no evidence presented regarding educational problems or their gravity; instead they are assumed as givens. Hence, the report is written much like a business plan with goals of the policy and steps that will be taken to improve the quality of education in American schools.

No Child Left Behind, outlines seven performance-based objectives to close the achievement gap: improving the academic performance of disadvantaged students; boosting teacher quality; moving limited English proficient students to English fluency; ensuring that all children can read by grade three; promoting informed parental choice and innovative programs; encouraging safe schools for the twenty-first century; increasing funding for Impact Aid; and encouraging freedom and accountability. Bush's educational blueprint vows "to increase accountability for student performance by focusing on what works, reducing bureaucracy and increasing flexibility."[4] Because he believes that "the federal government does not do enough to reward success and sanction failure in our educational system . . . and that it has not asked whether or not programs produce results or knows their impact on local needs,"[5] he has asserted his intentions of reforming the Elementary and Secondary Education Act (ESEA), limiting federal dollars to specific programs and goals to ensure improved results.

Believing that the United States is behind, Bush proposes that to close the achievement gap, accountability and high standards must be imposed through the following means: annual academic assessments, consequences for schools that fail to educate students, specifically the loss of Title I funds to be transferred to higher-performing public or private schools or accountability bonuses for states and schools in reward for demonstrated success in closing the gap; annual reading and math assessments (grades 4 through 8); a focus on reading in early childhood and the early grades; curricular emphasis on math and science; reading instruction and increased funds to schools for technology on a need-based formula; consolidation of overlapping and duplicate categorical grant programs; new state and local options in the form of charter schools that would operate on a five-year performance agreements; mandatory school reports to parents; and exemption from federal requirements for home schools and private schools.

Details regarding his program for rewards and sanctions include the following: provision of discretion to states and school districts to have the freedom to reform teacher certification or licensure requirements; provide alternative certification programs; reform of teacher tenure and implementation of a merit-based performance system; differential pay and bonuses to teachers in high-need subject areas and mentoring programs; excellence in teaching awards; shields from federal liability for teachers, administrators, and school board members regarding actions against students who are defined as disruptive, discipliary problems, so long as they do not engage in reckless or criminal misconduct; tax deductions for teacher up to $400 for out-of-pocket expenses for school supplies and professional enhancement; and parental disclosure regarding the quality of their child's teachers as defined by the state.[6] On related matters, Bush's plan promotes the establishment of science partnerships between states and institutions of higher education.

Promises to bring about swift change through the pervasive implementation of high-stakes testing, the rooting out of bad teachers, threats of reduction of resources to be followed by school closure, with an implicit notion of social Darwinist survival of the fittest in the market place, thus driving out of business bad schools, are at the heart of the Bush plan. Charter schools, vouchers, subsidies to private schools, as well as home schooling are intended to fill the void and provide choices to those ill served by the bad public schools. There is virtually no commentary about the consequences of this plan for the overwhelming number of poor, working-class, and children of color in particular who will be trapped in troubled schools, starved of resources, with teachers and staff under siege, without adequate funds to make up the difference between vouchers and tuition for highly prized spaces in private schools or charter schools.

Accordingly, teacher education also comes under sharp scrutiny and is labeled as "low status and lacking in rigor," when in reality teachers "are starved of life space, robbed of funds, and generally ridiculed."[7] Again, teachers and teacher education institutions, primarily those at research institutions, come under assault as the culprits responsible for the poor performance of students, and hence schools throughout the nation.

Testing is posited as the remedy, the litmus test for assessing and guaranteeing quality regarding students, schools, and teachers. The idea of focusing on what works (to improve student test scores) is based on the assumption that test scores and results are reliable indicators of student learning, achievement, development, and growth. The faith in testing persists even though research indicates that "testing often lacks objectivity, validity, or fairness and appropriateness and is rarely apolitical . . . is seriously flawed, with various tests incompatible and incomparable, with transfer problematic—that is the relationship between tasks and tests and actual performance with very little consideration of cultural differences."[8] Furthermore, there is a seduction of simplicity regarding problem solving in that learning and achievement are purported as easy to identify and quantify, and that they can be accurately measured and reduced to numerical scores, the basis upon which students, teachers, and schools will be judged as succeeding or failing and, consequently, rewarded or punished.

According to the diagnoses and prescriptions of A Nation at Risk and No Child Left Behind, the remedies for school improvement and the achievement of excellence in student achievement and teachers' instruction appeal to common sense in that they argue that the matter of quality education is an easy thing to address, and that results will be readily achievable through testing, testing, and more testing, complemented by a system of sanctions and rewards. It will be merely a matter of shaping up or shipping out for bad students, bad teachers, and bad schools.

Situating Proposals for Reform in the Broader Context for Schooling

Very few of the major reports and educational reforms proposals that have emerged over the past two decades (A Nation at Risk, Task Force on Education for Economic Growth, the Education Commission of the States, the Twentieth-Century Fund, the Carnegie Commission for the Advancement of Teachers . . .) pay any attention to the world in which children and youth live today—the quality of life in their homes and communities, whether or not their parents are employed and making a living wage, and whether they have medical coverage. Most of those reports and the proposals that follow them are very quick to lay blame, particularly on children and their teachers. If children and teachers are not the objects of blame, then it's parents who are remiss, particularly those parents who are of working-class, poor, black, Latino/a, and immigrant backgrounds, and especially those parents for whom English is not their native tongue. With issues of educational achievement made the particular problem of these populations, and with the persistent discrepancies in testing results in reading, math, as well as college entrance exams, between them and white middle-class youth, the reforms that tout high-stakes testing and a return to basics take on the aura of ethnocentrism[9] and exhibit a xenophobic creed.[10] To achieve in America, one needs to speak English, jettison any other languages, take on particular behaviors, embrace particular values, leave their cultural baggage at the door of the school, work hard, and consistently pass a barrage of tests, with high scores. According to this version of achievement, teachers need to spend more time preparing students to take tests and school districts need to invest more money in administering testing and scoring results. Furthermore, according to such thought, there needs to be a sharp pendulum swing from the past, the 1960s and 1970s in particular, an era blamed for the moral and cultural decline and relapse, because of "permissiveness and looseness," as well as loss of coherence in a sense of national character given influences of the Civil Rights Movement, student protests and anti-war campaigns (VietNam in particular), the Women's Movement, the Gay and Lesbian Movement, as well as the continued influx of immigrants from the Southern Hemisphere.

Within the proposals for reform, "there is no mention of the largest and fastest growing sector in the world economy, military production and trade, and no mention of the costs regarding the health of the nation's economy and the corresponding neglect of our social and individual well being."[11] Further, "there is no mention of democratic citizenship and what this entails in terms of critically examining pervasive problems and issues of our times; no critique of the tenuous partnerships between business and schools and the dismal failure of earlier programs."[12] That which is really promoted is a closer linkage between education and the needs of businesses, instead of a discussion of what we need for the twenty-first century in terms of communication and higher-level cognitive and problem-solving skills, scientific and technical literacy and thinking tools to understand the world order go unmentioned. Further, while schools are strongly encouraged to function more like businesses, there is virtually no mention of the high numbers of businesses that fail, let alone the practice of government bailout of particular corporations and commensurate consequences for schools.

Yet, testing is purported as the antidote to school reform and improved student learning, in spite of that fact that many of the widely used tests are seriously flawed in several major respects, with the "testing juggernaut moving on, crushing logic and reason, no matter what researchers say."[13] One of the things that distinguishes Bush's plan from earlier ones, A Nation at Risk in particular, is that it specifically claims that "one of America's greatest attributes is our diversity," and goes on to comment on the importance of "addressing needs of children and youth from minority backgrounds."[14] Regarding students whose first language is other than English, this plan asserts the need for Limited English Proficiency (LEP) students to "master English as quickly as possible," to be assured "through the streamlining of ESEA Bilingual Education programs into performance based grant funding to states and local districts" who would exert control that would bear upon the continuation of such programs. As a part of ensuring local control, Bush's plan would also "free school districts to select teaching approaches that meet the needs of students," with a "prohibition of regulations on funds mandating particular instructional methods to educate students."[15] While, this proposition appears, on the surface, logical and commonsensical, it contains an underlying intent to eliminate those bilingual programs that support dual-language development and maintenance. Inherent criticisms of multiculturalism are infused herein, in that curricular transformation that is based on principles of including ideas, issues, and material from children's diverse experiences is seen as undermining literacy, knowledge of and respect for a romanticized notion of Western civilization, diluting the curriculum into sensitivity experiences, working on attitudes and feelings, and not intellectually defensible, thus political and ideological, or educationally sound. The deeply embedded values of individualism, competition, and alleged meritocracy infused in the predominant world view, decidedly Eurocentric and yet presented as universal, are presented as objective and value-free, whereas other perspectives are characterized as biased, limited, particular, and therefore catering to special interest groups and not the general good. While on one hand teachers are to be scrutinized and regulated with their performance assessed in relationship to the test scores of their students, they are promised that their interests will be protected and that they will be supported by being "granted control over their classrooms regarding the removal of violent or persistently disruptive students, through the implementation of zero-tolerance policies for curricular and extracurricular activities, to facilitate crime prevention and prosecution, through federal and state partnership programs to identify, prosecute, punish and supervise juveniles who violate state and federal firearms laws."[16] To complement this initiative, there will be increased funds for character education. Who will decide what character means, according to whose cultural frameworks, and who will develop the curriculum and decide upon the instructional materials and methods of assessment?

These provisions are designed to provide easy remedies and create safe schools and playgrounds, which any parent would want for their children. What is missing from the discussion is any attention to the implications of the proposal, the following considerations in particular: Which children will be targeted as those "at risk" of being disruptive and violent, given past practices of racial profiling and discrepancies in school discipline practices regarding punishment and suspension, which have resulted in Black and Latino youth, primarily males, as most likely to be the objects of discipline and exclusion from school? They have also experienced stiffer and swifter disciplinary actions and punishments than have white youth. Where will there be correctives for this? When one looks at the public's response to the violence in inner-city urban schools, white flight, fear and justifiable outrage as the carnage and loss of life that has resulted because of weapons in schools, gang-related conflict, and the loss of life of innocent bystanders, one sees that the violence that has erupted in suburban settings like Columbine in Littleton, Colorado, and other similar communities, predominantly white and middle class, the treatment of students, and the way in which their parents and communities have been portrayed are distinctly different. While there have been numerous eruptions of violence ending in death and carnage in such communities, these things are still treated as anomalies, exceptions to the rule, warranting compassion and understanding of individual troubled youth. These communities are not stigmatized as hotbeds of violence where dangerous groups of youth are out of control. But schools and school districts populated by children of color, Black and Latino in particular, wherein the majority of teachers are white and middle class, are portrayed as under siege, with teachers needing combat pay and protection from dangerous and unruly children and youth. What will result from these aspects of the Bush plan is that more children of color, males in particular, will be put out of school for one reason or another with no where else to go but to the street, marked as not worth the investment of time and energy, so that when the numbers are turned in regarding attendance and test scores, things will look much better and be used as indicators of school improvement. Meanwhile, such youth will be consumed by the machine of the informal economy, with many ending up as wards of jails and prisons, effectively written off as beyond hope and redemption.

To remedy the problem of student troublemakers, disruptive elements, and miscreants, school districts will be "granted unprecedented flexibility regarding how they may spend federal educational funds." Here again is the seductive language of control and choice, but by whom and for whom? Who constitutes the members of school boards, public and private? How will priorities be established? Whose interests will be served? In this era of high-stakes testing and the need to show results, with better numbers, where are the assurances of access and equity, due process, pledges "to increase funding for individuals with disabilities," to provide additional funds for technology, and to increase funds to improve the quality of public school buildings and facilities, notwithstanding? Where are the assurances that students who would be stigmatized as likely to bring down classroom and school test scores will be given the instructional and other support to enable them to stay in school and succeed? With further reification of testing and test scores, what will be put in place to put the breaks on reinstating tracking and official practices allowing for differential curriculum for those designated as needing remediation? When schools can be excluded from federal guidelines, and make choices based upon expediency, what and who will assure that, given necessary costs, investments for students with learning disabilities will continue, when there will clearly be other options for uses of valuable funds?

As with A Nation at Risk, the Bush plan proposes reforms that do not address the consequences of the sweeping initiatives and their implications for ordinary children and youth. They both allege that the issues are clear, that solutions will be simple, and that things must be done *now* to bring about desired change. They promise quick fixes to complex problems. Yet, as reflected in Albrecht's commentary on A Nation at Risk, "the fascination of the public and the media has blunted and obscured the carefully researched, thoughtful, and imaginative reports of Ernest Boyer, John Goodlad, and Theodore Sizer" and others."[17] Steeped in the language of *argumentum ad hominem*, A Nation at Risk, engages in negation and denial, espousing that there is such a thing as a typical American high school and, rendering a judgment of unfitness, suggests imperative correctives through the use of incantatory language such as should, ought, rights, and obligations.[18] According to Lehr, critical responses of this report from various scholars and professional organizations have gone unheeded.[19] For example, scholars of the English language arts profession have raised criticisms regarding the limitations of the arguments as well as the recommendations regarding the curriculum, standards, expectations, time use, the teaching profession, educational leadership, and support. In particular they question the following: the wisdom of a uniform curriculum that does not include consideration of personal experience; the emotional, intellectual development of individuals, the development of lifelong learners, readers, and writers; long-standing discriminatory practices in schools; challenges to testing and measurement that rely on multiple-choice questions that stress knowledge of discrete facts rather than understanding; lack of attention to issues of censorship of instructional materials and textbooks; absence of estimation of costs to be incurred as a consequence of a longer school day and longer school year; matters of leadership and other kinds of support; an overall failure of will and a desire to preserve the status quo, cloaked in the rhetoric of change.

Common shortcomings of A Nation at Risk and No Child Left Behind include a "lack of attention to the broader context of schooling, the need for structural change, and a recognition that schools cannot go it alone and that other institutions must also change, and that schools must increasingly stress the goals of self-fulfillment and social education."[20] Among critics of A Nation at Risk was a consensus that it had failed to address not only the broader purposes of education, but also the needs of disadvantaged students, any accounting of the financial costs of the proposed reforms, or any analysis of systemic problems [social, political, economic dynamics] that affect schools.[21] The fetishization of testing and test scores as a part of this web of deception meant that the public was presented with a program that purported to solve the problem while obscuring the reality that intelligence could not be easily quantified and "that intellectual qualities cannot be measured in the same way that linear surfaces are measured."[22] Students who scored low were castigated. So were their teachers, who were labeled as the least academically able of college students with the lowest college entrance exam scores using survey data from high school seniors and not students who were currently enrolled in teacher education programs or those who had completed them.[23] The consequent assault on teachers, who were subjected to evaluation systems fraught with questionable and outrageous practices, has resulted in demoralization, with devastating effects on teacher morale. Hence, the deskilling of teachers who often feel under siege of having to teach to tests, profiteering of test preparation materials, and resultant resistance and defensiveness in cheating by teachers as well as administrators who wish to escape the web of disciplinary actions, such as school probation, staff transferals, and threats of budget cuts, and more seriously, school closure.[24]

In the two proposals for reform of American education under examination, the sharp and severe criticism on American schools, especially in A Nation at Risk, is couched in accusatory and condemnatory language. To counter the argument, Hunt and Staton assert that "Our nation is indeed at risk [but that] the roots of this risk however, lie not in our educational institutions but in other realms, for example, in the sorts of contradictions between democracy and capitalism."[25] On one hand there is the impulse to educate citizens for active participation in government and public life of the country, by the provision of education through high school along with opportunities for post-secondary education and/or training, to virtually everyone to ensure not only literacy but also the development of independent and critical thinking for the exercise of one's own informed opinions. Yet on the other hand, there is a desire to ensure privileges and the commensurate power to sustain them by perpetuating a system that ensures inequalities invoking individualism, competition, exclusion of not only individuals but also groups on the basis of race and ethnicity, gender, class as well as other dimensions of difference. In a postindustrial society wherein information technology is the new fault line regarding knowledge and work, where things are becoming increasingly automated, and where knowledge professionals are among the most employable for lucrative jobs, individuals with poor or limited skills, will be increasingly relegated to either low-paying jobs in the service sector or the dustbin of surplus labor, forced to survive in the informal economy, become predators or prey in the world of the street, or be subjected to recidivist or long-term residence in penal institutions where redundant labor is housed.

According to Albrecht, " 'A Nation at Risk,' contains the seeds of mischief, in its unequivocal indictment of U.S. schools, high schools in particular, in that if its prescriptions were followed blindly we could adopt [its] recommendations and mislead ourselves into thinking that much [has] been accomplished when [very] little has."[26] Instead of bringing about improvement in the learning and achievement of all students, the proposed reforms will "legitimize chasing kids out of school and will only hasten the disenfranchisement of students already unsuccessful and demoralized, because those who will be unable or unwilling to meet the new rigorous standards will be put out with schools absolved of any further responsibility."[27] As a consequence, the inequalities between racial and ethnic groups as well as social classes will be exacerbated, with students of color continuing to experience high and disproportionate dropout rates and poor preparation for college, with teachers teaching to the test(s) and a curriculum focusing on test preparation.[28]

The sensationalist and nationalistic language of A Nation at Risk, struck a chord and served as a rallying cry for those who had become disaffected with the performance of public schools, those who sought alternatives and wanted out because of the presence of others—minorities and immigrants— were wary about the curriculum and its straying from the classics and inclusion of multiculturalism and were concerned about raising taxes and loss of real wages and hence were persuaded by the rhetoric of the report that instead of supporting the investment of more money in failing public schools, other options like private and religious schools, home schooling, charter schools, and vouchers as the solution. Essentially this meant that public school systems, especially those in large urban areas, would be deprived of much needed funding, effectively siphoned off and made available to other entities, and that the privileged and those able to exercise choice, further encouraged by government subsidies, would be able to go elsewhere, where the Others were virtually absent. Such prospects appealed to the middle-class, predominantly white, as well as upwardly mobile working-class families who had developed a cynical view of public education that had been undermined by years of inadequate funding to support quality education. Conservative political forces, with their maligning of the federal government, an appeal to civil libertarianism, and a refusal to invest in social welfare and public institutions, vowed to reduce taxes and not to support new ones, with a consequent adverse effect upon public education. In this kind of climate, it is no surprise that the language of efficiency, control, standards, choice, rewards and punishment became the hallmark of the rhetoric of reform: make do with less, fund alternatives, and unleash experiments at public expense by funneling funds through private interest initiatives. Let the market sort things out as the final arbiter.

With this came the emphasis on testing and measurement: testing students and their teachers; dissemination of testing results in the name of informing parents of the quality of their schools and teachers; and thus making good and bad schools easy to identify. The real keys to improving education (e.g., involving students more actively in the learning process and cultivating their higher thought processes) are now difficult to get into the public agenda, which is now cluttered with the detritus of A Nation at Risk and its companion No Child Left Behind. Because these two proposals to reform American education focus on surface matters, they attempt to reduce a complex matter to one of unidimensionality and simplicity. Thus, they mislead the public into thinking that the solution is simple and clear—test and measure, label and categorize students, teachers and schools, reward and punish. These policies deliberately oversimplify the issues in order to divert public attention from more substantive issues.

Many Questions Unanswered and Consequences Unexamined

When we look at the gross inequalities in quality and kind of education experienced by different students in the nation's schools, we must turn our attention to such things as the way that schools are funded United States—based on property taxes. For example in the state of Illinois, in a newspaper article comparing the experiences of students in different school systems, the author reported that per capita expenditure per pupil ranged from as little as $3,987 to a high of $17, 911.[29] These vast differences translate into sharp distinctions in the quality of a school's facility, library holdings, instructional materials, the presence or absence of laboratories for science classes, number and kind of computers available for classroom instruction, and teachers' salaries. Without a change in policy regarding funding, how will no child be left behind, when many of them start virtually several laps behind others who are advantaged? Then there are additional dimensions of the funding problem: class size, number of support staff, and so forth. How will one address the differences in instruction in contexts wherein some students are in schools with class size averages between 15 and 20 and those that have class size averages of between 25 and 30? Implications of these differences on student learning and achievement elude attention and these kinds of details are neither examined nor explained in either A Nation at Risk or No Child Left Behind. Without attention to such matters, how can one believe that all children will be able to participate in viable educational initiatives in the name of excellence?

Then there is the matter of high dropout rates among students of color—African American and Latino/as in particular—with males experiencing disproportionately higher numbers as well as different strands of immigrant populations. Again, one must ask how will students who experience widely different educational programs, for example in elementary schools, catch up to those who enter with advantages that have accrued over time? As a case in point, in the literature on reading and literacy, the third grade is the fault line of divergent scores on reading tests that continue to widen as students matriculate through the upper elementary levels as well as high school. What will be the intervention at this point to forestall continued divergence in scores? Once students are tested and found to be behind the others, below grade level, or below the national average, what kind of instruction will they experience to improve their learning? What will be the nature of the prescribed curriculum? Once such students are tested again, even if they show improvement, will they, their teachers, and their schools be deemed worthy of further investment? According to Bush's plan, after a specified amount of time, approximately three years have elapsed, and a school has not shaped up sufficiently in producing students who pass the requisite tests, money is withdrawn and routed to alternative institutions and entities. As individuals take advantage of these options, what will happen to those left behind in these schools? Further, when the lemming flight from troubled schools is in full swing, and teachers and administrators move to other schools—private, charter, magnet, and alternative—what will happen to those educators who remain? Those who are stigmatized as well as their students as losers?

As for the schools that are successful, many of which succeed as the result of the social class of their students and the privileges that they bring to school and that receive bonuses for their "excellence," will these rewards not ensure further inequality between them and other schools less endowed? With the resultant concentration of high-achieving students in high-achieving schools, with highly paid teachers and administrators, will not others most surely be left behind? How will the resultant inequalities be remedied? Neither A Nation at Risk nor No Child Left Behind addresses these matters.

Even if one were to accept the idea of vouchers and charter schools as viable alternatives to public schools, how would one ensure broad access for students of color, students for whom English is not their first language, immigrant students, working-class students, as well as students with disabilities? When it comes to admission to the alternative institutions and choice initiatives, particular students, specifically those in flight from troubled or stigmatized schools will be suspect and therefore not identified or treated as ideal candidates for acceptance. Given historical practices, I believe that such individuals will be excluded. With the prospect that alternative and choice institutions will be exempted from federal requirements, what policies, procedures, and practices will be put in place to ensure that individuals perceived and judged as different will be treated fairly and gain entry into the highly prized schools? With the emphasis on test scores and placement, what will ensure that a diversity of students who could benefit from quality education would be admitted? Would such students not be screened out so that they would not be able to have an opportunity to bring student achievement test score averages, school scores, and school ratings down? Where will these students go? How will they be advised or steered to consider other options?

From a more sanguine perspective, suppose that some students of color, some working-class, some immigrant students, as well as those with disabilities who were in search of options to the public schools to which they had been assigned were given vouchers to attend a school of their choice. Would these students and their families have the same options as those more financially privileged? What would happen when the tuition of a school that one selects is significantly greater than the value of the voucher? How will the difference be made up? Scholarships? Loans? Regarding the latter, what would happen for those who would not qualify given limited family income, indebtedness, and so forth? Will students in this situation be eliminated solely on the basis of economics? What about the options of those who are unable to raise the necessary funds? Where will they go? To their second, third, or fourth choices? Back to an impoverished public school? Will they not be left behind?

Let us consider prospects for teachers and administrators as well. After those who have scored high on for example a national teachers' exam have gotten jobs ostensibly at the best schools, most likely increasingly privatized, where will the others go? Charters, magnets, alternative schools? How will they be sorted out among the remaining spaces? The same must be asked regarding school administrators and principals. According to the Bush plan in particular, those who have gotten the best results in raising and maintaining high test scores for students will be the most sought after. They would receive bonuses. What will be the plight of principals and others who have been in schools where students have presented challenges in terms of their achievement as demonstrated on test scores, but who have nevertheless made improvement and grown let us say a few grade levels within a year, but who remain below the averages that count? What will be their fate? And for those who have administered schools in which student achievement persists below the indicators for success, what will their choices be? On a related matter, what will be the consequences for morale among teachers, forced into competition with one another because of the rush to dash across the finish line in testing to beat the others? What will come of collaborative efforts and collegiality among teachers? What will come of the relationships between schools and their feeder schools, when one is designated as behind or failing?

Issues related to curriculum and pedagogy also raise matters of concern. In terms of the former, there are serious implications for the content of the curriculum and the nature of courses that students take. With a return to the five new basics as proposed by A Nation at Risk, there is an assumption that this will ensure that students get the knowledge they will need to pass tests and be successful in life. Furthermore, I can foresee a movement to return to the good old days of the Western civilization focus with a homogenizing intent, as a corrective to the drift to cacophony and as a consequence of multiculturalism and issues of diversity and difference, which are cited as responsible for lowered standards and low literacy scores. In this regard, Stotsky specifically argues that multicultural classroom instruction has undermined our children's ability to read, write, and reason.[30] To restore curricular order, is this assault on inclusion of diversity and difference not a harbinger for a return to a more classic and traditional curriculum wherein Eurocentric perspectives and values will be recalibrated at the core?

In the wake of an attempt to establish curricular control, a focus on teachers will be a next logical step. When one considers that becoming an educator, a teacher in particular, is not based on training and the transmission of strategies, tactics, and internalization of best practices, but rather academic and professional preparation to understand and negotiate the complexities of teaching and learning as well as working within complex and dynamic organizations that have particular cultures,[31] then one has to question what will be the future for those who see education as holistic, intended to engender intellectual, affective, ethical, aesthetic, as well as physical development of others, and not merely to pass tests? Will schools be able to retain a corps of educators who will make teaching their career, if they must be perpetually tested, regulated, disciplined, rewarded, and punished based on the test scores of their students? Will teachers who believe in education for creative, transformative, democratic ideals, stay and not be turned away or driven out by policies and practices designed to deskill them and render them mere extensions of the testing industry? If they stay, where will they be? In the successful schools? The alternatives? If they choose to stay in failing schools, how long will they last? What will sustain their spirit in schools on probation, under threat of closure and eroding funding? And when they leave, who will remain for the students left behind and what kind of education will be provided for them?

The same questions need to be posed regarding school administrators, principals in particular. Perhaps for some, maybe many, there will be an inevitable lure of prospects for increased funding and bonuses for success as rewards for increased and high test scores of students. Their own survival will depend upon this. In this kind of climate, what kind of education will they promote and advocate? What educational goals and objectives will they seek to achieve? What kind of leadership will they provide regarding curricular design, courses, requirements, and electives? Which teachers will they recommend for retention? For dismissal? For probationary status? How will they reward and sanction particular pedagogical practices? How will they respond to and deal with differences between themselves and teachers regarding the aims and purposes of education? Will those who challenge the testing juggernaut be stigmatized, silenced, and drummed out of the profession? And for those in educational leadership positions, what will become of those who themselves question the wisdom of reducing assessment of school success and failure, teacher success and failure, student success and failure, to the matter of test scores? Further, regarding the distribution of leadership, which schools will be able to attract the "better" and "most qualified" principals and other administrators? And consequently, who will be left to administer the less successful and failing schools?

Conclusion

Taken collectively, the questions that I have posed above regarding the implications of the proposed educational reforms and their effects upon students, teachers, and individuals in administrative roles such as principals, address issues that warrant serious consideration and reflection, given their short- and long-range impact on education in the United States. Instead of jumping on the bandwagon for testing, testing, and more testing, and a reductive approach to education and learning, individuals and groups who question the assumptions of the proposals for educational reform and their consequences should engage in discussion and debate that challenge the direction that is being chartered, and work to forge a new direction. In my view the United States needs to develop a new culture of education, learning, and achievement that is based on situating the local within the context of the global, with an appreciation of what it means to live within an increasingly interdependent system. We as a nation need to participate in a serious dialogue in which we revisit what it is that we believe should constitute our vision of an educated person for the twenty-first century: what kinds of knowledge, skills, dispositions, habits of mind, and values do we think are important and necessary to prepare individuals as citizens of not only this nation, but also the global society? The dialogues need to take place in homes, communities, schools, and other public forums, between and among educators, policymakers, parents, and other constituents of educational institutions.

It is for these reasons, along with a glaring lack of attention to the implications of the above issues that I have raised, that the proposals for school reform such as A Nation at Risk, and No Child Left Behind are empty rhetoric, indeed ruses, which while claiming to be in the nation's interest and thus in the interest of everyone, are really designed with the intent to perpetuate the given order of things, sustain privileges, provide additional funds to the haves and therefore widen the gap between them and the have-nots. This is what makes the proposals suspect in that once implemented, they will support the existing racial/ethnic and class differences, domestically, and at the same time work to enforce the existent global order: the overdeveloped postindustrialized, information-age societies on one axis, and the underdeveloped, marginally industrialized, poor, struggling economies, many of which remain agrarian, producing subsistent goods and products, on the other. The educational policies and complementary role of educational institutions in the United States will serve to reinforce a hierarchy with increasingly differential opportunities for quality education, quality of life, and active participation in the public life of the nation.

The implications of such proposals for educational reform being enforced are startling. They will result in not only many, many children left behind, in the nation, but also many countries and societies in the world left behind, given the consequences of an educational system that stresses competition, winners and losers, rewards and punishment, the desire and need to be number one, the drive to consume even more resources and monopolize access to them, and a resultant callous disregard for the welfare of others emanating from a belief that one has earned and indeed deserves privileges at the expense of others.

Notes

1. Joel Spring, *The Sorting Machine Revisited* (New York: Longman, 1989), viii.
2. Joel Spring, *The Sorting Machine Revisited* (New York: Longman, 1976), 2.
3. Daniel Tanner, "The American High School at the Crossroads," *Educational Leadership* 41, no. 6 (March 1984): 6.
4. George W. Bush, *No Child Left Behind* (Washington, D.C.: Committee on Education and the Workforce, 2001), 2.
5. Ibid., 2.
6. Ibid., 13.
7. Doran Christensen, *The Politics of Educational Reform: What Vested Interests Are at Stake?* (Chicago: American Educational Studies Association, 1987), ERIC Reproduction Service ED 290735, 5.
8. Melvin Howards, *Testing: Illusions of Measurement*, ERIC Reproduction Service, 1987 ED300393, 1.
9. See Abdul A. A-Rubaiy, *Current Voices of Reforms in American Education: Ethnocentrism Or Globalism* (Houston Tex.: Comparative and International Education Society); ERIC Document Reproductive Service, 1984, ED265646.
10. See Gerald W. Bracey, "Why Can't They Be Like We Were?" *Phi Delta Kappan* 73, no. 2 (October 1991): 104–17.
11. Tanner, "The American High School at the Crossroads," 7.
12. Ibid.
13. Howards, *Testing*, 17.
14. Bush, *No Child Left Behind*, 16.
15. Ibid., 17.
16. Ibid., 20–21.
17. James E. Albrecht, "A Nation at Risk: Another View," in *Phi Delta Kappan* 65, no. 10 (June 1984): 684.

18. Clifford Adelman, *War and Peace among the Words: Rhetoric, Style and Propaganda in Response to National Reports on Higher Education* (ERIC Document Reproductive Service, 1985), ED264758, 46.
19. Fran Lehr, *Responses of the English Language Arts Profession to* A Nation at Risk, Urbana, Ill.: ERIC Clearinghouse on Reading and Communication Skills; Springfield, Va.: ERIC Document Reproductive Service, 1984, ED250690, 1.
20. William E. Gardner, *"A Nation at Risk: Some Critical Comments," Journal of Teacher Education* 35, no. 1 (January–February 1984): 15.
21. Sandra L. Hunt and Ann Q. Staton, "The Communication of Education Reform: A Nation At Risk," *Communication Education* 45, no. 4 (October 1996): 9.
22. Howards, 2.
23. Christensen, *The Politics of Educational Reform*, 11.
24. W. James Popham, *The Truth about Testing: An Educator's Call to Action* (Alexandria, Va.: Association for Supervision and Curriculum Development, 2001).
25. Hunt and Staton, "The Communication of Education Reform," 12.
26. Albrecht, "A Nation at Risk," 684.
27. Ibid., 685.
28. Pauline Lipman, "Bush's Education Plan, Globalization, and the Politics of Race," *Cultural Logic* 4, no. 1 (2001): 10.
29. Stephanie Banchero. "Equity Not in School-Funding Equation," *Chicago Tribune* (December 30, 2001): sec. 1, 19.
30. Sandra Stotsky, *Losing Our Language: How Multicultural Classroom Instruction Is Undermining Our Children's Ability to Read, Write, and Reason* (New York: Free Press, 1999).
31. Gary Griffin, editor "Changes in Teacher Education: Looking to the Future," *The Education of Teachers*. The Ninety-Eighth Yearbook of the National Society for the Study of Education. Chicago, Ill.: Distributed by the University of Chicago Press, 1999).

INTRODUCTION TO CHAPTER 14

Kevin Vinson's and E. Wayne Ross' chapter is unique to this volume not only for its focus on the rise of enforcement-oriented high stakes testing in schools but by explaining this phenomenon in terms of its relation to corporate mass media produced spectacle. The chapter, drawing on the work of Debord, Baudrillard, Foucault and the tradition of critical pedagogy, elaborates the inextricable links between enforcement-oriented school policy and the cultural politics of mass media.

CHAPTER 14

Controlling Images

The Power of High-Stakes Testing

KEVIN D. VINSON AND E. WAYNE ROSS

Surveillance, Spectacle, and the Power of High-Stakes Testing

Increasingly today conceptualizations of public schooling rest upon the influence of dominant and dominating *images* rather than on more authentic understandings of the complex realities of classroom life. We create our interpretations of what is, what was, and what should be based on what is presented within the mainstream "news" media and what we see in the movies and on television. This especially holds true in the ever more powerful contemporary social/cultural/political/economic/pedagogical settings of standards-based educational reform,[1] most clearly, perhaps, within the current move toward high-stakes standardized testing, a regime in which both the cultural knowledge and the behavior of students, teachers, administrators, parents, classrooms, schools, and districts are not only (in)validated but also disciplined. Simply, the convergence of a number of phenomena related to image and high-stakes testing, including various means by which scholars might seek critical and practical insight, the mechanisms by which image and high-stakes testing both reflect and are reflected by societal circumstances, the enforcing consequences of such actualities, and the techniques by which both might be resisted define the scope of this chapter's efforts.

We recognize first that this "hegemony of the image" mirrors and is mirrored by—is made possible by and is reinforced by/reinforcing of— several developments in contemporary U.S. and international society, particularly within the realms of technology and globalization. It is, for instance, consistent with the advent of the possibility of 24/7 access to video monitors and cameras, in terms both of *seeing* and of *being seen*. This emerges, for example, in the proliferation of web cams, around-the-clock broadcast and cable (and satellite and Internet) television, state-sponsored privacy-moni-

Kevin D. Vinson is assistant professor in the Department of Teaching and Teacher Education in the College of Education at the University of Arizona.

E. Wayne Ross is Distinguished University Scholar and chair of the Department of Teaching and Learning in the School of Education and Human Development at the University of Louisville.

toring (e.g., the FBI's "Carnivore"), the multiplication of media outlets, and the explosion of "reality" television programs (e.g., *Survivor*, *Big Brother*, ad infinitum, ad nauseam). Moreover, it is constructed within an economic environment of conglomeration and oligopolification, a globalized setting in which media giants merge their abilities to control even more strongly access to both technology and the (re)production of public images (e.g., AOL, Time Warner, *and* AOL-Time Warner).

Contemporary regimes of high-stakes testing must be understood within such contexts, as mutually (re)inforcing and (re)productive, and as specific instances of the hegemonic dominance of media images. How often, for example, do individuals and groups determine the "effectiveness" of particular schools by relying on reported test scores—*media images*—whether or not they have any firsthand information on what actually occurs in any unique school? As public education increasingly comes to dominate U.S. political discourse, to what extent do such standardization policies universalize the cultural and behavioral interests of the economically, politically, and culturally powerful, especially as "liberals" and "conservatives" continue to merge around a singular idealized view of schooling (e.g., the No Child Left Behind Act of 2001).[2]

As society's rulers coalesce and more generally use both *surveillance* (the disciplinary observation of the many by the few) and *spectacle* (the disciplinary observation of the few by the many) as conjoint means of controlling individuals and groups, high-stakes testing represents not only the plane on which the school-society link is played out, but also a reinforcing context within which the interests of the wealthy and powerful work to legitimize what counts as both knowledge and appropriate behavior.[3] This is particularly the case with national education policy, which continues to be determined by the representatives of elite cultural and economic ideologies (e.g., in post–*A Nation at Risk* commissions comprised of key corporate leaders [e.g., IBM's Lou Gerstner], union officials [e.g., former American Federation of Teachers chief Al Shanker], and politicians [e.g., the National Governors' Association] convened for the purposes of determining the nature and *meanings* of U.S. public schooling). In effect, such powerful elites control not only public/media images of education, but also how they are (re)produced vis-à-vis the contents of "official knowledge"[4] and "proper" school behavior.[5]

In this chapter we consider the mutual relationships between images of public schooling and the operations of high-stakes testing, particularly regarding the degree to which they work to enforce, control, and discipline both cultural knowledge and behavior. Moreover, we interrogate the extent to which both seek to "normalize" as "correct" the interests of the economically and politically powerful. Drawing on the literatures surrounding the notion of *image, surveillance, spectacle*, and high-stakes standardized testing, we pursue: (1) the role of image in the contemporary societal merging (or coexistence) of surveillance and spectacle; (2) high-stakes testing as contextualized image; (3) the consequences of such conditions; and (4) Debord's constructions of *dérive* and *détournement* as modes of resistance.

In short, our contention is that high-stakes testing and test scores work as, and must be perceived in terms of, image and how image is constructed environmentally within the existing surveillance-spectacle arrangement. High-stakes testing as spectacle-surveillance–induced image then works to control groups and individuals via the specific mechanisms and technologies of the *gaze*—of seeing and being seen—and operate in support of potentially dangerous and oppressive consequences that must be resisted. As we conclude, *dérive* and *détournement* provide *an* incomplete, yet plausible, counter-maneuver, one aimed toward superseding the lifeless pedagogical status of standardization and standardized test scores.

Image: Schooling, Surveillance, and Spectacle

Our images of schooling fundamentally work to control—they operate locally, dynamically, and contingently as both cause and effect, aim and outcome, of *power* (i.e., such that image and power are mutually [re]productive). Set both physically and ideologically within the contextual complex of multiplicities that characterizes (post)modern U.S./global, capitalist, hyper/cyber/virtual society, power and image blur: *power* creates and is created by *image*(s), while *image*(s) simultaneously create(s) and is (are) created by *power*. At issue, namely, is *controlling images,* that is both control *of* images and control *by* images.

Understanding image demands engaging the milieus within which image is produced. In our interpretation this means focusing on the extraordinary conditions of (post)modern, global society. Most especially we consider the present disciplinary backdrop of surveillance and spectacle. It is within their coming together—their merging—that images are produced, maintained, and propagated, and within which they establish and exercise their (re)inforcing power. As images, test scores cannot approach the heuristic and quotidian complexities of contemporary schooling, no matter their makers' intentions. They can and do, however, proliferate as mechanisms of control.

Surveillance and Spectacle

Antiquity had been a civilization of spectacle. "To render accessible to a multitude of men [*sic*] the inspection of a small number of objects": this was the problem to which the architecture of temples, theatres and circuses responded. With spectacle, there was a predominance of public life, the intensity of festivals, sensual proximity. In these rituals in which blood flowed, society found new vigour and formed for a moment a single great body. The modern age poses the opposite problem: "To procure for a small number, or even for a single individual, the instantaneous view of a great multitude." In a society in which the principal elements are no longer the community and public life, but, on the one hand, private individuals and, on the other, the state, relations can be regulated only in a form that is the exact reverse of the spectacle: "It was to the modern age, to the ever-growing influence of the state, that was reserved the task of increasing and perfecting its guarantees, by using and directing, towards that great aim the building and distribution of buildings intended to observe a great multitude of men at the same time."[6]

Contemporary pedagogical images, including those associated with high-stakes testing, must (and can only) be understood contextually and against certain overlapping and contiguous sociocultural, economic, and political currents—changes in technology, the advent of state-sponsored infotech, global and corporate capitalism, and the "triumph" of the U.S. "one-party system." More precisely (and significantly), we must understand that they reflect and are reflected by such settings as they create and are created by a characteristic feature of twenty-first century life in the United States: namely, the imperative (in terms of desire *and* opportunity) of *seeing* and *being seen* (i.e., both *how* we are seeing and being seen and *that* we are seeing and being seen; related notions include the "cult of celebrity," Warhol's "fifteen minutes of fame," and Orwell's *Big Brother*). This imperative induces a fundamental disciplinarity, an enforced conformity, and a perceived necessity to standardize and become standardized.

What are these contexts and changes? In terms of technology one might again consider several fairly recent developments, including the advent of 24/7 television "broadcasting" via hundreds of cable/satellite channels, the Internet, and the proliferation of web cams—making it possible to see and be seen simultaneously, continuously.

Economically—within the environment of state-sponsored, global, corporate capitalism—consider how daily, round-the-clock updates reveal the scope to which stock prices and market capitalization figures increase or decrease irrespective of profit or profit potential—here, apparently, corporate image, how such institutions are *seen* (their "get rich quick" manipulations)—matter more than fundamental soundness or past and present performance (let alone social, political, environmental, and/or cultural awareness and sensitivity). This even in the aftermath of Enron, ImClone, and Martha Stewart.

Politically, note the degree to which the current race to the "middle" waged between the major political parties (e.g., year 2000 presidential candidates Bush and Gore) depends less on any authentic issue advocacy and more on how they are *seen* (and how they themselves see voters). In effect, this leads to the establishment of a one-party system in which powerful Republicans seek to appease their right wing (e.g., Patrick J. Buchanan, the Christian Coalition) while simultaneously staking a claim in the "center" (aka "compassionate conservatism") and powerful Democrats their left wing (e.g., Ralph Nader, environmentalists, the "New Democrat"). As a result, real difference is marginalized and traditional allies (e.g., Nader via the Democrats and Buchanan via the Republicans) are forced out and compelled to accept an existence *viewed* as extremist and nonmainstream. This would be, perhaps, not so problematic were it based less on *mere* image (i.e., polling data, focus group results, public relations, advertising) and more on a heartfelt dedication to significant issues, beliefs, and disagreements. For both sides the goal seems to be less one of defending and promoting the collective social good, and instead one of ensuring first *that* they are in fact seen, and second that *how* they are seen (Democrats *and* Republicans) is as "conservative" but not *too* conservative and "liberal" but not *too* liberal.

At heart, these contexts—sociocultural, economic, and political—(re)establish the priority of sight—the "gaze"—as a mechanism of discipline and social control. More specifically, they create and are created by the conditions within which the convergence of surveillance and spectacle occurs, and form in part the setting for what might be called a "new disciplinarity," a mode of often subtle coercion grounded in the extreme potentials of incessant seeing and being seen, of the gaze, of both surveillance *and* spectacle. It is of course here that images—including those related to schooling—reside and must be confronted.

For Foucault, surveillance represented a disciplinary power built out of the (eventually automatic and invisible) possibilities of the many being visible to the few (à la the architecture of the modern prison created according to the design of Bentham's panopticon). At present, elements of surveillance exist in such features of society as nannycams, Carnivore (the FBI's e-mail-tapping framework), and Echelon (the government's [NSA's] program for monitoring virtually all worldwide telecommunications), each of which must be further positioned within the Bush administration's post-September 11 creation of a Department of Homeland Security, the U.S.A Patriot Act, and TIPS (the Terror Information and Prevention System, citizens-as-spies).[7]

Spectacle, conversely, presupposed for Foucault a mode of disciplinarity based on the processes of antiquity, of the few being visible to the many (à la the ancient architectures of theaters, circuses, temples, and so forth). Yet according to philosopher Guy Debord in *The Society of the Spectacle*, spectacle describes *contemporary* society as well.

> The whole of life of those societies in which modern [italics added] conditions of production prevail presents itself as an immense accumulation of spectacles. All that once was directly lived has become mere representation.
>
> The spectacle is not [merely] a collection of images; rather, it is a social relationship between people that is mediated by images. . . . In form as in content the spectacle serves as total justification for the conditions and aims of the existing system. It further ensures the permanent presence of that justification, for it governs almost all time spent outside the production process itself. [Moreover, the] language of the spectacle is composed of signs of the dominant organization of production—signs which are at the same time the ultimate end-products of that organization.[8]

For Debord, the spectacle defines a society in which everywhere reality is replaced by images—images that obtain and pursue a "life of their own" distinct (not merged with) reality. It presents a form of alienation in which "being" means "appearing" and where, moreover, the image, as distorted and disconnected, mediates all social relationships. As he argued, the components and characteristics of this spectacle include:

1. the dominance of image over lived experience,
2. the privileged status of the commodity,
3. the promotion of abstract (exchange) value and labor,

4. alienation,
5. passive observation (by spectators) and contemplation (over living or experiencing),
6. a specific economics and ideology, and
7. isolation/separation/fragmentation/lack of community, and
8. the denial of history.

For Debord the spectacle maintains its own regime of control and discipline, one opposed to surveillance and to the panopticon, grounded in the fact that it exists purely for its own reproduction, and thus subordinates all of human life to its needs. It controls by isolating and fragmenting, denying history, distorting reality, alienating, and monopolizing communication (one way, to its advantage). It works ultimately to deny that which can promote change (i.e., community, dialogue, and so forth) in that those who want it maintained control images—the dominant form of social life—such that they might mystify underlying and hierarchical relations of power. They therefore control social relationships and do so via the mechanisms of the *spectacular.*

What makes today unique, however, is the merging or at least coexistence of the two, making it *possible* and among some people (even) *desirable* to see and be seen continuously and simultaneously (i.e., because of the Internet and cable/satellite/wireless technologies). In the extreme, the potential becomes more real that society will (or at least *could*) be understood as nothing but a medium through which everybody *can* watch everybody all the time and across and throughout all space—nothing more than a totality of images and spectacular relationships. Standards Based Educational Reform (SBER) in fact represents the extent to which this setting occurs, and presents a case not only by which this merger can be understood but also one that can itself be understood against and according to surveillance and spectacle. (An example here of the workings of surveillance is the official "monitoring" of testing procedures; an example of spectacle occurs in the media reporting of test scores. Both, in the end, privilege image over authenticity and work as a means of social control, political/economic dominance, and conformity.)

In the next section we consider high-stakes testing and media-reported test scores as images produced within the coalescence of spectacle and surveillance. We pursue how within this environment high-stakes standardized testing functions as a regime of enforcement and how it operates according to controlling images.

High-Stakes Testing and Enforcement

At bottom, high-stakes standardized testing, coupled with the publication of individual students', schools', districts', and states' scores, seeks to legitimize certain dominant and dominating images of culture, knowledge, behavior, economics, and politics in an overall effort to discipline and enforce certain "norms" consistent with the privileged interests of the wealthy and powerful. As such tests, elements of broader SBER schemes, spread they necessitate questions relevant to the power of surveillance and spectacle. They enable at multiple levels a media-sponsored, hierarchical relationship between forceful groups of elites and schools, with their diversified range of stakeholders positioned simultaneously as both the few observed (disciplined) by the many *and* the many observed (disciplined) by the few.

Image-Power, Surveillance-Spectacle, and Schooling

High-stakes standardized testing/SBER and those who authorize and endorse it aim to impose a certain set of images relative to "good" or "effective" education, including those of the "good" student, the "good" teacher, the "good" school, the "good" parent, "good" curriculum, and "good" instruction. These strive to enact a certain standardized and standardizing semantics of knowledge, learning, and behavior that work organically in the interests of the economically and politically powerful. The pressures of surveillance-spectacle compel those involved to conform lest they be criticized as not good, as deficient, and in need of even greater authoritarian oversight (e.g., state take-over, "reconstitution," privatization, and so forth).

More troubling though is the ethical dimension of the system. The implications are that some teachers, students, schools, curricula, and so forth are *better* than others. Undoubtedly this is true. Yet a problem emerges as these judgments are founded solely on reported test scores. The illusion is that without ever entering a given classroom one might be qualified to evaluate its inhabitants, their actions, their values or characters, and their relationships *simply* as a result of testing. This is the case with many policymakers and journalists (as well as other "seers" or "gazers"). Based on test scores, people draw conclusions about good and bad schools, effective and ineffective teachers, hardworking and "lazy" students, involved and uninvolved parents, and challenging and unchallenging curricula. They forget or ignore the fact that many low-scoring schools perform miracles, that their teachers and students are just as likely to be dedicated and committed (and "intelligent") as those in other settings, that schools where test scores are high do not own a monopoly on caring parents, and that content—most likely standardized anyway—is neither necessarily "better" nor "worse" than in higher-scoring schools.

Such frameworks employ representatives of dominant political and economic ideologies to reflect their own interests via the public schools (often with "token" representation among the less powerful). They present a standardized purpose (e.g., a "mission statement"), standardized content (e.g., mandated curriculum standards and guides), standardized methodologies (in some cases, for instance, even legislating phonics), and standardized assessments (high-stakes tests). (The October 2, 2001, headline in the *Baltimore Sun* proclaimed: "Uniform Teaching Program Advances: Panel, national group recommend statewide curriculum for Md.; A call for 'consistency.'") Elite and hegemonic images of the good are standardized. High-stakes testing is a means of enforcement of these images/interests. Teachers, students, parents, and principals are coerced toward such images via the tools of surveillance and spectacle. Surveillance operates (principally) on the micro level as educational managers observe and encourage *particular* activities and procedures. Spectacle operates (principally) on the macro level as the media report specific test scores frequently identified school-by-school and district-by-district. With respect to schooling, surveillance and spectacle are mutually empowering, circular, leaving teachers and students (and others) in an unfortunate position relative to the disciplinary gaze—observed by small numbers of powerful officials *and* by large numbers of the general public. Needless to say the pressures to "appear" a certain way, to conform to the dominant image, are immense.

This arrangement ignores the complex multiplicities of context, of the interplay among economics, history, beliefs, traditions, cultures, ideologies, and so on. They obfuscate or neglect the fact that in most cases test scores indicate not "learning" per se, but instead prevailing circumstances, including conditions of local wealth, political might, and racial, cultural, ethnic, and linguistic diversity—not, as SBER/high-stakes testing supporters claim, merit, intelligence, or hard work, but rather the extent to which teachers and students (and communities) are "like" the testmakers. They make possible, in fact, a state of increased privilege for the already privileged and inordinately reflect and reward the norms of domination.

The works of theorists such as Bakhtin, Barthes, Boorstin, McLuhan, and Baudrillard provide valuable insights into understanding the intricacies of high-stakes testing/test scores not only as images but also as instruments of sociopedagogical enforcement. Bakhtin[9] challenges us to pursue the processes by which such images implicate a certain representation of space-time (or "chronotope"), one that perhaps benefits a certain contextual reality (that of those who [wish to] control strategically our access to and interpretation of time, space, and schooling). Barthes asks that we critique not only the *denoted* ("literal") representations of pedagogical images (e.g., test scores—"objectively," for instance, whether they have increased or decreased, or whether "achievement" is higher or lower) but their *connoted* ("cultural") representations as well (e.g., that some children are inherently "better" than others). Boorstin begs the issue of testing as "pseudo-event," that which is "unreal," and exists principally for the purposes of its own publication and circulation, particularly given that "somebody [the media themselves, government officials] has an interest in disseminating, magnifying, advertising, and extolling [tests] as events worth watching or worth believing" so that someone might at some point ultimately "get [his or her] money's worth." McLuhan implies a set of consequences specific to the specific medium—newspaper reports of school success, for example—and argues that we confront their effects on human interaction, as "extensions" of our senses, and on their ability to "eliminate time and space factors in human association" such that the very social and psychological characteristics of schooling are altered—"the medium is the message." And Baudrillard compels the public to consider how test scores may in fact be "more real" than the "reality" of classrooms, schools, teachers, and students themselves—the extent to which they exist as copies/images without originals and in reference to no "underlying" reality—as "simulacra" and "simulations."

Consequences

Many potential consequences of this image/high-stakes testing/surveillance-spectacle conglomeration are already well known. As critics such as Haney, Kohn, McNeil, and Ohanian,[10] among others, have pointed out, under such a regime both curriculum and instruction narrow, pedagogy weakens, innovation declines, "achievement gaps" expand, teacher-centeredness increases, and (perhaps most ironically these days) more children are in fact "left behind." And, as we have already pointed out, connections between formal school knowledge and the economy generally solidify (often via the involvement with politicians and educational managers of corporate and financial leaders). As we also note, however, there are of course risks to the extent that SBER (curriculum standards, high-stakes testing) may be oppressive,[11] disciplinary,[12] antidemocratic,[13] inauthentic and opposed to the collective good.[14]

Further, though, there are consequences more specifically connected to the association of and between surveillance and spectacle. The spiral or circular (if not convergent) and mutually (re)productive character of the relationship helps ensure (1) that both in fact are strengthened and (2) that (therefore) school discipline and enforcement (in terms both of content and behavior) are tightened and subsequently made more effective, especially via the technologies of image.[15]

Resistance

Resisting the enforcing characteristics of controlling images, such as those inherent in SBER/high-stakes standardized testing regimes, presents a number of somewhat new and unique pedagogical challenges. The first rests with the odd and relatively broad coalition of elites who support them. This group includes wealthy and powerful groups and individuals located across the political-economic spectrum. Within this context "natural" alliances lose their meaning, as was the case when Nader fought the Democrats and Buchanan the Republicans in election year 2000. It is increasingly difficult here to recognize one's supporters and one's adversaries. The second, perhaps more important challenge exists via the very pervasiveness of the surveillance-spectacle complex. Although the various philosophies of image presented by Bakhtin, Barthes, Boorstin, McLuhan, and Baudrillard offer insights into what questions to ask and what answers to pursue, it is the theoretical work of Foucault and (especially) Debord and his colleagues that provide the critical starting points for contesting the authority of the technological, political, pedagogical, and socioeconomic gaze.

Dérive *and* Détournement *as Revolutionary Pedagogy*

Foucault's work on "resistance" is perhaps more straightforward than might be expected, even though, arguably, he never laid out an explicit program for liberation or revolution. As Gordon rightly suggests, "it may be objected that Foucault never locates his theoretical enterprise 'on the side of' resistance by undertaking to formulate a strategy of resistance." This means, in effect, the possibility that "the cunning of [any given revolutionary] strategy is taken as being the exclusive property of [distinct] *forms* [italics added] of domination."[16] It is, in other words, localized and specific, contingent. But for Foucault this doesn't mean that revolutionary resistance can't occur—it does occur, *period*—but only that any resistant act is neither inherently and universally good nor inherently and universally bad; it is inherently neither better nor worse than any other. "People do revolt. . . ."[17] Revolution and resistance are neither predictable, inevitable nor objective. But they do happen.

His thinking rests on a number of premises, most importantly the understanding "that power, with its mechanisms, is infinite," though not *necessarily* "evil" or "omnipotent." [18] Foucault cautions against various resistant tendencies in which some individuals have the authority to distinguish appropriate or proper revolutionary behaviors at the expense of others, and recognizes that revolutionaries must take into account not only those actions that are most directly "political," but also those that are "merely" of "evasion or defense." He warns of the problematics of some revolutionary strategies by which one regime charged with normalizing is replaced by another charged with the same coercive capacities. And yet, for Foucault power in all its guises demands some mode of resistance of the strongest sort: "The rules that exist to limit [power] can never be stringent enough; the universal principles for dispossessing it of all the occasions it seizes are never sufficiently rigorous. Against power one must always set inviolable laws and unrestricted rights."[19] He implies, subtly, the potential of an even more anarchic or hyperdemocratic and "profounder logic of revolt" in which the "whole species of rationality and the status of a whole regime of truth can be made to open itself to interrogation,"[20] a striking and radical resistance aimed toward the entirety of disciplinary power.

With respect to high-stakes testing as image, and within the convergence of surveillance and spectacle, this view allows for a number of tangible and more typical techniques, including those of boycott, refusal, organizing, political action, and so on. What Foucault frankly contests is the universal and immanent or natural rightness of one over the other, the preeminence of some action as against other action, the certainty that what replaces today's system will *necessarily* be an improvement, and the rash confidence that the essential problematics of pedagogical power will simply fade away.

Guy Debord and other members of the Situationist International (SI)[21] indicate other, less widely known techniques relevant to superseding "the society of the spectacle" and its effects, techniques not yet extensively explored for their conceivable and critical pedagogical significance, yet of special interest given their promise vis-à-vis the controlling and enforcing propensities of high-stakes testing.

The first, the *dérive*, literally "drifting," implies "[a] mode of experimental behavior linked to the conditions of urban society: [it is] a technique of transient passage through varied ambiances."[22] According to Debord:

> The dérive entails playful-constructive behavior and awareness of psychogeographical effects; which completely distinguishes it from the classical notions of the journey and the stroll.

In a dérive one or more persons during a certain period drop their usual motives for movement and action, their relations, their work and leisure activities, and let themselves be drawn by the attractions of the terrain and the encounters they find there. The element of chance is less determinant than one might think: from the dérive point of view cities have a psychogeographical relief, with constant currents, fixed points and vortexes which strongly discourage entry into or exit from certain zones.[23]

For the SI "psychogeography" referred to "[t]he study of the specific effects of the geographical environment, consciously organized or not, on the emotions and behavior of individuals."[24]

On the second, *détournement,* literally "diversion," the SI wrote:

Short for: detournement of preexisting aesthetic elements. The integration of present or past artistic production into a superior construction of a milieu. In this sense there can be no situationist painting or music [per se], but only a situationist use of these means. In a more primitive sense, detournement within the old cultural spheres is a method of propaganda, a method that testifies to the wearing out and loss of importance of those spheres.[25]

It "involves," according to Jappe, "a quotation, or more generally a re-use, that 'adapts' the original element to a new context."[26]

It is [moreover] also a way of transcending the bourgeois cult of originality and the private ownership of thought. In some cases the products of bourgeois civilization, even the most insignificant ones, such as advertisements, may be reemployed in such a way as to modify their meaning; in other cases, the effect may be to reinforce the real meaning of an original element . . . by changing its form.[27]

For Debord himself *détournement* suggested

the reuse of preexisting artistic elements in a new ensemble [via t]he two fundamental laws of detournement . . . the loss of importance of each detourned autonomous element—which may go so far as to lose its original sense completely—and at the same time the organization of another meaningful ensemble that confers on each element its new scope and effect.[28]

Together *dérive* and *détournement* sprang from Debord and his colleagues' "dreams of a reinvented world" where one might "supercede dead time," a world of experiment and play, of "discovering that a world of permanent novelty could exist, and finding the means to start it up."[29] According to Marcus:

These means were two: [jointly] the "dérive," a drift down city streets in search of signs of attraction or repulsion, and "détournement," the theft of aesthetic artifacts from their contexts and their diversion into contexts of one's own device. . . .

[Ideally] to practice détournement—to write new speech balloons for news-paper comic strips, or for that matter old masters, to insist simultaneously on a "devaluation" of art and its "reinvestment" in a new kind of social speech, a "communication containing its own criticism," a technique that could not mystify because its very form was a demystification—and to pursue the dérive—to give yourself up to the promises of the city, and then to find them wanting—to drift through the city, allowing its signs to divert, to "detourn," your steps, and then to divert those signs yourself, forcing them to give up routes that never existed before—there would be no end to it. It would be to begin to live a truly modern way of life, made out of pavement and pictures, words and weather: a way of life anyone could understand and anyone could use.[30]

As techniques of resistance aimed toward the enforcement elements of high-stakes testing (as controlling images, within the setting of surveillance-spectacle), what might *dérive* and *détournement* mean? What might they look like? How might they be applied? And how might they work?

Applied to schooling and high-stakes testing, the *dérive,* the more difficult of the two, demands first a reunderstanding of the geographical shifts brought on by changes in gaze-based technologies and the related global expansion of U.S. capitalism. It requires further a consideration of the architectural evolution induced by surveillance-spectacle and its effects (as discussed above). Today, with respect to education, *dérive* necessitates "drift-ing" not only through the teletecture and cosmotecture of contemporary schools (schools as virtual space, schools as casinos), but also through the cyberspace "city" of the Internet. It begs a critical confrontation with an entirely new set of psychogeographies.

In each instance, note again that images dominate and that surveillance and spectacle converge or coexist. This means, in that *dérive is a social act,* that students and teachers would move communally, cooperatively, drifting as it were through buildings but also through cyberspace/virtual space/hyper-space, through the cosmotecture and teletecture of contemporary schooling, as they were attracted or repelled, as their emotions and behaviors were piqued. These drifters would, for instance, be "free" to enter or exit testing sites (both physical and virtual) as they were encouraged or discouraged to do so, and they would seek simply to experience, to disrupt, and to play. They would surf websites, confronting relevant images, come and go, utilize moni-tors and web cams for "travel," compelled toward or away from various zones, from, say, "official" image bases, from control, and from the enforc-ing effects of standardization schemes. Conceivably, albeit in the extreme, they could drift in and out of—even "hack" into—testing locales and inter-rupt them, create with them, toy with them. They could, moreover, enter and exit classrooms, schools, central offices, government domains, and media positions where high-stakes testing is enacted and where, in the end, control-ling images are most oppressively enacted. All as a means of resistance.

With respect to *détournement,* the implications for resistance are perhaps clearer, especially within the contexts of image, surveillance, and spectacle. Again, to quote Jappe, *détournement* involves "a quotation, or more gener-ally a re-use, that 'adapts' the original element to a new context" such that a given image either (1) "may be reemployed in such a way as to modify [its] meaning"; or (2) such that "the effect may be to reinforce the *real* [italics added] meaning of an element . . . by changing its form."[31] Consider first, for example, this plausible (though made-up) newspaper headline:

Presidant Bush Announces Education Package—Called No Child Left Behind, Plan Emphasizes Increased Testing

In and of itself, this seems (or may seem to some) relatively innocuous, even positive, in that the administration will be devoting federal attention to schools and seeking to ensure that no child is left behind by testing them all on a regular basis to measure their progress. Suppose, however, that as a mode of resistance the headline is juxtaposed next to a chart providing data on test scores, wealth, ethnicity, language, and "dropout" rates, for instance in Texas, President Bush's home state. The power and significance of the image then changes as it becomes evident that in Texas, under a system that the president aims to impose on the country as a whole, some children indeed were/are left behind, and those who are share similar characteristics relative to wealth, language, and ethnicity.[32] The image has been "reused" or "reemployed" and its importance and meanings have shifted.

As a second example, imagine this newspaper headline:

State Assessment Scores Show Many Schools Failing

Suppose, further, an accompanying chart with the names of schools or districts in one column and mean standardized test scores in a second column, perhaps with pass-fail cutoff scores indicated.

Now consider recent (mind-boggling but true) news reports that within a particular state funding has been provided to equip upper school system management with personal wireless telecommunication devices (at a cost of thousands of dollars), while because of budget cuts at the school level parents have been asked to donate supplies, including toilet paper, as a means to save money that might otherwise have to be diverted from instruction. (According to some reports, some schools actually have engaged in a system of bartering donated supplies, again, including toilet paper, in order to obtain necessary educational material.) Now, reimagine the image. The headline:

State Assessment Scores Show Many Schools Failing

The chart? Column one, names of schools or districts; column two, number of rolls of donated toilet paper (with appropriately arbitrary pass-fail levels reported). As with the first case, both meaning and significance have been changed.

At the heart of *détournement* rests the notion that in all instances either the image is altered to "fit" the context, or the context is altered to "fit" the image. Such processes—or pedagogical strategies—enable students, teachers, and others to confront and combat the enforcing/enforcement properties of high-stakes testing *as* image. What they require, though, are access to and facility with those technologies that make such enforcement possible— computers, the Internet/World Wide Web, web cams, and so forth—as well as an understanding—a *critical consciousness*—of controlling images, surveillance, and spectacle. Joined with *dérive* and Foucauldian techniques, *détournement* provides an untapped mode of relatively and authentically situated and critical resistance, *praxis*. (We should note also that there is no reason why this would not apply to other images, for example those promulgated via film, television, and so on.)

Summary and Conclusions

Ours is an age of image, and of "image profiteers,"[33] a time and place where seeing and being seen matter, where visual media rule and where the tools exist to make possible an absurd if not frightening new world in which everyone *can* watch (can *control*) everyone all the time, *Brave New World* and *1984*, a new world that is neither neutral nor predictable, one rife with unseen and untheorized problems, possibilities, dangers, and consequences. It is an age characterized in part by what Frank Rich calls "the mediathon," the "all coverage all the time" infotainment treatment of such events as the O. J. Simpson trial, the Clinton–Lewinsky affair, and the ongoing Gary Condit–Chandra Levy scandal (stoppable it seems only by the monumental disaster of the World Trade Center/Pentagon tragedies of September 11). It is an age of hyperreality, of the endless bombardment of individuals by an evermore exhausting array of never-ending, at times indistinguishable, multimedia images, an age in which seemingly the copy can (does) function as more real and authentic than the original (if any such thing still exists) and in which even "serious" media/image purveyors often are (deservedly) suspect.[34]

As fads and fashions, endorsements and sponsorship deals, cosmetic surgery, Hollywood special effects, "reality" television, and even military operations demonstrate, image matters (even if, *contra* Andre Agasi and Canon, it isn't *everything*). Consider, for example, the words of Lieutenant Colonel Gregory C. Sieminski on the importance of image even in the naming of military operations:

> Applying the four guidelines [for choosing a name] will result in an effectively nicknamed operation, an outcome that can help win the war of images. In that war, the operation name is the first—and quite possibly the decisive—bullet to be fired. Mold and aim it with care.[35]

The military establishment and its backers know that "reality" itself may not be enough to garner support on behalf of any given mission, and that therefore the public must be "convinced" (or coerced) to follow along on other, more "imaginary" grounds (e.g., Operation Enduring Freedom and not Operation Kill bin Laden, or the Department of Homeland Security and not the Department of Homeland Surveillance). It is about looks and appearances at least as much as it is about the characteristics and importance of aim, threat, strategy, and tactics. Unfortunately, the same may be said perhaps about schooling and high-stakes testing.

The predominance of image must be understood within the prevailing context of surveillance and spectacle, a context that reinforces and is in turn reinforced by the presence of dominant and dominating images. Within this setting the mechanisms and technologies of seeing and being seen struggle against those of *not* seeing and *not* being seen according to a multiple and complex interplay among desire, possibility, existence, and necessity.

Contemporary schooling as contested site moves within and across these borders. Its participants engage in oppression *and* resistance, a disciplinary drama in which they are positioned simultaneously as both the many observed by the few and the few observed by the many. Standardization regimes coerce educational stakeholders toward a privileged image supported by and supportive of the interests of the most wealthy and powerful among us, all in the name—the *appearance*—of democracy, achievement, and economic opportunity. And, not surprisingly, the "copy" frequently *is* more "real" than the "original."

Within the convergence of surveillance and spectacle high-stakes testing functions as a mechanism of enforcement, proceeding as a matter both of control *by* images and control *of* images, a circularity in which power is an effect of image and image is an effect of power—*image-power* or *power-image*. Certain dominant images, established and maintained by elite educational managers, force a disciplinary and antidemocratic conformity on the part of (among others) teachers, students, and schools toward the interests of the (same) wealthy and powerful minority who sanction the contents, policies, procedures, and consequences of high-stakes testing in the first place. Those who control images produce images that control—power produces (and maintains and reinforces) images, images produce (and maintain and reinforce) power—all in their own power-laden interests.

We offer the practices of *dérive* and *détournement* not as absolutes or final statements, but as quotidian and incremental praxis, a tentative set of steps toward reestablishing the place of living and authenticity as against alienation, passivity, antidemocracy, conformity, and injustice. For in the end, high-stakes testing and SBER are not the whole story but merely a piece of the bigger story, one in which we and our children are author and character, subject and object, player and played on. Perhaps this is our true test. If so, then the stakes are high indeed.

Notes

1. See Kevin D. Vinson and E. Wayne Ross, "In Search of the Social Studies Curriculum: Standardization, Diversity, and a Conflict of Appearances," in *Critical Issues in Social Studies Research for the Twenty-First Century*, edited by W. B. Stanley (Greenwich, Conn.: Information Age Publishing, 2001); and Kevin D. Vinson, Rich Gibson, and E. Wayne Ross, *High-Stakes Testing and Standardization: The Threat to Authenticity* (Burlington, Vt.: John Dewey Project on Progressive Education /University of Vermont, 2001, available at www.uvm.edu/~dewey/monographs/ProPer3n2.html

2. See also Kevin D. Vinson, "Image, Authenticity, and the Collective Good: The Problematics of Standards-Based Reform," in *Theory and Research in Social Education* 29 (2001): 363–74; and Vinson and Ross, "In Search of the Social Studies Curriculum."

3. See E. Wayne Ross, "The Spectacle of Standards and Summits," *Theory and Research in Social Education* 27, no. 4 (1999): 440–46.

4. See for example, Michael W. Apple, *Official Knowledge: Democratic Education in a Conservative Age* (New York: Routledge, 1993).
5. See for example, Alfie Kohn, *The Schools Our Children Deserve: Moving Beyond Traditional Classrooms and "Tougher Standards"* (Boston and New York: Houghton Mifflin, 1999).
6. Michel Foucault, *Discipline and Punish: The Birth of the Prison*, trans. Alan Sheridan (New York: Vintage Books, 1979), 216–17.
7. For a critical view of the "new" surveillance, see Jeffrey Rosen, "A Watchful State," *New York Times Magazine* (October 7, 2001): 38–43, 85, and 92–93.
8. Guy Debord. *The Society of the Spectacle*, trans. D. Nicholson-Smith (New York: Zone Books, 1995), 12–13.
9. Mikhail M. Bakhtin, *The Dialogic Imagination: Four Essays by M. M. Bakhtin*, edited by Michael Holquist, trans. C. Emerson and M. Holquist (Austin: University of Texas Press, 1981); Roland Barthes, *Image-Music-Text*, trans. S. Heath, (New York: Hill and Wang, 1977); Daniel J. Boorstin, *The Image: A Guide to Pseudo-Events in America* (New York: Vintage Books, 1987), 40; Marshall McLuhan, *Understanding Media: The Extensions of Man* (Cambridge, Mass. and London, UK: MIT Press, 1994), 9; Jean Baudrillard, *Simulacra and Simulation*, trans. S. F. Glaser (Ann Arbor: University of Michigan Press, 1994).
10. Walt Haney, "The Myth of the Texas Miracle in Education," *Education Policy Analysis Archives* 8, no. 41 (2000), available at epaa.asu.edu/epaa/v8n41; Alfie Kohn, *The Case Against Standardized Testing: Raising the Scores, Ruining the Schools* (New York: Heinemann, 2000); Linda McNeil, *Contradictions of School Reform: Educational Costs of Standardized Testing* (New York and London: Routledge, 2000); Susan Ohanian, *One Size Fits Few: The Folly of Educational Standards* (New York: Heinemann, 1999).
11. See Iris Marion Young, "Five Faces of Oppression," in *Rethinking Power*, edited by T. E. Wartenberg (Albany: State University of New York Press, 1992); and Paulo Freire, *Pedagogy of the Oppressed* (New York: Continuum, 1970).
12. See Foucault, *Discipline and Punish*.
13. John Dewey, *Democracy and Education: An Introduction to the Philosophy of Education* (New York: Macmillan, 1966).
14. See Vinson, "Image, Authenticity, and the Collective Good"; and Vinson, "National Curriculum Standards and Social Studies Education: Dewey, Freire, Foucault, and the Construction of a Radical Critique," *Theory and Research in Social Education* 23 (1999): 50–82.
15. See Kevin Vinson and E. Wayne Ross, "In Search of the Social Studies Curriculum."
16. Colin Gordon, "Afterword," in *Power/Knowledge: Selected Interviews & Other Writings 1972–1977*, edited by Colin Gordon (New York: Pantheon, 1980), 256.
17. Michel Foucault, *Michel Foucault: Power*, edited by J. Faubion, trans. R. Hurley, et al., (New York: New Press, 2000), 452.
18. Ibid.
19. Ibid., 453.
20. Gordon, "Afterword," 258.
21. For example, see Len Bracken, *Guy Debord: Revolutionary* (Venice, Calif.: Feral House, 1997); Anselm Jappe, *Guy Debord*, trans. D. Nicholson-Smith (Berkeley: University of California Press, 1999); Ken Knabb, *Situationist International Anthology*, edited by and trans. Ken Knabb (Berkeley, Calif.: Bureau of Public Secrets, 1981); and Greil Marcus, *Lipstick Traces: A Secret History Of The Twentieth Century* (Cambridge: Harvard University Press, 1989).
22. Situationist International, "Definitions," in *Situationist International Anthology*, edited by Ken Knabb (Berkeley, Calif.: Bureau of Public Secrets, 1981), 45.
23. Guy Debord, "Theory of the *Dérive*," in *Situationist International Anthology*, edited by Ken Knabb (Berkeley, Calif.: Bureau of Public Secrets, 1981), 50.
24. Situationist International, "Defintions," 45.
25. Ibid., 45–46.
26. Ibid., 59.
27. Ibid.

28. Debord, "Theory of the *Dérive*," 55.
29. Marcus, *Lipstick Traces*, 168, 170.
30. Ibid., 170.
31. Jappe, *Guy Debord*, 59.
32. See Haney, "The Myth of the Texas Miracle"; and Kevin D. Vinson and E. Wayne Ross, "What We Can Know and When We Can Know It," *Theory and Research in Social Education* 29, no. 2 (2001): 204–11.
33. Maureen Dowd, "We Love the Liberties They Hate," *New York Times* (September 30, 2001): 13.
34. Frank Rich, "The Age of the Mediathon," *New York Times Magazine* 84 (October 29, 2000): 13; Francis Fukyama, *Our Postmodern Future: Consequences of the Biotechnology Revolution* (New York: Farrar, Strauss and Giroux, 2002); Todd Gitlin, *Media Unlimited: How the Torrent of Images and Sounds Overwhelms Our Lives* (New York: Henry Holt/Metropolitan, 2001).
35. Gregory C. Sieminski, "The Art of Naming Operations, *Parameters* (U.S. Army War College Quarterly) (Autumn 1995): 81–98, available at carlisle-www.army.mil/usawc/parameters/1995/sieminsk.htm.

INTRODUCTION TO CHAPTER 15

Robin Truth Goodman's chapter looks at the culture of the World Cop by discussing how popular detective fiction is instructing citizens on the meaning of the police. It considers how the increase in global policing functions intersects with an ideological assault on the public sphere generally, including on public education. "Dick Lit" uniquely analyzes how popular discourses of feminism are bolstering the successes of expanding corporatism and militarism. As well, it shows how popular literature can be complicit in teaching people to consent to global capitalist policies that fundamentally undermine democratic institutions.

CHAPTER 15

Dick Lit

Corporatism, Militarism, and the Detective Novel

ROBIN TRUTH GOODMAN

In the wake of the terrorist attacks of September 11, 2001, on the World Trade Center and the Pentagon, world politics has assumed the shape of a criminal investigation. Not only has the so-called war on terrorism included what the *New Yorker* magazine has called "probably the most important criminal investigation in American history," but also civil society itself has been opened up as a field of hidden clues, suspicions, and criminal secrets of foreign aggressions. Part of this, the *New Yorker* goes on, has to do with how "[t]he new antiterrorism bill, passed after minimal hearings and debate, breaks down Cold War–era barriers between foreign intelligence and domestic law enforcement to an unprecedented degree." In other words, evidence formerly found in intelligence operations on foreign governments, where warrants were not demanded and civil protections not upheld, could now serve as part of a criminal case. Says Morton Halperin, defense expert and former Clinton official, "[u]nlike a law-enforcement tap, the government never has to tell the subject that they've done it. If the government thinks you're under the control of a foreign government, they can wiretap you and never tell you, search your house and never tell you, break into your home, copy your hard drive, and never tell you that they've done it."[1] "Historically," Halperin continues, "the government has often believed that anyone who is protesting government policy is doing it at the behest of a foreign government and opened counterintelligence investigations of them." Taking its meaning from the Nixon administration's active work to criminalize political protest[2] and the constructed opposition between civil liberties and public or personal safety, political dissent—now more than ever—appears as an act of war.

The substantive collapse between domestic policing and international interventions witnessed in the *New Yorker* article is not an outgrowth of the September 11 crisis, but rather had already made its way into popular

Robin Truth Goodman is an assistant professor in the Department of English at Florida State University. She is the author of *Infertilities: Exploring Fictions of Barren Bodies* (University of Minnesota Press, 2000) and co-author with Kenneth J. Saltman of *Strangelove: Or How We Learn to Stop Worrying and Love the Market* (Rowman & Littlefield, 2002). She is also the author of *World, Class, Women: Feminism, Global Literature, and the Politics of Education* (Routledge, 2003).

common sense through means of what is now conventionally called the policies of the "World Cop." The advances of policing onto the global stage are
realigning power, law, and the nation-state, and are, in turn, creating new
narratives that allow an ethics of war to make sense in popular consciousness. In addition, they participate in subordinating the idea of "law" as
defending common or public interest in the nation-state to a more globalized
version of "law" as a militarized tool of imperialism. As Michael Holquist
has pointed out, "[y]ou cannot have detective fiction before you have detectives,"[3] and neither can you have global policing without an ideological
production to frame it. How does the public *learn* to think about the police,
and how do these lessons indicate the meanings behind the ways the new
international order drives domestic law, and how domestic law, in turn,
frames the pursuit of global justice? As Henry Giroux has argued:

> Educational work is both inseparable from and a participant in cultural poli-
> tics because it is in the realm of culture that identities are forged, citizenship
> rights are enacted, and possibilities are developed for translating acts of inter-
> pretation into forms of intervention. . . . The politics of culture not only recon-
> stitutes and maps how meaning is produced, it also investigates the connections
> between discourses and structures of material power, the production of knowl-
> edge and the effects it has when translated into daily life.[4]

This chapter turns to popular detective fiction in order to trace how the
idea of the police has come to dominate international politics and what the
implications of this are for future democratic action. In particular, it looks at
Sara Paretsky's 1994 popular detective novel *Tunnel Vision*.[5] *Tunnel Vision*
narrates the ascendance of the "feminist" police-detective/entrepreneur over
the forces of urban corruption, domestic disorders, illegal labor, international
drug mafias, and money launderers in order to reestablish an ethical freedom
to do business anywhere. In the novel, the protagonist-detective V. I.
Warshawsky is dating an African American cop,[6] insinuating a collaboration, but also a tension between the freedom of the private sector in its white
adventurism and the lugubriousness of the public sector mired in the ghetto
as it enforces domestic law. Vic's detective service sets up an ethical call for
free surveillance that surpasses legal restrictions and domestic territory,
elevating the privacy, autonomy, and muscularity of the private eye and its
business above a wretched public sector overdependent on the state, its banal-
ity, its responsibilities, its institutions, its borders, and its laws. In fact, Vic
and the cop break up before the end of the novel because Vic refuses to follow
the legal code. Presenting the only choice as between inadequate public institutions and a militarized culture of the bottom line—that is, between the
superpowered individual and the ineffectual state—the vilification of state
functions that *Tunnel Vision* performs has broad implications for the future
of the public sphere. It undermines the possibilities for imagining an actively
political and democratic civil society not bogged down in state bureaucracies and legal routines nor subjected to an ethics of private profit through
heroic military triumph. The weakness of the nation-state and the necessary
turn toward extralegality presented in *Tunnel Vision* symptomize a cynicism

about public life which, in the popular consciousness, raises suspicions about all things public and all public places for developing democratic cultures, from welfare to schools to the police themselves.

From the World Cop to the Just War

The internationalization of the police is combining with the internationalization of capital to change the relationship between ethics and sovereignty while it refashions ideologies of the nation-state and its public institutions as forces of limited or particularistic legal jurisdiction and power. In their book *Empire*, Michael Hardt and Antonio Negri have attributed the extension of the policing function in the idea of the "World Cop" to two basic transformations in the world order: "the banalization of war and the celebration of it as an ethical instrument." "Two distinct elements are combined in this concept," they go on. "[F]irst, the legitimacy of the military apparatus insofar as it is ethically grounded, and second, the effectiveness of military action to achieve the desired order and peace."[7]

An ethics of war is neither new nor particularly prevalent or credible today, though it is tempting to try to figure the rationale for a "just war," what its causes and contours would be and how it could be fought. As Richard Falk has argued, the founding charter of the United Nations defined the "just war" as a multilateral action, with respect for sovereignty, which creates the conditions for negotiating the ceasing of aggression throughout the world, or, as the founders themselves promised, "to save succeeding generations from the scourge of war." Yet, Falk continues, the Security Counsel's confidence in its abilities to end war through consensual alliance did not pan out, as its "peacekeeping" missions, from Korea to the Gulf War, "entailed an ambitious set of encroachments on sovereign discretion that seemed to go beyond ... the foreign policy establishments of all leading countries." "It would undermine confidence in the UN," Falk goes on, "if the extent of its authority could be shaped arbitrarily and on a case-to-case basis by the political will of its most powerful members,"[8] that is, according to a logic of exceptions rather than as rules. "Police action," as Michael Klare has pointed out, has increasingly emphasized unilateral action, meaning counterterrorism, counterinsurgency, and low-level warfare designed to ensure U.S. world dominance and the subordination of its allies over time. This means, while still investing in conventional weapons, the 2003 military budget will include "power projection" capabilities as well as a "wide array of new equipment ... four AC-130U flying gun platforms (of the type used to pound enemy positions in Afghanistan) and converting four Trident ballistic-missile submarines into "strike submarines" that will carry Tomahawk land-attack cruise missiles and will be able to infiltrate small squads of Special Forces commandoes into the coastal areas of hostile powers" and will also fund "nuclear warfare and space-based systems": "[T]he Defense Department will no longer organize its forces to counter specific military threats posed by clearly identifiable enemies, but instead will acquire a capacity to defeat *any* conceivable type of attack mounted by *any* imaginable adversary at *any* point in time—from now to the far-distant future. Put differently, this is a mandate for the pursuit of *permanent military supremacy*" [original emphasis].[9]

Hardt and Negri define the "just war" from the biblical tradition, where "the concept rests primarily on the idea that when a state finds itself confronted with a threat of aggression that can endanger its territorial integrity or political independence, it has a . . . right to make just war," and then dismiss this definition as "something troubling."[10] This definition of *bellum justum*, they say, routinizes repression at the same time as it makes the enemy into an absolute. Based on an inarguable protocol of self-determination, the infusion of policing language and policing techniques demonstrates a growing need for ethical rationales behind "the imperial model of authority"[11] and a sentimentalization of military technologies, even as it contradictorily undermines the ethical argument of imperialism. As well, the international police function of the neoliberal state advocates a seemingly unbreakable peace ideologically sustained by perpetual war.

On the other hand, Hardt and Negri continue, "the imperial process of constitution tends either directly or indirectly to penetrate and reconfigure the domestic law of the nation-states, and thus supranational law powerfully overdetermines domestic law."[12] For example, the Patriot Act, passed into law after the terrorist attacks of September 11, contained provisions to curtail national sovereignty: in particular, a section that would extend the use of U.S. courts to countries suing companies for illegal commerce and tax evasion—with an eye to gauging money laundering, fraud, corporate smuggling, and terrorists' financial networks—was voted down in the House and only partially restored as a narrowed-down version in the Senate.[13] Severely restricting the nation-state's abilities to protect its public institutions and domestic production, this and other "free-trade" arrangements let corporate activity transcend the laws and responsibilities of a nation-state. Recently, these corporate protections have worked to allow the tobacco industry to avoid tariffs and taxes in foreign countries like Colombia, undersell local brands, and increase advertising without increasing legal imports, even as they, to a certain degree, protect the bank accounts of terrorist organizations.

The rise of global corporate power cannot be divorced from the militarization of justice. Increasing needs for energy, for example, to accommodate an ever-expanding consumer market has led to an establishment of military bases in the Middle East with predictable repercussions. In Afghanistan of the 1990s, the U.S. support for Unocal's oil pipeline projects—in an attempt to transport petroleum from Turkesmenestan and other oil-rich countries in the Caspian Sea region while avoiding Iran—resulted in the build up of the Taliban as the *mujaheddin* most likely to ensure stability: " 'The Taliban will probably develop like the Saudis did. There will be Aramco, pipelines, an emir, no parliament, and lots of Sharia law. We can live with that,' said one US diplomat."[14] Clearly, building a culture open to market forces is more important that creating democratic institutions.

The question that U.S. policymakers faced was whether to intervene in a peacekeeping mission in order to out-compete the Argentinean oil company Bridas along with the Russian and the Iranian transportation networks, or to let the Pakistanis arm the Taliban until stability was reached. The decision to follow a hands-off policy in Afghanistan meant an eventual cutting-off of support, instigating a fiscal crisis in the Taliban's regime, and a subsequent diminishment of public services, including schools. As a result, with a waning of employment opportunities and the closing down of schools for both boys and girls, Afghani male youth crossed the border into Pakistan to be educated in private *mishras* where they were trained in fundamentalism and militancy. Under the direction of Madeleine Albright and the Clinton admininistration in 1997, the United States changed its course, targeting the Taliban as causing instability in the region through its drug trafficking, terrorism, and Islamic fundamentalism. Now the world is reeling in the after-effects of these decisions. In the midst of a war on terrorism, with the richest country on earth leveling the poorest nation, with the number of civilian dead uncounted and a new government only recently installed and already challenged through assassination and fragmentation and weak public support, with millions of desperate refugees facing a brutal winter, with prisoners of war being kept in eight-by-six cages in Guantanamo, with esteemed professionals like Alan Dershewitz announcing on *60 Minutes* that he thought torture should be made legal in the name of the Constitution, and with an executive promise of the war's indefinite extension, there is something disturbing in the idea of police action defining the principles of universal justice. Certainly, national sovereignty is not the defining principle or the ultimate goal of the police-war.

Clearly, the biblical tradition of defending sovereignty does not stand up in the face of the police, as the police themselves participate in waging aggressions against other nations' territorial integrity, political independence, and public interest. The provision against violations to "territorial integrity or political independence" of a sovereign nation would apply to U.S. actions in Nicaragua and Panama, for example, putting the global police on the wrong side of the equation, that is, on the side of the "threat" to territorial integrity and political independence—on the side of the criminal—rather than on the side of the right to make just. As well, respect for national sovereignty would mean setting up legal restrictions to corporate management of other nations' legal, political, economic, and financial systems, including trade and taxes.

Nor is it particularly clear in the contemporary U.S. domestic scene that the notion of the police presupposes ethical conduct when a 1999 Amnesty International report documented "patterns of ill treatment across the USA, including police beatings, unjustified shootings and the use of dangerous restraint techniques to subdue suspects,"[15] or when a 2000 Amnesty International report recognized "[t]he continued use of the death penalty" along with "a nationwide pattern of police brutality; the physical and sexual abuse of prisoners, inhuman or degrading conditions of confinement and the mistreatment of asylum seekers" as "serious human rights violations."[16] Is there a contradiction between the sacralization of imperialist action in the name of policing and the general popular distrust of the domestic police to ensure safety? How does the global spread of industrial management appear as part of a national juridical tradition even as just policing action within the nation-state proves to be in disarray, fundamentally and violently in opposition to the public it is supposed to be protecting?

The State of the Police

Most scholarship on detective fiction focuses on one of three styles of analysis: one, they engage in outlining the generics of genre; two, they set out to reveal detective fiction as an instance of the surveillance or disciplinary society and the birth of the modern subject described in Michel Foucault's work; or three, they see in detective fiction the development of modern methods of logic like deduction or, in the case of Jacques Lacan and Umberto Eco, semiotics. The first approach evolved in the 1970s as part of a newly formulated interest in popular culture within strains of postmodern theory analyzing the breakdown between high and low cultural forms. It tries to develop what John Cawelti called "the formulaic pattern of the detective story" like "raciocination and mystification," "the proportion of inquiry to action," a "tension between violence and order"[17] and the like, in order to create a sense of seriousness, even scientivism, around the study of the popular and the mass-produced.

The second approach tends to concern itself more with the social, but in ways that virtually deny the actual practice of the police. This is due mostly to Foucault's own attempts to theorize power as occurring in microsites and local networks outside of the centralizing idea of power embodied in the state. In D. A. Miller's exemplary study *The Novel and the Police*, for instance, policing tends to signify everything but policing: "Disciplinary power," he writes, "constitutively mobilizes a tactic of tact: it is the policing power that never passes for such, but is either invisible or visible only under cover of other, nobler or simply blander intentionalities (to educate, to cure, to produce, to defend)."[18] More recently, Christopher Wilson has taken the concept of the Foucaultian surveillance society out into the streets and read it alongside the history of community policing from the time of Stephen Crane's carousing in the Bowery in the mid-1890s to the present, only to conclude that policing is less a matter of communities wanting to be free of crime and less a matter of tactical politics than about cultural narratives' "policing of representation" or about the panoptical features of realism. Even recognizing that "the formerly ward-based policing of ... cities had been transformed into a new ... professionalism based in boot camp paramilitarism, aggressive automobile patrol, and intelligence gathering on even the most innocuous of citizen groups," Wilson still goes on to conclude that "the current political mantra of 'more police officers on the street' "[19] is no more egregious than the desire for spectatorship within a media society. Building on classical linguistics as it appeared within psychoanalysis and then deconstruction, the third type of criticism even goes further in reducing the politics of policing to a linguistic or representational mechanism, where, as Lacan himself says, "it is that the displacement of the signifier [e.g., the dead body or missing statue] determines the subjects in their acts."[20]

What these theoretical paradigms fail to show is how the current obsession with policing shapes the political identities of today's citizens. I recently asked a group of students what they thought made the inner city dangerous, and they told me it was the police. One of those students wrote her final research paper on the "Code of Conduct" for New York City's police. She called her precinct and asked some of her relatives who were in the police force to get her a copy of this document, and when nobody came through, she started asking police on the beat if they could tell her anything about it: the police she asked did not even know that such a code existed. A segment on the *MacNeil/Lehrer News Hour* explained the difficulties of counting and assessing crime statistics in Philadelphia. The pictures illustrating the story were of white men in suits in board rooms and offices discussing methods of investigation cut against scenes of police cars cruising through bombed out urban sections where suspicious dark bodies lurked. Behind the scenes, three young white men with glasses sat in front of computers writing programs that would map concentrations of crime, overviewing and rationalizing not only where crimes were occurring, but also the problem neighborhoods where future crimes would be committed, expanding red blobs on a screen. The function of the police was to isolate communities of danger where the state's arm of law and order had an obligation to enforce its controls.

Increasingly, the role of the police has become a focus of controversy as the police force in many parts of the country has been imposing a draconian rule over public spaces and private lives. As David Cole states:

> The videotaped beating of Rodney King by officers of the Los Angeles Police Department encapsulated for many blacks the treatment they expect and fear from police. . . . In 1994, the Mollen Commission reported on widespread police corruption and brutality in the Bronx. . . . The Mollen Commission found that police corruption, brutality, and violence were present in every high-crime precinct with an active narcotics trade that it studied, all of which have predominantly minority populations. It found disturbing patterns of police corruption and brutality, including stealing from drug dealers, engaging in unlawful searches, seizures, and car stops, dealing and using drugs, lying in order to justify unlawful searches and arrests and to forestall complaints of abuse, and indiscriminate beating of innocent and guilty alike. The commission found that police officers and supervisors often accepted lying and brutality as necessary aspects of the job.[21]

The perceived need for policing and the perceived dangers of city streets, even as crime statistics show decreasing rates of crime nationally, reflect a general sense of insecurity intensifying with capital's deregulation and the weakening of public supports and democratic outlets. The flexibility of the contemporary workforce appears as one possibility for explaining the rise in perceived danger and feelings of insecurity, in addition to a general popular and cynical distrust of public institutions and politics to work effectively in the public interest. As Zygmunt Bauman notes, "The extant political institutions, meant to assist [citizens] in the fight against insecurity, offer little help. In a fast globalizing world, where a large part of power, and the most seminal part, is taken out of politics, these institutions cannot do much to offer security or certainty. What they can do and what they more often than not are doing is to shift the scattered and diffuse anxiety to one ingredient ... alone—that of safety, the only field in which something can be done and seen to be done."[22] The fear of crime and the call for stricter and harsher policing displaces blame for insecurity onto the poor, thereby incapacitating criticism of the structures and distributions of power. It also marks the decrease in the rights of self-determination for citizens in the face of the rise in corporate governance.

The establishment of the police force as an arm of the state in charge of civic metropolitan protection occurred in London in 1829, mostly as a symbolic "embodiment of an emerging system of law," with the detective branch installed in 1842 and consisting of plain-clothed officers mostly commandeered to patrol the ranks of working-class dissent.[23] In the United States, cultural historian Robin Kelley has traced the history of the police through the civil patrollers of the antebellum south, who were hired specifically to run down and catch runaway slaves and "geared almost entirely to the maintenance of slavery." While private detection in the form of the Pinkerton agency was allied with abolitionist and labor politics in the north, Kelley argues that modern-day urban police grew out of what he calls "planter class . . . terrorist groups"[24] like the Ku Klux Klan and the Knights of the White Camellia. Urban policing in the states became institutionalized at the turn of the century through the replacement of party bosses' political appointments by formal academies, but it was Franklin Delano Roosevelt who professionalized the force through exams, uniforms, inspections, and pistol practice, and Nixon who escalated and militarized the police to face the explosion of civil disobedience in the civil rights struggle and the peace movement and who thereby first managed to link rhetorically the menace of crime and drugs to the rise of resistance politics. This led to a federalization, a rationalization, and a militarization of law enforcement.

As policing is increasingly a cultural presence through which most people today are forced to negotiate their relations with power, and as, at the same time, policing is used as a technique of international relations and imperialist infiltrations, it is important at this time more than ever to think about what the popular police imaginary entails, what kind of ethics such ongoing confrontations implicate, and how other types of social organization can be formulated. Contemporary political movements on the left have been organizing and rallying with ever more intensity against what has quickly become an Orwellian culture: university faculty suspended for speaking in dissent; foreign university students monitored for their course selections; immigrants detained for practicing free association; over 1,200 people arrested, held, and interrogated, most without formal charges; and the prospect of secret military tribunals giving the executive branch of the federal government expanded powers of public apprehension. As David Cole has warned,

> Secrecy has become the order of the day. Criminal proceedings are governed by gag orders—themselves secret—preventing defendants or their lawyers from saying anything to the public about their predicament. . . . The Patriot Act authorizes never-disclosed wiretaps and secret searches in criminal investigations without probable cause of a crime, the bedrock constitutional predicate for any search. . . . A major impetus behind George W. Bush's presidential order authorizing the trial of suspected terrorists in military tribunals was the desire

to avoid the constitutional necessity of disclosing classified evidence to the defendant in an ordinary criminal trial. In military tribunals, defendants have no right to a public trial, no right to trial by jury, no right to confront the evidence or to object to illegally obtained evidence and no right to appeal to an independent court.[25]

Even before September 11, with two million people in jail; with four white policemen shooting and killing an unarmed black man in the Bronx; with the police sexually assaulting a Haitian man in Brooklyn; with Rodney King, Leonard Peltier, and Mumia Abu-Jamal; with the police violently cracking down on demonstrators at a Mathew Shephard vigil in New York, at the 2000 Democrat and Republican Conventions in Los Angeles and Philadelphia, and at protests in Seattle and Washington D.C., as well as in Prague and Genoa, against the increasingly undemocratic nature of global capitalism; with New Jersey cops profiling criminals through race, the excessive use of force by the police was one of the dominant repressive measures of power, infecting the quality of people's lives, their sense of security, and the very nature of their freedom. Even as police departments have been subjected to investigations, reforms, restructuring, and punitive measures as a result of such spectacles saturating the media, police repression continues, in the brutal shooting of unarmed black teenager Timothy Thomas in Cincinnati, leading to violent riots and martial law, as well as in a video of police in Inglewood, California, throwing mentally challenged African American teenager Donovan Jackson against a car and then punching him. The current intensification of policing, in fact, started in 1967 when President Lyndon Johnson took policing away from the Treasury and the Food and Drug Administration and put it in the hands of a new "super agency" that would spend "billions of dollars in an effort to reshape, retool and rationalize American policing" by doling out "military weaponry, communications technology, and special training," targeting gangsters and drug traffickers as well as ordinary street users and demonstrators against the war. Since then, as Christian Parenti has pointed out, public spaces are militarized: " 'order' is achieved by 'flooding' Black neighborhoods with swarms of police, including SWAT teams and canine units. It is the strategy of colonial war: peace through superior fire power."[26] Schools are being increasingly patrolled and guarded by police with or without arms. Public parks like New York's Washington Square are filmed day and night by police cameras posed on top of neighboring buildings to scout out petty drug dealers. Under new court precedents, our rights of privacy under search-and-seizure limitations are being ever more narrowly defined. Parents are being encouraged to inform on their kids under fear of being sued or brought up on criminal charges, even have them arrested for wearing the wrong clothes or for writing what are seen as controversial or dangerous words and phrases, even while friends are turning in fellow students for behaving in the radically expanding array of ways currently considered "off-color." Any theory of the police that stops at representational politics or circumvents the very real operations and reconfigurations of a centralized state threatens, at the very least, to miss the point.

Novel Policing

Sara Paretsky's novels participate in the tradition of hardboiled detective writing which came out of the 1930s and focused on a tough-guy urbanism, as well as out of a Sherlock Holmes' characterization with the investigator operating as a quasi-Nietzschian inspired superhero genius who is able to solve crimes by slicing together bits of empirical knowledge and subjecting them to the logic of deduction. Starting in the 1980s, the novels also fit into a new trend in detective fiction which pits a female detective against a patriarchal police force and an equally patriarchal criminal class, posing feminism as a condition of independence, justice, empathy, and freedom that will lead capitalism out of its self-interested and shackling corruptions. As Priscilla Walton and Manina Jones have pointed out, "During the period between 1976 and 1980 ... [t]he number of women's mystery novels in general increases sharply, from 166 to 299, with the boom between 1981 and 1985. But the increase in professional investigators is even more remarkable: it more than triples from 13 (between 1976 and 1980) to 43 titles between 1981 and 1985, and continues at the same rate—almost tripling again from 1986 to 1990, to 124, and again in the (incompletely documented) period between 1991 and 1995, to 366."[27] What Walton and Jones do not consider, however, is how this boom in female or feminist detective fiction corresponds with the growth and the militarization of policing as well as an expansion of neoliberal culture. Though they claim that this trend in detective fiction represents a renewed enthusiasm for the feminist values of the 1970s, the way Vic's feminist agency connects ethics with a shrinking of public protections in favor of a fast-paced, transcendent heroism of capital does not necessarily bode well for a future of liberation for everyone.

V. I. Warshawsky is a lawyer with an ethical social conscience who goes into private detective practice because she finds more freedom working on a contract basis than she did as a public defendant. *Tunnel Vision* starts out when V. I.'s building in the Chicago loop is being torn down to make room for more profitable real estate, and the novel quickly turns into a plot of urban decay and corrupt multinational developers versus the underdogs, the not-for-profits, the abused women and children, the down-and-outs, and their champion, the entrepreneur. As Vic is investigating why the small Century Bank turned down the not-for-profit Home Free's request for a loan for the Lamia Project (a women's carpentry collective that would build homes for single mothers), she comes into her all-but-demolished office one day to find Deirdre Messenger's corpse on her desk, her brains spilling out on the keyboard, and the only witnesses to the crime a homeless family who had been living in the boarded-up building but who had disappeared without a trace. In the end, it turns out that the bank, protected by large financial interests and a crooked politician, had been using Home Free as a front for laundering large sums of money alongside a whole host of other crimes, including recruiting nonunionized, illegal, Romanian immigrants as construction workers and breaking the Iraqi sanctions.

Traditionally in detective fiction, the police are shown to be ineffectual buffoons, as in Sherlock Holmes, or bumbling bureaucrats who always arrive just a bit too late, as in many of the hard-boileds. Like the hero in the western who is marginal to the law in order to restore it, there is usually tension between the detective and the law, as the detective tends to operate on the fringes of the law, closer to lawlessness and criminality, often deriving his wisdom, insights, heroism, and tactics from his affinity with the ghetto. In *Tunnel Vision,* however, as the police operate at a high level of competence as law enforcers sometimes smothered in overwork, the detective's power emanates from her correspondence with the lawlessness of multinationals and international finance. Her abilities to trespass, pick locks, break and enter, and hack into harddrives parallel the abilities of her opponents to, on the one hand, break into her office and warp her databases, and, on the other, to take the law into their own hands, breaching Senator Alec Gantner's own Boland Amendment, which forbade financial deals with terrorist organizations, going against the laws of the nation-state. The Gantner family's agricultural production corporation, or Gant-Ag, is bypassing trade barriers by selling corn to Saddam Hussein in exchange for cash payments to an offshore bank in the Cayman Islands. The Cayman Island bank then launders the money, jet-lifting it to Gant-Ag's private strip from where it can be deposited in Century, a small bank formerly supporting Chicago housing renewal, women's projects, family shelters, social services, and the like. When Deidre Messenger learns of this and threatens to reveal it, she is subcontracted to be killed.

For the Gant-Ag interest, as for Vic, the police represent an "intervention in people's lives."[28] V. I. is dating a black police officer named Conrad Rawlings. The banker, the senator's son, and the director of Home Free find Conrad trespassing in Gant-Ag's cornfields and plan to kill him for obstructing their business: an expected midnight plane flying from the Caymans and stacked with cash. Blakely, the financial big-wig behind Gant-Ag's operations, accuses Conrad of infringing on his rights to privacy, so that the right to privacy gets interpreted as only serving to facilitate criminal interests: "You may be a Chicago policeman," he says to Conrad, "but our security force found you trespassing on our property."[29] In the same way, Vic finds not only the cops, but the public sector in general trespassing on her business, searching her under suspicion, threatening to arrest her for illegal investigations, restricting her access to those she needs to protect. When she tries to appropriate evidence from one of Deirdre's daughter Emily's schoolteachers, for example, the teacher tries to refuse by insisting on the students' rights to privacy. Vic counters with an assertion that Emily's private life is important and should be opened to the investigation and yet is overlooked by the police and the lawyers who are focusing on the public aspects and the legal codes.[30] Conrad makes the similarities between Vic's methods and those of the criminals quite clear: "I remember last year," he says, "someone broke into this place and trashed it pretty good. That seem reasonable to you?"[31] Conrad's partner, Terry Finchley, also highlights the causes of police foot-dragging when he says, "Not being a private citizen like Vic, I need a warrant."[32] Unlike Vic, the police can only gather evidence by following the procedures and regulations of the nation-state: respecting privacy and domestic borders, establishing "probable cause," filling out "a few hundred

forms,"[33] where Vic could get around stalking laws, trespass, and imper-
sonate the police with impunity. In other words, restrictions on policing
protecting citizens' right to privacy are obstructing, rather than catalyzing,
the pursuit of justice.

Vic's similarities with the international drug and financial mafia do not
end with her proclivity to break the law. Indeed, Vic's frequent run-ins with
criminal organizations require her often to carry a gun, and she sometimes
finds herself in the midst of shoot-outs and dangerous explosions so intense
that both injury and death are to be expected. Vic's expertise is to be able to
respond to whatever the situation calls for, thinking quickly, using whatever
equipment she comes upon, always, like the criminals themselves, able to
innovate, with both intellect and pure strength, to overcome whatever singular, exceptional danger presents itself. Being pursued by a rolling plane, she
finds a cart that she quickly figures out how to drive, managing to work the
controls, the brake, and the gears with her right hand as she fires shots from
the gun in her left.[34] Vic's need to carry arms is justified in the way she might
be threatened unexpectedly, without any regularity or law, and so would
need to be prepared for the unexpected defense: "I heard them an instant
before I saw them, an instant that got the Smith & Wesson into my hand,
safety off. Three hooded shadows rose at the top landing. I fired."[35]

The implication here is that feminism and feminist values have given
women the right and the encouragement to be tough because they have at last
achieved economic independence. This conclusion contradicts other claims
of popular or academic feminism that would maintain that women's challenge to a culture of "toughness" will save the world from militarism. In an
article much lauded in feminist circles as a response to the September 11
crisis (though written during the Clinton administration), renowned feminist scholar Cynthia Enloe argued that the "privileging of military concerns
over other important U.S. international goals"—like ending the use of land-
mines, signing on to the international Criminal Court, and backing the UN
convention acknowledging the rights of children in war—"is about the male
politician's angst over not appearing 'manly.'" If only those in charge of
international policy decisions would engage in feminist analysis, Enloe
continues, "the peculiar American contemporary political culture that
equates military experience and/or military expertise with political leadership" would self-destruct, and war would end. In other words, war results
from a peculiarly American cultural form of manliness that demands toughness and aggression and missile defense systems and zero-tolerance crime
policies, or rather "a political competition to appear 'tough,'"[36] not from
economics or from asserting hegemonic control over resources and workers,
as though if women were to gain power, the global demand for oil, for
example, would suddenly disappear as just another appearance of manliness. Enloe's analysis misses three vital points: (1) that feminism advocated
"toughness" in women as a mark of economic independence and the success
of feminism, as *Tunnel Vision* demonstrates; (2) that militarism arises not
from men's desires to appear "manly" but from the expansion of
consumerism and its labor needs, implicating women as much as men, and
even demanding "toughness" and "manliness" in women as a mark of femi-

nism; and (3) that attributing and naturalizing gender traits—both masculinity and femininity—are the very strategies global capitalism itself has wielded in order to deepen its exploitation. In Enloe's view, masculinity is "tough" while femininity and feminism are "relational" and "soft," but it is precisely by mobilizing these very attributes of gender that the economic system currently exploits women and femininity in order to pursue economic interests in the name of ethics. Justice for women depends not on "feminizing" the public but rather on abolishing an economic system relying on relations of domination and submission, so that feminist critique must be in the forefront of finding new ways of viewing the public beyond the metaphorics of femininity or of a muscular, technological instrument of security.

Vic's recourse to militarism, as she shoots down the plane or fights down an aggressor, is justified on the basis of an "abstract concept of justice," where she restores the law that she has, in fact, been the one to break. The difference between Vic's trespasses and the criminality of those she pursues is that Vic is acting in the interest, as Conrad points out, of her "own private version of justice":[37] to defend what she and others see as otherwise defenseless people. Conrad rejoins,

> Look, Vic, it's why we have laws and give jobs to people like me to enforce them—so everyone doesn't go buzzing through the streets defining justice however it suits them that morning. It's bad enough we got a million guns in this town so every second jerk can play Shane if he wants to.[38]

What is clearly not operative in Vic's abstract concept of privatized justice is a viable public sphere. Aside from the police with their hands tied up in the legal code, *Tunnel Vision*'s public appears on the one hand as criminal violence and on the other as homeless, victimized, abused, feminized, hystericized, and helpless. As Vic rescues the homeless woman Tamar and Emily and the kids in their charge from the tunnel under The Loop where they had hidden, she describes them as utterly defenseless, even degenerate in their misery:

> I grabbed the nearest figure, a small child. He struggled briefly, then stood still and began to wail softly. The rest of them stopped. There were more than four, but how many I couldn't tell in the light of my failing flashlight. Above the smell of mold and coal and rats the stench of urine and fear rose to smite me. . . . One of the larger figures tried to pry my hand from his arm but her fingers were weak and she couldn't free the child. His own arm underneath my hand felt frail . . . "Emily?" . . . If she hadn't started to talk I would not have known her. Her frizzy hair was matted to her head, her face pinched and gray with hunger and filth. Her blue jeans and shirt hung on her shrunken body.[39]

Both Tamar and Emily have run underground to escape the law—Tamar as a witness to Deirdre's murder and Emily as an innocent suspect for her mother's murder. They are, too, both victims of abuse, Tamar having been beaten by her husband and Emily raped by her father. The public programs where they each land after Vic rescues them serve the function of offering them therapy rather than collective action and organizing for ending patriarchal violence and domestic abuse. The physical, mental, and emotional dereliction they exhibit—individually and collectively —, as well as their feminine frailty, foreground the political inefficacy of fighting for justice, advocating instead learning to "heal" and be cared for in order to accommodate oneself to the system that is.

The novel's feminism hinges on Vic's ability to be a "solo operator."[40] As Priscilla Walton and Manina Jones profess, "This ... draws attention to the female private eye's role as a practical feminist whose investigations advance, in effect, a *working* feminism that seems to reconcile feminist theory and everyday practice."[41] "Too pigheaded to make a good employee,"[42] Vic's feminist independence rides not only on her private pursuit of justice in her distrust of lawyers, courts, and police, but also in her ambitions to make a career in private business, mostly by being subcontracted into jobs. Even though she makes less money through her contract deals than she would in a firm, her business sense, adventurism, and hustling talent—what she calls her "blue-collar work ethic,"[43] which she claims to have inherited from her mother—places her above the conventions of femininity, particularly with regards to mothering. As Deirdre herself contends, "All you women who went on to have careers are the same. ... You don't think those of us who stayed home and put our children and husbands first are worth anything."[44]

In fact, as Deirdre discovers the plot about the airlifts while working to support her husband's bid for a judgeship, Deirdre's dependence on her husband and his finances as well as her allegiance to her family lead to her demise. Contrasted to Vic's feminist, entrepreneurial independence, Deirdre's feminine reliance on her husband's income ends punitively as she, quite literally, gets her brains knocked out of her, and the uselessness of Deirdre's economic rationality is further reinforced as her brains appear squashed and squished over various tools of work, from Vic's keyboard and computer screen to her documents, databases, and, ultimately, the murder weapon. Vic's careerism frees her from particularly feminine forms of mental illness shown in women's lack of autonomy, symptomized as both victim psychology (Deirdre never leaves her brutally abusive husband and ends with her head, quite literally, mixed up) and substance dependence (Deirdre is an alcoholic).

The novel, then, explains the punishment that Deirdre incurs as resulting from overdependence, meaning, in the novel's logic, that she has failed in her feminist ethic. The disciplining of women for the "antifeminist" crime of overdependence spills out across class lines and ends up: (1) further feminizing the public sphere for its hysteria and overdependence; (2) maligning mothering as punishable for its overindulgent caring of kids and for sacrifices for the family, even while giving lip-service to developing institutions for protecting mothers rather than dismantling patriarchy;[45] and (3) censuring all women's needs for public interventions, like the homeless woman Tamar Hawk's and then Emily's repeated appearances in places of public assistance, schools, public hospitals, therapy sessions, and shelters. Ultimately, *Tunnel Vision* does not challenge gender roles or suggest alternatives to the general oppression of women: women are still the victims, the needy, the desperate, and the helpless. Rather than providing a new theory of gender relations and equality as much contemporary feminism has been developing, this feminism is used to pathologize femininity as weak, needy, and dependent as femininity is seen as forming the baseness and depravity of the public sphere. Vic's ethic to support charities and female labor organizations funded by benevolent loans and hand-outs does not signify an end to the exploitation of women's labor or the end of inequality or the end of abuse or the sudden leveling of opportunities and wages, but rather that Vic can rise above this degraded female existence and become the promise of self-determination, independence, singularity, heroism, and success only when—unlike the women's collectives—she is armored with her own capital. Her reward in the end is a $10,000 check from one of her benefactors, allowing her to add two employees to her small business payroll. Foregrounding the public's only recourse as pity, terrorized and abused women demand Vic's muscular protection and justify the growth of her business as well as her avoidance— alongside criminal capital—of the patriarchal police code, the law of the nation-state, and other people's civil protections.

Vic's "abstract concept of justice" is intertwined with police law enforcement, even somewhat protected by it, but still above it. In fact, Conrad's job as enforcer of the law is limited because working the ghetto has become routinized like service work: "[s]ix gunshots, one fatal, a stabbing, a hit-and-run where the guy dragged the body halfway down Western Avenue before it came loose, and a baby in a garbage can,"[46] he lists when Vic asks about his night at the office. Meanwhile, Vic's work for justice is praised by her professor Manfred Yeo as more about the exceptional, singular event or crisis rather than the work-a-day world of the urban police or the bureaucrat: "jumping from bridges," he announces, "is much more exciting than filing writs of certiorari . . . I'm ashamed," he goes on, "of too many of our graduates for putting billable hours ahead of justice."[47] As Hardt and Negri explain the right of the police to intervention within today's global politics, "In order to take control of and dominate such a completely fluid situation, it is necessary to grant the intervening authority the capacity to define, every time in an exceptional way, the demands of intervention . . . reduc[ing] right and law to a question of pure effectiveness."[48] In the diminishment of the nation-state's role to produce legal norms and regulations, law gets constituted increasingly through contingency and exception, as in the 2000 U.S. presidential elections, where the Supreme Court justices made a decision they themselves deemed an exception to the rule of precedent, or in a war on terrorism, where the enemy is identified through his potential ability to perform the heretofore unimaginable violence. The new order is constituted by the crisis of the singular, exceptional event, represented by the ethnic terrorist or the drug lord, which, now transferred from urban settings into a global arena, the policing postimperial power is able to control through what seems like moral action but is really the condition of unilateral supremacy.[49] Outside of the foundations of justice, law, and governance as universalized philosophically in the modern state, the enemy as exception gets placed in the position of the criminal to be policed, and the private detective is praised as the one to catch the criminal by working beyond the law.

The marginalization of the domestic police, or the marginalization of the law of the nation-state, means a justice without justice, or a justice defined through superior muscularity, through force of arms, and through winning, where the possibility of public debate or public scrutiny under state legal protection has lost its moral force and had its deathly remains squished under a corporate extralegality. At the same time, a centralization of the international police as the cornerstone of foreign policy has produced an ideology of militarism as the only ethical force against barbarism, terror, and excess when militarism is actually what is creating these very outcomes. It is important to make a claim for the possibility of a noncontingent, nonexceptional drive for justice, for ethical norms, and for institutions to enforce them, both domestically and internationally. An effort must be made to redefine just practices in the new international order, taking into account that the public debates over the role of the police fundamentally play out concerns over a multinationalism replacing the waning protective power of the nation-state, the public it might sustain, and what its new forms of justice will be. As clearly protectionism and isolationism are not viable, ethical, or optimal options, global institutions—schools, courts, information networks, collective and deliberative assemblies, credit arrangements, culture industries, legislative bodies, enforcement—must be formed to protect public interests and democracy everywhere. The question is, how can this civil society, its institutions, and its practices be imagined and built differently than as either blood-thirsty individualist competitors warring over a piece of the pie or as pathetic and sickly urchins whimpering before the state's sordid mother-love?

Notes

1. Jeffrey Toobin, "Crackdown: Should We Be Worried About the New Antiterrorism Legislation?" *New Yorker* (November 5, 2001), available at www.newyorker.com/FACT/?011105fa_FACT2.
2. "Enter Richard Nixon: inveterate red-baiter, enforcer in the McCarthyite mob, and a former vice president, whose "political obituary" had been broadcast by ABC in the wake of his 1962 California Gubernatorial race. Surveying the approaching cloudbursts of the late 1960s, Nixon argued that "the deterioration of [respect for law and order] can be traced directly to the spread of the corrosive doctrine that every citizen possesses an inherent right to decide for himself which laws to obey and when to disobey them." As Dan Baum pointed out, "Nixon, like many who would follow in his wake, was linking street crime to the civil disobedience of the civil rights movement." Christian Parenti, *Lockdown America: Police and Prisons in the Age of Crisis* (London and New York: Verso, 1999), 6–7.
3. Michael Holquist, "Whodunit and Other Questions: Metaphysical Detective Stories in Postwar Fiction," in *The Poetics of Murder: Detective Fiction and Literary Theory,* edited by Glenn W. Most and William W. Stowe (San Diego, New York, London: Harcourt Brace Jovanovich, 1983), 154.
4. Henry A. Giroux, *Stealing Innocence: Youth, Corporate Power, and the Politics of Culture* (New York: St. Martin's Press, 2000), 25–27.
5. Sara Paretsky, *Tunnel Vision* (New York: Dell, 1994).
6. Robin D. G. Kelley has pointed out how the state is often maligned in political rhetoric through its association with what is seen as its African American dependents: single mothers and children of the ghetto. "I have rarely heard vitriol as vicious as the words sprouted by Riverside (California) county welfare director Lawrence Townsend: 'Every time I see a bag lady on the street, I wonder, "Was that an A.F.D.C. mother who hit the menopause wall—who can no longer reproduce and

get money to support herself?"'" Robin D. G. Kelley, *Yo' Mama's Disfunktional!: Fighting the Culture Wars in Urban America* (Boston: Beacon Press, 1998), 2.

7. Michael Hardt and Antonio Negri, *Empire* (Cambridge, Mass. and London, Engl.: Harvard University Press, 2000), 12, 13.

8. Richard Falk, "Reflections on the Gulf War Experience: Force and War in the UN System," in *The Gulf War and the New World Order: International Relations of the Middle East,* edited by Tareq Y. Ismael and Jacqueline S. Ismael (Gainesville, Fla.: University Press of Florida, 1994), 32.

9. Michael Klare, "Endless Military Superiority," *The Nation* (July 15, 2002): 15, 12.

10. Hardt and Negri, *Empire,* 12.

11. Ibid., 17.

12. Ibid.

13. See Mark Schapiro, "Big Tobacco: Uncovering the Industry's Multibillion-Dollar Global Smuggling Network," *The Nation* (May 6, 2002): 18.

14. Ahmed Rashid, *Taliban: Militant Islam, Oil & Fundamentalism in Central Asia* (New Haven, Conn.: Yale University Press, 2000), 179.

15. Amnesty International, *United States of America: Race, Rights and Police Brutality* (New York: Amnesty International USA, 1999), 1.

16. Amnesty International, *The Case of Mumia Abu-Jamal: A Life in the Balance* (New York: Seven Stories Press, 2000), 8.

17. John G. Cawelti, *Adventure, Mystery, and Romance: Formula Stories as Art and Popular Culture* (Chicago and London: University of Chicago Press, 1976), 106, 107, 108.

18. D. A. Miller, *The Novel and the Police* (Berkeley: University of California Press, 1988), 17.

19. Christopher P. Wilson, *Cop Knowledge: Police Power and Cultural Narrative in Twentieth-Century America* (Chicago and London: University of Chicago Press, 2000), 217, 10.

20. Jacques Lacan, "Seminar on 'The Purloined Letter,'" in *The Poetics of Murder: Detective Fiction and Literary Theory,* edited by Glenn W. Most and William W. Stowe (San Diego, New York, London: Harcourt Brace Jovanovich, 1983), 154.

21. David Cole, *No Equal Justice: Race and Class in the American Criminal Justice System* (New York: New Press, 1999), 23–24.

22. Zygmunt Bauman, *In Search of Politics* (Standford, Calif.: Standford University Press, 1999), 5.

23. Dick Hobbs, *Doing the Business: Entrepreneurs, the Working Class, and Detectives in the East End of London* Oxford: Clarendon Press, 1988), 34, 40.

24. Kelley, "'Slangin' Rocks . . . Palestinian Style': Dispatched from the Occupied Zones of North America," in *Police Brutality: An Anthology,* edited by Jill Nelson (New York and London: W. W. Norton & Company, 2000), 25, 26.

25. David Cole, "National Security State," *The Nation* (December 17, 2001), available at www.thenation.com/doc.mhtml?i=20011217&s=cole.

26. Christian Parenti, *Lockdown America* (New York: verso, 1999), 6, 87.

27. Priscilla L. Walton and Manina Jones, *Detective Agency: Women Rewriting the Hard-Boiled Tradition* (Berkeley and Los Angeles: University of California Press, 1999), 28.

28. Paretsky, *Tunnel Vision,* 34.

29. Ibid., 437.

30. Ibid., 148–49.

31. Ibid., 250.

32. Ibid., 155.

33. Ibid., 104, 217.

34. Ibid., 440.

35. Ibid., 261.

36. Cynthia Enloe, "Masculinity as a Foreign Policy Issue," *Foreign Policy in Focus* 5, no. 36 (October 2000), available at www.foreignpolicy_infocus.org.

37. Paretsky, *Tunnel Vision,* 447.

38. Ibid., 250.

39. Ibid., 311.
40. Ibid., 438.
41. Walton and Jones, *Detective Agency*, 37.
42. Paretsky, *Tunnel Vision*, 437.
43. Ibid., 70.
44. Ibid., 86.
45. "The problem is—there are shelters for women with children. Of course, there are. But they aren't always safe places. And most of them are only open at night, so you have to figure out something to do during the day" (Paretsky, *Tunnel Vision*, 11).
46. Ibid., 70.
47. Ibid., 48–49.
48. Hardt and Negri, *Empire*, 16–17.
49. Slavoj Žižek has also criticized how the concept of the universal embedded in the nation-state necessitates the exception. According to Žižek, in the new univerasalist transnationalism of the New World Order, the universalist practices of the nation-state—like humanitarianism or multiculturalism—give rise to a violent return of the excluded because the identity of the community can never be fully articulated or can only be fully constituted in the suspension of the political. In other words, negotiation and struggle are replaced by a technocratic collaboration or universal consensus between parties, where opposition appears only as "pure Evil" usually manifest as racism: "The Otherness excluded from the consensual domain of toler-ant/rational post-political negotiation and administration returns in the guise of inexplicable pure Evil. . . . What defines postmodern post-politics, therefore, is the secret solidarity between its two opposed Janus faces: on the one hand the replace-ment of politics proper by depoliticized 'humanitarian' operations (humanitarian protection of human and civil rights and aid to Bosnia, Somalia, Rwanda, North Korea . . .); on the other, the violent emergence of depoliticized 'pure Evil' in the guise of 'excessive' ethnic or religious fundamentalist violence" ("Carl Schmitt and the Age of Post-Politics," in *The Challenge of Carl Schmitt*, edited by Chantal Mouffe (London and New York: Verso, 1999), 32–33).

INTRODUCTION TO CHAPTER 16

Eugene Provenzo's chapter focuses on the educational role of violent video games in teaching youth and adults to think about war as fun and exciting by transforming real violence into spectacle and rendering ethical and political concerns out of the picture. Like Vinson and Ross, Provenzo is concerned with the complexities of challenging representational violence in spectacle form. The chapter offers a historical account of not only how the gaming industry has commodified the images of state power but also how the military has used violent video games for training. It calls for discussion of the place for such technology in a democratic society.

CHAPTER 16

Virtuous War

Simulation and the Militarization of Play

EUGENE F. PROVENZO, JR.

President Dwight D. Eisenhower commented in his 1961 Farewell Address that a "conjunction of a vast military establishment" was being setup in the United States, which was unique in the American experience. According to Eisenhower, "The total influence—economic, political, even spiritual—is felt in every city, every statehouse, every office of the federal government." Eisenhower believed that we had to guard against this trend. The domination of the nation's scholars by federal project allocations, and the funding associated with them, he warned, threatened the survival of American democracy.[1]

Video games and the entertainment industry may seem a long step from the type of situation feared by Eisenhower. Yet, in point of fact, recent alignments among academia, the video game industry, and the military represent precisely this phenomenon. I argue in this chapter that the recent establishment of the Institute for Creative Technologies (ICT) at the University of Southern California potentially represents the type of conjunction of the military establishment that Eisenhower warned against over forty years ago. I believe that when the military blurs the line between war and entertainment, through the use of video games to train soldiers, and then shares its work with the entertainment and amusement industry, it is quite literally militarizing critical aspects of play and its function as a learning experience.

A major part of this phenomenon is related to the increasing role of simulations in the construction of postmodern culture and to the rapid evolution and development of computers and computer simulations. Essentially, a simulation substitutes a model or simulacra for the real. As the French social

Eugene F. Provenzo, Jr. is a professor at the University of Miami. His research on computers and video games has been reviewed in the *New York Times*, *The Guardian*, *Mother Jones* and the *London Economist*. He has been interviewed on National Public Radio, ABC *World News Tonight*, the CBS *Evening News*, *Good Morning America*, BBC radio, Britain's Central Television and Britain's Channels 2 and 4, as well as Australia's *LateLine*. He is the author of *Video Kids: Making Sense of Nintendo* (Harvard University Press, 1991) and *Beyond the Gutenberg Galaxy: Microcomputers and the Emergence of Post-Typographic Culture* (Teachers College Press, Columbia University, 1986).

and culture theorist Jean Baudrillard maintains, what is left is "the generation by models of a real without origin or a reality: a hyperreal. The territory no longer precedes the map, nor survives it. Henceforth, it is the map that precedes the territory—*precession of simulacra*—it is the map that engenders the territory."[2]

The military has a long history of using simulations in the modern era. During the 1920s, for example, the British military developed elaborate war game scenarios for tank and mobile armored training outside of Salisbury, England. Two years before the Gulf War, Iraq ran computer simulations for the invasion of Kuwait. General Norman Schwarzkopf, just a few weeks before Iraq's invasion of Kuwait, sponsored a computer-simulated command post exercise, code named "Exercise Internal Look '90," in which 350 high-ranking members from each of the military services fought a war with Iraq.

Using simulations to train people in the military makes perfect sense. Having navy pilots practice landings on an aircraft carrier in a flight simulator is an excellent way to give them pre-flight experience before they get into the cockpit of an actual plane. Highly realistic combat simulations are probably the best way to give military trainees a sense of what warfare is really like without putting them in harm's way.

The connection between the use of simulations and the entertainment and amusement industry and the American military is by no means new. In 1931, the navy purchased its first flight simulator from Edward Link. Interestingly, while the navy bought one flight simulator, amusement parks across the country bought fifty of the machines. A device originally intended for military instruction became a popular amusement for the general public. James Der Derian explains how this tradition continues today, as video games based on military hardware such as the Commanche helicopter, the F-22 Fighter Plane, and the *Seawolf* SSN-21 submarine literally appear "on the shelves almost as soon as the weapon system first appears."[3]

The link between video games and military culture has, in fact, existed for over two decades. In the early 1980s, military recruits at Fort Eustis, Virginia, played the video arcade game *Battle Zone* in which realistic silhouetted enemy tanks, helicopters, and armored personnel carriers were targeted and destroyed. Ronald Reagan, the military's commander in chief during this period, argued that video games probably helped people prepare for the military.[4]

The use of video games both to train individuals to wage war and to entertain and amuse the general public is disturbing. The definition of what is a game and what is the reality of war is easily blurred. During the Gulf War, for example, the American public was presented with warfare as though it were just another video game. Throughout early 1991, Americans spent night after night watching smart bombs and missiles zero in on their Iraqi targets. War looked just like the video games in the arcades. Following the Gulf War, video games based on military scenarios from the conflict became hugely popular. Spectrum Holobyte, for example, released a tank game based on the army's SIMNET land combat training program. Absolute's *Super Battletank* put the player into the cockpit of an M-1A Abrams tank in Kuwait. As J. C. Herz explained in *Joystick Nation*:

Operation Desert Storm was just the ticket. It was the greatest thing to happen to interactive entertainment since Sonic the Hedgehog. Everyone in America had seen missile footage through laser guided sites on television. Now they could play the war on their very own home computers. Within a year of the Gulf War, Spectrum Holobyte released a tank game based on the Army's SIMNET land combat training program. Shortly thereafter Absolute's *Super Battletank* put you into the cockpit of an M-1A! Abrams tank in Kuwait, where in a curious reversal of America's Gulf War odds, you got to play the U.S. Armed Forces as underdog.[5]

The violence of the Gulf War was being translated into a "look alike" video simulation for the general public. Of course, what the video games and the government's carefully edited film and video footage of the Gulf War did not show, was the actual death and destruction caused by the smart bombs and missiles as they zeroed in on the targets, a point commented on at length by Jean Baudrillard in his 1991 book *The Gulf War Did Not Take Place*.[6]

The line between the reality of warfare and entertainment has recently become even more confused by efforts on the part of the United States military to link the development of military simulations with the entertainment industry. In August 1999, the secretary of the Army, Louis Caldera, announced that the Army was awarding the University of Southern California $45 million to set up a research center to create military simulations. At the new center, the Institute for Creative Technologies, film students and video game designers are being brought together to create state-of-the-art multimedia systems that can be used for military training. Part of the idea behind the program is that technology developed for the military can also be used by the entertainment industry. Louis Caldera, secretary of the Army, describes this as "a win-win for everyone."

According to the institute's website, the "entertainment industry brings expertise in story, character, visual effects, gaming and production" to the institute, while the "computer science community brings innovation in networking, artificial intelligence, and virtual reality technology." Schools at the University of Southern California that work closely with the institute include the School of Cinema-TV, the School of Engineering, the Information Sciences Institute, Integrated Media Systems Center, and the Annenberg School of Communication. What is at work here is the merging of academic, entertainment, and military segments of American culture.

I believe that there are two questions that particularly need to be addressed concerning this merger: (1) What are the implications of the linking of the military with the entertainment industry and the Academy? and (2) How does the introduction of the art of simulation through video game technology change the public's understanding of the meaning of war?

What are the implications of the linking of the military with the entertainment industry and academia? War, in reality, is about killing your enemy. As the cyber war theorist James Der Derian explains: "what separates and elevates war above lesser ("Copernican") conceits is its intimate relationship to death. The dead body—on the battlefield, in the tomb of the unknown soldier, in the collective memory, even on the movie screen—is what gives its special status, what trumps any lesser issues."[7] For Der Derian there is "the corporal gravitas of war," which cannot be avoided.

By merging simulated war with video game technology, the difference among war and play and entertainment becomes profoundly confused. Nowhere is this more clear than in the case of the development of first-person shooter video games. Blowing one's opponent away is the basic activity of most first-person shooters. The game *Doom* is typical. *Doom* was first introduced on the Internet in 1993. Marketing of the game by its manufacturer Id Software was brilliant: users were able to download the first two sequences of the game for free. Once hooked, they would have to pay for subsequent episodes. A total of fifteen million games were downloaded worldwide and 150,000 sold directly.[8]

The advertisement for *Doom II* sums up the games attitude quite nicely: "Bloodthirsty DEMONS from Hell. GUT-SPATTERED Hallways. A Big-Ass, Nasty GUN in your hand. Life is GOOD."[9] When you actually play the game, you can choose any of five Skill Levels ranging from: "I'm too young to die"; "Hey, not too rough"; "Hurt me plenty"; "Ultraviolence"; and "Nightmare."

Doom II sold 1.5 million copies.[10] The series was completed with *Final Doom*. The realism provided by *Doom* is perhaps best reflected in the fact that the *Doom II* game was adopted by the U.S. Marine Corps for training recruits. *Doom II* had many features that made its use attractive to the military.

In 1995, under financial pressure to keep costs down while providing the best training possible, the marine corps turned to off-the-shelf video and computer games to see if they could be adapted for military use. As Lieutenant Colonel Rick Eisiminger, team leader of the Modeling and Simulation Office for the marines explained: "We were tasked with looking at commercial off-the-shelf computer games that might teach an appreciation for the art and science of war."[11] Dozens of games were reviewed and it was determined that *Doom II* could readily be adapted to the marine corp's needs.

In the Marine version of *Doom II*, military images and weapons are superimposed on the original game using digital photographs. The game is played with a four-man team—just like an actual marine combat or "fire unit." Compared to training people with live ammunition, instructing military through the use of a game such as *Doom II* provides an inexpensive and safe means by which to provide recruits with hours of practice at relatively little cost. They are also perceived as being very effective. As Lieutenant Colonel David Grossman, a former professor of psychology at West Point, argues, first-person shooter video games like the *Doom* series "are murder simulators which over time, teach a person how to look another person in the eye and snuff their life out."[12]

Teaching a person how to kill another as part of a simulation—more specifically, through the use of a video game—is probably a very useful activity for the military. It is reasonable to assume that organizations such as the institute for Creative Technologies have as their purpose the creation of the most realistic and accurate simulations possible (i.e., when someone is shot or killed, they want the experience to be as close to reality as possible).

But when this technology is disseminated to the entertainment and amusement industries, it has profound implications. Suddenly, we have made the reality of death, Der Derian's "corporal gravitas of war," an entertainment and amusement. The line between the reality of death and fantasy and play suddenly becomes obscured. In this context, it is worth noting that Eric Harris, who, along with Dylan Klebold, was responsible for the Columbine High School shootings in April 1999, created his own customized version of the first-person shooter video game *Doom*. Harris's version had two shooters, extra weapons, unlimited ammunition, and victims who could not fight back. His modification of the game clearly included the key features for the Columbine shooting that he and Klebold carried out.[13]

While using simulation and video game technology may be a highly efficient way of training people for battle, making this technology available to the entertainment industry, where it can eventually filter its way into use by children and adolescents, let alone civilian adults, seems highly irresponsible. Will future killers like Harris and Klebold use video game simulations to practice their monstrous acts? Should the military be creating the next generation of simulations that will then be made into games to be played by children? Or, should the military limit its development of games to be what they should be—sad, and perhaps necessary, teaching machines in the tragic art of war?

Issues raised in the above discussion clearly relate to our second question: *How does the introduction of the art of simulation through video game technology change the public's understanding of the meaning of war?* We are obscuring the reality of war—more specifically the death of other human beings. This phenomenon is discussed by Der Derian who believes that a new type of warfare—what he refers to as "virtuous war"—is being created by the military, academics, and the entertainment industry. According to him:

> Unlike other forms of warfare, virtuous war has an unsurpassed power to commute death, to keep it out of sight, out of mind. Herein lies its most morally dubious danger. In simulated preparations and virtual executions of war, there is a high risk that one learns how to kill but not take responsibility for it. One experiences "death" but not the tragic consequences of it. In virtuous war we now face not just the confusion but the pixilation of war and game on the same screen.[14]

In this context, I remember very clearly watching the Gulf War unfold in front of me on my television set in early 1991. Each night, smart bombs and missiles zeroed in on their Iraqi targets. The images that appeared in the military briefings, and as part of the extended newscasts, were very seductive. On the television screen they looked like the scenarios we had seen in some arcade game. These images made the reality of death seem like an amusement. War had become a matter of carefully controlled surgical strikes. Communication centers, military bunkers, and tanks were targeted on a pinpoint basis, with what seemed to be virtually no harm done to the civilian Iraqi population or to our troops.

Of course, the reality we eventually learned about was that the Gulf War was not a video game, but a tragic event involving the hideous death of thousands of people. This becomes evident as still news photographs showing bombed-out tanks and the charred remains of Iraqi soldiers made their way into the world's newspapers and magazines.

War, which has been redefined through the use of simulation technologies—whose reality has been altered by pixilated objects running across a computer or television screen—has profound implications for the military and the general population. Just as television brought the Vietnam War into American homes, where it could be seen and reflected on, thus changing the character of the war, so too does "virtuous war" change the meaning of war.

Paul Patton in his introduction to the English translation of *The Gulf War Did Not Take Place*, argues that by making the Gulf War into a media event, its reality was profoundly altered. As he explained, a simulacrum of war was presented. Thus:

> In this sense, while televisual information claims to provide immediate access to real events, in fact what it does is produce informational events which stand in for the real, and which "inform" public opinion which in turn affects the course of subsequent events, both real and informational. As consumers of mass media, we never experience the bare material event but only the informational coating which renders it "sticky and unintelligible."[15]

In a certain sense, the introduction of video game imagery into the coverage of the Gulf War represents a profound reshaping of the metaphor of war. If war is death, then by representing warfare as a game and simulation—something that is digital rather than analogue—then the meaning of death is altered. The reality of war, of death, their horror and violence are mediated. We might well reflect on Baudrillard's notion that "At a certain speed, the speed of light, you lose even your shadow. At a certain speed, the speed of information, things lose their sense."[16] The face of war becomes "like a surgical operation" that cosmetically alters and modifies the specter of death.[17]

James Der Derian argues that "virtuous war has an unsurpassed power to commute death, to keep it out of sight, out of mind."[18] As a result, Der Derian is concerned that "we learn to kill but not take responsibility for it."[19] We have seen the principles of virtuous war in play in the Gulf War, in Kosovo where simulation has heavily influenced planning, and in the violent and shattering fantasies of Eric Harris and Dylan Klebold in the April 1999 Columbine High School shootings.

In Orson Scott Card's remarkable novels *Ender's Game* and *Ender's Shadow*,[20] children in the future are placed in a simulation where they think they are being trained to play a game, but in reality are fighting a war. The tragedy of the novel—the power of its story—is that we act without fully knowing what we do. I believe that this is what could become the tragedy of the military's use of video games and their collaboration with the entertainment industry and academia. By making war into a game, we obscure the meaning of war. We make it easier to participate personally in the act of killing others, and to accept images of war on our television screens. We also make it easier to accept and integrate these images into our experience and day-to-day lives.

By simply accepting simulated war and the types of activities sponsored by the Institute for Creative Technologies, we not only allow the meaning of war to be diminished, but expand the role of the military in the creation of our leisuretime activities and the learning that formally occurs through the process of play—even in process of "playing" something as seemingly innocent as a video game. As a result, we see new manifestations of social and cultural influences emerge, manifestations that resonate with President Eisenhower's warning over a generation ago concerning the potential influence of the military on our culture.

In conclusion, in light of the themes outlined in the other chapters in this book, as well as the specific arguments of this chapter, we should reflect on Der Derian's argument that "This conjunction of an immense military establishment and a large arms industry" as part of the development of a system of "virtuous war" is

> new in the American experience. The total influence—economic, political, even spiritual—is felt in every city, every statehouse, every office of the federal government.... In the councils of government we must guard against the acquisition of unwarranted influence, whether sought or unsought, by the military industrial complex. The potential for the disastrous rise of the misplaced power exists and will persist.... We want democracy to survive for all generations to come, not to become the insolvent phantom of tomorrow.[21]

Simulated war, "playing" war as entertainment and amusement, obscures the reality of war and potentially threatens the integrity of our democracy. We need to question the linking of the military with the entertainment and amusements industries and academia. The issue is not a trivial one, but is instead a profound reflection of how the meaning of war is being redefined by the culture of simulation and the substitution of the real for the hyperreal.

Notes

1. Quoted in James Der Derian, *Virtuous War: Mapping the Military-Industrial-Media-Entertainment Network* (Boulder, Colo.: Westview Press, 2001), viii.
2. Jean Baudrillard, *Simulations*, trans. Paul Foos, Paul Patton, and Philip Beitchman (New York: Semiotext(e), 1983), 2.
3. Der Derian, *Virtuous War*, 89.
4. Eugene F. Provenzo, Jr., *Video Kids: Making Sense of Nintendo* (Cambridge: Harvard University Press, 1991) 133.
5. J. C. Herz, *Joystick Nation: How Videogames Ate Our Quarters, Won Our Hearts and Rewired Our Minds* (Boston: Little Brown, 1997), 207–208.
6. Jean Baudrillard, *The Gulf War Did Not Take Place*, trans. and with an introduction by Paul Patton (Bloomington: Indiana University Press, 1995).
7. Der Derian, *Virtuous War*, 166.
8. Herz, *Joystick Nation*, 84.
9. Ibid., 86.
10. Id Software web site: http://www.idsoftware.com.

11. Rob Riddell, "Doom Goes to War," *Wired 5*, no. 4 (April 1997). Available at www.wired.com/wired/archive.
12. Deborah Claymon, "Video-Game Industry Seeks to Deflect Blame for Violence," *Miami Herald* (July 2, 1999): 3E; and David Grossman and Gloria DeGaetano, *Stop Teaching Our Kids to Kill: A Call to Action Against TV, Movie & Video Game Violence* (New York: Crown Publishers, 1999).
13. Craig A. Anderson and Brad J. Bushman, "Effects of Violent Video Games on Aggressive Behavior, Aggressive Cognition, Aggressive Affect, Physiological Arousal, and Prosocial Behavior: A Meta-Analytic Review of the Scientific Literature," *Psychological Science* 12, no. 5 (September 2001): 353.
14. Der Derian, *Virtuous War*, xvi.
15. Baudrillard, 1995, 10.
16. Ibid., 48.
17. Ibid., 28.
18. Der Derian, *Virtuous War*, xvi.
19. Ibid.
20. Orson Scott Card, *Ender's Shadow* (New York: Tom Doherty Associates, 1985); Orson Scott Card, *Ender's Shadow* (New York: Tom Doherty Associates, 1999).
21. Der Derian, *Virtuous War*, p. viii.

INTRODUCTION TO CHAPTER 17

William Reynolds and David Gabbard explain the threats to community and schooling posed by the rewriting of public memory by the cultural pedagogies of Hollywood films. The chapter begins by outlining some of the history of the government's effort to use propaganda to help overcome the Vietnam syndrome that led to the recent meeting between top Bush advisor Karl Rove and Hollywood executives in October 2001. The chapter then uses the 2002 Vietnam film *We Were Soldiers* to illustrate how the rewriting of the public memory of that war is actively involved in producing pedagogies that are favorable to both the expansion of corporate power and the War on Terrorism. It concludes by insisting that educators are also in powerful positions to produce public memory in democratic ways. The chapter is unique to the volume for both its attention to public memory and film pedagogy in relation to corporatization and militarization.

CHAPTER 17

We Were Soldiers

The Rewriting of Memory and the Corporate Order

WILLIAM M. REYNOLDS AND DAVID A. GABBARD

The antiwar movement spawned by America's colonial war of aggression against the people of Vietnam placed new limitations on the government's ability to initiate direct military interventions against any nation or people who may have had the audacity to refuse their assigned role within the global economy. Prior to Vietnam, such interventions could be conducted in plain sight, because a majority of the public could be counted on to support the government's actions as part of a "just war." Vietnam changed all of that. It created a groundswell of widespread public dissent against the use of military force for anything other than obvious defensive purposes. This strong antiwar sentiment even surfaced in debates over military spending, posing a serious threat to the state's Pentagon welfare system of economic planning. Since the end of World War II, the state relied on the fear mongering and anticommunism of Cold War propaganda to rationalize the expenditure of massive public subsidies for high tech research and development. In the wake of Vietnam, however, even the fear of "godless commies" could not abate the rising tide of public distrust concerning the role of the U.S. government and its military in world affairs. Such public opposition to overt militarism came to be known as the Vietnam syndrome. Because such "sickly inhibitions against the use of military force"[1] can greatly interfere with the ability of the state to defend and advance corporate interests abroad, there have been tremendous efforts made to remedy the public of this condition or, at least, to aid the government in working around it.

The Reagan administration, for example, understood this situation perfectly well. They were particularly frustrated by the limitations that it

William M. Reynolds is professor of curriculum studies in the Department of Curriculum, Foundations and Research at Georgia Southern University. He has authored, co-edited and co-authored books including *Reading Curriculum Theory: The Development of a New Hermeneutic* (1989), *Understanding Curriculum as a Phenomenological and Deconstructed Text* (1992), *Inside/Out: Contemporary Critical Perspectives in Education* (1994), *Understanding Curriculum: An Introduction to the Study of Historical and Contemporary Curriculum Discourses* (1995) and *Curriculum: A River Runs Through It* (Peter Lang, forthcoming). *Expanding Curriculum Theory: Dis/positions and Lines of Flight* (Lawrence Erlbaum, forthcoming). His current interests are Deleuzian philosophy, film studies and their connection to curriculum studies.

placed on their abilities to engage in direct military intervention in Central America during the early 1980s. It was, after, the Vietnam syndrome that led the Reagan team to engage in unprecedented levels of covert operations in such countries as Nicaragua, where Congress had actually banned U.S. aid to the Contras, those factions of the military who had supported the former dictator, General Anastasio Samoza. In an effort to garner greater public support for the policies that these covert operations were caring out (illegally), the Reagan administration's National Security Council created the Office for Public Diplomacy (OPD), staffed by members of the U.S. Army's Fourth Psychological Operations Command Group (PSYOPS). Headed by Cuban-born Otto Reich,[2] the OPD's "main mission was to inflame fears about Nicaragua and its left-wing Sandinista government that had come to power by overthrowing a corrupt, U.S.-supported dictator"[3] (the previously mentioned Samoza). More specifically, the OPD planted stories in the U.S. media supporting the Reagan Administration's Central America policies during the 1980s. Reich would later describe the OPD as a "vast psychological warfare operation of the kind the military conducts to influence a population in enemy territory"—such is the state's understanding of those sectors of the population who might remain infected with the Vietnam syndrome.

Among the range of lies perpetrated by Reich and the OPD, was the "news" leaked to the press regarding the arrival of Soviet MiG fighter jets and chemical weapons in Nicaragua, as well as false accusations that top-level members of the Nicaraguan government were involved in drug trafficking. The latter accusation was especially ironic, given that the CIA itself had been involved in drug trafficking in order to help finance the Contra rebels, (dubbed "freedom fighters" by Reich, the OPD, and, of course, Reagan) military operations. In keeping with the standards of Cold War propaganda, the intent of these efforts at "domestic diplomacy" was to overcome the public's Vietnam syndrome and win support for the Reagan administration's Central American policies. To do so, they sought to convince Americans that the Sandinistas, as well as other groups in the region threatening to upset the "favorable business climates" within the region constituted a "clear and present danger" to the security of the United States. Press reportage that contradicted this message and thereby reinforced the Vietnam syndrome invited retribution from the OPD as Reich was not above using his position to bully the press for not telling the "right" story. In April 1984, he met with executives at CBS to upbraid them for their news division's unpatriotic coverage of Nicaragua that month. He did the same with reporters and editors from National Public Radio in October of that same year. In the following year, Reich and the OPD circulated a story accusing U.S. reporters of producing favorable coverage of Nicaragua's Sandinista government in exchange for sexual favors from Nicaraguan prostitutes.[4]

Though the OPD was shut down just prior to the Iran-Contra hearings, for rather obvious reasons, the basic structure and function of that group has been restored under the administration of President George W. Bush. Using September 11 as pretext for citing a need for such an organization, (the need to publicize the U.S. government's perspective on the war against terrorism), the Bush team has created what they call the Office of Strategic

Influence (OSI). Though the name may have changed, the same people in charge of the OPD are now in charge of OSI—the Fourth PSYOPS group. Their primary task, of course, entails working to ensure that news media across the country and around the world tell the right story about the current war on terrorism, including Bush's justification for the pending attack on Iraq. Even Otto Reich has been brought back into the operation. Bush signed him into his current position as assistant secretary of State for Western Hemisphere Affairs while Congress was on recess, avoiding a potentially embarrassing confirmation hearing. Meanwhile, John Poindexter, another shadowy figure from the Iran-Contra scandal, heads up Bush's Information Awareness Office. Charlotte Beers oversees yet another related agency—the Office of Public Diplomacy and Public Affairs, while John Rendon and his public relations firm, The Rendon Group, are under a $100,000 a month contract to track foreign news reports and offer advice on media strategy

All of this provides crucial background information for understanding the significance of Karl Rove's[5] meeting with top Hollywood executives in the aftermath of September 11 at the posh Peninsula Hotel in Beverly Hills on October 17, 2001. Interestingly enough, given this chapter's analysis of *We Were Soldiers*, Sherry Lansing, chair of Paramount Pictures film division, and Jonathan Dolgen, head of Viacom's entertainment group, hosted the event. Though downplayed in the media as having been generally unproductive, the meeting did provide Rove the opportunity to enlist Hollywood's support in the war on terrorism. As reported by Marc Cooper for *The Nation*, Rove stressed

> that he had no intention of giving marching orders to Hollywood. "The industry will decide what it will do and when it will do it," he said as he emerged from the Sunday morning meeting. Instead Rove briefed the Hollywood executives on a seven-point message that the White House would like to stress:
>   1. that the war is against terrorism, not Islam;
>   2. that Americans must be called to national service;
>   3. that Americans should support the troops;
>   4. that this is a global war that needs a global response;
>   5. that this is a war against evil;
>   6. that American children have to be reassured; and
>   7. that instead of propaganda, the war effort needs a narrative that should be told, said a straight-faced Rove, with accuracy and honesty.[6]

Simply put, the current Bush administration has solicited the cooperation of Hollywood in its on-going war against the Vietnam syndrome, hoping to ensure that future Hollywood productions will present all the right images and send all the right messages to the public concerning any future military interventions or strikes that the state might carry out in its potentially endless war on terrorism. In other words, Rove's meeting with top executives from the film and entertainment industry ought to be viewed as an effort to instruct Hollywood on how it should begin thinking about (re)presenting the future before it happens. In keeping with Rove's seven points, those representations should avoid invoking any public challenge to U.S. foreign and military policy that might lead to a relapse into the deepest throws of the Vietnam syndrome. While the Bush administration has begun shaping how the future will be represented, Hollywood has already begun rewriting the past.

The Rewriting/Reconstruction of Memory: *We Were Soldiers*

Memory is not being erased as much as it is being reconstructed.[7]

Real life is becoming indistinguishable from the movies.[8]

It is significant to analyze the ways in which memory is being rewritten and reconstructed in the wake of the terrorist attacks of September 11, 2001. Post September 11 films such as *Windtalkers, We Were Soldiers, Collateral Damage,* and others have helped to create a militaristic notion of individual heroism and nostalgia for victory, thereby rewriting history in ways that affirm the material interests of the corporate order and the state that fights to further it. The corporate order through various movie conglomerates produces films, which work to rewrite our history.

Paramount Pictures, the company that produced the film *We Were Soldiers,* is a behemoth of a corporation and is one of the top-four corporations involved in film production and distribution. Viacom International (a home shopping company) purchased Paramount in 1993. It owns Paramount Pictures, Spelling Films, Paramount Home Video, Republic Entertainment, Paramount Television, Spelling Entertainment, MTV, MTV2, Nickelodeon, Nick at Nite, Nick at Nite's TV Land, VH1, Showtime, The Movie Channel, Flix, Paramount Stations Group, and eleven televisionstations. It jointly owns USA Network, Sci-Fi Channel, Comedy Central, *South Park,* All News Channel, Sundance Channel, and United Paramount Network. In publishing it owns Simon and Schuster and Macmillan. In retail and recreational companies it owns Blockbuster, Paramount Parks (six theme parks), theaters (Famous Players, United Cinemas International, and Cinamerica, prime distribution sites for films), and Bubba Gump Shrimp Restaurants. It also owns miscellaneous companies such as Viacom Consumer Products (Paramount toys, brand T-shirts, games), Viacom Entertainment Stores, and on and on. This list indicates that Paramount Pictures is a corporate giant in the film industry and that films that are produced in this historical period are a matter of extensive negotiations, packaging, and distribution.

Particularly interesting is the manner in which corporately produced Vietnam War films can be used in a post-September 11 society to rewrite history and convey certain aspects of heroism and militarism for both youth and adults in developing dispositions and attitudes necessary for a prolonged war on terrorism, which may include attacking "rogue" nations. For example, *We Were Soldiers* premiered in theaters on the same day that Operation Anaconda began in Afghanistan. Henry Giroux has provocatively analyzed films about Vietnam and demonstrated certain aspects of the ways in which they rewrote and developed our subjectivities in the Reagan era.[9]

At the height of the Reagan era, Hollywood rewrote the Vietnam War in the image of an unbridled and arrogant national machismo. Films such as

Uncommon Valor (1983), *Missing in Action 2, The Beginning* (1985), *Rambo: First Blood, Part II* (1985), and *The Hanoi Hilton* (1987) used Vietnam as a backdrop to celebrate heroic rescues. Chemical warfare, forced settlements, and the burning of villages on the part of the U.S. military were written out of history, as Hollywood invented wooden macho men intent on saving the real victims of Vietnam, the MIAs, from the demonized Vietnamese.[10]

Giroux continues that what was at issue in this rewriting of history was a Reaganite construction of the image of masculinity that coincided with a conservative image of national identity and patriotism. Times have changed. We have a "compassionate conservative" president in George W. Bush. In the age of "compassionate conservatism," family values, faith-based education, and a long-term war against terrorism, films such as *We Were Soldiers* must first construct different notions of warriors. The soldiers in this Vietnam are not the pot-smoking, acid-dropping, hippies of the films of the 1970s. They are not the berserk chopper commander from *Apocalypse Now,* also of the Air Calvary, who liked the smell of napalm in the morning and played Wagner as he attacked. Nor are they the steely Rambo, Chuck Norris kind of killing machines characteristic of the 1980s and 1990s. The new Vietnam War soldier is the good soldier, a family man, and an everyday hero, who will fight for his country. That is reinforced by the conservative idea that Vietnam was not a quagmire flawed from the outset or an aggression. It was a war fought by noble and heroic men. There is still the attempt to rewrite the Vietnam War but for other purposes. Now conceptualizations of good soldiers and film portrayals such as this can construct notions more in-line for the war on terrorism. It can allow a prolonged war, the acceptance of heavy causalities, the spread of the war to other locations and nations to seek out evil. The evil empire of the Reagan times, communism, has been vanquished according to the conservative metanarrative, and now it has been replaced with a more deceitful, cunning, and mobile evil. There is once again a just cause to rally around. We must as the first war slogan said seek "Infinite Justice." One of the last scenes in *We Were Soldiers* is the small fluttering and battle-tattered American flag. Symbols are powerful and there is no absence of American flags in this current milieu. Films can assist in mobilizing the necessary dispositions for war by rewriting the wars that have come before and the images associated with them. We are reminded by opening credits and promotional talk shows on television that the authenticity and transparent truth of this film derives from the fact that it is based on a actual Vietnam battle and the book *We Were Soldiers Once and Young: Ia Drang, The Battle that Changed the War in Vietnam* written by Harold G. Moore, and Joseph L. Galloway. Like documentary realist films that obscure the motivated representation undergirding their production, such appeals to realism efface the process of memory rewriting in which the cultural work engages.

There are many issues that arise in *We Were Soldiers* and in this chapter we will focus on only two: (1) The movement made in this film from the lone macho heroic rescuer to the development of the family man father/soldier; (2) The manner in which the nature of individual heroism is a way to obtain a military victory no matter what the cost, which is consistent with the corporate order's notion of success of the individual and overcoming adversity individually.

The film deals with the circumstances surrounding an incident in November 1965, 450 U.S. soldiers of the First Battalion, Seventh Calvary were dropped into a small clearing in the Ia Drang Valley. Two thousand North Vietnamese soldiers surrounded them. The film deals with the heroic actions of the soldiers and their commander Lieutenant Colonel Harold Moore. The film does portray the North Vietnamese soldiers more as human beings than in previous Vietnam films, but that is not the primary purpose of this film. And, although the film is emotionally moving, the interesting facets are those that rewrite our identities for a new post–September 11 era.

Gone are the days of *Rambo: First Blood* (1982), *Rambo: First Blood 2* (1985), and *Rambo III* (1988). "The image of Sylvester Stallone as Vietnam veteran John Rambo, brandishing a rocket-launcher whilst parading his musculature, became an icon of American masculinity in the mid-1980s.[11] That hero has been replaced in this era by the more compassionate one. He is a combination actual person and film hero. We witness this even in an unabashedly action-oriented film like *Collateral Damage*, in which Arnold Schwarzenegger, still brandishing impressive weaponry, plays a family man/fireman seeking revenge on Colombian guerrilla terrorists for killing his wife and young son. Here is the individual hero/father fighting as an individual. When we look at the character of Moore in *We Were Soldiers*, he is not the muscled caricature of a John Rambo, but a family man. He has 5 children and a devoted wife. That essential ingredient of compassionate conservative middle-class family values is present in a nostalgic way. In one scene he happens into one of the children's bedrooms as the kids are engaging in horseplay and he tells them it is time for bed. But, before they head off to bed they need to say their prayers. And, a potential conflict between Moore's Catholicism and his wife's Methodism is resolved as he suggests that they pray for the family. Once again, those family values are reinforced.

Moore is a military man through and through, but he is also the good father/husband. And that characteristic is with him as military leader. At one point in the film, he is watching his young officers train. He is convinced that the most compassionate young officer, the one that tends to his men's foot injuries with care, will make an outstanding officer and the young gung-ho officer who "wants to be a hero" does not measure up to a compassionate officer. This is quite a change from John Rambo. Moore, continuing with his family orientation, describes to his men that they need, like the Native Americans, to fight as a family and that his officers and men need to learn to take care of each other.

MOORE: "When this thing starts that is all we are going to have."

That sentiment has been repeated in the year since September 11, 2001, in many contexts even T-shirts that proclaim "United We Stand."

One final aspect of this father/soldier image occurs when the young lieutenant Jack Gagin is in the chapel and Moore comes to visit him on the occasion of his daughter's birth. They have a talk about the family and the military.

GAGIN: "What do you think about being a soldier and a father?"
MOORE: "I hope that being good at one helps you to be better at the other."

Moore then asks Gagin what he thinks and Gagin replies that he and his wife, Barbara had spent a year in Africa building a school for children who had been orphaned by a warlord who lived across the border and didn't like their tribe. Gagin says he knows that God has a plan for him, and he hoped it was to protect orphans. Moore suggests they ask God about it. So, Moore prays.

> Our Father in Heaven before we go into battle, every soldier among us will approach you each in his own way. Our enemies, too, according to their own understanding ask for protection and for victory. So, we bow before your infinite wisdom and we offer our prayers as best we can. I pray you watch over men like Jack Gagin that I lead into battle and use me as your instrument in this awful Hell war to watch over them. Especially if they are men like the one beside me deserving of a future in your blessing and good will. Amen. Oh yes and one more thing dear Lord, about our enemies. Ignore their heathen prayers and help us blow these little bastards straight to Hell. Amen, again.

These are not the type of soldiers we witnessed in films like *Platoon* and *Apocalypse Now*. They are rewritten post September 11 Vietnam family men, heroes much more in line with the needs of an identity for a fight against terrorism and a new compassionate conservative, corporate, militaristic agenda, interestingly reflecting all the values and commitments of the agenda of family values, religious beliefs, and a hard edge toward the enemy.

Just before Moore leaves for Vietnam, he spends time with his daughter talking about war. She asks her father, what is war? He replies that it is when people from another country try to take the lives of other people and then soldiers like him know it is their job to stop them. Our memories of the early years of the Vietnam War are constituted into a more appropriate image for the age of terrorism.

Another facet of these family values is the work of the wives at home while the men are fighting. After the battle starts, telegrams announcing the deaths of the officers arrive by taxi at the houses of the soldiers families. Moore's and Gagin's wives decide to deliver these telegrams together to the families of the men killed in action, a very poignant moment in the film and consistent with reinforcing family values and individual acts of courage, to which I turn next.

Individual heroism consistent with the individualism of competitive corporate capitalism is another way *We Were Soldiers* is told. As the film portrays this story it constitutes and rewrites memories for those of us who were alive during the Vietnam period and for that younger generation, it constructs their memories. The film is full of episodes of individualist heroic deeds and sacrifices. And, there certainly were such acts during the Vietnam War. Though like the other stages of Vietnam War films, this one removes from examination the political context of the cold war and the history of U.S. imperial aggression. It does demonstrate that individual valor and ingenuity are most important in victory, no matter what the cost. Sergeant Major Plumley, a gruff and seasoned veteran, finally speaks to one young soldier after the man spends a day and night surrounded by the enemy and in an almost constant firefight. Apparently individual heroism makes an acceptable soldier. The young compassionate officer Gagin is killed in a heroic effort to leave no man behind. He is mortally wounded attempting to carry his wounded comrade off the field and out of harm. The brave few finally outsmart and through many instances of individual valor turn the tide of the battle by aggressively attacking. Rugged individualism, a long-standing requirement of a capitalist, corporate, military society is again reconstituted in this film. It is the way to succeed in business and the way to succeed on the battlefield.

Reconstructing Memory

> Not least to blame for the withering of experience is the fact that things, under the law of pure functionality, assume a form that limits contact with them to mere operation, and tolerates no surplus, either in freedom of conduct or in autonomy of things, which would survive as the core of experience, because it is not consumed by the moment of action.[12]

Movies such as *We Were Soldiers* need to be analyzed, for they offer the potential of a critical reading of how the politics of war films can conceal the ideological and hegemonic principles used to legitimate militarism and a particular brand of heroism that supports particular political ideologies. Films, such as this, work to change our memories about the way that war operates. Just as Vietnam War films operated to produce a particular conservative image of nationalism and patriotism in the 1980s, Vietnam War films can, post-September 11, serve the same function with a different image. As a popular culture text this film functions:

> Through discursive practices and ideological practices that are both pedagogical and political. As part of a larger cultural apparatus, [it] signifies the centrality of film as a medium of popular culture, a centrality that must be addressed not simply as a pedagogical apparatus actively involved in diverse identity formations but also for the crucial role it plays in the construction of national identities in the service of global expansion and colonialism.[13]

The portrayal of individual heroism and victory over sometimes overwhelming odds becomes commonplace and the tactics of corporate capitalism and militarism become, if not accepted, at least presented as less despicable. Popular culture must be taken seriously as it, through reconstructing our memories and ideas of what constitutes militarism and heroism, produces our identities. Popular films such as *We Were Soldiers*, immersed in the global brand-named corporate military order, help create and perpetuate it as they are created by it. The discursive critique of film is important pedagogical work. As we are tossed among the many discursive cinematic practices and portrayals that continually shift our subject positions as educators, academics, workers, citizens, parents, and children, we need to develop critiques of popular cultural artifacts like films recognizing that they too are developed within a particular political, ideological, historical period. These connections and intricacies might be the place to start to discuss with students their involvement and immersion in the global, branded corporate and military order. Start with what they consider to be legitimate knowledge.

What is needed are alternative visions of a democratic existence. There are tactical moments when we can temporarily find spaces to write ourselves and work ourselves out of the very things that imprison us, however, temporary those moments may be. These visions of existence are not based on conservative, militaristic principles, the simulacra of a brand named lifestyle, or a celebration of a community safe and secure in relinquishing freedom, nor the narrow visions of upper middle-class life with its resplendent material possessions and vacuousness. Educators must remember that Hollywood does not have a monopoly on rewriting public memory. Hollywood's products provide a meaningful starting point for critical educators to challenge the conservatizing versions of history in films such as *We Were Soldiers*. Cultural and curriculum studies producers have an opportunity in their educational practices to re-write memory in ways that strengthen democratic public values, civic virtue, and collective action by encouraging engagement with and memory of a progressive past of struggle for social justice.

Notes

1. Norman Podherz, quoted in Noam Chomsky, "Media Control" (1991/1993). Available at www.zmag.org/chomsky/talks/9103-media-control.html#apr.
2. Otto Reich also helped write the Helms-Burton Act that maintains the U.S. embargo against Cuba.
3. Jeff Cohen, "The Return of Otto Reich: Will Government Propagandist Join Bush Administration?," *FAIR* (June 8, 2001), available at http://www.fair.org/articles/otto-reich.html.
4. Ibid.
5. Karl Rove served as chief strategist for George W. Bush's presidential campaign and now serves as Bush's top advisor, managing the Office of Public Affairs, the Office of Public Liaison, and the Office of Strategic Initiatives.
6. Marc Cooper, "Lights! Cameras! Attack! Hollywood Enlists," *The Nation* (December 10, 2001), Available at http://www.brycezabel.com/mediapage/thenation.htm.
7. Henry A. Giroux, *Impure Acts: The Practical Politics of Cultural Studies* (New York: Routledge, 2000), 10.
8. Theodor Adorno and Max Horkheimer, "The Culture Industry: Enlightenment as Mass Deception," in *The Cultural Studies Reader*, 2nd ed., edited by S. During (New York: Routledge, 1999), 31–45.
9. Henry A. Giroux, *The Mouse that Roared: Disney and the End of Innocence* (New York: Rowman & Littlefield Publishers, 1999); and Henry A. Giroux, *Breaking into the Movies: Film and the Culture of Politics* (Malden, Mass.: Blackwell Publishers, 2002).
10. Giroux, *The Mouse that Roared*, 151n.
11. Yvonne Tasker, *Spectacular Bodies: Gender, Genre and the Action Cinema* (New York: Routledge, 1999).
12. Adorno and Horkheimer, "The Culture Industry."
13. Giroux, *Breaking into the Movies*.

INTRODUCTION TO CHAPTER 18

While the proceeding chapter examines the interrelations between cultural production and the building of consent for the war terrorism, in particular with regards to film, Michael Apple pays close attention to how individual Americans, himself included, experienced the events of September 11. His chapter is important for highlighting why dangerous forms of patriotism flourish as well as the role of teachers in addressing September 11.

CHAPTER 18

The Politics of Compulsory Patriotism

On the Educational Meanings of September 11

MICHAEL W. APPLE

The volume of material that has been published on the September 11 tragedy has been extensive. While some of it has been filled with an uncritical acceptance of official views on the subject, a good deal of it has been considerably more nuanced and self-critical about the role that the United States may have played in helping to generate the conditions that led to the kinds of despair that might make some people believe that such action could be a "legitimate" response to U.S. hegemony. I do not think that there is any way to justify the acts of September 11. But I do think that they cannot be understood in isolation from the international and national contexts out of which they arose. I will leave an exploration of the international context to others.[1]

In this chapter, I want to do something else. I wish to focus on the most local of levels: the complicated ways in which September 11 was experienced phenomenologically by teachers such as myself, and the little known effects it had on pedagogy and on the urge to have schools participate in a complicated set of patriotic discourses and practices that swept over the United States in the wake of the disaster. Given this focus, parts of my analysis will need to be personal. I do this not because I think that I have any better purchase on reality than the reader, but because all of us may be better able to understand the lived effects of September 11 by exploring what it meant to identifiable social actors like myself. Thus, I start at the personal level, but my aim is to participate in a collective project in which people from many different social locations and positions tell the stories of what September 11 meant, and continues to mean, for their lives and educational practices.

Michael W. Apple is John Bascom Professor of curriculum and instruction and educational policy studies. He teaches courses in curriculum theory and research and in the sociology of curriculum. His major interests lie in the relationship between culture and power in education. He is the author of *Educating the "Right" Way: Market, Standards, God, and Inequality* (RoutledgeFalmer, 2001), *Official Knowledge: Democratic Education in a Conservative Age* (Routledge, 2000), and numerous other books on the cultural and political dimensions of education and curriculum.

Horror and Hollywood

"Damn. Who could be calling now?" My annoyance was palpable. This was one of the increasingly rare mornings that I had been able to carve out uninterrupted time to devote myself to serious writing. I ran from my computer to the phone, hoping not to lose the line of thought I was struggling with. The call was from one of my most politically active students.

"Michael, do you have your TV on? Put it on *now, quickly!* The World Trade Center is *collapsing*. It's unbelievable. We're in for a new McCarthyism! What do you think we should *do!*"

I put the television on. You'll forgive me, but the first words out of my mouth were "Holy shit!" I sat. I watched. But this was decidedly not passive watching. Mesmerized is exactly the wrong word here. As the buildings collapsed, my mind was filled with an entire universe of competing and contradictory emotions and meanings. This wasn't the O. J. slow-motion caravan. Nor was it like my experience of being a young teacher when Kennedy was assassinated. Then, I was giving a spelling test at the time the shooting was announced over the school's loudspeaker. I kept giving the test, too shocked to do anything else. Yes, like the Kennedy experience there now was the intense shock of the surreally slow-motion plane, of the collapsing towers, and worst of all of people jumping out of buildings. But I had changed and so had the cultural assemblage around which one made interpretive sense of what was happening.

At nearly exactly the same time as I felt immense horror at the World Trade Center disaster, something else kept entering into the lenses with which I saw the images on the screen. The key word here is exactly that—screen. It seemed almost unreal. The explosions weren't large enough or dramatic enough to seem "real." It was as if I expected Bruce Willis to come running out of the collapsing buildings after a fireball of gargantuan proportions lit up the sky. The fireball was "too small." The scene of the plane as it headed for the second tower—a scene broadcast over and over and over again, as if there was something of a perverse politics of pleasure at work—was too undramatic, to "unemotional" (as if it needed a musical crescendo to tell us of the impending tragedy). The only word I can use to describe that part of this welter of meanings and emotions was that even though I had prided myself on being critically conscious of the ways that our dominant commodified cultural forms worked, I too had been "Hollywoodized." The horror of death meets *The Towering Inferno*. But the falling bodies always brought me back to reality. It was *that* sight that brought the carnage back home.

Like many people I am certain, I sat and watched—for hours. Interviews, screaming people running away, running toward, but always running—or seeking cover. Another plane—this one missing. What was its target? Then came the news that the Pentagon was hit. This created an even more complex set of interpretations and readings. Why did I have even more complicated emotions now? I had marched on the Pentagon against the Vietnam War. I had been tear-gassed there. It was the seat of American military might and power. Somehow it *deserved* to be a target. And yet, real people were killed there, real people who worked there, not only out of choice but because, in a U.S. economy that was what is best called military Keynesianism (use government funding to prop up the economy, but by channeling huge amounts of that money into military-related enterprises), the Pentagon and similar sites were where many of the jobs *were*.

Then, by that night and throughout the days and nights that followed, the ruling pundits took charge of the public expression of what were the legitimate interpretations of the disaster. The visual construction of authority on the screen and the spoken texts themselves will provide critical media analysts with enough data to once again demonstrate how power is performed in public, how the combination of somber setting, the voices of righteousness, and the tropes of patriotism and vengeance all work together to create a mighty call not for justice but for vengeance.[2] (This is one of the reasons that I and many others joined forces to create the Justice not Vengeance movement in towns and cities throughout the nation.)

In understanding this, I try to remember that the media not only help us construct the nature of the problems we face, but they are powerful mobilizing tools. And everywhere one turns after September 11 there are voices of the media saying the same thing. Dissident voices are not totally silent, but the shock has affected them as well; and their messages are muted. We are at war. Terrorists are here. Freedom has taken a horrible blow. But God is on our side. We cannot afford the luxury of worrying about civil liberties. Lenient policies toward immigrants, the defunding and depowering of the FBI and the CIA, our diminished military strength, all of these and so much more were nearly the only official response. There must be one unitary reply. Track "them"down in all places at all costs. Find their supporters wherever they may be, especially if they are here. Any questions about *why* so many people in so many nations might have been mistrustful of—indeed hated—the US is seen as nearly unpatriotic; they could not be tolerated at this time. Oh, these questions might be worth asking, but after "we" had destroyed the threat to our very way of life that international terrorism represented. Of course, even asking the question "Why do they hate us?" is itself part of the problem. At the same time, I also realize that by constructing the binary of "we/they," the very nature of the question establishes center/periphery relations that are fully implicated in the production of a reactionary common sense. Good/bad terms have always dominated the American political landscape, especially in terms of international relations.

How can we interpret this? Speaking very generally, the American public has little patience with the complexities of international relations and even less knowledge of United States' complicity in supporting and arming dictatorial regimes; nor does it have a developed and nuanced understanding of U.S. domination of the world economy, of the negative effects of globalization, of the environmental effects of its wasteful energy policies and practices, and so much more, despite the nearly heroic efforts of critics of U.S. international policy such as Noam Chomsky.[3] This speaks to the reality of the selective tradition in official knowledge and in the world beyond our borders that the news portrays. Even when there have been gains in the school curriculum—environmental awareness provides a useful example—these have been either adopted in their safest forms[4] or they fail to internationalize their discussions. Recycling bottles and cans is "good"; connections between profligate consumption of a disproportionate share of the world's resources and our daily behavior are nearly invisible in schools or the mainstream media. In this regard, it is helpful to know that the majority of nonbusiness vehicles purchased in the United States are now pick-up trucks, minivans, and sport utility vehicles—a guarantee that energy conservation will be a discourse unmoored in the daily practices of the United States consumer and an even further guarantee that the relationship between U.S. economic and military strategies and the defense of markets and, say, oil resources will be generally interpreted as a fight to protect the "American Way of Life" at all costs.

I mention all this because it is important to place what happened in the wake of September 11 in a context of the "American" psyche and of dominant American self-understandings of the role the United States plays in the world.[5] In the domestic events surrounding September 11, *we* had now become the world's oppressed. The (always relatively weak) recognition of the realities of the Palestinians, or the poor in what we arrogantly call "the third world" were now evacuated. Almost immediately, there were a multitude of instances throughout the nation of people who "looked Arabic" being threatened and harassed on the street, in schools, and in their places of business. Less well known, but in my mind of great importance since they show the complexities of people's ethical commitments in the face-to-face relations of daily life, were the repeated instances of solidarity including university and community demonstrations of support for Islamic students, friends, and community members. Yet these moments of solidarity, though significant, could not totally make up for such things as Islamic, Punjabi, Sikh, and other students in high schools and at universities being threatened with "retaliation" and in the case of some Punjabi secondary school students being threatened with rape as an act of "revenge" for September 11. This documents the connections between some elements of national identity and forms of masculinity, a relationship that cries out for serious analysis.[6]

At the universities, some teachers ignored the horror, perhaps for much the same reason I had dealt with the Kennedy assassination by simply resorting to normality as a defense against paralysis. In other classes, days were spent in discussions of the events. Sadness, disbelief, and shock were registered. But just as often, anger and a resurgent patriotism came to the fore. Any critical analysis of the events and of their roots in the hopelessness and despair of oppressed peoples—as I and a number of my colleagues put forward in our classes and seminars—had to be done extremely cautiously, not only because of the emotionally and politically charged environment even at a progressive university like my own, but also because many of us were not totally immune from some of the same feelings of anger and horror. Even for progressive educators, the events of September 11 worked off of the contradictory elements of good and bad sense we too carried within us and threatened to pull us in directions that, in other times, would have seemed to be simplistic and even jingoistic. But at least for me and the vast majority of my colleagues and graduate students, the elements of good sense won out.

Given these elements of good sense, it was clear that pedagogical work needed to be done. But this wasn't a simple issue, since a constant question, and tension, was always on my mind. How could one condemn the murderous events, give one's students an historical and political framework that puts these events into their larger critical context, and provide a serious forum where disagreement and debate could fruitfully go on so that a politics of marginalization didn't occur in the classes—and at the same time not be seen as somehow justifying the attacks? While I had very strong feelings about the need to use this as a time to show the effects of U.S. global economic, political, and cultural policies, I also had strong "teacherly" dispositions that this was also *not* the time to engage in a pedagogy of imposition. One could not come across as saying to students or the public, "Your understandings are simply wrong; your feelings of threat and anger are selfish; any voicing of these emotions and understandings won't be acceptable." This would be among the most counterproductive pedagogies imaginable. Not only would it confirm the already just-near-the-surface perceptions among many people that somehow the left is unpatriotic, but such a pedagogy also could push people into rightist positions, in much the same way as I had argued in my own work about why people "became right."[7] This required a very strategic sense of how to speak and act both in my teaching and in my appearances on national media,

Take my teaching as a major example. I wanted my students to fully appreciate the fact that the U.S.-led embargo of Iraq had caused the death of thousands upon thousands of children each year that it had been in place. I wanted them to understand how U.S. policies in the Middle East and in Afghanistan itself had helped create truly murderous consequences. However, unless their feelings and understandings were voiced and taken seriously, the result could be exactly the opposite of what any decent teacher wants. Instead of a more complicated understanding of the lives of people who are among the most oppressed in the world—often as a result of Western and Northern economic and political policies[8]—students could be led to reject any critical contextual understanding largely because the pedagogical politics seemed arrogant. In my experiences both as an activist and a scholar, this has happened more often than some theorists of "critical pedagogy" would like to admit. [9]None of us are perfect teachers, and I am certain that I made more than a few wrong moves in my attempts to structure the discussions in my classes so that they were open and critical at the same time. But I was impressed with the willingness of the vast majority of students to reexamine their anger, to put themselves in the place of the oppressed, to take their more critical and nuanced understandings and put them into action. Indeed, one of the things that was striking was the fact that a coalition of students in my classes was formed to engage in concrete actions in their own schools and communities, as well as in the university, to interrupt the growing anti-Islamic and jingoistic dynamics that were present even in progressive areas such as Madison and the University of Wisconsin.

This politics of interruption became even more important, since these complicated pedagogical issues and the contradictory emotions and politics that were produced in the aftermath of September 11 were felt well beyond the walls of the university classroom. At times, they also had the effect of radically transforming the politics of governance of schooling at a local level in communities throughout the United States. One example can serve as a powerful reminder of the hidden effects of the circulation of discourses of patriotism and "threat" as they move from the media into our daily lives.

Patriotism, the Flag, and the Control of Schools

More than 1,200 persons packed the auditorium. Flags were everywhere, in hands, on lapels, pasted on jackets. The old and trite phrase that "you could cut the tension with a knife" seemed oddly appropriate here. The tension was somehow *physical*; it could literally be felt, almost like an electrical current that coursed through your body. And for some people present at the hearing, the figures behind the front table deserved exactly that. They needed to be electrically shocked, indeed were almost deserving of something like the electric chair.

Months before the September 11 disaster, the seeds of this conflict had been planted in what were seemingly innocuous ways. Smuggled into the state budget bill was a bit of mischief by conservative legislators seeking to gain some arguing points for the next election. There was a section in the budget authorization bill that required that students in all public (state funded) schools publicly recite either the Pledge of Allegiance or play the national anthem (*The Star Spangled Banner*, a strikingly militaristic song that has the added benefit of being nearly impossible for most people and certainly most children to sing). Even though the legislation allowed for "nonparticipation," given the long and inglorious history of legislation of this kind in the United States, there was a clear implication that such lack of participation was frowned upon. This was something of a time bomb just waiting to explode. And it did. In the midst of the growing patriotic fervor following September 11, the Madison, Wisconsin, School Board voted to follow the law in the most minimalist way possible. For some Board members, the law seemed to be the wrong way to teach patriotism. Rote memorization was not the best approach if one actually wanted to provide the conditions for the growth of thoughtful citizenship. For others, the law was clearly a political ploy by conservative legislators to try to gain more support among right-wing voters in an upcoming election, which was felt to be a close call. And for other board members, there were a number of principles at stake. The state should not intervene into the content of local school board decisions of this type. Further, not only had the new law not been subject to close public scrutiny and serious debate, but it threatened the cherished (at least in theory) constitutional right of freedom of dissent. For all of these reasons, a majority of people on the school board voted not to have the reciting of the Pledge or the singing of the anthem.[10]

Within hours, the furor over their decision reached a boiling point. The media made it their major story. Prominent headlines in a local conservative newspaper stated such things as "School Board Bans Pledge of Allegiance," even though the board had actually complied with the formal letter of the law, and even though the board had indeed held public hearings prior to their actions where many people had objected both to the law and to the saying of the Pledge and the singing of the anthem. Conservative politicians and spokespersons, colonizing the space of fear and horror over the destruction of the World Trade Center, quickly mobilized. "This could not be tolerated." It was not only unpatriotic, but it was disrespectful both to the women and men who died in the disaster and to our military overseas. To those being mobilized, it also was a signal that the board was out of touch with "real" Americans, one more instance of elite control of schools that ignored the wishes of the "silent majority" of "freedom loving" and patriotic Americans.

The populist notes being struck here are crucial, since hegemonic alliances can *only* succeed when they connect with the elements of "good sense" of the people.[11] Popular worries over one's children and the schools they attend, in a time of radical corporate downsizing and capital flight, worries about social stability and cultural traditions that are constantly being subverted by the commodifying processes and logics of capital, and so much more, allow conservative groups to suture these concerns into their own antipublic agenda. Thus, rampant and fearful conservatism and patriotism are not the only dynamics at work in this situation, even though the overt issue was about the Pledge and the anthem. None of this could have happened without the growing fear of one's children's future and over the nature of an unstable paid labor market, and especially without the decades-long ideological project in which the right had engaged to make so many people believe that "big government" was the source of the social, cultural, and economic problems we face.[12]

Yet, there were more conjunctural reasons for this response as well. It is always wise to remember that while the state of Wisconsin was the home of much of the most progressive legislation and of significant parts of the socialist tradition in the United States, it also was the home of Senator Joseph McCarthy—yes, the figure for whom McCarthyism is named. Thus, behind the populist and social democratic impulses that have had such a long history here, there lies another kind of populism. This one is what, following Stuart Hall,[13] I have called "authoritarian populism," a retrogressive assemblage of values that embodies visions of "the people" that has been just as apt to be nationalistic, antiimmigrant, anticosmopolitan, anticommunist, pro-military, and very conservative in terms of religious values.[14] In times of crisis, these tendencies can come to the fore. And they did, with a vengeance.

We cannot understand any of this unless we understand the long history of the struggles over the very meaning of freedom and citizenship in the United States.[15] For all of the protagonists in the school board controversy, what was at stake was "freedom." For some, it was the danger of international terrorism destroying our "free" way of life. Nothing must interfere with the defense of "American freedom," and schools were on the front lines in this defense For others, such freedom was in essence meaningless if it meant that citizens couldn't act on their freedoms, especially in times of crisis. Silencing dissent, imposing forms of compulsory patriotism, these acts were the very antithesis of freedom. A hidden curriculum of compulsory patriotism would, in essence, do exactly this.

This documents an important point. Concepts such as freedom are sliding signifiers. They have no fixed meaning, but are part of a contested terrain in which different visions of democracy exist on a social field of power in which there are unequal resources to influence the publicly accepted definitions of key words. In the words of one of the wisest historians of such concepts:

> The very universality of the language of freedom camouflages a host of divergent connotations and applications. It is pointless to attempt to identify a single "real" meaning against which others are to be judged. Rather than freedom as a fixed category or predetermined concept, ... it [is] an "essentially contested concept," one that by its very nature is the subject of disagreement. Use of such a concept automatically presupposes an ongoing dialogue with other, competing meanings.[16]

The realization of how concepts such as democracy and freedom act as sliding signifiers and can be mobilized by varying groups with varying agendas returns us to a point I made earlier, the ideological project in which the economic and cultural right have engaged. We need to understand that widely successful effects of what Roger Dale and I have called "conservative modernization" have been exactly that—widely successful.[17] We are witnessing—living through is a better phrase—a social/pedagogic project to change our common sense, to radically transform our assumptions about the role "liberal elites," of government and the economy, about what are "appropriate" values, the role of religion in public affairs, gender and sexuality, "race," and a host of other crucial areas. Democracy has been transformed from a political concept to an economic one. Collective senses of freedom that were once much more widespread (although we need to be careful of not romanticizing this) have been largely replaced by individualistic notions of democracy as simply "consumer choice." While this has had major effects on the power of labor unions and on other kinds of important collective social movements, it also has created other hidden needs and desires besides those of the rational economic actor who makes calculated individual decisions in a market.[18] I think that these needs and desires have also played a profound role in the mobilization of the seemingly rightist sentiment I have been describing.

Underneath the creation of the unattached individualism of the market is an almost unconscious desire for community. However, community formation can take many forms, both progressive and retrogressive. At the time of September 11, both came to the fore. The Madison School Board's decision threatened the "imagined community" of the nation, at the same time as the nation actually seemed to be under physical threat.[19] It also provided a stimulus for the formation of a "real" community, an organization to "win back" the space of schooling for patriotism. The defense of freedom is sutured into the project of defending the nation, which is sutured into a local project of forming a (rightist) counter-hegemonic community to contest the antipatriotic and ideologically motivated decisions by urban liberal elites. Thus, the need to "be with others," itself a hidden effect of the asocial relations of advanced capitalism, has elements of good and bad sense within it. Under specific historical circumstances these elements of good sense can be mobilized in support of a vision of democracy that is inherently undemocratic in its actual effects on those people in a community who wish to uphold a vison of freedom that not only legitimates dissidence but provides space for its expression.[20]

In saying this, do not read me as being totally opposed to ideas of nation or of the building of imagined communities. In my mind, however, social criticism is the ultimate act of patriotism. As I say in my book *Official Knowledge*, rigorous criticism of a nation's policies demonstrates a commitment to the nation itself. It says that one demands action on the principles that are supposedly part of the founding narratives of a nation and that are employed in the legitimation of its construction of particular kinds of polities. It signifies that "I/we live here" and that this is indeed our country and our flag as well. No national narrative that excludes the rich history of dissent as a constitutive part of the nation can ever be considered legitimate. Thus, in claiming that the board had acted in an unpatriotic manner, the flag-waving crowd and the partly still inchoate movement that stood behind it in my mind was itself engaged in a truly unpatriotic act, one which showed that the national narrative of freedom and justice was subject to constant "renegotiation" and struggle over its very meaning.[21] The September 11 tragedy provided the conditions for such struggles at a local level, not only in the classrooms at universities such as my own but in the ordinary ways we govern our schools.

I could spend many more pages describing what happened with the school board. But, even with the forces arrayed against it, the threat to call a special election to oust all of the board members who voted against the mandatory Pledge and anthem singing stalled. The recall campaign failed by a wide margin. The conservative organizers were not able to get anywhere near the number of votes needed to force a new election. This is a crucial element in any appraisal of the lasting effects of September 11. In the face of resurgent patriotism and anger, in the face of calls for an enhanced national security state and for schools to be part of the first line of defense, at the local level in many communities wiser heads, ones with a more substantive vision of democracy, prevailed. Yet, this is not the end of this particular story. The pressure from the right did have an effect. The board left it up to each individual school to decide if and how they would enforce the mandated patriotism. This decision defused the controversy in a way that has a long history in the United States. Local decisions will prevail; but there is no guarantee that the decisions at each local school will uphold a vision of thick democracy that welcomes dissent itself as a form of patriotic commitment.

It is unclear then who really won or lost here. But one thing is clear: no analysis of the effects of September 11 on schools can go on without an understanding of the ways in which the global is dynamically linked to the local. Such an analysis must more fully understand the larger ideological work and history of the neoliberal and neoconservative project and its effects on the discourses that circulate and become common sense in our society. And no analysis can afford to ignore the contradictory needs and contradictions that this project has created.

Oh, and one last thing, a complete analysis would require that we look at the effects of the commodified products of popular cultural forms of entertainment that each of us use to "see" the momentous events taking place all around us. Critical cultural analysts have taught us many things. Yes, we participate in guilty pleasures. (How else to explain my framing of the disastrous events of September 11 in terms of Hollywood images?) And, yes, we can read any cultural form and content in dominant, negotiated, and oppositional ways. But it might be wise to remember that—at least in the case of the ways in which Michael W. Apple experienced the horrors of the planes and buildings and bodies on September 11—all three went on at the same time. Recognizing our own contradictory responses may be a first step in finding appropriate and socially critical pedagogic strategies to work with all of our students in interrupting the larger hegemonic projects—including the redefinition of democracy as "patriotic fervor"—that we will continue to face in the future.[22]

Notes

1. See for example, Noam Chomsky, *9–11* (New York: Seven Stories Press, 2002).
2. Michael W. Apple, *Official Knowledge*, 2nd ed. (New York: Routledge, 2000).
3. Noam Chomsky, *Profit Over People* (New York: Seven Stories Press, 1999).
4. Nancy Fraser, *Unruly Practices* (Minneapolis: University of Minnesota Press, 1989).
5. Even though I have used this word before in my text, I have put the word "American" in quotation marks for a social purpose in this sentence, since it speaks to the reality I wish to comment on at this point in my discussion. *All* of North, Central, and South America are equally part of the Americas. However, the United States (and much of the world) takes for granted that the term refers to the United States. The very language we use is a marker of imperial pasts and presents. See Edward Said's *Orientalism* (New York: Random House, 1978) for one of the early but still very cogent analyses of this.
6. Marcus Weaver-Hightower, *The Gender of Terror and Heroes?* (New York: Teachers College Record, forthcoming).
7. Michael W. Apple, *Cultural Politics and Education* (New York: Teachers College Press, 1996).
8. William Greider, *One World, Ready or Not* (New York: Simon and Schuster, 1997).
9. This is one of the reasons that, even though parts of the points may have been based on only a limited reading of parts of the critical pedagogical traditions, I have some sympathy with a number of the arguments made in Carmen Luke and Jennifer Gore's *Feminism and Critical Pedagogy* (New York: Routledge, 1992)— and not a lot of sympathy for the defensive overreactions to it on the part of a number of writers on "critical pedagogy." Political/educational projects, if they are to be both democratic and effective, are always collective. This requires a welcoming of serious and engaged criticism.
10. The reality was actually a bit more complicated than such a simple act of prohibition. The Madison School Board *did* actually comply with the law by having the music of the anthem played over the loudspeaker. Thus, if a school was determined to, say, have the anthem, only an instrumental version was to be played. This would eliminate the more warlike words that accompanied the music. Some members of the board felt that in a time of tragedy in which so many innocent lives had been lost, the last thing that students and schools needed were lyrics that to some glorified militarism. The solution was a compromise: play an instrumental version of the anthem. This too led to some interesting and partly counterhegemonic responses. At one school, a famous Jimi Hendrix rendition of The *Star Spangled Banner* was played over the loudspeaker system. This version—dissonant and

raucous—was part of the antiwar tradition of music during the Vietnam-era protests. This raised even more anger on the part of the "patriots" who were already so incensed about the board's vote.

11. See Apple *Cultural Politics and Education* (1996), and Michael W. Apple, *Educating the "Right" Way: Markets, Standards, God, and Inequality* (New York: Routledge, 2001).

12. See Michael B. Katz, M. B., *The Price of Citizenship* (New York: Metropolitan Books, 2001); Apple *Cultural Politics and Education*; and Apple, *Educating the "Right" Way* (2001).

13. Stuart Hall, "Popular Democratic vs. Authoritarian Populism," in *Marxism and Democracy*, edited by Alan Hunt (London: Lawrence and Wishart, 1980).

14. See Apple, *Educating the "Right" Way* (2001).

15. See Eric Foner, *The Story of American Freedom* (New York: Norton, 1998).

16. Ibid., xiv.

17. Roger Dale, "The Thatcherite Project in Education," *Critical Social Policy* 9 (1989–90): 4–19 and Apple, *Educating the "Right" Way*.

18. See Apple, *Educating the "Right" Way*; and Linda Kintz, *Between Jesus and the Market: The Emotions that Matter in Right-Wrong America* (Durham, N.C.: Duke University Press, 1997).

19. Benedict Anderson, *Imagined Communities* (New York: Verso, 1991).

20. Of course, the conservative groups that mobilized against the board's initial decision would claim that they were exercising dissent, that their members were also engaged in democratic action. This is true as far as it goes. However, if one's dissent supports repression and inequality, and if one's dissent labels other people's actions in favor of their own constitutional rights as "unpatriotic," then this is certainly not based on a vision of "thick" democracy. I would hold that its self-understanding is less than satisfactory.

21. In this regard, it is important to know that the Pledge of Allegiance itself has *always* been contested. Its words are the following:

> I pledge allegiance to the flag of the United States of America, and to the republic for which it stands, one Nation, under God, with liberty and justice for all.

Yet, the phrase "under God" was added during the midst of the McCarthy period in the early 1950s as part of the battle against "God-less communists." Even the phrase "to the flag of the United States of America" is a late addition. The Pledge was originally written by a well-known socialist and at first only contained the words "I pledge allegiance to the flag." In the 1920s, a conservative women's group, the Daughters of the American Republic, successfully lobbied to have the words "of the United States of America" added as part of an anti-immigrant campaign. They were deeply fearful that immigrants might be pledging to another nation's flag and, hence, might actually be using the pledge to express seditious thoughts.

22. I would like to thank James A. Beane for his comments and for his help on the material used in this chapter.

INTRODUCTION TO CHAPTER 19

Peter McLaren and Ramin Farahmandpur's chapter offers the fullest exposition in the book of a critical/revolutionary pedagogy to challenge education as enforcement. Expanding on the discussion in the introduction to this book, the chapter first elaborates on the destruction of corporate globabalization. It then criticizes right-wing pedagogies of jingoistic patriotism following September 11 and then builds on the terrorism pedagogy of Kumamoto to offer concrete and practical suggestions on how to construct a critical pedagogy to address the issues raised by September 11.

CHAPTER 19

Critical Revolutionary Pedagogy
at Ground Zero

Renewing the Educational Left after September 11

PETER MCLAREN AND RAMIN FARAHMANDPUR

This chapter addresses the importance of teachers developing their abilities to engage students in discussions on terrorism and creating pedagogical spaces inside classrooms in which students can express their concerns about the September 11 tragedy and their fears about the possibility of future attacks. One way to approach this task is to discuss, debate, analyze, and reflect upon the social and historical construction of such concepts as terrorism and patriotism. We believe that such concepts are not only ideologically constructed, but they are also intended to represent a narrow vision of the complex social world in which we live. Teachers can assist students develop a "language of critique"[1] to guide them in investigating how such concepts are "selectively" employed by the ruling class to represent and reproduce existing relations of power among dominant and subordinate groups in society. For example, teachers can help students to understand how contemporary right-wing forces have taken advantage of the September 11 tragedy by making patriotism synonymous with the ideology of Americanism, and how terrorism is portrayed to represent violence by Arabs against Westerners and not vice versa.

We believe that educators have a moral and ethical obligation to provide a forum in which students can question and critique the right-wing's efforts to rally people around its domestic and foreign U.S. policy initiatives. This

Peter McLaren is currently a professor of education in the Division of Urban Schooling at the Graduate School of Education and Information Studies. He has authored and edited approximately forty books and monographs on critical pedagogy, the sociology of education, critical literacy, critical ethnography, cultural studies, and social theory. His works have been translated into eleven languages. He became the inaugural recipient of the Paulo Freire Social Justice Award on April 26, 2002.

Ramin Farahmandpur is an assistant professor in the the Department of Educational Policy, Foundations and Administrative Studies at Portland State University. He recently completed his Ph.D. in the field of Curriculum Theory and Teaching Studies at the Graduate School of Education and Information Studies at UCLA. Farahmandpur has co-authored a number of articles (with Peter McLaren) on a variety of topics ranging from globalization, neoliberalism, critical pedagogy, and critical multiculturalism. Currently he is co-authoring a book with PeterMcLaren entitled: *Globalization and the New Imperialism: Towards a Revolutionary Pedagogy* (Rowman & Littlefield, forthcoming).

demands scrutinizing efforts by the media punditocracy and the right-wing elements to make patriotism synonymous with capitalism and consumerism. In this context, critical media literacy can play an important role in deepening students' understanding of the tragic events surrounding the September 11 attacks by providing them with the necessary pedagogical tools to decode and interpret images, sound bites, and texts produced by the mainstream media. To unmask the contradictions between patriotism and consumerism, between patriotism and democracy, and between patriotism and Americanism requires students to have access to a *language of critique*. In writing this chapter, we hope to contribute toward their development of this language by illuminating what we believe to be some of the more essential connections between corporatism and militarism that are the focus of this book. We also hope to offer pedagogical strategies, a *language of possibility*, that critically minded educators might use to preempt any sense of helplessness that might be engendered through the exploration of such themes.

Whose Terror?

Understanding the causes of terrorism constitutes the first step that students and teachers can undertake in its eradication. Chalmers Johnson's[2] model of "blowback" (i.e., a term first used by the Central Intelligence Agency [CIA] but adopted by some leftists to refer to actions that result from unintended consequences of U.S. policies kept secret from the American public) offers a lucid framework for analyzing the attacks of September 11. Johnson argues what the mainstream media reports as the malign acts of "terrorists" or "drug lords" or "rogue states" or "illegal arms merchants" often turn out to be "blowback" from earlier covert U.S. operations." Blowback related to U.S. foreign policy occurred when the United States became associated with support of terrorist groups or authoritarian regimes in Asia, Latin America, or the Middle East, and its clients turned on their sponsors. In Johnson's sense, September 11 is a classic example of blowback, in which U.S. policies generated unintended consequences that had catastrophic effects on U.S. citizens, New York City, and the American and indeed global economy. The events of September 11 can be seen as a textbook example of blowback since bin Laden and the radical Islamic forces associated with the al-Q'aeda network were supported, funded, trained, and armed by several U.S. administrations and by the CIA. The CIA's catastrophic failure was not only to have not detected the danger of the event and taken action to prevent it, but to have actively contributed to producing those very groups who are implicated in the terrorist attacks on the United States on September 11. The book *Whiteout: The CIA, Drugs and the Press* by Cockburn and St. Clair reveals just how assiduously the CIA assisted the opium lords who took over Afghanistan and helped to usher the Taliban into power, eventually helping in the financing of Osama bin Laden's al-Q'aeda network.[3]

The United States imposes severe economic sanctions on Muslim countries that commit human rights abuses and for accumulating weapons of mass destruction. At the same time the United States ignores Muslim victims of human rights abuses in Palestine, Bosnia, Kosovo, Kashmir, and Chechnya.

Through vast weapons sales, the United States props up its economy. Yet it insists on economic sanctions to prevent weapon development in Libya, Sudan, Iran, and Iraq. And, as Steve Niva points out, "The U.S. pro-Israel policy unfairly puts higher demands on Palestinians to renounce violence than on Israelis to halt new settlements and adhere to U.N. resolutions calling for an Israeli withdrawal from Palestinian lands."[4]

More broadly speaking, we believe that the events on September 11 should be examined in the context of the crisis of world capitalism. Here we are not so much referring to corporate executives—"the Ebola viruses of capitalism"—as we are the globalization of the productive forces under free trade liberalization. Here we follow a number of the central assertions of William Robinson, namely, that in recent decades the capitalist production process itself has become increasingly transnationalized.[5] We have moved from a world economy to a new epoch known as the global economy. Whereas formerly the world economy was composed of the development of national economies and national circuits of accumulation that were linked to one another through commodity trade and capital flows in an integrated international market, while nation-states mediated the boundaries between differently articulated modes of production, today national production systems are reorganized and functionally integrated into global circuits, creating a single and increasingly undifferentiated field for world capitalism. We are talking here about the transnationalization of the production of goods and services (globalization) and not just the extension of trade and financial flows across national borders (internationalization). The new global financial system disperses profits worldwide as the world becomes unified into a single mode of production and single global system bring out about the organic integration of different countries and regions into a global economy.

The consequences of the restructuring of the world productive apparatus are staggering. We agree with Robinson that technological changes are the result of class struggle—in this case, the restraints on accumulation imposed by popular classes worldwide. Global class formation is occurring, with supranational integration of national classes accompanying the transnational integration of national productive structures. This has accelerated the division of the world into a global bourgeoisie (the hegemonic global class fraction) and a global proletariat. That is, dominant groups fuse into a class or class fraction within transnational space. There is an emergent capitalist historic bloc sustained by a transnational capitalist class and represented by a transnational bourgeoisie. The United States is playing a leadership role on behalf of the emerging transnational elite; that is, the United States is taking the lead in developing policies and strategies on behalf of the global capitalist agenda of the transnational elite. It follows from this that revolutionary social struggle must become transnationalized as power from below in order to counter transnationalized capitalist power from above.

Today's marketplace is really a continuation of the core ideology of Reaganism, what Manning Marable describes as free markets, unregulated corporations, an aggressive militarization abroad, and the suppression of civil liberties and civil rights at home. In a sense the United States is now closer to the Reagan ideal of the national security state "where the legitimate functions of government were narrowly restricted to matters of national defense, public safety, and providing tax subsidies to the wealthy."[6] It is the flourishing of Reagan's "military Keynesianism"—"the deficit spending of hundreds of billions of dollar on military hardware and speculative weapons schemes such as 'Star Wars.' "[7]

It is also clear that today world capitalism is trying to reestablish itself in transnationalized formations, since its current forms are virtually unsustainable. In other words, the transnational capitalist elites are seizing opportunities to use military force to protect their markets and create new ones. In fact, a more dangerous threat than individual acts of terror today resides in the multifarious contradictions internal to the system of world capitalism. Throughout its history, U.S. capitalism has tried to survive in times of crisis by eliminating production and jobs, forcing those in work to accept worse conditions of labor, and seizing opportunities that might arise in which the public would support military action to protect what the United States defines as its vital interests. Developed and underdeveloped population groups occupying contradictory and unstable locations in an increasingly transnational environment, coupled with cultural and religious antagonisms among the capitalist actors, creates conditions of desperation and anger among the factions of the oppressed. We do not say this to give credibility to terrorism as a response to such anger, but to seek to understand and prevent the conditions in which terrorism is ignited. Marable warns: "The question, "Why Do They Hate Us?', can only be answered from the vantage point of the Third World's widespread poverty, hunger and economic exploitation."[8]

Given this daunting global challenge, it is important that educators ask the following: Is there a viable socialist alternative to capitalism? What would a world without wage labor be like? Without living labor being subsumed by dead labor? Would a world without the extraction of surplus value and the exploitation that accompanies it be a safer and more just world, a world less likely to be infested with the conditions that breed terrorism?

Unmasking Neoliberal Globalization

Contrary to the myths that have been circulated by the corporate-owned media, globalization does not, in any sense of the word, bring about the conditions for political harmony or economic stability. Neither does it furnish mutual economic growth to those nations, particularly Third World countries, who are forced to participate in the global economy under the leadership of the United States. The big scandal of our time, write Petras and Veltmeyer,[9] is that globalization fabricates the ideology that all countries benefit equally from the internationalization of trade. Yet, globalization is not by any stretch of the imagination, as we have been repeatedly told by corporate pundits, an "irreversible" and unstoppable process that arose from certain social and historical conditions. In fact, we contend that globalization is a process orchestrated by advocates of neoliberal social and economic policies. Yet we do not have to resign ourselves to the inevitability of neoliberal globalization.

It is worth noting that under the banner of globalization, corporate overworlders claim that the internationalization of capital is the solution to the declining rate of profit. For the cheerleaders of the free market, including Milton Friedman, globalization is the cure to the accumulation crisis of capital. However, we unequivocally dismiss the claims that globalization represents, by and large, a qualitative leap in capitalist production. In our view, globalization represents a number of fundamental developments in capitalist economic crisis that include, among other things,

- a short-term solution to long-term declining productivity;
- the intensification of competition among the leading imperialist nations, most notably, the United States, Japan, and Germany (the largest Western industrial economies who have shifted part of their production to Third World countries);
- the internationalization of investment and speculative capital;
- the international division of labor created by the integration of new technologies in an effort to raise productivity;
- the employment of new methods of flexible production largely derived from post-Fordist regimes of accumulation, and last but not least;
- the surging attacks by the right on behalf of the ruling classes on the working class and the poor.

In our opinion, the concept of globalization serves to detract attention from the broader objectives of U.S. imperialism: to establish political domination; to facilitate economic exploitation; and to loot the natural resources of Third World nations. In other words, the concept of globalization serves as a smokescreen to conceal the main objectives of U.S. imperialism's quest for global hegemony. As such, we believe that the concept of imperialism better reflects U.S. foreign policy objectives.

Finally, we should also mention that one of the objectives of neoliberal social and economic policies is liberating capital from any regulations that may be imposed upon it by government agencies. Part of the neoliberal social and economic policies is carried out through *privatization* -the *e-baying* of state-owned enterprises, industries, and public owned goods and services to the private sector, which is largely carried out under the banner of "efficiency" and "productivity"—two buzzwords employed to mask corporate theft of social resources. Furthermore, *deregulation* acts as a "buffer zone" to ward off any formidable threats against corporate profits in spite of the growing unemployment and environmental damage that it has caused, not to mention, reducing public expenditure on social services that include public education, and health services, childcare to cite a few examples. In the end, what it all comes down to is that the objective of the right is to abolish the concept of "public good" and to replace it with the ideology of "personal responsibility" of George Bush's compassionate conservatism.

The New Niche Market: Global Slavery

Capitalism is more than a sobering lesson for historians; it provides the ideal showcase for the tragedy of the human species. It not only includes men and women who are forced to work in hazardous working conditions, for barely endurable hours, and for much less than a living wage, but also children who labor perilously inside factories and sweatshops manufacturing numerous consumer goods (such as Nike shoes) that are shipped to consumer markets located in advanced capitalist countries. Capitalism does not screen its victims; anyone is fair game. It "sizes up" everyone. Anyone is ripe for exploitation. It should therefore surprise no one that capitalism is happily at war with children. Worldwide, nearly 250 million children are presently working (some estimate it is as high as 400 million). Nearly 90 million of the 179 million children in India work. Children in the southern region of India work sixteen hours a day, six days a week for a meager $1.30 a week salary. In Bangladesh, the number of working children is 6.1 million. In Thailand, there are nearly 13,000 child prostitutes (some estimate the figure to be closer to 800,000). In Nairobi, 30,000 children live on the streets. In Colombia, 28 percent of Bogota's prostitutes are young girls between the ages of ten and fourteen. In the United States nearly 290,000 children are illegally employed in various industries; this includes 59,600 children who are under the age of fourteen.[10] For the profiteers of capital, the children's war is a famously lucrative one; it must hurt so good to be able to exploit the most helpless of the world's populations.

Contrary to popular opinion, slavery is far from dead. Approximately twenty-seven million people worldwide are paid no wages and their lives are completely controlled by others through violence. According to Kevin Bales, "slavery itself keeps changing and growing."[11] Slavery has largely disappeared as "the legal ownership of one person by another," but it remains inescapably true that slavery is a growing industry worldwide, from the brothels of Thailand, to the charcoal mines of Brazil, to women in the West who have been kidnapped from Eastern Europe. According to Bales:

> At US $2,000 the young woman in a Thai brothel is one of the world's more costly slaves. People, especially children, can be enslaved today for little as US $45. The 11-year-old boy I met in India six weeks ago had been placed in bondage by his parents in exchange for about US $35. He now works 14 hours a day, seven days a week making *beedi* cigarettes. This lad is held in "debt bondage," one of the most common variations on the theme of slavery. Debt bondage is slavery with a twist. Instead of being property, the slave is collateral. The boy and all his work belong to the slaveholder as long as the debt is unpaid, but not a penny is applied to the debt. Until his parents find the money, this boy is a cigarette-rolling machine, fed just enough to keep him at his task. People may be enslaved in the name of religion, like the *Devdasi* of India or the *trokosi* of West Africa. They may be enslaved by their own government, like the hundreds of thousands of people identified by the International Labour Organisation in Burma. Whoever enslaves them, and through whatever trickery, false contract, debt or kidnap method, the reality for the slave is much the same.[12]

The reason slavery escapes our notice is because Western jobs are not threatened and multinationals are not undercut by slave-based enterprises. In fact, citizens of 74 percent of countries with high international debt load are regularly trafficked into slavery. For countries with a low international debt load, the figure is 29 percent. In 50 percent of countries with high international debt load, slavery is a regular feature of the economy, compared with just 12 percent of countries with low international debt load.[13] A recently leaked CIA report notes that as many as 50,000 women and children are forced to work as slave laborers in the United States each year. They are lured to the United States from Asia, Africa, Latin America, and Eastern Europe and serve largely as prostitutes, domestic servants, or bonded workers. In 1995, seventy-two Thai clothing workers were found imprisoned in a Los Angeles sweatshop. They were forced to work twenty-two hours a day for 62 cents an hour.[14]

Those who naively believe that slavery has disappeared in the United States may be surprised once they learn that in many prisons across the United States, slavery has been upgraded to "bonded labor." A number of corporations, including J.C. Penney, IBM, Toys R Us, TWA, and Victoria's Secret have shamelessly profited from prison labor. And what about the close to 50,000 women and children who are forced into prostitution, domestic servitude, and sweatshop labor each year?

The deteriorating working and living conditions for laborers in Third World countries is comparable—and in many respects exceeds— the horrid working and living conditions of the English working class as described by Frederick Engels in his book.[15] In Sri Lanka many workers must work fourteen hours a day; in Indonesia and the Philippines they work twelve-hour day shifts; and in the southern regions of China sixteen-hour workdays is the norm. Working conditions for many women in the United States is not much better than in developing countries. In Little Saigon, located in Orange County, California, the average minimum wage for undocumented immigrants working in illegal sweatshops has been reported to be $1 dollar an hour.[16] Inside sweatshops and factories around the world, young women are placed under incessant surveillance and subjected to humiliating working conditions by plant managers in order to ensure the efficient operation of production lines. For instance, young women are frequently given amphetamines to prolong working hours, and their menstrual cycles are placed under continual supervision to prevent pregnancy, a condition that is detrimental to business because it slows down production lines.[17] In the *maquiladoras*, women's biological reproduction is regulated and synchronized to the pulse of new methods of lean and flexible production in order to maximize profitability and minimize labor costs. Young women are forced to provide evidence that they are menstruating each month by participating in "monthly sanitary-pad checks."[18] As part of the contingent labor force, women are employed on twenty-eight-day contracts that coincide with their menstrual cycle. Those who are found pregnant are automatically fired and summarily released from the factory premises.

In 1998, Nike, with its global army of 500,000 contingent semiskilled workers in Third World countries has managed to amass a record revenue of $6.4 billion with the "assistance" of unregulated environmental laws and nonunionized cheap labor. In poor underdeveloped countries such as Haiti, hourly wages are reported to be 12 cents an hour, while in Honduras, workers' hourly wages are 31 cents an hour. The cost of manufacturing a pair of Nike shoes—whose retail price is $120.00—is estimated to be 70 to 80 cents in the dank sweatshops of Indonesia.

The recent assaults on welfare programs, bilingual education, multicultural education, and affirmative action boldly illustrates the incompatibility of capitalism with democracy. Mark Drey paints an eerie picture of contemporary capitalism at the end of the twentieth century:

> Communism may have been consigned to the desktop recycle bin of history, as free-market cheerleaders never tire of reminding us, and Marx may be an ironic icon of nineties retro chic, but the old bearded devil may have the last laugh: As we round the bend to the millennium, class war and the percolating rage of the "workers of the world" are emerging as the lightning-rod social issues of the coming century. Growing income inequality, accompanied by the hemorrhaging of U.S. manufacturing jobs because of automation or their relocation in the low-wage, nonunion "developing world," is sowing dragon's teeth. The disappearance of even unskilled factory work at a time when economic growth is insufficient to absorb dislocated workers is dire enough; that it is happening at a moment when traditional safety values no longer function—owing to the wasting away of the labor movement, the conservative dismantling of social services in favor of "market solutions" to social ills, and the ongoing buyout of representative government by corporate power—has created fertile soil for the apocalyptic politics of the disaffected.[19]

Contrary to popular mythology, money is not the source of capitalism's wealth; rather, its source is the sweat and blood of exploited workers. It is the savage manipulation of their labor power that creates revenue for the money moguls of the advanced capitalist West. Daniel Singer writes: "The obscene equivalence between the wealth of the world's top few hundred billionaires and the income of nearly three billion wretched of the earth illustrates this point."[20]

As we speak, there are an estimated five billion men, women, and children who are forced to subsist on $2 a day. Meanwhile, the two hundred largest corporations in the world, who have a combined 28 percent monopoly over global economic activities, merely employ 0.25 percent of the global workforce. To put things into perspective, the combined wealth of the eighty-four richest individuals in the world exceeds the GPD of China, which has a population of 1.3 billion.

The staggering disparities between the rich and the poor can no longer be cast aside. The contradictions inherent within capitalist social relations of production are transparent for those who are brave enough to face the truth about the current crisis of global capitalism. To cite one example, between 1997 and 1999, the average wealth of the rich who were lucky enough to be listed on the Forbes 400 list increased by $940 million. In sharp contrast, in the past twelve years, the net worth of the bottom 40 percent of the households in the United States declined by a dramatic 80 percent. Or take the example of the CEO of Disney, Michael Eisner, whose annual salary in 1998 was estimated to be $575.6 million. Compare that to the average annual salary of Disney employees, which stands at $25,070. We must question why, for example, the hourly wage of a worker in Guatemala is 37 cents an hour while Phil Knight, the CEO of Nike, has amassed a fortune of $5.8 billion.

The contradictions of capital in general, and the imperfections of the market in the advanced capitalist countries of the West in particular, are especially evident throughout the United States. Today, nearly 700,000 people are homeless on any given night in the United States. Annually, two million experience homelessness. Tragically, one out of every four homeless persons is an innocent child. In the majority of large metropolitan cities across the United States, homelessness is considered a crime. A number of innovative methods have been implemented to make homeless people invisible. In Chicago, for example, homeless people are arrested and prosecuted daily. These are the casualties of unceremonious economic excommunication. Before he became reinvented as the purebred embodiment of New York City itself, Rudolph Giuliani initiated a "quality-of-life" campaign in New York City that involved nightly sweeps and crackdowns on homeless people to ensure that they did not transgress the boundaries dividing the wealthy neighborhoods from the poor neighborhoods.

By a sheer will to obliterate the past, modern-day capitalists of the Enron school of ethics have unburdened history of its complexity and temporality and purified it of the stench of its victims. Capitalist accumulation can be experienced as an eternal "now," forever self-fellating and pleasure-giving, never reneging on its promise of eternal happiness. If there is any justice folded into the transcendent order of things, it is this: when Bush's chief Bubba, "Kenny Boy," Lay is invited to drink at Plato's River of Forgetfulness, he'll be persuaded by the prophet of Necessity to return to the Republic in his most unvarnished incarnation: a hog squealing at the trough, waiting to be served up as Sunday dinner for all those "whose pension funds were pumped dry to provide the hog wallow with loot."[21]

The United States is by far the most powerful capitalist country in the world. Consider the list of 497 billionaires (down from 551 before 2001 as a result of global recession) in the world; 216 billionaires are from the United States, followed by Germany with 35, and Japan with 25. The combined wealth of these 497 billionaires equals the incomes of the most impoverished half of the human population. Yet, in the wealthiest nation on earth, the United States, one out of every six children lives in poverty. According to a published report by the progressive think tank the Economic Policy Institute, one in four Americans were making poverty-level wages in 2000, and while major health care providers such as Johns Hopkins Hospital in Baltimore are developing special health coverage programs that offer "platinum service" to the rich (complimentary massage and sauna time with physical exams in the state-of-the-art testing labs), nearly forty million Americans go without health insurance.

The United States has declared the September 11 attacks to be an act of war. While these acts were indeed brutally warlike and a loathsome and despicable crime against humanity, clearly they did not constitute an act of war—an armed attack by one state against another—but rather acts of terrorism (which surely makes them no less hideous). Having failed to get authorization for the use of military force from the UN Security Council, Bush Jr. and his administration tried to get a formal declaration of war from the Congress but instead was given a War Powers Resolution Authorization (only one member of Congress, Barbara Lee, an African American representative from Oakland demonstrated the courage to vote against it as a matter of principle). The Bush administration then convinced NATO to invoke Article 5 of the NATO pact in an attempt to get some type of multi-lateral justification for U.S. military action. After failing on two further attempts to get Security Council approval for military action, the United States ambassador to the United Nations John Negroponte sent a letter to the Security Council asserting article 51 of the United Nations Charter, claiming that the United States reserves its right to use force against any state that it wishes as part of its fight against international terrorism (Negroponte was former U.S. ambassador in Honduras during the Contra war and oversaw funding of Battalion 316 that was all but wiped out in the democratic opposition; his confirmation was rammed through the day after the attacks).

The New Citizenship

President Bush now has his war mandate and is operating with a blank check for arming the military machine to its depleted uranium teeth and to unleash it against any individual or state that he alleges was involved in the attacks on September 11 or else sheltered, harbored, or assisted individuals in those attacks.[22] President Bush has made it unequivocally clear: those who are not with him are against him.

Such an attitude communicates an ominous message to America's youth regarding the roles and responsibilities of democratic citizenship. The Bush administration has stooped to the most deplorable levels of political opportunism by using the unforgiving and unforgivable attacks of September 11 as a pretext for ushering in a new realm of citizenship that irreparably fractures the once inseparable connection between democracy and justice. Reason has been sacrificed at the altar of unreflective action. Hatred of the Other that had been gestating for decades since the Reagan era has now been unleashed with the Bush/Cheney junta's furious assault on terrorism and all things turbaned, with the terrorists substituting for our former enemies: the Red Menace from the Georgian Steppes. Members of the ruling class have been the front-line defenders of the war on terrorism and are all too willing to sacrifice civil rights if it will protect their position in the global division of labor. The already complicated equilibrium of our cities has gone into frenzied fibrillations at the prospect of death and destruction suddenly reigning down upon our innocents. The ever-imminent but undefined hope that the world is getting better has been forever silenced by September 11. The reflective impoverishment of the American public—raised for generations on junk media K-Mart realism, trailer park fiction, and Diet Pepsi minimalism—has proven advantageous to President Bush, whose popularity as the Christian Crusader is at a record high according to recent homeland polls. Bush's mental glacier is in no danger of being shrunk by global warming. It continues to float the most hawkish ideas since Ronald Reagan past what seems to be an unsuspecting public convinced that only Bush has the mettle to wipe the planet clean of Muhammad's holy militia.

In this latest Bush era, it has become dangerous to think, to ask too many questions, or to look beyond the face value of whatever commentary is served up to us by our politicians, our military, and our so-called intelligence agencies and those who have disingenuously become their Beverly Hills lap dogs: the media. Among most media commentators, dialectical thought has been lamentably undervalued and shamefully under practiced. It is a world where it is safer to engage in rehearsed reactions to what we encounter on our television screens. It is safer to react in ways that newscaster/entertainers big on acrimonious scapegoating and short on analysis define for us as patriotic: applaud all actions by governmental authorities (especially those of the president) as if they were sacerdotal or morally apodictic. CNN has already declared it is "perverse" to focus on civilian suffering, exercising a racist arithmetic that deems civilian casualties in the United States to be inferior to those in Afghanistan. And it is clear that Fox television is little more than the *Pravda* of the Bush administration protecting George Bush, Jr. from public scrutiny and steadfastly supporting his "Enemy-of-the-month-club."

Former secretary of education, and candidate for President in the 2000 Republican primaries William Bennett has become one of Bush's most outspoken public defenders and has assumed the mantle of "philosopher king" of the Republican party. Bennett, who obviously benefited from Henry Kissinger's advice that anyone who wishes to become a recognized "expert" must learn to "articulate the consensus of those with power," has recently published *Why We Fight: Moral Clarity and the War on Terrorism.*23 An angry and indomitable cheerleader for the American war machine, Bennett continues to serve as a despotic mouthpiece and polemical hack for the most self-righteous and morally apodictic wing of the republican far right, mixing religious triumphalism (in Bennett's case, Catholic) with an overwhelming sense of his own importance and an absolute exclusion of any possibility of doubt or disillusionment on the issue of U.S. moral superiority in the world. Philosophically bankrupt, morally indignant, intellectually suspect, unburdened by an excess of imagination, and stamped with the temptation of careerism, *Why We Fight* is a half-baked criticism of the peace movement and what Bennett believes to be its benighted and morally dysfunctional leaders whom he blames for the failure of the United States to defeat the North Vietnamese and for aiding the enemies of civilization through their ongoing criticism of President Bush's permanent war on terrorism. Determined to give revenge by carpet bombing a moral justification and "payback" a philosophical warrant—not to mention the imprimatur of the republican elite—Bennett's book rewrites bald imperialism as a democratic obligation to free the world from evil doers. Bennett's unwavering support for the U.S. war machine and its politics of preemptive strikes is as blinkered as it is pernicious. His unforgiving absolutism and elitist adulation for Plato's republic betray a contempt for dialectical reasoning and a blind allegiance to conservative dogma. For Bennett, merely raising the question of why the terrorist attacks of September 11 happened is an act of moral turpitude and a betrayal of the homeland. Bennett refuses to connect the history of global capitalism to the history of U.S. foreign policy and avoids any discussion of the contradiction between its supposed leadership in the fight for democracy with its support for Latin American dictators, its training of death squad leaders in the School of the Americas, its clandestine overthrow of democratically elected socialist governments, its buttressing of anticommunist warlords in Southeast Asia, its slavish dedication to moneyed interests, and its willingness to punish all those who resist the encroachment of global corporatism.

A Primer for a Post-September 11 Critical Pedagogy

We believe that the study of terrorism can be and should be integrated as part of a broader multidisciplinary curriculum in classrooms. Bob Kumamoto has offered a number of steps that teachers can use part of their curriculum to help students explore terrorism in a systematic fashion.[24] Kumamoto's approach involves the study of history, economics, political science, geography, anthropology, social psychology, and sociology. Teachers can begin this project by dividing their students into several groups. Each group concentrates on one of the factors, or one of the majors areas related to terrorism. For example, one group of students can examine how oil from the Middle East and the U.S. arms sales to Israel contribute to the ongoing conflicts and tensions in that region of the world. From a sociological standpoint, students can study how the harsh and brutal living conditions endured by Palestinians in refugee camps contributes to terrorism. In addition, students can investigate geographical complexities of the Middle East region that have ignited disputes and quarrels over the Holy land and the occupied territories. In the political arena, students can find connections between the rise of Palestinian and Arab nationalism and U.S. economic and political interests in the region. Students can also examine Islamic fundamentalism through its historical opposition to Marxism and its embrace of capitalist social relations of production. From a historical perspective, students can explore the root causes of both Palestinian terrorism and Israeli state-sponsored terrorism in an effort to discover alternatives to both. Finally, by drawing upon the literature in social psychology, students can investigate the various motivating factors that cause individuals and groups to engage in terrorism and violence against innocent men, women, and children.

After their initial investigation, each group can report back to the class and share their findings. Teachers can then guide students to make connections between their findings and social and historical processes that have shaped that region of the world. For instance, teachers can assist students in making connections between acts of terrorism and practices such as colonization and imperialism. Second, students can explore the relationship between new media technologies and how acts of terrorism are reported to the public in specific geopolitical contexts. Third, students can examine how new "weapons of mass destruction" (biological, chemical, and nuclear), which may fall into the hands of terrorist organizations, can pose new threats to world peace and global stability. Other areas and topics that students can connect their findings to include state-sponsored terrorism, narco-terrorism, and eco-terrorism. For example, students can explore which states actively promote terrorism to protect their social, economic, and political interests.[25]

Contextualizing the September 11 terrorist attacks mandates that we also question United States' foreign policy along with its vital political and economic interests in the Middle East region, not to mention its support for the Israeli state. We believe that U.S. foreign policy has generated deep-seated bitterness and resentment among Arabs, and in some instances, it has been a motivating factor in the rise of Palestinian extremism. This is not to suggest that criticism be deflected from the anti-Semitism, sexism, and homophobia exhibited by Islamic fundamentalist groups (or by Christian fundamentalists, for that matter). Students of history can also try to find connections between their findings and the causes for the long-standing tradition of "Yankeephobia" in Latin American and South American countries. Further, students would do well to investigate how unjust labor practices of multinational corporations in Third World countries made U.S. citizens easy targets of anti-American sentiments. Finally, we want to remind students and teachers that the purpose of such activities is not to find justification or a rationale for terrorism and violence, but to understand what motivates individuals and groups to resort to political terrorism

Finally, we should remind teachers that exercising democratic rights demands that they engage their students in meaningful dialogues and discussion over social, economic, and political issues that affect their lives. As such, we want to differentiate between *formal* citizenship and *substantive* citizenship.[26] Whereas formal citizenship is linked to the legal dimensions of citizenship under capitalist democracy, in which political rights are disjoined and severed from economic rights; substantive citizenship is intimately connected to the "capacity of individuals to exercise those powers in actual debate, and in the resolution of political issues."[27] We believe that it is important for teachers to broaden and strengthen pedagogical spaces whereby students can exercise "substantive citizenship." Within the parameters of these social and political pedagogical spaces, teachers, students, and workers can undertake the task of self-empowerment by their direct participation in the decision-making processes over issues that have an immediate impact on their daily lives at both the local and community levels. These include, but are certainly not limited to, engaging in discussions and debates over issues such as housing, taxation, education, health services, and social programs.

Toward a Critical Revolutionary Pedagogy

Critical educators across the country must oppose what we are now seeing throughout the United States: a senseless xenophobic statism, militarism, erosion of civil liberties, and a quest for permanent military interventions overseas within the fracture zones of geo-political instability that have followed in the wake of the attacks, all of which can only have unsalutary consequences for world peace. This is particularly crucial, especially in light of the history of U.S. imperialism and in light of another of Said's trenchant observations, that "bombing senseless civilians with F-16s and helicopter gunships has the same structure and effect as more conventional nationalistic terror."[28]

As critical educators we are faced with a new sense of urgency in our fight to create social justice on a global scale, establishing what Karl Marx called a "positive humanism." At a time when Marxist social theory seems destined for the political dustbin, it is needed more than ever to help us understand the forces and relations that now shape our national and international destinies. As Bertell Ollman opines:

> I think what Marxism is about is to avoid the temptation of taking a stand based solely on our emotions. Marxism encourages us not to moralize about good and evil and who is more good or evil when you are confronted with many people capable of such actions. Marxism encourages us to contextualize what happened and who is involved; of how this happened in our world today and how it fits into history, into time. When you do that you can't avoid dealing with and trying to make sense of the role that the U.S. has played in its foreign policy and also in global capitalism. One must look at that and figure out ways of dealing with it so that we can handle not only September 11th but all of the September 11ths which are coming up ahead.[29]

One of the purposes of critical/revolutionary pedagogy is to work to bring about a global society where events of September 11, 2001, are less likely to occur. It does this through creating contexts in which revolutionary/transformative praxis can occur. Critical pedagogy is a politics of understanding, an act of knowing that attempts to situate everyday life in a larger geo-political context, with the goal of fostering regional collective self-responsibility, large-scale ecumenism, and international worker solidarity. It will require the courage to examine social and political contradictions, even, and perhaps especially, those that govern mainstream U.S. social policies and practices. It also requires a reexamination of some of the failures of the left.

In the face of such an intensification of global capitalist relations, rather than a shift in the nature of capital itself, we need to develop a critical pedagogy capable of engaging everyday life as lived in the midst of global capital's tendency toward empire, a pedagogy that we have called revolutionary critical pedagogy. The idea here is not to adapt students to globalization, but make them critically maladaptive, so that they can become change agents in anticapitalist struggles. The revolutionary multicultural unity sought by proponents of critical pedagogy is unflaggingly opposed to its class collaborationist counterpart represented by George Bush, Colin Powell, and Condaleeza Rice.

Without question, the attacks of September 11 have handed the capitalist ideological offensive and imperialism a major and unexpected victory. Parasitical capitalism under the banner of neoliberal globalization, and spearheaded by the WTO, IMF, and World Bank, has been disastrous for the world's poor. The struggle ahead for leftist educators will be difficult, but there are some signs of hope. In her book *Students against Sweatshops*, Liza Featherstone writes:

The triple extremities of war, terror, and recession could distract the public from capitalism's everyday inequities. On the other hand, they certainly dramatize the system's problems: Bush's tax breaks to corporations; the way every national burden, from economic slowdown to anthrax, is disproportionately shouldered by the working class.[30]

And while there is no direct connection between the current economic difficulties we are experiencing in the United States and working-class radicalism and militant resistance, it is more likely now that people are beginning to question more seriously the present system. One encouraging development that we are witnessing is a progressive radicalization of youth. Featherstone reports that

> Many activists say that the September 11 attacks have left people ever hungrier for forward-looking, optimistic social action. The global economic justice movement in particular may stand a better chance of being heard, at a time when Americans are suddenly looking at the world and wondering, "Why do 'they' hate us. . . ." For many, September 11 underscored the need to rethink America's role in the world, and to redress global economic inequality.[31]

The defeat of U.S. imperialism will require teachers to join antiwar efforts and peace movements across the nation. Inaction on this front may lead to escalating acts of terrorism both here in the "homeland" as well as throughout the world. Given the uncertainty that looms in our collective future, it is more important than ever before that educators participate in popular social movements—regional, national, and international—to resist the military adventurism and Enronization of the global lifeworld fueled by U.S. imperialism. As Michael Parenti has eloquently expressed: "Those who believe in democracy must be undeterred in their determination to educate, organize, and agitate, in any case, swimming against the tide is always preferable to being swept over the waterfall."[32]

Notes

1. See Henry Giroux, *Teachers as Intellectuals: Toward a Critical Pedagogy of Learning* (South Hadley, Mass.: Bergin and Garvey, 1988).
2. Chalmers Johnson, *Blowback: The Costs and Consequences of American Empire* (New York: Owl Books, 2000).
3. Alexander Cockburn and Jeffrey St. Clair, *Whiteout: The CIA, Drugs, and the Press* (New York: Verso, 1999).
4. Steve Niva, "Addressing the Sources of Middle Eastern Violence against the United States," in *Common Dreams News Center* (September 14, 2001), available at www.commondreams.org/views01/0914–04.htm.
5. See William Robinson, "Social Theory and Globalization: The Rise of a Transnational State," *Theory and Society* 30 (2001): 157–200.
6. Manning Marable, "The Failure of U.S. Foreign Policies," in *Along the Color Lines* (November28, 2001); available from www.manningmarable.net.
7. Manning Marable, "Terrorism and the Struggle for Peace," in *The Mail Archive* (October 25, 2001), available at mail-archive.com/brc-news@lists.tao.ca/msg00662.html.
8. Ibid.

9. See James Petras and Henry Veltmeyer, *Globalization Unmasked: Imperialism in the 21st Century* (Halifax, Nova Scotia: Fernwood Publishing, 2001).

10. David Kameras, "Bringing Home Child Labor: What it Takes to Make the Products We Buy," *America@Work* 3, no. 5 (1998): 12–16.

11. Kevin Bales, "Throwaway People," *Index on Censorship* 28, no. 1 (2000): 36–45.

12. Ibid., 38.

13. Ibid., 36.

14. Barry Grey, "Leaked CIA Report Says 50,000 Sold Into Slavery in US Every Year," in *World Socialist Web Site* (April 25, 2000) available at wsws.org/articles/2000/apr2000/slav-a03.shtml.

15. Friedrich Engels, *The Conditions of the Working Class in England* (Chicago: Academy Chicago Publishers, 1994)

16. James B. Parks, "This Holiday Season No Sweat," *America@Work* 2, no. 10 (1997): 11.

17. Ibid., 12.

18. Naomi Klein, *No Logo: Taking Aim at the Brand Bullies* (New York: Picador, 1999).

19. Mark Drey, *The Pyrotechnic Insanitarium: American Culture at the Brink* (New York: Grove Press, 1999), 262–63.

20. Daniel Singer, *Whose Millennium? Theirs or Ours?* (New York: Monthly Review Press, 1999), 216.

21. Alexander Cockburn, "The Hog Wallow," *The Nation* 275, no. 5 (2002): 8.

22. See Francis Boyle, " No War against Afghanistan!" in *Ratical* (October 18, 2001) [cited October 20, 2001], available at www.ratical.org/ratville/CAH/fab112901.html.

23. William Bennett, *Why We Fight: Moral Clarity and the War on Terrorism* (New York: Doubleday, 2002).

24. Bob Kumamoto, "The Study of Terrorism: An Interdisciplinary Approach for the Classroom," *Social Studies Review* 33, no. 1 (1993): 16–21.

25. These examples have been drawn from Kumamoto, "The Study of Terrorism."

26. Petras and Veltmeyer, *Globalization Unmasked*.

27. Ibid., 121.

28. Edward Said, "Islam and the West are Inadequate Banners," in *The Observer* ([September 16, 2001] [cited on September 18, 2001]), available at www.observer.co.uk/comment/story/0,6903,552764,00.html.

29. Bertell Ollman, *How to Take an Exam and Remake the World* (Montreal: Black Rose Books, 2001), 7.

30. Lisa Featherstone, *Students against Sweatshops* (London and New York: Verso, 2002), 104.

31. Ibid., 104–105.

32. Michael Parenti, *The Terrorism Trap: September 11 and Beyond* (San Francisco: City Lights Books, 2001), 111.

INDEX